Royalist Conspiracy in England 1649-1660

by DAVID UNDERDOWN

ARCHON BOOKS, 1971

Copyright © 1960 by Yale University Press
Reprinted 1971 with permission in an
unaltered and unabridged edition.

ISBN: 0-208-00960-4
Library of Congress Card Number: 74-122409
Printed in the United States of America

TO MY MOTHER

Preface

IN THE ELEVEN YEARS between the execution of Charles I and his son's Restoration, the English Royalists conspired repeatedly on behalf of their King over the water. The purpose of this book is to provide a consecutive narrative of these efforts; of the Royalist party as a movement dedicated to the overthrow of the Commonwealth and Protectorate governments, by force or clandestine negotiation with other opposition groups. This will involve a discussion of the structure of the Royalist party, and an analysis of the various personal and political factions of which it was composed. The following chapters will discuss not only the activities of the better-known leaders but also the fortunes of the Royalist rank-and-file, who in the end made an important contribution to the history of seventeenth-century England. They will be concerned not merely with the spectacular occasions when Cavalier plotting burst into the open in rebellions or assassination schemes, but also with the much longer periods of planning which made the violent phases possible. Royalist conspiracy, as we shall see, possesses a notable continuity.

There has been in recent years a marked revival of interest in the Royalists. Valuable studies of them have been made from the standpoint of both economic and social history, and their importance is unquestioned. This book is not an attempt to supplement or supersede them. No general study of Royalist conspiracy, however,

has previously been attempted. The standard histories of the Interregnum, including the great series by Gardiner, Firth, and Godfrey
Davies, discuss the subject incidentally. But for obvious reasons,
Royalist conspiracy only comes to the forefront of their narratives
in the dramatically violent or tragic moments, which do not by
themselves tell the whole story. A great deal of more specialized
work has been done on isolated incidents: the "Royal Miracle," the
rising of March 1655, the Restoration itself. In no case, however,
can these undeniably significant crises be seen in perspective, as
part of a continuous whole, and an attempt to remedy the deficiency
must be this book's primary justification.

The objection will probably be made that the numerical insignificance of the conspiring Royalists debars them from such extensive treatment. Their plots were uniformly unsuccessful, and the
Royalist party as a conspiracy can be seen as either comically or
tragically ineffective, according to taste. Monarchy, we know, was
restored in 1660, but by Monck and the moderates, not by the
discredited Cavaliers. There is enough truth in this oversimplifica-
tion for it to be taken seriously; however, even if it could be
sustained, the subject would still be worth investigating. A full
understanding of a revolutionary era demands a study of the conservatives as well as the revolutionaries. The Royalists were the
most intractable internal problem of every government between
1649 and 1660; none could establish itself permanently without
either assimilating or suppressing them. The Royalists' obstinate
refusal to respond to conciliation was one of the political constants
of the republic. The Levellers, a much smaller group, failed too;
yet few would deny that they deserve close attention.

The objection that the Royalist party was only a secondary factor
in the events leading to the Restoration cannot, of course, be summarily dismissed. Yet it would be a mistake to prejudge the issue.
Although a study of Royalist conspiracy cannot hope to resolve
more than one component in the complicated politics of the
Interregnum, it is a fact that no previous account of the period has
been able to draw on a continuous history of Cavalier sedition.
One factor in the equation has been missing. Behind our discussion
of the routine business of conspiracy will therefore lurk some larger

questions about the Restoration itself. Obviously no complete answers can be provided in a book that limits itself to the Royalist party—and to only the more violently inclined section of it at that —but this does not mean that the questions cannot be asked. And in observing how the Restoration was achieved, we shall be in a better position to evaluate the Royalists' part in it.

The historical importance of Royalist conspiracy is not limited to its impact on the politics of the Interregnum; it reaches far into the future of post-Restoration England. For years afterward, the Cavalier was a stock symbol of Tory mythology. Defeated in war but still holding fast to his allegiance during years of repression, his idealized portrait inflamed the passions of many to whom the phrase "Church and King" was as much the evocation of an heroic past as a contemporary party slogan. The Royalist conspirator passed by way of Restoration martyrologists and Tory ballad-mongers into the sentimental twilight of political controversy. Between the romantic figure of Tory legend and the debauched, hectoring rake into which the Cavalier was turned by unfriendly pens, there is an unbridgeable gulf. It is perhaps worth pausing to inquire of the reality behind the two opposing myths: to discover, if we can, how many Cavaliers actually conspired, who they were, and how effective. A second way in which Royalist conspiracy affected post-Restoration history lies in the careers of the Royalists themselves. Many went on to play a part—in a few cases distinguished, more often obscure—in the stormy politics of Charles II's reign. The experience of seditious intrigues against the republic, the attitudes which this experience helped to implant, and the personal connections formed by the active conspirators: none of these things are without future relevance.

Returning to the immediate contents of this book, some of the limitations of its subject matter must be mentioned. This cannot, obviously, be a complete study of the political, or even the merely conspiratorial, opposition to the Commonwealth and Protectorate. Much will be said about the other opposition factions, Presbyterians, Levellers, and the rest, but only from the standpoint of their relations with Royalist conspiracy, and of Royalist efforts to use them for their own ends. These other parties, and the neutrals and moderates of various hues who often disliked the republic just as intensely, may have contributed more to its downfall than did the Royalists. Their history deserves to be written; here it will be encountered only incidentally. It will, however, be necessary to see the activities of the Royalists in relation to this other, non-Royalist opposition.

It is also worth pointing out that I do not claim to have written a complete history of the English Royalist party. The fortunes of the Royalists abroad, whether in Europe or the colonies, have been regarded as only peripheral. An arbitrary definition of the conspiring Royalist party which excludes the exiles entirely would be impossible: among them were the King and his councilors, to whom the plotters looked for leadership. Countless lesser men, both active conspirators and inactive conformists, crossed and recrossed the seas, and were in exile at one time or another in the 1650's. The Royalists abroad will be discussed, however, only insofar as is necessary for a full understanding of the conspiracies. As for the Royalists at home, their earlier history, political ideas, religion, economic and social problems—all have to be compressed to the bare minimum required as background. These may be more important and rewarding subjects than mine, but they have already been described by other pens, and duplication can hardly be defended in a book that is already long enough. The outstanding recent account of the civil war, Miss C. V. Wedgwood's *The King's War,* includes the essential history of the Royalist party to 1647, and her next volume will no doubt carry the story into my period. Among much else, her narrative shows clearly how even in wartime the party was wrecked by the same organizational and financial problems that beset it when it became a conspiracy. For the Royalists in general I have relied heavily on Paul H. Hardacre's *The Royalists during the Puritan Revolution,* a valuable study recent enough to absolve any other author from retracing the same ground. Mrs. Joan Thirsk's excellent articles on confiscated lands have shown what can be done in the economic field, but much detailed work in local history remains before we can speak with certainty about the economic structure of the Royalist, as of other Interregnum parties. The reader will therefore look in vain for yet another set of generalizations (based on insufficient evidence) about the status of the gentry, whether Royalist or parliamentarian, rising or declining. The story of conspiracy is complicated enough to be worth unraveling for its own sake.

The subject of this study was first suggested to me by Sir Keith Feiling in 1950. Chapters 4–10 represent an expansion and revision of my B. Litt. dissertation, presented at Oxford in 1953. The subsequent completion of the book was assisted by a grant from the Research Grants Committee of the University of the South. Many friends on both sides of the Atlantic have contributed valuable assistance and advice; too many for me to do more than acknowledge them gratefully but collectively. I have profited especially by the suggestions of Paul Hardacre (in addition to the stimulus provided by his published work), Professor Hugh Trevor-Roper, and Robert Latham, of Royal Holloway College. John Webb, of Sewanee, read several chapters in manuscript and made many helpful observations. David Piper, of the National Portrait Gallery, gave expert advice on illustrations. To the staffs of the Bodleian Library, the British Museum, the Public Record Office, the Historical Manuscripts Commission, and the Sterling Memorial Library of Yale University I owe even more than most students for their patience, courtesy, and frequent anticipation of my needs. One obligation above the rest demands special and grateful acknowledgment: to Christopher Hill of Balliol College, Oxford, from whose unfailing wisdom and acute criticism these pages derive whatever merits they possess.

All dates, unless otherwise stated, are Old Style, except that the year has been regarded as beginning on January 1. Original spellings and punctuations have been retained in passages quoted; the use of *u, v, i,* and *j,* however, has been made to conform with modern practice. In direct quotations from ciphered correspondence, passages deciphered by the author have been given in square brackets.

D. U.

Sewanee, Tenn.
November 1959

Contents

Illustrations

Abbreviations

Add. MS   British Museum, Additional Manuscript.

BIHR   *Bulletin of the Institute of Historical Research.*

BM   British Museum.

Carte,   *A Collection of Original Letters and Papers, Concern-*
Papers   *ing the Affairs of England . . . 1641–1660, Found*
             among the Duke of Ormonde's Papers, ed. Thomas
             Carte, London, 1739.

CCC   *Calendar of the Proceedings of the Committee for*
             Compounding, ed. M. A. E. Green, London, 1889–92.

CClSP   *Calendar of the Clarendon State Papers,* ed. O. Ogle,
             W. H. Bliss, W. D. Macray, and F. J. Routledge, Ox-
             ford, 1869–1932.

CJ   *Journals of the House of Commons 1547–1714, 1803–.*

Clarendon,   *The Life of Edward Earl of Clarendon . . . in*
Con.   *Which Is Included a Continuation of his History of*
             the Grand Rebellion, Oxford, 1857.

Clarendon, *History*	Edward Hyde, Earl of Clarendon, *The History of the Rebellion and Civil Wars in England,* ed. W. D. Macray, Oxford, 1888.
ClSP	*State Papers Collected by Edward, Earl of Clarendon,* ed. R. Scrope and T. Monkhouse, Oxford, 1767–86.
CSPD	*Calendar of State Papers, Domestic Series, 1649–1660,* ed. M. A. E. Green, London, 1875–86.
DNB	*Dictionary of National Biography.*
EHR	*English Historical Review.*
Gardiner, *C&P*	S. R. Gardiner, *History of the Commonwealth and Protectorate,* 2d ed. London, 1903.
HLQ	*Huntington Library Quarterly.*
HMC	Historical Manuscripts Commission Report.
LBM	*The Letter-Book of John Viscount Mordaunt 1658–1660,* ed. Mary Coate, Camden Society, London, 1945.
LJ	*Journals of the House of Lords 1578–1714.*
NP	*The Nicholas Papers: Correspondence of Sir Edward Nicholas, Secretary of State,* ed. G. F. Warner, Camden Society, London, 1886–1920.
OPH	*The Parliamentary or Constitutional History of England,* London, 1761–63.
SPDI	State Papers Domestic, Interregnum (Public Record Office).
TRHS	*Transactions of the Royal Historical Society.*
TSP	*A Collection of the State Papers of John Thurloe, Esq.,* ed. Thomas Birch, London, 1742.
VCH	Victoria County History.

1. Exit Tyrannus

ROYALISM WAS TRANSFERRED from the planes of military and political action to that of conspiracy on January 30, 1649, when Charles I stepped from the central window of Inigo Jones's Banqueting House to meet his executioner. For the Royalists, as for the whole English nation, the bleak horror of that leaden winter day was the ultimate crisis of the revolutionary era. The King was dead, and his successor an inexperienced youth in exile. Even after the defeats of the first civil war, the fact that Charles I had been in England and able to bargain with his enemies had given the Royalist party at least the semblance of leadership, and the possibility of restoring him to power by negotiation. The King's alliance with the Scots had brought on the second civil war, and again he had been put to rout. The victorious Army had proceeded to purge Parliament of the Presbyterian moderates, and then to pass the point of no return by bringing Charles I to trial. Already subject to virtual exclusion from the political life of the country, and to serious measures of economic discrimination, the Royalists were now confronted with the alternatives of throwing up the sponge or working for the restoration of their new monarch by conspiracy. A significant number chose the second course.

Before their efforts are described, a brief survey of the political state of England in 1649 is required; an examination of the impact of the King's execution on the major political groups or parties. I have already several times referred to the Royalists as a "party." In the present climate of historical opinion the whole concept of party is regarded with justifiable suspicion. As I shall find it convenient to continue to apply the term to the Royalists on many occasions throughout this book, and to discuss their relations with other "parties" (Presbyterians, Independents, and their successors), a brief comment on the meaning of the term may be useful.[1] We have, of course, to forget everything we know about "party" in later times; even the most coherent of Interregnum parties had only a rudimentary unity of policy, little permanence, and no organization or discipline at all. A seventeenth-century party was indeed no more than an indefinite aggregation of all those who, at a given moment, happened to think alike on the major political issues. The fact that they thought alike at one time was no guarantee that they would think alike a year, or even a month later; especially on the parliamentary side party alignments were essentially transient and unstable. "Party," moreover, accounts for only one segment of the political spectrum. There was always a large number, probably a majority of the "political nation," of moderates, trimmers, and opportunists whose party allegiance was doubtful, variable, nonexistent, or definable only in terms of local, county issues.

As for the party labels themselves, there is a simple defense for the traditional terminology: contemporary usage. The terms "Royal party," "Cavalier party," and "King's party" were commonly used by people of all shades of opinion. Without much subtlety, they identified as a group those who had supported Charles I in the first civil war, or who after the war were in favor of restoring the Crown's original powers, without binding limitations. Descriptions such as "Presbyterian" and "Independent" are more complicated, especially the former; but again I plead contemporary usage. A few other preliminary cautions should be mentioned. Neither of the two major groups into which the formerly

1. For some valuable insights into the nature of "party" in this period see J. H. Hexter, *The Reign of King Pym* (Cambridge, Mass., 1941), and "The Problem of the Presbyterian Independents," *American Historical Review*, *44* (1938–39), 29–49; also George Yule, *The Independents in the English Civil War*, Cambridge, 1958.

united parliamentary party divided by 1649 possessed the same coherence or permanence as the Royalist party. And, in spite of the names, the issues on which they parted company were by no means exclusively religious; if they had been we should be discussing churches, not political factions. "Presbyterian" can often be equated with "moderate," and after 1648 with "neutral"; yet there were moderates and neutrals who did not think of themselves as Presbyterians. There is another reason for not discarding the old label. The Royalists could identify a Presbyterian when they saw one, even if we cannot, and for them the name evoked a much more powerful emotional response than the word "moderate" would have aroused. So then, to the Presbyterians.

For all the horror that it produced in the ranks of the Royalists, the act of regicide had quite as decisive an impact on these Presbyterian moderates. Their breach with the Independents was now irreparable; a fact that was bound to affect their relations with the Cavaliers. The prospects of cooperation between Royalists and Presbyterians depended on one's estimate of the width of the gulf dividing them. Superficially it did not appear unbridgeable. The Presbyterian leaders inherited quite as strong an attachment to the established constitution and social order as did their Royalist opponents. In 1647 the Presbyterians had attempted to halt the revolutionary forces which they had helped to unleash six years before but which now seemed to be getting both politically and socially out of hand. Their terms of compromise, the restrictions on monarchy and episcopacy proposed in the Isle of Wight Treaty, were not clearly defined, and failed to stimulate the enthusiasm for an unequivocal position that could inspire both Royalists and Independents. Such is the way of compromises. Charles I's alliance with the Scots in the second civil war had placed the English Presbyterians in an awkward dilemma. Although a few of them went over to the King, the majority were unable to swallow their distaste for an opportunist alliance between their old enemies and the despised Scots, an alliance which, moreover, did not meet their minimum terms. Most of the Presbyterians joined the already swollen ranks of the neutrals, and this was the position they maintained, with increasing difficulty, for ten more years. The numerical strength of this Presbyterian "middle group" should not be exaggerated; yet the influence of personalities like Fairfax (whose retirement from public life after 1649 qualifies him as a Presbyterian), Manchester, and Stamford was always great enough to be a potentially disturbing weight in the political balance.

By 1649 the Presbyterians were distinguished from the Royalists by differences of degree rather than irreconcilable principle. There was disagreement about the guarantees needed to safeguard the settlement of 1641, and about the vexed question of ecclesiastical authority, and these things were important. They were not, on the other hand, fundamental in terms of practical politics. Both parties agreed on the essentials of settlement: on the Crown, the traditional constitution and social order, a national church; and both wished to stem the tide of further change. Some Presbyterians urgently stressed the possibilities of compromise. Sir William Waller's long philosophical and historical argument for kingship was not essentially opposed to that of Hyde and the Royalist moderates who had supported the reforms of 1641. "That which I aim at," says Waller in his *Vindication,* "is the re-establishment of a monarchy circumscribed and entrenched, and as I may say, fortified with good laws." A little further on, indeed, Waller acknowledges Charles II as King "by a clear and individual right of succession, as next and immediate heir, without reference to any condition or limitation." [2] Most Presbyterians were probably more rigid about the conditions, but a serious effort might have ironed out the differences. Many of Charles II's advisers, and the best ones at that, stood firmly by the limitations imposed in 1641, and however little the Royalists liked the thought of presbytery, Charles I had been willing to promise it for three years for the sake of a Scots army. The two parties were kept apart as much by the bad blood of the civil war as by any fundamental disagreements making compromise impossible. The problem of the Presbyterian alliance was to be one of the vital choices confronting the Royalists for years to come.

For the other main faction of the old parliamentary party, the Independents, the consequence of the King's execution was less

2. *Vindication of the Character and Conduct of Sir William Waller* (London, 1793), pp. 301, 307.

complicated: it established them in power. Militant Independency had captured the New Model during the war, and since Pride's Purge the Army was the ultimate arbiter of the nation's destinies. Although the Rump leaders, Vane, Heselrige, and their friends, might strike classical republican attitudes, behind them were the looming figures of Cromwell and Ireton. The Independents, whether inside or outside the Army, were wedded to policies which could be stomached by neither Royalists nor Presbyterians. They rejected the Presbyterian concept of a state church, and advocated a religious toleration limited by the exclusion of Roman Catholics and Anglicans, but which encouraged the existence of the more extreme Protestant sects. The Independents were also distinguished by their reliance to a far greater degree than the Presbyterians on social classes below the rank of the substantial gentry, whose conservatism conditioned the other two parties. The Rump, the Independents, the Army: here were the three related entities with which the Royalists had no hope of compromise, and from which they could expect the olive branch of conciliation only if they were willing to abandon their principles.

There was, however, one offshoot from the Independents which was almost as hostile to the Rump as were the Royalists themselves: the Levellers. And the King's death was not without consequences for them too. No doubt the Levellers were a small minority among the politically articulate, but they had more than made up for it by their vociferous championship of the soldiers' grievances in 1647, during the tension between Army and Parliament. Cromwell, indeed, found it necessary to accept Leveller collaboration until the danger of a restoration of the King on Presbyterian terms had been averted. After that he no longer needed them, and they received the *coup de grâce* in Burford churchyard on May 14, 1649. Although "Freeborn John" Lilburne remained the idol of the underprivileged, and although some of their other spokesmen, such as John Wildman and Edward Sexby, behaved as though they had a party behind them, the Levellers were never again a serious threat to Army discipline. However, the depth of their hatred for Cromwell and the Rump leaders who had betrayed them, the liveliness of their propaganda, and the fact that they had little to lose by violence all had significant implications for the Royalists. The objection that Leveller democracy was even further opposed to Royalist principle than was Independent oligarchy could be answered by either side with the argument that in times of crisis ends may have to be temporarily subordinated to means. A Royalist-Leveller alignment was a remote possibility in 1649; nevertheless some Royalist conspirators found it worth considering.

When discussing the Royalists' chances of obtaining support from Presbyterians and Levellers, we should bear in mind the absence of cohesion in both groups. The Royalists, however, were still a distinct party in a rather special sense, distinct even from the Presbyterians who were now moving haltingly toward alliance with them. Their identity was more sharply defined by the facts that they had fought alone in the first civil war and had not suffered the same fragmentation as their enemies. Their ultimate goal could be simply expressed: the restoration of the King, either by force or negotiation, but in any case without limiting conditions. To a considerable degree, however, the Royalists' sense of solidarity was emotional rather than rationally political. Devotion to the mystique of kingship combined with loyalty to the Crown as a symbol of shared experiences in camps, on battlefields, and not least at the hands of puritan sequestration committees. Wartime comradeship, mass political outlawry, and the burdensome financial exactions also entailed by defeat—these meant something very different to their new-found Presbyterian friends, if friends they were.[3] Romantic traditions have a habit of taking root most rapidly among the defeated, and the bitter unity which the passage of events had forged was not allowed to fade with blurring memories of Marston Moor and Naseby. The habit of conspiracy helped to keep it alive for a faithful few. More potent for the majority were the discriminatory measures with which Parliament tried to legislate Royalism out of existence: exclusion from political power, both national and local; and especially the pressures of sequestration and composition.

3. For a brilliant discussion of the emotional and ideological basis of Royalism see Keith Feiling, *History of the Tory Party, 1640–1714* (Oxford, 1924), chap. 3.

It would be wrong to assert that the Royalists were exclusively a class party, but it is nonetheless true that their main strength was based on the ownership of land, in other words, on the aristocracy and gentry. The landowning class was of course sharply divided, and it provided the leaders on both sides. The bigger landowners, however, were more often on the King's side than on the Parliament's. In 1642 the House of Lords divided two to one for the King, the Commons nearly three to two against him.[4] Daniel Defoe's Cavalier, an excellent composite portrait of the average Royalist, was the son of "a gentleman of a very plentiful fortune, having an estate of above £5,000 per annum, of a family nearly allied to several of the principal nobility." [5] Although many Royalists were less affluent, the country gentleman of moderate means and interest was generally typical of the party's leaders. Now land, although more durable and respectable than financial wealth, was also less easy to mobilize for war purposes. After 1643 the Royalist effort rapidly degenerated into a gallant fight against odds and better generalship. The burdens of the war itself were also inevitably greater for the defeated side than for the victors. Thus even without the additional exactions imposed by Parliament, the Cavaliers were already seriously weakened before the war was over.

The sequestration system made certain that they would not recover easily. Local county committees, directed from London by a parliamentary Committee for Sequestrations, were the first weapons used to reduce their territorial strength. Sequestration reduced income; composition often made a serious drain upon capital. The imposition of delinquency fines, payable before the estate could be removed from sequestration, became the standard procedure after the autumn of 1644. It was handled by the Committee for Compounding at Goldsmiths' Hall, and soon turned into one of the most lucrative sources of parliamentary revenue. It is unnecessary to illustrate the impact of the system in a study that is prin-

4. Paul H. Hardacre, *The Royalists during the Puritan Revolution* (The Hague, 1956), p. 5. D. Brunton and D. H. Pennington, *Members of the Long Parliament* (London, 1954), pp. 14, 187. Mary F. Keeler, *The Long Parliament 1640–1641*, American Philosophical Society, Memoirs, 36 (Philadelphia, 1954), 12.

5. Daniel Defoe, *Memoirs of a Cavalier* (London, 1926), p. 1.

cipally concerned with conspiracy. Many sequestered Royalists were forced to mortgage the fraction of their estate allowed them to support their families. Later, to pay their composition fines, they had to borrow on unfavorable terms, or sell part of what was left, in a buyers' market. The Royalists were also subjected to heavy assessed taxes, collected by the Committee for the Advance of Money; after June 1648 they alone had to pay them. Composition was in itself a considerable deterrent to conspiracy. Only one additional penalty could be imposed on the Royalist who was strong-minded enough to refuse to compound: outright confiscation. If, however, he had paid his fine and recovered his estate, he would hardly take the risk of being punished again. The tendency of many determined loyalists to take the fatal step of compounding was regarded by the exiled leaders in 1649 with an alarm that bordered on despair.[6]

There were many other irritating restrictions on the Royalist gentry. By 1649 they were shut out of local government, as well as national affairs, by the removal of Royalist JP's and members of borough corporations. A series of new laws in 1649 and 1650 strengthened the inhibitions. To hold almost any office, and even to obtain the protection of the law, it became necessary to take the Engagement to be "true and faithful" to the Commonwealth. Some were too scrupulous to perjure themselves, but backed by the King's authority to use "what liberty their consciences shall give them," a good many were willing to take the oath, "in policy," as Whitelock noted. Even for those who swallowed their pride and took the Engagement, however, the remaining regulations made it impossible to retain their habitual leadership in politics and society.[7]

6. For composition procedure see *CCC, 1*, preface, and *5*, intro. For its effects, H. E. Chesney, "The Transference of Lands in England, 1640–1660," *TRHS*, 4th ser. *15* (1932), 181–210; and Hardacre, *Royalists*, pp. 19–32, 64–69.

7. *Letters and Papers Illustrating the Relations between Charles the Second and Scotland in 1650*, ed. S. R. Gardiner, Scottish Historical Society, 17 (Edinburgh, 1894), 48 (cited as *Charles II and Scotland*). Bulstrode Whitelock, *Memorials of the English Affairs from the beginning of the reign of Charles the First to the happy Restoration of King Charles the Second* (Oxford, 1853), *3, 141*. See also S. R. Gardiner, *C&P, 1*, 193, 246; Hardacre, *Royalists*, p. 65; and A. C. Wood, *Nottinghamshire in the Civil War* (Oxford, 1937), pp. 129–30.

This discrimination against the Royalist gentry deprived the great lords of opportunities for exercising the patronage that was theirs in normal times. Many lesser men, younger sons of the poorer gentry, had no obvious place to turn for the employment that would have maintained them in respectable idleness, or would have helped them up the ladder of advancement. Patronage on the Royalist side was not, of course, completely destroyed: noblemen like Hertford and Southampton still maintained their dependents, and there were a few openings for employment abroad. In October 1652 Thomas Paulden, one of the defenders of Pontefract, wrote to his father in this strain:

> I am promised from a person of great qualitie (whom I cannot here name) to have a particular care taken of mee & now in order to it I am providing my selfe for Fraunce. I hope I shall bee there wth.in a monneth at furthest if you please to give mee yor. leave wch. I hope you will not deny mee when I tell you yt. it is a fortune wch. many men of farre greater condicon then my selfe would bee glad to meete wth. & besides I know no other way of living by wch. I can possibly subsist my selfe above halfe a yeare longer.[8]

There were many like Paulden for whom the choice was between exile and an empty future governed by their enemies; whichever alternative was chosen, there would be strong temptations to look for excitement and reward in the life of the professional conspirator. The interruption of the normal system of patronage thus made its contribution to the instability of the Interregnum.

If young men of Paulden's stamp were unable to find protection in the households of the Royalist nobility at home, this was merely an indication that the nobility was having to relinquish its normal leadership. The consequences for the Royalist party were obvious enough: either it would not be led or it would have to find other leaders. To some extent, of course, the Royalists could look for leadership abroad; from the King and his scattered councilors. The difficulties of exercising that leadership from beyond the seas need hardly be stressed. To the normal hazards of communication were

8. Fairfax MS (Bodleian), 32, fol. 182.

added the obstacles of having to circumvent Commonwealth officials on the lookout for Royalist agents at the ports. The exiled leaders were also inevitably somewhat out of touch with their friends in England, having to assess a situation in which they were not themselves directly involved. There was not much sign of agreement on future policy even among the exiles, and the political factions at Charles II's Court were inextricably related to the internal politics of the Royalist party at home. A brief survey of these factions is therefore a necessary part of our discussion of the general state of the Royalist party at the time of the King's execution.

"It is scarce credible how great the divisions of the Royalists are here," one of Thomas Scot's agents reported from Paris in November 1651, and the same generalization might have been made at any time since Charles II's accession.[9] The dominant group in the King's Council in 1649 and for two years to come was the "Louvre" party, so named for its connection with the Queen Mother and her intimate adviser Jermyn. Henrietta Maria had been behind the original alliance with the Scots in December 1647, and the Louvre was still prepared to make compromising terms with all or any of the parliamentary parties in order to restore the monarchy at the earliest possible moment. For the present, as a government spy interpreted their attitude, Jermyn and his faction regarded the Presbyterian party as being "much more considerable then ye Episcopall," and were skeptical of the Royalists' ability to promote effective risings alone.[10] Entrenched in the Council and supported by such men as Lords Percy and Culpeper and the Secretary Robert Long, the Louvre thus continued the alignment with both Scots and English Presbyterians: "this Franco-Scottish policy of *realpolitik*," as the historian of the Tories (and Royalists) justly describes it.[11]

The main opposition to the Louvre opportunists came from the rigidly "Old Royalist" group led by Hyde, Hopton, and Sir Edward Nicholas, and supported by Ormond in Ireland. Put simply, their

9. *CSPD, 1651–52*, p. 2. Quoted from the original MS by Eva Scott, *The King in Exile* (London, 1905), pp. 440–41. The report was not, as stated by this author, made to Thurloe, who was not yet responsible for intelligence.

10. Stowe MS (BM), 185, fol. 111. The author of this paper is Joseph Bampfield.

11. Feiling, p. 75.

objection to the Presbyterian alliance was that it abandoned important principles without practical benefits. In 1648 the Scots invasion, as Hyde could show, had led to damaging Cavalier abstentions. Instead of the still only half-converted Presbyterians, Hyde argued, it was better to rely on the Old Royalists whose loyalty was assured. The short-term successes of such a policy might be less spectacular, but in the long run it would enable the King to be restored on his own terms. If the Royalists had the patience to wait on events, they would win the allegiance of moderate men of all parties when the nation returned to its senses. In the meantime it was important to work for the downfall of the Rump by conspiracy, but it would be futile to expect the Cavaliers to risk their necks for a King whose entrance into the country would be at the head of an army of Scots Covenanters. Until 1651, however, Hyde's arguments were disregarded, and he was sent off to Spain on a joint embassy with Lord Cottington.[12]

Both the Louvre and the Hyde-Nicholas groups were distinguished by attachment to certain policies. The third of the court factions was less clearly defined, and was united only by personal jealousies of the men in the other two. It was an ill-assorted collection of political adventurers of whom Lord Gerard and the Attorney General, Sir Edward Herbert, were the most prominent; they looked to Prince Rupert for leadership, and were known as the "Swordsmen." Many of the personal quarrels which made it difficult for the Swordsmen to cooperate with the other factions go back to the first civil war: to Rupert's feud with Lord Digby, for example. On the whole the Swordsmen adopted a negative, obstructive attitude to whichever of the other parties happened to possess the King's ear. Until September 1651 they denounced the Louvre; then, when Hyde returned to favor, they attacked the patient methods which replaced the Presbyterian alliance.[13]

Each of the most prominent exiled leaders had his own following

12. On Hyde's policy see B. H. G. Wormald, *Clarendon: Politics, History and Religion* (Cambridge, 1951), pp. 161–72, 185–98.

13. Clarendon, *History*, Bk. XII, §§ 60–64, 121–25; XIII, §§ 121–34; XIV, §§ 62–77, 90–91. Carte, *Papers*, *1*, 299–472. See also Scott, *King in Exile*, passim; Gardiner, *C&P*, *1*, 61–62, 194–205; and Thomas H. Lister, *Life and Administration of Edward, first Earl of Clarendon* (London, 1837–38), *1*, 326–28, 365–69, 378–88.

of personal adherents in England, although none were sufficiently organized to be regarded as parties paralleling the ones at Court. There is no doubt that the great majority of the English Royalists suspected the Louvre policy, resented concessions to Presbyterianism, and violently disliked the use of the Scots. "As the hatred of the Queen and her governing made many rebels in the beginning of the English rebellion," one correspondent wrote from England, "so the same apprehensions begin to work afresh even in those who have all this while suffered in the King's cause." According to Lord Hatton, Jermyn and his friends were regarded as the "chiefe saints in the Presbyterian Kalender," and Nicholas heard that several plans to seize ports and strongholds in England were in abeyance because of dissatisfaction with the Louvre policies.[14] Remembering 1648, or at least their own version of it, the Royalists were determined not to be pushed into action again unless the Presbyterians engaged first; "for feare of a desertion as formerly," an agent reported from England in 1650. After a period of hesitation, the new King revived the Scots alliance on even less palatable terms, by the Treaty of Breda. This, the betrayal of Montrose, and the King's treatment by the Kirk when he went to Scotland did nothing to increase the English Royalists' enthusiasm for the Louvre projects. They were, of course, in a hideous dilemma. Loyalty dictated that they should do all they could to assist the King; yet they could not refrain from a quiet cheer when the Scots felt the hammer blows of Cromwell's Army and the Kirk's grip on the King weakened. A Commonwealth print summarized the attitude of many Royalists in a report of opinion in Dorset in October 1650: "They stood as spectators, and tried fair play, and prayed for the Presbyterians destruction." [15]

In discussing Royalist reactions to the Presbyterian alliance, we have been anticipating the events of 1650. It is time to retrace our steps by a year, to the more immediate consequences of the execution of the King. The terror of the act of regicide was driven home by the new Commonwealth during the next few months, when

14. Carte, *Papers, 1,* 414, 417; *NP, 1,* 151–53, 186–90.
15. *Charles II and Scotland,* p. 133. *A Perfect Diurnall of Some Passages and Proceedings of, and in Relation to the Armies,* No. 47.

more of the leaders of 1648 paid the penalty. On March 9, after trial by what John Evelyn called "the Rebels' new Court of Injustice," Hamilton, Holland, and Capel were beheaded. On April 25 Col. John Poyer was shot, having lost when he and two others condemned with him by court martial drew lots for the privilege of being executed. In August, Col. John Morris, who had held on in beleaguered Pontefract for a few hopeless weeks after the King's death, was condemned with his cornet, Michael Blackburne, at York assizes, and also put to death. Although Norwich and Owen, the other two prisoners arraigned with Hamilton, were reprieved, and although the announced intention of proceeding against other prisoners was not carried out, "Cromwell's New Slaughter-house," in Clement Walker's title-phrase, struck fear and horror into the whole Royalist party.[16]

"Broken and subdued," was Clarendon's later description of his friends in England, and indeed their morale could scarcely have been lower. "The whole stocke of his patience is excersized in the encounter of these sad times," a correspondent said of John Ashburnham, Charles I's former attendant at Hampton Court. Ashburnham himself groaned that his heart was "full of sorrow and mourning for the death of our deare master of holy and glorious memory"; nevertheless his response to recent events had been not to embark on further resistance, but to compound, and in the same letter that he uttered this noble sorrow, to recommend that Secretary Nicholas should do so too.[17] "When we meet," said Sancroft, "it is but to consult to what foreign plantation we shall fly." Scholarly divines like Sancroft were not really serious in their talk of seeking sanctuary in the colonies, but there were others who were. One of them was a Worcestershire Cavalier named Henry Norwood, who afterward recalled that "a very considerable number" of the Royalist gentry "did fly from their native country, as from a

16. *Diary of John Evelyn*, ed. E. S. de Beer (Oxford, 1955), 2, 548. Clement Walker, *History of Independency* (London, 1648–51), Pt. III. Gardiner, *C&P*, *1*, 10–11, 41–42. For announcements of other projected trials in 1649 see *CJ*, *6*, 157, 165; *CSPD, 1649–50*, p. 39.

17. Clarendon, *History*, Bk. XII, §§ 41, 150. *Correspondence of Isaac Basire*, ed. W. N. Darnell (London, 1831), p. 96. *CCC*, p. 1863. *NP*, *1*, 111. For Ashburnham see *DNB*, and Keeler, p. 89.

place infected with the plague." Norwood and two of his friends landed as castaways on an island off the Virginia coast early in 1650. They were soon rescued, and welcomed by others of their kind who had recently come from England; among them Sir Thomas Lunsford, Sir Henry Chicheley, and Major Philip Honywood. There have been too many dangerous generalizations from Norwood's experiences and those of others like him; the legend that Virginia was densely populated in these years by crowded shiploads of aristocratic émigrés will not bear examination. Nevertheless, the Royalist colonies did provide a temporary refuge for a few who could see no hope of further resistance in England.[18]

The Royalists who fled to Europe were much more numerous, and their opportunities of returning home much greater. Many had gone abroad at the end of the first civil war, often finding employment in foreign armies. Some of the travelers had good reason to leave in a hurry. On the nights before and after the King's execution several prominent prisoners took advantage of the concentration of attention upon Charles to escape from their own jails: Lord Loughborough from Windsor; the Presbyterian Major General Massey from St. James'; and that spinner of tall tales, Sir Lewis Dyve, from Whitehall. Loughborough reached Rotterdam early in March, at about the same time, the report of his arrival stated, as "very many persecuted Cavaliers." [19] To control the flow of fugitives, the Council of State ordered that passes to go beyond the seas were to be granted only to those who would give security not to act against the state. Although travelers were sometimes arrested for not having passes, for example at Gravesend in August 1649, the enforcement of these regulations left much to be desired. Traffic in

18. *Memorials of the Great Civil War,* ed. Henry Cary (London, 1842), 2, 118. Norwood, "A Voyage to Virginia" in *Tracts and Other Papers,* ed. Peter Force (Washington, 1836–46), 3, No. 10. For a decisive refutation of the "Cavalier legend" see Thomas J. Wertenbaker, *Patrician and Plebeian in Virginia,* Charlottesville, Va., 1910. For Norwood see P. H. Hardacre, "Further Adventures of Henry Norwood," *Virginia Magazine, 67* (1959), 271–83.

19. James Heath, *Chronicle of the Late Intestine War* (London, 1663), pp. 419–20. *Perfect Diurnall of Some Passages in Parliament,* No. 288. Carte, *Papers, 1,* 232. Dyve's embroidered account is mentioned in *Evelyn,* ed. de Beer, *3,* 40.

counterfeit passes was common, and a group of officials, including Cromwell's former secretary, turned it into a lucrative racket. John Evelyn preferred to travel with forged documents and bribe the searchers rather than take the Engagement. A fair proportion of the defeated Royalist party was thus able, legally or illegally, to find temporary relief from the gloomy discontents of England.[20]

For the much greater number who remained, the choices ranged from complete submission to violent opposition, with infinite gradations in between. No absolute distinction can be drawn between the conspiring and the conformist wings of the Royalist party, for many Cavaliers drifted from one to the other and back again. Nevertheless, the two groups can be roughly separated. Most of those who compounded and took the Engagement were necessarily closer to the conformist attitude. Their loyalty might be unabated, but they would leave it to others to risk their necks. Perhaps necks would not have to be risked at all; the Rump might collapse of its own weight, although if that was to happen its essential prop, the Army, would have to disintegrate. Perhaps the Presbyterians could be persuaded to play the major role in overthrowing the Commonwealth; if so, it would be advisable for the Royalists to hold themselves in reserve and be ready to profit from the confusion. Many who chose to sit back and await better days looked with disfavor on the activities of the violent minority, whose exploits in their eyes only led to an intensification of repression. Some of the conformists, or "prudentialists," tried to make the best of both worlds; putting themselves at the head of a movement ostensibly dedicated to conspiracy and then using their influence for restraint.

The situation which confronted the Royalist party after the execution of Charles I was not, therefore, as simple as it might superficially appear. For those who decided that a restoration of Charles II by Royalist action alone was still a practical possibility,

20. *Bibliography of Royal Proclamations of the Tudor and Stuart Sovereigns, 1, England and Wales,* ed. Robert R. Steele, Bibliotheca Lindesiana, 5 (Oxford, 1910), 343–45. *Evelyn,* ed. de Beer, *3,* 15–16. *CSPD, 1649–50,* pp. 215, 543. *Cromwelliana: A Chronological Detail,* ed. M. Stace (Westminster, 1810), p. 61. Wilbur C. Abbott, *Writings and Speeches of Oliver Cromwell* (Cambridge, Mass., 1937–47), *2,* 85.

the road ahead could hardly be a smooth one. Paradoxically, in spite of the low ebb which the Royalist cause had reached in January 1649, active conspirators could always count on a definite, although inarticulate, pro-monarchist sentiment smoldering beneath the surface. Although powerless to express itself against the bared swords of a triumphant Army, the very existence of this obstinate, unthinking attachment to the old order was a constant encouragement to conspiracy. Drunken toasts to Charles II were common enough, and seditious abuse of the "Parliament rogues" and their "stinking lousy committee." In this atmosphere the Royalists, like all resistance movements, could keep up their spirits with defiant gestures and nocturnal slogan-writing. The night after the King's execution, papers proclaiming Charles II were secretly dispersed in London, and all during 1649 there were mutinous proclamations of the King in the provinces: at Malton in Yorkshire, Preston, Twickenham, and Norwich. The Act prohibiting the proclamation of another king was pulled down when it was posted at Exeter, and when on May 30 the Lord Mayor was at last persuaded to announce the abolition of monarchy in London, there were rumblings of disapproval from the bystanders.[21] However encouraging all this might be, it had little bearing on the Royalists' real problem: the construction of an underground movement that would translate vague sympathies into effective action.

Although the Roman Catholics must have been aware of them, few other Royalists in 1649 had much appreciation of the problems that confronted organizers of a national conspiracy. The difficulties of maintaining communications, of making arrangements involving substantial numbers of men without destroying the necessary secrecy; the psychological problem of persuading lukewarm supporters that it was occasionally worth taking risks in order to keep the cause alive—all these were obstacles whose extent was only slowly realized. Whether it was best to leave major decisions

21. Whitelock, *3*, 11, 65, 138, 148. Heath, pp. 415–16. *CSPD, 1649–50,* pp. 290, 292–93, 298, 300. *Perfect Diurnall of . . . the Armies,* No. 10. *Depositions from the Castle of York,* ed. James Raine, Surtees Society, 40 (1861), p. 40. See also Gardiner, *C&P, 1,* 12, 39, 57; and for some more examples, *Middlesex County Records,* ed. J. C. Jeaffreson, Middlesex Record Society (London, 1886–92), *3,* 192–205.

to the leaders abroad, or whether the King should appoint an accredited council to meet secretly in England, was another matter to be decided. If the latter, who would the leaders be, and how far would their authority be obeyed? Would it be possible to strike a satisfactory balance between the excessive recklessness which would get the innocent into trouble and discourage the men of substance, and the apathy-creating caution which might be logically unchallengeable, but which would allow the cause to wither away for lack of inspiration? Even supposing a network of conspiracy could be constructed, what was the best policy for it to follow—the promotion of an insurrection by Royalists alone, or a combined conspiracy with the Presbyterians? Finally, how effectively would the Royalists be able to dodge the government's inevitable countermeasures?

With all these problems before them, the condition of the Royalists in 1649 can scarcely be described as hopeful. Reeling under the blows of sequestration and composition, shocked by the execution of Charles I, and terrorized by the High Court of Justice's series of savage examples, they faced an implacable government, determined to suppress the ungodly (the Royalists) in the name of the divine right of the elect. Unable to forget their hostility to the Presbyterians, they lacked confidence in their leaders abroad who continued an unpopular Scots alliance, and set the worst examples of factionalism and intrigue. Yet the vitality of the Royalist ideal was never extinguished, and within a remarkably short time the party entered the lists against the Commonwealth as a conspiratorial movement.

After the execution the statue of the dead King at the Exchange had been taken down, and in its place appeared the inscription *Exit tyrannus, Regum ultimus.* For more than eleven years the Royalists struggled to show that this was not the last word.

2. The Beginning of Conspiracy

FOR THIRTY WEARY MONTHS after the King's execution, the fortunes of the English Royalists were inseparably linked with those of the Scots and the minority of Presbyterians in England who were willing to rise above a disgusted neutrality. During this period the rough outline of a Royalist underground organization came tentatively into being, survived precariously for a few months, and was shattered even before the downfall of the Scots army which it was intended to support. As we have seen, it was not a propitious time for creating an effective resistance movement out of the wreckage of the royal armies. Horror and revulsion at the act of regicide were not necessarily accompanied by a desire for immediate action, at least for the vast majority of the gentry who called themselves Royalists. The existence of a widespread smoldering dislike of a government whose main claim to authority was the sword was the only source of encouragement for the optimistic. But it was not by riotous proclamations of the new King, or by healths drunk on loyal, tipsy knees, that Charles II would be restored. If the Royalists were to enjoy any part in that still unlikely event, much preliminary spadework was necessary.

The essential foundation for any future action was the formation of a recognized chain of command. Whichever of his three available alternatives Charles eventually chose—invasion by a mercenary force from Europe, by Ormond's Irish, or by the Scots—an organ-

18

ized network of conspiracy to mount a supporting rebellion was essential, and would require elaborate preparation. Ideally, such preparations could best be directed by the party's leaders in England, men on the spot, men whose authority would be unhesitatingly accepted by those of inferior rank. A committee of just such men was proposed in November 1649. The idea was first broached by Sir Gilbert Talbot, formerly Charles I's resident at Venice, and was passed on to Secretary Nicholas by William Coventry. "It is thought fitt here," Talbot observed, "that the King fix a Councell of some few sober and discreet men here, who may meete constantly and consult upon all matters that may concerne his Majesties service, as the meanes to unite the heartes of all the sober Royalysts." Three of the most influential peers still in England, Richmond, Hertford, and Southampton, were obvious candidates for membership, Talbot suggested.[1]

The proposal was bound to commend itself to Nicholas and all who agreed that Charles' best hope lay in the English Cavaliers themselves, rather than in compromises of principle with Catholics or Presbyterians. Apparently Charles also approved. On December 4 Nicholas duly passed on to Coventry the news that the King had responded favorably.[2] In spite of Nicholas' enthusiasm, however, Talbot's proposal was quietly pigeon-holed, and it is not hard to see why. The unpopularity of the Presbyterian alliance among the English Royalists meant that any committee of their leaders either would be hostile to Jermyn and the ruling group in the King's Council or would not be truly representative. Jermyn, Percy, and Long were not likely to promote the creation of an accredited body in England that would focus opposition to their own policies. Charles did not commit himself to the Scottish terms until May 1, 1650, when the Treaty of Breda was completed, but his reluctant progress toward this position made a formal link with the Old Cavalier leaders less and less possible. Conspiracy in England was not entirely excluded from the Louvre scheme, but it took a distinctly secondary place to the action in Scotland.

1. *NP, I,* 154–55. For Coventry see *DNB;* for Talbot, *Archaeologia, 35* (1853), 338 n.
2. *NP, I,* 154 n.

There was another serious obstacle to the creation of an authorized council in England: the unwillingness of the great lords to risk their necks and estates. The three peers recommended by Talbot were all men of massive prestige and authority; all three had served Charles I assiduously, and had attended him to the end; but not one of them would accept new and dangerous responsibilities. Hertford, as we shall see, was eventually drawn into the conspiracy in the western counties, but his age and preference for retirement left the real command to his son Beauchamp. Southampton, reserved and pessimistic, had no recorded contact with his Cavalier friends in the two years before Worcester. Richmond, who had refused to participate in the Kent rising in 1648, soon made his attitude clear. He was suggested as a suitable commander for the Royalists of the Southeast when Charles decided to encourage them to rise in 1650. Thomas Coke, an agent recently arrived from Holland (he was the son of Charles I's Secretary of State and had been MP for Leicestershire), visited him at Cobham in July and tried to persuade him to accept the dangerous honor. Richmond replied that he "was no soldier nor ever meddled in busines of that nature . . . and did desire but to live quietly." It was a common response: the cautious abstention of men of property and prestige was to be a constant obstacle to Royalist plotting throughout the succeeding decade.[3]

The arguments for living quietly were solid enough. Already the Commonwealth was fully alive to the dangers of Royalist conspiracy. At first the Council of State had assumed collective responsibility for intelligence. But on July 1, 1649, sole responsibility was vested in the regicide Thomas Scot. Scot's diplomatic agents were often employed to spy on the Royalists abroad, and as the exiles were never noted for control over their tongues, the results were sometimes informative. Much will be said about Scot's informers in England; they were too many to enumerate here, "swarming over all England as Lice & Frogs did in Egypt," Clement Walker indig-

3. HMC, *Portland, 1,* 582, 596–97. *CSPD, 1650,* pp. 233–34. *Charles II and Scotland,* pp. 132–33. On the general attitude of the Royalist peers see Clarendon, *Con.,* § 22. For Hertford, Richmond, and Southampton see *DNB,* and Clarendon, *History,* Bk. VI, §§ 384–86; for Coke, Keeler, pp. 137–38.

nantly complained. Such agents frequently acted as trepanners, or
agents provocateurs, involving simple-minded Royalists in fake
conspiracies and then turning them over to the authorities—
"Decoy ducks," they were often called.[4] In the autumn of 1650 Scot
was given an energetic assistant. Capt. George Bishop, an ardent
scripture-quoting Independent from Bristol, was made secretary to
the Committee for Examinations, taking over the detailed supervision of domestic intelligence. Another of Scot's instruments, less
regularly employed, was John Wallis, Savilian Professor of Geom-
etry at Oxford. Wallis had created something of a stir by deciphering the King's papers after Naseby, and claimed to have originated
the science of cryptography. Wallis pretended to be a political neutral, interested in deciphering merely as an intellectual exercise,
but he gave Scot valuable service. Wallis' indifference to politics
was sometimes useful to Royalist suspects; the Presbyterian Robert
Harley, for instance, was able to escape punishment when some of
his letters were intercepted, through his kinship with Lady Vere to
whom Wallis was chaplain. Decipherers like this could not have
operated without the government's control over the mails. Not only
were letters intercepted, they were also copied, and when the forger
was skillful enough, the originals were retained as evidence, while
indistinguishable duplicates were sent on to the unsuspecting
recipients. Samuel Morland later became the greatest practitioner
of this dangerous art, but Bishop also had men who could do it.
The Royalists had good reason to respect Scot's intelligence system.
"Hee doth thinke you deale with the devill; that as soon as thinges
bee thought off, you knowe them," one of Bishop's men reported
after a conversation with the Marquis of Newcastle.[5]

4. "Thomas Scot's Account of his Actions as Intelligencer during the
Commonwealth," ed. C. H. Firth, *EHR, 12* (1897), 116–26. Walker, *Independency,* Pt. III, 34.
5. "Scot's Account," *EHR, 12,* 121. *Original Letters and Papers of State
. . . Found among the Political Collections of Mr. John Milton,* ed. John
Nickolls (London, 1743), pp. 49–50, 77. *CClSP, 2,* 45. HMC, *Portland, 8, 9.*
For Bishop's career see Nickolls, p. 49; *CSPD, 1649–50,* pp. 149, 443, 459,
578, 585, 597; *1650,* pp. 339, 348, 400, 461, 481; and John Latimer, *Annals
of Bristol in the Seventeenth Century* (Bristol, 1900), pp. 250, 349. For Wallis
and Morland see *DNB;* the latter's account of methods used in intercepting
and transcribing letters is in HMC, *Buccleuch, 2,* Pt. I, 49–51. John Wildman

In the absence of leadership from the peers and in the face of the government's vigilance, Royalist conspiracy was slow to develop any organized characteristics. Among the early preoccupations were the provision of regular intelligence about affairs in England, and of extremely limited financial supplies for the exiles. Intelligence came sometimes from professional intelligencers, sometimes from the friends or relatives of members of Charles II's entourage. Sir Richard Browne, the King's ambassador in Paris, received information on English affairs from his son-in-law, the diarist John Evelyn, until Evelyn left for France in July 1649. Secretary Nicholas had an English intelligencer in 1649, and Hyde received regular news from his kinsman William Hyde. William Coventry was also receiving letters in the summer of 1649, from a paid intelligencer with copious financial needs: he was not satisfied by a bill of exchange for a mere £100. One of the most interesting of the intelligencers was that scurrilous denizen of Grub Street, Marchamont Needham, the editor of *Mercurius Pragmaticus*. In March 1649 Needham addressed two letters of intelligence to the King himself, but he was a journalist rather than a mere private scribe, and there is no record that the correspondence continued. No one trusted him, least of all the Royalists. After a spell of imprisonment in the summer and autumn, Needham sold his services to the Commonwealth, and no one was surprised. This by no means exhausts the roll of Royalist intelligencers in 1649—among others in regular communication with the exiles was that zealous prebendary of Durham and fellow of St. John's, Cambridge, Dr. John Barwick—but it is sufficient to show the variety of their sources of information.[6]

Just as important as reliable knowledge of events in England was money to make independent action possible. In August 1649 Charles II issued a number of promissory notes for his financial

was not impressed by the crude methods used in Scot's time: "A Brief Discourse Concerning the Businesse of Intelligence," ed. C. H. Firth, *EHR, 13* (1898), 530.

6. *Evelyn* (ed. 1857), *3*, 36–52. *Memorials of the Civil War*, ed. Robert Bell (London, 1849), 2, 90–120. Carte, *Papers, 1*, 224–99. *CClSP*, 2, 1–4. HMC, *Pepys*, pp. 282, 299–300, 307. Peter Barwick, *Life of the Reverend Dr. John Barwick*, tr. H. Bedford (London, 1724), pp. 114–16. On Needham's activities at this time see *DNB*, and Gardiner, *C&P, 1*, 252–55.

agents; the recipients included Evelyn's acquaintance Lady Catherine Scott, daughter of the Earl of Norwich; Lord Percy; and John Birkenhead, one-time editor of *Mercurius Aulicus*. Some money must have been collected on them; we know of £1,000 contributed by Lady Savile, and the Presbyterian clergy were active in London. It is impossible, however, to guess at the total amount involved. The English Cavaliers, preoccupied with sequestration and composition, had little money to spare, and potential collectors were easily discouraged. One financial agent of whom much was hoped, the antiquary Gervase Holles, never went to England at all; his instructions were drawn up at Jersey in December 1649, and that is the last we hear of it. The experience of Colonel Keynes, a Royalist agent who was in England in April 1650, was evidently typical: "I found generally in all so great an apprehension of the difficultye of returne without discovery of persons that I could not presume of any certainty in that kind." [7]

Meanwhile the first flickerings of more active sedition were beginning. Some of it can be dismissed as spurious chatter. Capt. Thomas Verney, no very trustworthy source, reported in March that he was in touch with a group of firebrands plotting to seize a town in the south of England. At about the same time another doubtful character, Major John Bernard, enlisted his old colonel, Eusebius Andrews, in a tentative discussion of conspiracy, but when Andrews left London in May they had not advanced beyond vague talk. Better evidence of subterranean discontent can be found in the proceedings of the Council of State. There were arrests at Chester at the end of March, and occasional rumblings in Kent. On April 13 the Council ordered an investigation of suspicious meetings at a Gravesend tavern. It was discovered that Royalist agents frequently passed through the town on their way in and out of the country: the inn was closed, and its private pier demolished. On May 12 a warrant was issued for the arrest of Col. Philip Froude,

7. *Original Letters Illustrative of English History*, ed. Sir Henry Ellis (London, 1824–46), *3*, 327; 2d ser. *3*, 351. CClSP, *2*, 19–22. HMC, *Portland*, *2*, 27–28. *Evelyn*, ed. de Beer, *2*, 560; *3*, 13. *Barwick*, p.128. *Charles II and Scotland*, p. 95. CSPD, *1649–50*, pp. 420–21. HMC, *Buccleuch*, *1*, 533–39. *Complete Collection of State Trials*, ed. T. B. and T. J. Howell (London, 1816–28), *5*, 70–71.

of Gillingham, and a number of others suspected of a design against the state; a few days later a certain Marcellus Rivers was imprisoned on a similar charge. None of this was very serious, but it shows that the Cavalier party was not regarded as quite extinct.[8]

Two developments early in September 1649 strengthened the goverment's belief that Cavalier plotting was no longer confined to the disconnected efforts of obscure adventurers. The first was the discovery of renewed activity by the Levellers, and evidence of collusion between them and the Royalists. Actually the evidence was slender. John Lilburne, pouring out a torrent of invective from the Tower against Cromwell, had indeed come round to a belief that a restored monarchy might in certain circumstances be reconciled with popular liberties. There is, however, no indication that he was in contact with Royalist agents in any serious way. A few months earlier, that unattractive rascal Tom Verney had approached him with a proposal for raising men to support the mutineers Cromwell was pursuing to their doom at Burford. Lilburne suspected, probably correctly, that Verney was being paid to trepan him, and the intrigues of this bankrupt sponger did nothing to inspire him with confidence in the Royalists. The Council, however, was anxious to tar all its opponents with the same brush. On September 8 there was a Leveller mutiny at Oxford, and the government assiduously spread stories that it was Royalist-inspired. The only evidence for such an allegation was a letter from a certain "T.F." in the Fleet prison (no doubt Verney again) to Lord Cottington, advising a Leveller alliance as the best hope of success for Charles II. This proved absolutely nothing. The only hint from the Royalist side suggesting that Royalist-Leveller discussions may really have occurred in this period is a statement by Thomas Coke in April 1651. Coke asserted that at the time of Lilburne's trial (October 1649), Leveller overtures were transmitted to the Earl of Cleveland by Sir Sackville Crowe, but there is nothing to corroborate this. The supposition of Royalist-Leveller contact in Septem-

---

8. *CSPD, 1649–50,* pp. 84, 140, 532, 534. HMC, *Pepys,* pp. 292–93. Howell, ed., *State Trials,* 5, 9. *Cromwelliana,* p. 54. For Legge and Werden see *DNB;* for Froude, *CCC,* p. 1325; for Verney, F. P. and M. M. Verney, *Memoirs of the Verney Family* (London, 1892–94), *1,* 135–55; *2,* 408; *3,* 138–78.

ber 1649 rests almost entirely on the statements of government propaganda, and its only importance lies in the fact that it led to increased vigilance on the part of the authorities.[9]

The second reason for the Council's alertness was more substantial. On September 17 Charles II arrived in Jersey from St. Germain. This did not mean that he had decided to repudiate the Scots, or to pin all his hopes on the English Royalists; nevertheless, there were immediate signs of rejuvenation in the Cavalier ranks. Hopes grew that Charles might be seriously contemplating a descent into the country, and loyal voices were raised in seditious conversations in many parts of England. Eusebius Andrews arrived back in London in August, and soon the whispered proposals of the friendly Major Bernard began to take on more definite shape. An old scheme of Andrews', to seize the Isle of Ely, might profitably be revived, Bernard suggested, and he produced a number of friends of doubtful antecedents to assist. One of these, John Benson, was a servant of Sir John Gell, a well-known Presbyterian officer who harbored a strong grievance against his parliamentary employers because of long outstanding arrears of pay. Benson correctly stated that Gell might easily be won over, and although Cromwell's victories in Ireland convinced the plotters that the time was not ripe for the attempt on Ely, they pressed for Gell's adherence. By the end of the year Andrews was busily arranging meetings with conspirators who were, Bernard told him, promoting designs in other areas. They showed a curious inability to fulfil their appointments, but Andrews was too innocent to suspect the truth. He was already in the toils of *agents provocateurs;* he was not arrested immediately only because the government preferred to give him enough rope to hang himself. Others were more fortunate in being secured before they put their necks into the noose. Among those rounded up before the end of 1649 on suspicion of Royalist plotting were Lord Blayney, a certain William Roberts in Kent, and Edward Penruddock, one of the King's Gentlemen of the Privy Chamber. The

9. Verney, *Memoirs, 3,* 142–46. *OPH, 19,* 192–93. *CSPD, 1649–50,* pp. 303–4, 314–15. *Perfect Diurnall of Some Passages in Parliament,* Nos. 319–21. *CJ, 6,* 293. HMC, *Portland, 1,* 591. See also Gardiner, *C&P, 1,* 160–64.

Council took other precautions. Local authorities in Derbyshire and Oxford were told to break up potentially dangerous gatherings at race meetings and bowling matches; officials were empowered to search carriers' packs for Royalist propaganda; and a report was made to Parliament on Cavalier activities in the London area.[10]

More serious to the government were the organized conspiracies that began to be promoted from Court soon after the King's arrival in Jersey. There was a significant increase in the number of agents from abroad, accredited to seek out the county leaders, and well furnished with commissions, instructions, and advice. One of the busiest was Lord Gerard's brother-in-law, Col. Roger Whitley of Aston Hall, Flint, whose instructions were dated from Jersey on October 5. Whitley was authorized to return to England, to deliver letters and commissions to the leading Cavaliers in his native district, and to "bring ym to speedy Resolucons, to take up Armes." Specifically, he was empowered to treat with Sir Thomas Myddelton of Chirk, John Booth of Dunham Massey, and other Presbyterians of the Northwest; to attempt to reduce strongholds such as Beaumaris castle; and to discover who would be the most acceptable commander for a rising in the area. Little is known about Whitley's prosecution of this mission; but it may be significant that early in 1650 there were reports of seditious meetings at Shrewsbury (the Presbyterians were blamed), and that two men from the Isle of Man were arrested at Chester on a charge of attempting to betray the garrison. In March 1650 Whitley foolishly involved himself in a ridiculous scheme to seize Bardsey Island, and he himself, one of his Gerard kinsmen, and half a dozen other Royalists were arrested. However disastrous its ending, Whitley's mission is another reflection of the growing desire of the anti-Louvre group in Charles II's Council to revive the spirits of their friends in England.[11]

The stimulus given English Royalists from Court was not con-

10. Howell, ed., *State Trials*, 5, 3–9. Bell, 2, 105. HMC, *Pepys*, p. 255. *CSPD, 1649–50*, pp. 323, 333–38, 347, 400, 411, 413, 434, 547.

11. *CSPD, 1650*, p. 204. HMC, *Leybourne-Popham*, p. 58. *Perfect Diurnall of the Armies*, Nos. 8–9, 12–15. Whitelock, 3, 144, 147, 160. Egerton MS 2542, fols. 14–15. For Whitley see *Archaeologia, 35*, 338 n.; for Myddelton, *DNB;* for John Booth, *LBM*, p. 27 n.

fined to sending isolated agents to organize areas where activity was not yet visible. In some places the Cavaliers were themselves beginning to form local cadres capable of being expanded into more formal military units should the time be ripe. In October 1649 commissions were sent to Royalist leaders, self-appointed or otherwise, in many different counties. By far the most important of the new local organizations was one in the Southwest of England. Even before the King's landing in Jersey, the most vigorous signs of Cavalier resistance were to be found in the West. Cornwall had always been strongly for the King; and although the puritan clothworkers of Somerset and the counties to the east had been buttressed by families like the Pophams and Horners, there was still a heavy sprinkling of Royalist squires in those counties. Resistance was encouraged from beyond the seas. Charles II's garrisons were still holding out in Jersey and the Scillies, Ormond fighting successfully in Ireland. On February 19 Lord Hopton, cruising off the Cornish coast with twenty ships from Scilly, issued a declaration to "the Gentlemen and Inhabitants of Cornwall," calling them to be ready to support armed action against the usurpers. The Commonwealth authorities quickly took precautions, and travelers in the West that summer were frequently stopped and questioned. The danger from sea-borne Royalists, however, was not over.[12]

The first real outbreak inspired by Royalists in the islands occurred at Weymouth and nearby Portland in July. Weymouth was a useful bridgehead for invasion, and the rugged Isle of Portland, connected with the mainland by a narrow isthmus, had obvious strategic possibilities. The idea was to seize the two places with nearly 1,000 men from Jersey and one of the northern French ports; although nothing is known about preparations for the descent, disaffection in the Dorset towns was real enough. Soldiers in the Weymouth garrison were implicated, and rumor had it that there was a plan to cut the throats of all who refused to join them. The leading spirit in the affair was Capt. "King" Gardiner, of Portland, who had fought in Dorset in the first civil war. "A very active trecherous fellow," the Commonwealth prints describe him. Gardi-

12. Add. MS (BM) 4180, fol. 10. Mary Coate, *Cornwall in the Great Civil War* (Oxford, 1933), pp. 251–53.

ner and a number of other townsmen were arrested before their plans were ready, but they created a mild flutter of alarm for a few days.[13]

When the Court arrived in Jersey, the disaffection of the western Royalists received official encouragement. A few months of discussions and clandestine journeyings by the itinerant adventurers who were always available for such employment, produced a fairly coherent system of conspiracy. It was a promising organization, and by 1650 was calling itself the Western Association. The first sign that something was afoot was the departure of an agent named Richard Pile from Jersey in September 1649. Pile was a Hampshire man who had been one of the King's surgeons since 1642, and had followed the younger Charles into exile; he had, as we shall see, some connection with Secretary Nicholas. No direct traces of Pile's mission have survived, but it may not be entirely coincidental that within a few weeks of his disappearance from Jersey, Nicholas was drawing up a set of instructions and commissions for three leaders in the West. Sir John Paulet in Hampshire, Col. Francis Wyndham in Somerset, and Col. Robert Phelips in Dorset and Wiltshire were each authorized to take charge of preparations for a rising in their respective counties. At the same time a general declaration was drafted, calling on the gentry of Devon and Cornwall to support any attempt the King might make with his forces from abroad. Paulet, apparently, made no response to the commission, but Wyndham and Phelips were among the principal architects of the Western Association. They were both Old Royalists from civil war days, stout performers in the fighting in the West; the former as Governor of Dunster, the latter at the siege of Bridgwater.[14] They were not alone in stirring up the dull embers of Royalism. Early in

13. *Perfect Diurnall of Some Passages in Parliament*, Nos. 312–13. *The Kingdomes Weekly Intelligencer*, No. 321. Whitelock, *3*, 71. HMC, *Pepys*, p. 300. A. R. Bayly, *The Great Civil War in Dorset* (Taunton, 1910), pp. 358–59. There is a reference to Gardiner's part in the civil war in Bayly, p. 72; perhaps the William Gardner, merchant, of Weymouth, mentioned in *CCC*, pp. 2995–96. He proved to be a recalcitrant prisoner: *Perfect Diurnall of the Armies*, Nos. 3, 65. There was some discussion of hanging him as a spy: Nickolls, p. 27.

14. *CSPD, 1649–50*, pp. 325, 354–55. For Pile see *CSPD, 1660–61*, p. 556; for Paulet, G. N. Godwin, *The Civil War in Hampshire*, London, 1904; for Wyndham, H. A. Wyndham, *A Family History 1410–1688: The Wyndhams*

1650 suspicious meetings of local Cavaliers created alarm at Plymouth. A few days later two disguised Royalist agents were arrested at Sir Charles Trevanion's house in Cornwall: Col. Walter Slingsby, one of Hopton's most trusted officers; and a companion who was thought, incorrectly, to be Sir John Berkeley.[15]

Charles II reached Breda to begin final negotiations with the Scots commissioners on March 16, 1650. Two days later an agent arrived from the West: a certain Colonel Keynes, evidently Alexander Keynes of Radipole, Dorset. Keynes was sent by three separate Royalist groups, one in London, one of Catholic peers, and one in the West, with the double object of acquainting the King with their existence, and of urging him not to desert Montrose. The first two groups need not concern us, but the overtures from the West were important. In Cornwall, Keynes announced, the influential Arundells, Sir John of Lanherne, and Colonel Richard of Trerice, undertook to raise the county, provided they could be assured of support from Scilly, preferably under the command of Sir Richard Grenville, the King's disgraced General in the West. Grenville, they suggested, should be sent to reinforce his nephew at Scilly, and in any national rising should be Lieutenant General under the old Marquis of Hertford.[16]

Keynes was quickly sent back to inform the Arundells that arms and ammunition were already being assigned to Scilly. The Cornish leaders were instructed to integrate their plans with those in other parts of the country, and to be prepared to seize Pendennis

---

of *Norfolk and Somerset* (London, 1939), pp. 189, 196–278; for Phelips, *DNB* (under "Phelips, Sir Robert, 1586?–1638"), and *Archaeologia, 35,* 343 n.

15. *CSPD, 1649–50,* pp. 478, 480. *Perfect Diurnall of the Armies,* Nos. 7–8. Sir Richard Baker, *Chronicle of the Kings of England . . . ,* continued by Edward Phillips (London, 1674), p. 611. Whitelock, *3,* 140. Ibid., p. 116, also notes the arrest of Slingsby and Berkeley under October 1649, but other accounts contradict this. Berkeley cannot have been Slingsby's companion, as he was abroad at this time: *CClSP, 2, 32,* 50. For Slingsby see *CCC,* p. 1800, and Sir Ralph Hopton, *Bellum Civile,* ed. C. E. H. Chadwyck Healey, Somerset Record Society, 18 (London, 1902), 16, 23, 28, 62, 90–103.

16. *Charles II and Scotland,* pp. 36–38. For Keynes see *CCC,* pp. 1654–56; and F. A. Keynes, *Gathering Up the Threads* (Cambridge, 1950), p.106. In the autumn of 1650 Thomas Coke talked to him about a design on Poole: *HMC, Portland, 1,* 577. He then went into exile and was in Paris in 1653: *CClSP, 2,* 259. For the Arundells see Coate, *Cornwall in the Civil War;* for Richard Arundell, *DNB,* and Keeler, p. 88.

and Plymouth. That the Weymouth project was not dead is indicated by the hope that it would be "prosecuted with all industrie, diligence, and secrecy." Keynes left Breda on March 31, while Charles was still wrestling with the inflexible Scots, and in the latter part of April traveled busily around the West. He carried the King's answer to Sir John Arundell, visited Wyndham and Phelips, and talked to the former about the Weymouth design. Among Keynes' other hosts were John Coventry, son of Charles I's Lord Keeper; old Sir Henry Berkeley of Yarlington; Giles Strangways of Melbury Sampford, Dorset; and Edward Kirton of Castle Cary, steward to the Marquis of Hertford—all of them disabled Royalist MP's and men of substance. Finally, Keynes was present at the inaugural meeting of the Western Association.

This interesting gathering was held at Salisbury in April 1650, under the common disguise of a race meeting. There were two delegates from each of the six counties in the area, and although not all the names have come down to us (Somerset is not accounted for), there is enough evidence to form some idea of the quality of the Association's chief men. Hampshire was represented by Sir William Courtenay, a recusant of modest means but good family; and Sir Humphrey Bennett of Shalden, another man of middle rank who had commanded a troop of horse in the civil war and distinguished himself at the second battle of Newbury. Strangways, a much wealthier man (he and his father had been fined £10,000 for delinquency), represented Dorset; and from Devon there were Sir Henry Carey and one of the Seymours of Berry Pomeroy. The Cornish delegates were Sir John Arundell and Sir Chichester Wrey, of St. Ives. Wrey's presence followed a violent local quarrel: his Royalist integrity had been questioned and he had been called a turncoat by Sir Jonathan Trelawney. There was a duel, but no one was hurt, and Wrey removed any remaining doubts by going to the Salisbury meeting. The others present included Keynes and the surgeon Richard Pile.[17]

17. *Charles II and Scotland*, pp. 48–49, 94–100. HMC, *Portland*, *1*, 577. For Berkeley, Coventry, Kirton, and Strangways see Keeler, pp. 108–9, 143–44, 241–42, 352–53; for Courtenay, *CCC*, p. 1841; for Bennett, ibid., p. 1944, also Hopton, *Bellum Civile*, pp. 69–70, 83, S. R. Gardiner, *History of the Great Civil War* (London, 1886–91), *2*, 45–50, and *CClSP*, *2*, 32; for Wrey,

All these, with the exceptions of Keynes and Pile, were solid and responsible men, typical of the Royalist party's backing among the country gentry. None, however, possessed a fraction of the influence of the remaining participant in the Salisbury conference, a personage who immediately assumed command of the Western Association. This was Henry, Lord Beauchamp, son of the Marquis of Hertford, and in view of his father's senescent inactivity, the effective head of the great Seymour connection, with its estates in half a dozen counties and a prestige unsurpassed in the West. According to Thomas Coke, Beauchamp had already been sent a commission as General of horse for the western counties. A few weeks after the Salisbury conference Beauchamp wrote to the King, acknowledging "yt trust which your Majesty was pleased so far above my merrit to impose in mee." By May 1650 the Western Association was effectively in existence, and possessed an assured and authoritative commander.

The conference broke up after three or four days, but some of the lesser lights, Keynes, Pile, John Seymour, and Courtenay, went on to re-assemble at the last-named's house a week later, "there to receive our finall dispatch from my Lord Beauchamp." This "finall dispatch" summarized the general conclusions of the conference. There were, Beauchamp and his friends thought, reasonable prospects of launching a Royalist rebellion in the West, but only if certain conditions were fulfilled. The conditions were important. A rebellion could only succeed if the Rump's forces in the West, not impressively strong in Beauchamp's judgment, were drawn off to fight the Scots; if reinforcements to the number of 2,000 foot were landed in Devon or Dorset; and if there were no general arrests of the western gentry in the meantime. On May 31, when Charles was already in the Presbyterian toils, Beauchamp again insisted on the need for foreign forces in a report on his discussions with the county commissioners; although loyally disposed, they could do nothing without an organized invading force.[18]

LBM, p. 22 n.; for Trelawney, *DNB*, and *CCC*, p. 1508. The duel between the two latter is reported in *Perfect Diurnall of the Armies*, No. 17.

18. *Charles II and Scotland*, p. 96. HMC, *Portland*, *1*, 577, 583. *NP*, *1*, 178–79. For Beauchamp see the article on his father in *DNB*; for John Seymour, *LBM*, p. 163 n.

The conclusion of the Scots alliance gave some hopes that the first of Beauchamp's conditions might be fulfilled. The other two, however, were impossible. The required forces from abroad were never obtained, partly because the pro-Scottish element in Charles II's Council was not enthusiastic about the idea, more decisively because there were none available. Robert Long firmly put the case against foreign assistance in a letter to Ormond: "We have no foreign forces, nor money to raise them; and if we had, it will be difficult to get shipping to transport them . . . Besides an entire body of foreign forces . . . will be extremely disagreeable to the English. All the King's friends in England advise the King to agree with the Scots." In the last two sentences Long was merely expressing the Louvre's interested skepticism about the practicability of action in England; in the first sentence, on the other hand, he was stating hard facts. Various negotiations were on foot to find men in Europe to supplement the meager reserves in the islands; but all of them, whether through the Duke of Lorraine, the German Von Karpfen, or the Danish Count Waldemar, came to nothing.[19]

As for the western leaders' third condition, that they must be able to bring their plans to maturity without the interruption of a purge, the fact was that the Commonwealth was never likely to relax sufficiently, especially with war threatening in Scotland, to make this possible. The Association was not actually broken until 1651, but even in 1650 there were signs that the authorities in the West were on their guard. At about the time of the Salisbury meeting there was a round-up of suspects in Cornwall (Trevanion, Slingsby's host in January, was among the victims), and although most of them were released on security, Beauchamp and his fellow plotters were suitably impressed. There were similar warning signals in Somerset, where five men of lesser stamp were arrested at Wells in mid-April and consigned to Exeter jail. Talk of the revival of Royalist hopes must have already been spreading in tones louder than the discreet whispers of the gentry, for the five Wellensians had talked loosely of a rising due to take place around the beginning of May. Fortified with Dutch courage and good Somerset cider, they denounced supporters of the Commonwealth as rogues

19. Carte, *Papers, 1,* 373–74. Gardiner, *C&P, 1,* 196, 200, 240–41.

and traitors, drank healths to their confusion, and talked gleefully of cutting their throats. In Dorset, too, there were arrests, the Sheriff being instructed to take into custody Capt. John Holmes and three others on a charge of treason. Nor were matters helped in May by the dispersal of another declaration, ostensibly from Hopton at Scilly, calling on the western gentry to rise in support of a descent from the islands. The Cornish authorities were still investigating a plot to betray Pendennis, and took the opportunity of making further arrests.[20]

In spite of these early discouragements, it is worth taking stock of the Association's progress in the latter part of 1650. There was much coming and going by the lesser agents, Keynes, Pile, and John Seymour. After leaving Courtenay's house on May 1, they traveled as far as Winchester together (with some narrow escapes on the way) and then parted, Keynes for London and the Continent, Pile and Seymour for the West. Seymour was soon sent to make further representations to the King of the need for assistance from abroad; he followed Charles to Scotland and did not return to the West until December. Pile and the more substantial men of the Association must have occupied their time in lining up supporters, and perfecting their plans for a rising. Thomas Coke was not impressed with the preparations, and after a conversation with Pile told the King on August 2 that the West was still unready, blaming Beauchamp for the shortcomings. This criticism was hardly disinterested, for Beauchamp had been highly suspicious of the newly arrived agent, with good reason as events were to show, and had refused to cooperate with him.[21]

Beauchamp was soon to have bad news for those who demanded definite assurance of invasion from abroad. The failure of Charles II's hopes from Germany early in 1650 had left him with no alter-

20. *Charles II and Scotland*, p. 97. *CSPD, 1650*, p. 535. Whitelock, 3, 179–93. *Perfect Diurnall of the Armies*, Nos. 19–21, 23. *The Declaration of the Right Honourable Ralph Lord Hopton*, May 1650. *The Scots Remonstrance*, May 1650.

21. *Charles II and Scotland*, pp. 97, 133. *CClSP*, 2, 67, 73. HMC, *Portland, 1*, 577. Carte, *Papers, 1*, 465. *NP, 1*, 199. Add. MS 4180, fols. 25, 43. A month after Keynes' visit to the West his wife, trying to recover his estate, petitioned that he was dead in Germany: *CCC*, pp. 1655–56.

native but to accept the Scottish terms. Hopton and Nicholas, however, continued to look for a means of escape, turning now to Charles' brother-in-law, the Prince of Orange, to supply what Beauchamp and his followers demanded. The defeat of Charles' northern allies at Dunbar in September produced further arguments for an agreement with the Dutch. Already (in July, apparently) Charles had written from Scotland appealing to William to lend him 2,000 men to be landed, prophetically, at Torbay. Early in October the King warned Sir John Grenville at Scilly to be ready to descend on Cornwall to support him. No one could tell how much interest this aroused in the Prince's ambitious mind, and he did not commit himself. On October 27 he died, and Charles had to look elsewhere for a champion. Nicholas, nursing hopes of William's compliance to the end, decided that the tragedy utterly wrecked "the Business in the West." Some of the local leaders had reached the same conclusion before the Prince's death, for both Sir John Arundell and Wrey obtained licenses to go to London and compound before the end of October.[22]

A western rising was therefore a remote prospect in the latter part of 1650; the organization, however, did not disintegrate. When Coke was questioned by the Council of State in April 1651, he showed how the Seymour interest had produced a widespread network of conspiracy throughout the western counties. This was particularly true in Somerset and Wiltshire, where Hertford and Beauchamp had brought in wealthy men like Sir Charles Berkeley of Bruton, and Sir Edward Rodney of Rodney Stoke, a cousin of the Seymours'. Rodney's brother, Coke declared, had been sent to Breda with an account of the Somerset preparations, and there had been talk of designs on Dunster (in which Francis Wyndham was implicated), and on the Holms islands in the Bristol Channel. Hertford's brother, Lord Seymour, was active in Wiltshire, and so was Col. James Long, a nephew of the Secretary of State. In Devon, Beauchamp had lined up an array of Seymours, Courtenays, and Careys, as well as the much respected Sir Hugh Pollard of

22. HMC, *Portland, 1,* 594–95. *ClSP,* 2, 546. *NP, 1,* 199, 206. *Evelyn,* ed. H. B. Wheatley (London, 1879), *4,* 201. Nickolls, p. 49. *Perfect Diurnall of the Armies,* No. 47. Coate, *Cornwall in the Civil War,* p. 259.

King's Nympton, a former MP and Governor of Dartmouth. He had had fair success in Dorset, and in Cornwall he had added to Trevanion, Wrey, and the Arundells men like Sir Peter Courtenay, one of Sir Bevil Grenville's old officers, and members of such stout Cornish families as Rashleigh, Prideaux, Tremaine, and Polwheele.

The plot's ramifications also extended northward into Gloucestershire and Hereford. In Gloucester the most prominent figure was the sixth Lord Chandos; aristocratic, but spendthrift and impoverished, he had relapsed into a comfortable neutrality in the civil war after an early appearance on the King's side. In May 1650 Beauchamp suggested that he should be made the Association's Lieutenant General of horse, but this was not found possible. According to Coke, Chandos and Sir Henry Lingen, one of the leading Cavaliers in Herefordshire, planned a local rising a few months later, no doubt in conjunction with that of the Western Association. Word was received in Scotland that Chandos was able to raise no less than 4,000 men—obviously one of those sweeping exaggerations which make it impossible to estimate the Royalists' real strength. Coke was instructed to investigate. He managed to see Chandos, but the peer was "very shy" and returned evasive answers to all Coke's questions. Even so, there is no doubt that the western design was taken seriously at Charles II's court as well as at Whitehall. Long after the last hopes of foreign help had vanished, the dispatch of commissions for Beauchamp and his friends continued.[23]

The Western Association is a noteworthy exception to the generally low level of Royalist organization in 1650. In other parts of the country plans were much less forward, and a mood of apathy and resentment prevailed. Charles II secretly told Beauchamp that he did not regard himself as bound by any of his promises to the Scots, but although many suspected as much, it cannot have in-

---

23. HMC, *Portland*, *1*, 578–80, 583–84, 588–89. *NP*, *1*, 180–81, 199. Egerton MS 2542, fols. 56, 69. *Evelyn*, ed. Wheatley, *4*, 198. For Chandos, Lingen, and Pollard see *DNB*; for Berkeley, S. W. Bates Harbin, *Members of Parliament for the County of Somerset* (Taunton, 1939), p. 139; for Rodney, Keeler, p. 324.

creased their love for the alliance.[24] Much of what we know of
Royalist conspiracy in the summer and autumn of 1650 comes from
the confession of Thomas Coke after he was arrested. Informers
are not always to be trusted, but whenever it can be checked Coke's
evidence usually seems reliable; in the West, for instance, his account is substantiated by Keynes' reports and by other correspondence. We can therefore accept Coke's information as fairly accurate
within the limits of his knowledge; intercepted letters and reports
of government spies can be used to supplement his statements.

Coke, as we have seen, came to England from Holland in June
1650, with the dual task of continuing the negotiations with the
London Presbyterians begun by Silas Titus, and of helping to coordinate the local conspiracies emerging in the provinces. His arrival coincided with a period of more than usual tension. All
delinquents had been ordered out of London in March, and an
emergency High Court of Justice set up to deal summarily with
those suspected of sedition. The air was thick with rumors of arrests and other repressive measures. An *agent provocateur* had been
at work in Staffordshire, persuading some of the local gentry (Sir
Robert Shirley among them) to sign an incriminating paper, which
he then turned over to the authorities. More arrests were made in
London at about the same time, some for being in the capital without permission, others, including that of Dr. John Barwick, on
suspicion of deeper designs. There were recurrent troop movements, a new Militia Act was passed, horses were seized for the service of the state, and extra vigilance ordered at the ports. On July 18
Captain Robert Levinz was hanged in Cornhill after trial by court
martial for distributing Royalist commissions. Finally, in August,
the High Court of Justice claimed its first victim, when the unfortunate Eusebius Andrews was executed; Bernard had trepanned him
into committing his intentions to paper.[25]

In the midst of all this Coke found little to encourage him. Ac-

24. *NP, 1,* 180–81, 199.
25. Howell, ed., *State Trials,* 5, 1–42. *CSPD, 1650,* pp. 159–60, 165–67,
187, 193, 203, 256, 263, 533–36. Whitelock, *3,* 191. *Perfect Diurnall of the
Armies,* Nos. 22–23. Walker, *Independency,* Pt. III, 34. *Barwick,* pp. 117–22.
Evelyn, ed. de Beer, *3,* 14. See also Gardiner, *C&P, 1,* 247, 250, 267; *2,* 5–7.

cording to his later statements, the exiled leaders had divided the country into local associations, for which commanders had been appointed, most of them still abroad. Besides Beauchamp in the West, there was an Eastern Association under the Duke of Buckingham; a Northern one under the Marquis of Newcastle; the Earl of Derby, still holding the Isle of Man, was responsible for the Northwest; Lord Gerard for the Southeast; and the Presbyterian Lord Willoughby for Lincolnshire.[26] A survey of these general areas suggests that apart from the West, the organization existed only on paper.

It is appropriate to begin with London and the home counties, for of all possible successes, a Royalist coup in the capital would be the greatest. The conspiracy in London, however, was so predominantly Presbyterian that its details lie outside the scope of this discussion.[27] Gerard, the assigned commander in Kent after Richmond's refusal, was in exile, but he had agents operating in the county, one of them John Heath, a son of the former Chief Justice. Heath and another Kentishman, Richard Thornhill of Olantigh, directed matters in the county, usually from a safe retreat at Rotterdam. Coke received a list of the subordinate officers from Thornhill. Among them were the Earl of Northampton's brother, Sir William Compton, who had estates in the county and had risen there in 1648; two wealthy London merchants, Sir Nicholas Crisp and Sir George Stroud; and such prominent local names as Culpeper, Boys, and Mennes. It seems that Dover was the chief objective: the necessary port for an invading force.[28] In Surrey most of Coke's acquaintances were former parliamentarians or neutrals. Edward Bysshe, the Garter King-at-Arms, asserted that he could

26. *Charles II and Scotland*, pp. 154–55.

27. The fullest account is Leland H. Carlson, "A History of the Presbyterian Party from Pride's Purge to the Dissolution of the Long Parliament," *Church History*, *11* (1942), 108–22. See also HMC, *Portland*, *1*, 584–88, 596–99; and *Charles II and Scotland*, p. 155.

28. *Charles II and Scotland*, pp. 154, 156. *NP*, *1*, 199, 238–39. HMC, *Portland*, *1*, 582, 597. *CSPD*, *1650*, pp. 233–34, 279–80; *1651*, p. 130. Carte, *Papers*, *1*, 465–66. Nickolls, p. 39. For Heath see *DNB* (under "Heath, Sir Robert, 1575–1649"), *LBM*, p. 123 n., and *ClSP*, *3*, 207; for Thornhill, *CCC*, pp. 2255, 2853–54, and *Evelyn*, ed. de Beer, *4*, 9 n. A fuller account of Compton will be given below, pp. 79–80.

raise 1,000 men at short notice, and several other prominent neutrals were sympathetic: Sir Francis Stydolf of Norbury Park, George Evelyn of Wotton, and men of that stamp. Sir Richard Onslow was also said to be well disposed, but "so totally guided by the Presbyterian Ministers" that the Cavaliers would not trust him. In Sussex, on the other hand, Coke's conspirators were mostly Old Royalists: Sir Edward Ford the water engineer, John Ashburnham, the Irish peer Lumley. Coke also implicated Cromwell's friend Richard Norton, one of the recently excluded Presbyterian members. He was summoned before the Council but promptly allowed to go; perhaps Coke confused him with his Royalist namesake, Sir Richard Norton of Rotherfield, Hampshire, who had been arrested a few months earlier.[29]

There is nothing in Coke's disclosures to suggest that Royalist preparations in the Southeast can bear comparison with those in the Western Association. The same is true of the Midlands and the Northeast: in both regions the commander was running the conspiracy from abroad. Loughborough, the midland leader, had been kicking his heels in Holland since his escape from prison in January 1649. In December 1650 a Royalist emissary named Stafford came to Nottingham with instructions from Loughborough. He met some of the local gentry, perhaps at the house of Sir Thomas Williamson of East Markham, and heard much inflated talk of their raising a body of horse, having a hundred men ready in Nottingham town, and disaffecting the castle garrison. Captain Bishop was soon on the track of Loughborough's friends. The most prominent of the Old Royalists was Sir Charles Compton, another of the Earl of Northampton's brothers; but neither the Compton nor the Hastings interest was exerted with the force of the Seymours' in the West. The Presbyterians were more active. According to Coke, the ministers at Northampton and Leicester were in touch with their conspiring brethren in London; and most of the fiery spirits in

29. HMC, *Portland, 1,* 581–82, 599–600. *CSPD, 1650,* pp. 487, 520; *1651,* pp. 200, 227, 252, 256. Nickolls, pp. 50, 54. For Bysshe, Ford, Lumley, and Onslow see *DNB;* for Stydolf, *Evelyn,* ed. de Beer, *3,* 157 n.; for Sir Richard and Colonel Norton, *Hampshire Notes and Queries, 5* (1890), 64–65, and Godwin, *Civil War in Hampshire.* On George Evelyn's political sympathies, see *Evelyn,* ed. de Beer, *1,* 6–7.

Coventry, Warwick, and Stratford were also of the Presbyterian stamp.[30]

The situation in Yorkshire was not very different. The commander, the courtly Newcastle, was a man of prestige; but he suffered from the usual financial difficulties of exile and preferred a cultivated retirement. In December 1650 he too had his agents in the North; Stafford traveled with one as far as Newark. A plan to seize Hull and Scarborough, ports for the forces Newcastle was trying to procure in Germany, was the main feature of the plot. At Scarborough, Newcastle was said to be relying on Sir Hugh Cholmley, who had come over to the King in 1643, and there was a rumor that the Governor was well-inclined, backed by some of the local Presbyterians. Stafford was told that all was ready at Hull, where money had been promised to advance the design. Coke's belief that Fairfax was involved (he had been empowered to offer him an earldom and £10,000 a year) was undoubtedly mere guesswork—the first of many such rumors. As in nearly every county outside the West, there is a significant absence of prominent Royalist names in the vague rumors about the development of conspiracy in Yorkshire before the end of 1650.[31]

On the other side of the Pennines there were much busier preparations. This was no accident. Lancashire was close to the King's forces in Scotland, and its great feudal magnate was a fanatical Royalist. The Earl of Derby was well placed in his Manx stronghold to maintain surreptitious correspondence with his friends and tenants. Two of his men had been arrested at Chester in February 1650, and three months later a consignment of arms was impounded by the authorities at Liverpool. The agent Stafford found a ready response when he arrived in December to distribute his commissions. Men had been engaged in Chester and Liverpool, and at Manchester and Bolton he found "the most resolved people

30. HMC, *Portland, 1,* 578–81, 585. Nickolls, pp. 47, 50, 65–66, 77. Williamson is the only prominent Royalist with the initials "Sir T.W." in the list in Wood, *Notts. in the Civil War,* p. 122. For Compton see *LBM,* p. 67 n.; for Loughborough, below, pp. 78–79.

31. Nickolls, pp. 47, 50, 65. HMC, *Portland, 1,* 579–80, 585–88. *CSPD, 1650,* pp. 213, 294, 385, 452. *Charles II and Scotland,* pp. 154–56. For Cholmley see *DNB; BIHR, 3,* 189; and Keeler, pp. 134–35.

that ever I met withall." Fourteen regiments could be raised in the Northwest, Stafford optimistically decided. Carlisle was to be secured, to open the way to a party of horse from Scotland, and representatives of the Scots army had been secretly to Chester to discuss the preparations. Some of the credit for these signs of organization should probably go to Col. John Booth, a Cheshire Presbyterian who had been Governor of Warrington in 1644, had changed sides in the second civil war, and was again under suspicion of Royalist activity in 1650. Coke was instructed to confer with him, and traveled to Warrington for that purpose in July. By this time Booth had wisely left the county, but Coke met him later in London and heard that he regularly assisted Royalist agents through Lancashire on their way to Scotland. Soon afterward Booth was arrested and his horses and arms seized. He was released in October, but it was some time before he managed to clear himself completely.[32]

The last of Coke's regions, the east coast, was supposedly divided between Buckingham and Willoughby. The latter had gone to Barbados by the time Coke came to England; Buckingham was in Scotland and might have been expected to exercise his nominal power of command. Buckingham corresponded with Coke, but there is no evidence that he played any direct role in the eastern counties. The real organizer in East Anglia was Col. Thomas Blague, Governor of Wallingford for the King in the civil war. As early as January 24, 1650, Charles assured his supporters in Norfolk and Suffolk that he had never trusted anyone but Blague in his dealings with them. In June Blague traveled to England with Coke. He had commissions, Coke recalled, apparently intended for Sir Henry Felton, a Suffolk moderate, and one of the Pastons. He also talked about a design against Yarmouth and the adjoining islands, mentioning that he had an agent in the port; it may be significant that on July 22 the Council of State received information about a plot to seize the adjacent peninsula of Lovingland. By the begin-

32. Nickolls, pp. 35, 47, 50. Whitelock, *3*, 196. HMC, *Portland, 1*, 589–90. *Charles II and Scotland*, pp. 133, 154–56. *CSPD, 1650*, pp. 174, 376–77, 452, 523.

ning of August Blague had returned to the Continent, but he left his servant Curtis behind to maintain communication.[33]

As the year 1650 drew to its close the English Royalists showed increasing signs of again becoming a dangerous threat to the Rump. There was still much hostility to the Scots alliance, and a general reluctance to appear alongside such doubtful friends as the English Presbyterians; but progress was being made. There was great variety in the state of preparedness attained in different parts of the country; but where, as in the Western Association, great families like the Seymours had taken the lead, a recognizable local organization had emerged. Unfortunately the West was not typical of the general state of the party, and in many places the leaders were still unwilling to respond even when a lead was given from abroad. The most serious deficiency was the absence of any central directorate, the result of the Louvre's skepticism about the effective strength of the Cavaliers. In these circumstances, it was obvious that the Royalists were still incapable of acting alone. Local risings to support a Scots invasion might, however, still be possible, especially if the King could respond to the popular demand for forces from abroad. Beyond this, the most that could be hoped for was that the Western Association might furnish a pattern for more effective action on a larger scale.

33. Cary, *2, 418. Charles II and Scotland*, pp. 4, 132, 155. *CClSP*, 2, 41. HMC, *Portland, 1,* 578, 580. *CSPD, 1650*, p. 248. For Willoughby see *DNB*; for Blague, *Archaeologia, 35,* 337 n.; for Felton and Paston, G.E.C., *Complete Baronetage* (Exeter, 1900–09): and *Acts and Ordinances of the Interregnum*, ed. C. H. Firth and R. S. Rait (London, 1911), *2,* 40, 304, 473, 670, 1075, 1080, 1333.

3. Worcester and the "Miraculous Preservation"

"UPON THE ROUTE AT DUNBARR, the royall partie were much comforted in seeinge us destroy their enemy, as well as ours," Captain Bishop smugly observed.[1] Yet however few the Royalists' regrets at the defeat of unwanted allies, the Scots were still the foundation of their sovereign's plans. Given the internal weaknesses of the King's party, there was nothing for it but to swallow their distaste, and hope that in the flush of victory Presbyterianism might somehow be circumvented. Officially, therefore, the Royalist plan for 1651 remained substantially what it had been in 1648: an invasion from the north, supplemented by risings in Cromwell's rear. The first essential of the design became a fact in August, when Leslie crossed the border. The risings, however, did not materialize. The underlying reason why they did not was the general loathing of the Scots, but three more specific reasons can also be identified: the absence of supporting foreign forces, the discouraging results of a premature rising in Norfolk in December 1650, and the betrayal of a large part of the Royalist plans by Thomas Coke and Isaac Birkenhead.

The first point can be swiftly dealt with. Projects were still on foot in 1651 to seize strategic places such as Lovingland or Mersea

1. Nickolls, p. 49.

42

Island, to provide ports of ingress for invading Hessians or Lorrainers. Ely, Crowland, and other fen strongholds were also closely
watched by the Council of State. For the Royalists of the east coast
there was still, however, the old stumbling block: there were no
Hessians or Lorrainers. Early in August 1651 Bishop received information about the visit of a Norfolk agent to the exiles at Dort:
"Nothinge would bee done there," he reported, "except they could
have a party land." [2]

Before this occurred the local Royalists had learned their lesson.
The Norfolk insurrection carries us back to August 1650, when
the conspiracy first began to spread. Blague was still the commander
in absentia, correspondence was maintained with agents in London, and meetings of local enthusiasts held under the protection
of an oath of secrecy. By autumn many of the Cavalier gentry were
involved. Coke heard that 1,500 horse and as many foot soldiers had
been listed, well provided with arms and ammunition. Although
this was the usual statistical flight of fancy, the conspirators took
themselves seriously. One of the chief centers of activity was Downham Market; early in November a new arrival there opened a
fencing school as a cover for the comings and goings of conspirators.
Unfortunately for Blague, his absence allowed the plot to get out
of control. By mid-November even a casual observer could tell that
something was brewing: there was a vague feeling of uneasiness,
and rumors circulated of vast, imaginary disasters that had befallen
the Commonwealth's armies in Ireland and Scotland. Suspicious
hunting parties were attended by sporting gentlemen wearing
swords: "an unusuall Weapon to kill game with," Colonel Rich,
the parliamentary commander in Norfolk, remarked. Then there
was a great gathering for a football match near Norwich, a disorderly and expectant gathering, which seemed to be waiting for a
watchword.

About November 28 the watchword came, apparently by accident. The Norfolk conspiracy soon began to look alarmingly like a
local rebellion. There were four main centers: Downham, Swaff-
ham (some fifteen miles to the east along the Norwich road),

2. Nickolls, p. 77. *CSPD, 1651*, pp. 29, 235, 305–6, 330, 398, 401. Egerton
MS 2542, fol. 70.

Thetford in the south of the county, and Easton Heath, three miles from Norwich. At all of them the numbers were inconsiderable; perhaps fifty at Downham, a few more at Easton Heath, and probably less at the other two. The three parties from the outlying areas moved toward Norwich, counting on support inside the city; some said that 1,500 men were waiting for a chance to rise, and that the gates were open in readiness. Rich, with three troops of his regiment, moved swiftly to intercept, 200 dragoons were called up from Lynn, and the county militia mustered to support them. The undisciplined Royalists scattered without a fight; some of them almost ran into one of Rich's troops, defying it with nothing more lethal than a few half-hearted cheers for Charles II. The remainder abandoned their arms and horses and disappeared with indecent haste. "They fled for fear of pursuers," a Norfolk official told Speaker Lenthall, "but none then pursued them but the terror of their own fault." This was not quite true, for upwards of forty prisoners were taken, but the affair was certainly a matter for laughter rather than alarm. An impressive cache of arms near Norwich (enough for 2,000 men, according to local gossip), was dumped in a convenient pond. A hopeful Royalist agent who landed at Aldeburgh the day after the comedy conscientiously fished them out; but there was no one to use them.

Most of the prisoners taken in this pathetic affray were men of humble rank and no estates; a few exceptions are worth identifying. Sir Ralph Skipwith was arrested with his chaplain, and sent to the Tower. Three other gentlemen, the aged and previously neutral Sir John Tracy; Sir Thomas Guibon, a local parliamentarian; and Richard Godfrey were committed to the Serjeant-at-Arms, but all were discharged within a few months, and they were probably not deeply implicated. Three of the principal suspects escaped to Cambridge and were thought to have found concealment in the colleges. Col. John Saul, Governor of Crowland in the civil war, was less fortunate: after Parliament had set up a High Court of Justice to deal with the prisoners (it was recognized that no local jury would convict), he was found guilty and executed at Lynn. A parson named Thomas Cooper, now a schoolmaster, suffered a similar fate at Holt in front of his own school door; a certain Major George

Roberts was hanged at Walsingham; and one of the influential Hobart clan went to his death at Dereham. Altogether twenty-four prisoners were condemned, of whom twenty were executed and another dozen or more sentenced to varying terms of imprisonment. The list includes a brewer, a woolen draper, a merchant or two—obscure men, unfortunate enough to suffer for the incompetence of their leaders.[3]

The repercussions of the Norfolk fiasco were felt far beyond the immediate limits of the conspiracy, upsetting the confidence of all but the most stouthearted. Mopping-up operations continued in Norfolk and the surrounding counties for several weeks, and there were many arrests of prominent Royalists in other areas. Country houses were searched for arms, and even that innocuous loyalist Sir Justinian Isham came under suspicion. The worst blows were struck in Hampshire, where the Western Association was seriously damaged by the securing of Sir Humphrey Bennett and Sir William Courtenay. Bishop was still convinced that a general rising was imminent. The Norfolk affair, he decided, had been an accidental forerunner of a national design timed to go off before Christmas, with the aid of a foray from Scotland and more substantial forces from abroad. Bishop, however, overestimated the enemy's preparedness.[4]

The Royalist schemes in the remainder of the country were soon broken by the Council of State. It was, unfortunately, in the one area where preparations were on a scale comparable to those of the

3. Zachary Grey, *An Impartial Examination of the Fourth Volume of Mr. Daniel Neal's History of the Puritans* (London, 1739), appendix, pp. 105–8. Nickolls, pp. 33–39, 49. *Perfect Diurnall of the Armies*, Nos. 52, 55–57, 60. HMC, *Portland, 1*, 545, 578, 580. *CJ, 6*, 504–6. *CSPD, 1650*, pp. 465, 472, 481; *1651*, pp. 48, 462. *England's Black Tribunal* (London, 1737), pp. 162–63. *Norfolk Quarter Sessions Order Book 1650–1657*, ed. D. E. H. James, Norfolk Record Society, 26 (London, 1955), pp. 28, 32. For Skipwith see *CCC*, pp. 581, 1553–54; for Cooper, A. G. Matthews, *Walker Revised. Being a Revision of John Walker's Sufferings of the Clergy* (Oxford, 1948), p. 266; for Tracy, *CCC*, p. 2340, and R. H. Mason, *History of Norfolk* (London, 1884), p. 298; for Guibon, W. A. Shaw, *The Knights of England* (London, 1906), *2*, 209.

4. Nickolls, pp. 35–36, 49–50, 54, 56. *CSPD, 1650*, pp. 449, 456, 487, 568. *Correspondence of Bishop Brian Duppa and Sir Justinian Isham 1650–1660*, ed. Sir Gyles Isham, Northants. Record Society, 17 (Lamport, 1951), p. 25.

Western Association that the damage was done: the Northwest. The leaders in this region included Col. Robert Werden of Chester, who after a brief spell in prison in 1649 had helped to put Coke in touch with John Booth; Col. Edward Vernon, a younger son of Sir Edward Vernon of Sudbury; Col. Vere Cromwell, son of the Earl of Ardglass; and Col. John Shalcross of Derbyshire, who claimed to be able to raise a good force from among the local miners. Their plans included the assembling of a series of county rendezvous, which would combine with the Lancashire Royalists at Warrington. Derby would send a party from the Isle of Man, and a detachment of cavalry from Scotland, under either Buckingham or Massey, would find a passage through the border counties; the whole Scots army was not required. Sir Philip Musgrave, who had been Governor of Carlisle in the first civil war and had commanded the rearguard in Hamilton's invasion in 1648, was now in close touch with Derby and the Manxmen, and was said to be busy preparing the way for them in Cumberland.[5] The agent primarily responsible for maintaining communication with the forces in Scotland and the Isle of Man was Capt. Isaac Birkenhead, a brother of Charles I's wartime "Oxford Aulicus." [6]

All these elaborate plans were upset in March, when Birkenhead was captured at Greenock while embarking for the Isle of Man. Some of his companions, including Musgrave, managed to escape to the island, but Birkenhead's papers provided the Council of State with the information they needed. Birkenhead's later activities indicate that he must have been a cooperative witness: he was voted £20 for his services, and in the three following years undertook a number of secret missions in the Council's employment. His papers were sufficiently alarming to spur the Council into action: militia

5. Cary, 2, 418. HMC, *Portland, 1,* 578–79, 582, 589–90. Carte, *Papers, 1,* 442–43; 2, 28. For Musgrave see *DNB;* for Vernon, *CCC,* p. 1373, *LBM,* p. 23 n., and *Collections for a History of Staffordshire, 7,* Pt. II (1886), 118; for Cromwell, G.E.C., *Peerage, 1,* 193–94; for Shalcross, *CCC,* pp. 1031–32.

6. Not, as stated by Gardiner (*C&P, 2,* 12), John Birkenhead himself. Isaac turned traitor and worked for the Council of State: see below, p. 62, and *Severall Informations and Examinations Taken Concerning Lieutenant Colonell John Lilburn* (July 1653), pp. 1–4. He died in 1655: HMC, *5th Report,* Appendix, p. 176. John Birkenhead survived until 1679: *DNB.*

forces were rapidly alerted, and regulars under Harrison sent to the
Northwest. Birkenhead's disclosures also put the authorities on the
trail of Thomas Coke. He managed to conceal himself for a few
days, but on March 29 was taken at a house in the Strand, and
having been proclaimed traitor for his failure to surrender, his life
was at stake. He proceeded to save it by giving the fullest possible
information about the Royalist plans that lay within his power;
and throughout the month of April poured out an elaborate account of both Royalist and Presbyterian conspiracy. He also tried
to recover the list of Kent supporters for his captors, and wrote to
Thornhill to that purpose, but the Rotterdam Royalists were suspicious, and tricked the messenger into returning to England without an answer. The names of Coke and Birkenhead soon became
Royalist bywords for treason, and their disclosures ended all chance
of a serious rising, forcing Charles into even greater dependence
upon the Scots.[7]

The government made good use of its information. Orders to
move more troops into Lancashire, and special warnings to important garrisons like Windsor and Colchester, streamed out of Whitehall during March and April 1651. Among the large number of
Presbyterian and Royalist leaders arrested on suspicion in Lancashire and the surrounding counties were Cols. Shalcross and John
Booth. Two of their associates, Colonel Ashurst and Sir Thomas
Tyldesley, got away to the Isle of Man, but the plot was shattered
beyond repair. Coke's recollections of the missing Kent list led to
the questioning of the cautious Richmond and the securing of Sir
Thomas Peyton, Sir John Boys, and many other leading gentlemen
in the county. The authorities were already beginning to unravel
the Presbyterian conspiracy in London; Coke gave them all the
additional evidence required for its destruction. Chandos in
Gloucestershire, Lord Windsor in Worcestershire, and the Yorkshire peer Belasyse were among the more prominent of those secured in other areas. In many cases these arrests led to only brief

7. Heath, p. 522. *CSPD, 1651*, pp. 88, 93–94, 98, 119, 122, 130, 222, 522–23.
Carte, *Papers, 1*, 465–66. *NP, 1*, 238–39. *CJ, 6*, 550–55, 579–80. Steele, *Procla-
mations, 1*, 354. See also Gardiner, *C&P, 2*, 12 ff. Coke's confessions are in
HMC, *Portland, 1*, 576–604, and *Charles II and Scotland*, pp. 154–57.

periods of restraint; but when they were released, as many were during the summer, it was usually on security heavy enough to deter them from again provoking the Commonwealth's anger.[8]

Coke's disclosures had serious consequences in the Western Association. Beauchamp's supporters had already been disappointed by the King's inability to assist them with foreign forces, and had been weakened by the capture of the Hampshire commanders, Bennett and Courtenay. The organization was still intact, however, at the time Coke was arrested. Beauchamp was in touch with the King in Scotland and his advisers abroad through the Devonian John Seymour. Seymour, who had been sent to ask Charles for foreign troops, returned empty-handed about Christmas 1650. Nicholas received a memorandum from him in March, in which the western Royalists asked to be given advance warning if the King intended to fight a decisive battle in Scotland, and made suggestions as to how their orders to rise should be transmitted. On April 3 Beauchamp was advised that it would be impossible to give notice of the King's intentions, Nicholas suggesting instead that the Westcountrymen should have scouts ready in Lancashire and Westmorland. Beauchamp and some of his friends were in London during the spring, no doubt to coordinate their plans with those in other regions, and there was tension throughout the West.[9]

One of the essential bases, Scilly, was soon lost to Charles. Blake's fleet forced Sir John Grenville to sign articles of surrender on May 23, and the last chance of invading the West disappeared. By this time the Western Association had been systematically wrecked by a roundup of its leaders. There were arrests in Cornwall, Hampshire, and Somerset, where Sir Edward Berkeley and Sir Edward Rodney were among those put under restraint. By April 16 Beauchamp was in the Tower. Imprisonment there was a Seymour family tradition, Hertford consolingly told his son: "It seems it is a place entailed upon our famylie, for wee have now helde it five

8. *CSPD, 1651*, pp. 68–246 passim, 522–26. *Perfect Diurnall of the Armies*, Nos. 68, 71, 73. HMC, *6th Report*, Appendix, p. 434. HMC, *Portland, 1*, 575–76. See also Gardiner, *C&P, 2*, 15, and Carlson, *Church History, 11*, 119–21.

9. Nickolls, pp. 50, 54. HMC, *Portland, 1*, 577, 579, 583–84. *NP, 1*, 231–32. Egerton MS 2542, fol. 69.

generations." Nicholas and his fellow exiles could ill afford to be as philosophical. Coke and Birkenhead had "totally ruined" the King's plans in England, the Secretary complained, their treason "being like to prove the ruin of most of his Majesty's best affected subjects in England, as well presbyterians as others." There was nothing left but the Scots.[10]

Before the Scots were ready to march, the English Cavaliers had more to suffer. They had to watch the proceedings of the new High Court of Justice, which in June and early July sat to deal with Christopher Love, chosen as an example for his Presbyterian friends in London. They had to watch the passage of the Parliament's first Act of Confiscation on July 16. They had to watch the suppression of a feeble and premature Royalist rising in Cardigan. A few of the rebels were killed (some accounts say as many as forty), and a number of prisoners taken, mostly Joneses, Jenkinses, and Lloyds. Meanwhile Leslie was performing elaborate, pointless maneuvers with his new Scots army in the hills south of Stirling, and Cromwell was moving across the Forth to cut off their supplies.[11]

On July 31 Charles II and Leslie began the southward march. The invasion of England was the last despairing gamble of a bankrupt policy. The Royalist organization which had been designed to support it lay in ruins; the mood of the King's former friends was still compounded in equal parts of resentment at the Scots connection, and disinclination to believe that any good would come of it. As Cromwell foresaw, there could be little hope of any substantial appearance of Englishmen to swell the Scottish ranks. "All the rogues have left us," Hamilton rejoiced after Argyll's withdrawal, but the rogues were not the only ones to go. At least one Royalist officer who had been willing to fight north of the border refused to accompany the advance. This was Col. John Pinchbeck, a Devon man who had been at Scilly until its surrender. Taken prisoner by Monck, he announced "that he went

10. *CSPD, 1651*, pp. 150, 152, 169, 179, 193–94, 234, 525. HMC, *12th Report*, Appendix 9, pp. 47–48. Whitelock, *3*, 296. *Perfect Diurnall of the Armies*, No. 69. *NP, 1*, 237, 240–41, 253–54.

11. Gardiner, *C&P, 2*, 15–29. For the Cardigan affair see *CSPD, 1651*, pp. 264–67; *CJ, 6*, 591; Cary, *2*, 279; Whitelock, *3*, 312, 314; *Perfect Diurnall of the Armies*, Nos. 81–82.

as farre as Glasgow with the King's forces, but could have noe satisfaccion to goe further with him." Pinchbeck's defection, small in itself, was a poor omen for the campaign, if it was to depend on the enthusiasm of the English Royalists.[12]

On August 6 Charles, already much weakened by desertions, reached Carlisle. In spite of the frustration of the plan to launch a general rising, much was still expected from Lancashire, with its strong infusion of Presbyterians and Roman Catholics, both equally hostile to the Commonwealth. Yet, Clarendon recalls, the King's army "was very little increased by the access of any English." There were a few exceptions. The most notable was Derby, who landed with a small force from the Isle of Man and tried to raise his friends and tenants. The results were disappointing. Manchester and some of the other south Lancashire towns provided a fair sprinkling of recruits, but the presence of Old Royalists like Tyldesley, who returned with Derby, Lord Widdrington, recently one of Charles II's entourage, Roger Whitley, and Edward Roscarrock, another fugitive from Scilly, frightened most of the Presbyterians back into their cave of neutrality. Massey, sent to rouse them, carelessly allowed a letter from the Scots ministers to be made public, warning against too close an alliance with the Cavaliers; the damage was never repaired. A meeting of the local gentry called by Derby at Warrington broke up in anger when the Earl refused to take the Covenant. Sir Thomas Myddelton, of whom much had been expected, immediately arrested the King's messenger and sent the letter he carried up to Parliament. The fact that he had recently given heavy security to the Council of State may help to explain his promptness. On August 25 Derby's little army was scattered to the winds by Robert Lilburne at Wigan. Widdrington and Tyldesley were among the killed, 400 prisoners were taken, and only Derby and a few companions managed to escape and limp south to join the King at Worcester.[13]

12. *Scotland and the Commonwealth . . . August 1651 to December 1653,* ed. C. H. Firth, Scottish Historical Society, 18 (Edinburgh, 1895), p. 2. Whitelock, *3,* 334. See also Gardiner, *C&P, 2,* 34–35. Pinchbeck is mentioned in Coke's confession: HMC, *Portland, 1,* 588.

13. Gardiner, *C&P, 2,* 35–40. Clarendon, *History,* Bk. XIII, §§ 58–72. Allan Fea, *After Worcester Fight* (London, 1904), pp. 56–58. *CSPD, 1651,* p. 200.

In the "faithful city" Charles was welcomed by the Mayor and other civic dignitaries, who obligingly opened the jails and released a number of Royalists imprisoned during the recent purge. Apart from this windfall, the number of Cavaliers who came in was little more impressive than in Lancashire; and there were scarcely any from further afield than the immediate locality. Francis, Lord Talbot, the Earl of Shrewsbury's son, appeared with sixty horse. Other recruits included Sir John Packington, Sir Walter Blount, Sir Ralph Clare, Sir John Winford, Thomas Hornyold of Blackmore Park, and John Washburn of Wichenford, the two latter each bringing some forty men apiece. Others who had been equally zealous during the civil war stayed carefully away. Sir Rowland Berkeley of Cotheridge had been a stout man for Charles I, but would have nothing to do with the Scots. He ignored several invitations to join the King, he told his father-in-law a few days after the battle. On the morning of September 3, if Berkeley's story is to be believed, the King sent a party of horse to induce him to change his mind. Berkeley spent the whole day dodging the fighting, and managed to get home only after five hair-raising hours. Sir Rowland provides a good case history of the lengths to which Old Royalists would go to escape compromising themselves with the Scots. The response to Charles' summons to the Pitchcroft meadow was, therefore, imperceptible. The country at large remained quiet, actively enrolling in the militia to fight the invader, or at best staying passively neutral. From the cowed and dispirited remnant of the Western Association there was not the slightest murmur of revolt. Later some found it politic to regret their inaction. By 1656 Lord Newport, whose house at High Ercall lay not far distant from the King's line of march, was "so penitent for his behaviour to the K. . . . at his being at Worcester as that he desired to expiate his crime." To Secretary Nicholas it all appeared "an abominable shame and dishonour," but in the mood of September 1651 the reasons are not far to seek.[14]

Cary, *2*, 321, 333–35. For Tyldesley and Widdrington see *DNB*, and for the former, also *BIHR*, *12*, 204; for Roscarrock, *CSPD, 1651*, p. 216, and Coate, *Cornwall in the Civil War*, pp. 199–200.

14. Gardiner, *C&P*, *2*, 40–41. Fea, *After Worcester Fight*, p. 62; Berkeley's own account of his activities, HMC, *10th Report*, Appendix 6, pp. 175–76,

And so it was that on the anniversary of Dunbar, Cromwell built his bridges of boats, and after some sharp fighting by Teme and Severn and at Perry Wood, achieved his "crowning mercy." It was not a difficult battle to win against a demoralized and heavily out-numbered adversary, and this, the most overwhelming of Oliver's victories, was also the most decisive. For Worcester ended all military danger to the Commonwealth from any imaginable direction, be it Scottish, Presbyterian, or Cavalier. As Charles followed the fleeting Scots in headlong gallop out of St. Martin's gate in the waning light of a September evening, he was also flying from the whole disastrous policy of the Presbyterian alliance, in which his father had entangled the monarchy almost four years before. The events of the next astonishing month were to demonstrate that the personal loyalty of Royalists of all ranks of society had been little abated; but it was loyalty to the Crown as an ideal, and had nothing to do with acceptance of its policies. Many would have echoed the King's wry agreement with the smith at Bromsgrove, that the rogue Charles Stuart deserved to be hanged "more than all the rest, for bringing in the Scots."

The consequences of Worcester for the Royalist party were in the end profound: abandonment of the Presbyterian alliance and a return to influence by Hyde, Nicholas, and all who wished to maintain the strict integrity of the Old Royalist tradition. But while the King was a hunted fugitive such reorientations of policy would have to be postponed. The tale of Charles' wanderings between September 3 and October 15, 1651, when he sailed for France, has been told often enough, and has acquired a substantial crust of hoary legend and dubious anecdote.[15] As we are primarily

suggests that Blount's list reprinted by Fea should be treated with caution. Clarendon, *History*, Bk. XIII, § 71. *CClSP*, *3*, 134 (quoted from MS 51, fol. 309). *NP, 1*, 268. For Clare, Newport, and Packington see *DNB;* for Talbot, G.E.C., *Peerage, 11*, 719; for Berkeley, *Diary of Henry Townshend*, ed. J. W. Willis Bund, Worcs. Historical Society (London, 1920), *CCC*, p. 1449, and *The Berkeley Manuscripts*, ed. Sir John Maclean (Gloucester, 1883–85), *2*, 88.

15. Contemporary narratives of the escape are reprinted in Allan Fea, *The Flight of the King* (London, 1897), and *After Worcester Fight;* and in *The Royal Miracle*, ed. A. M. Broadley, London, 1912. Clarendon's account is interesting but inaccurate; *History*, Bk. XIII, §§ 83–106. There are adequate accounts in Gardiner, *C&P, 2*, 49–57; Scott, *King in Exile*, pp. 220–83; and Arthur Bryant, *King Charles II* (London, 1931), pp. 11–40.

concerned with the Cavaliers rather than with their King, it is legitimate to substitute summary for detailed narrative, swallowing our regrets at the loss of so much picturesque, if hackneyed, adventure. One reason for not ignoring the escape altogether is the need to stress that it was less a matter of miracle or accident than Restoration myth might suggest. The credit, indeed, should go not to providence but to the only two segments of the Royalist party which had ever possessed even the bare skeletons of organization: the recusants and the Western Association.

The first phase of the escape was the responsibility of the Catholics. As resistance in Worcester disintegrated into rout, Charles and his entourage had instinctively taken the same line of retreat as the broken Scottish regiments. A halt near Kidderminster enabled Derby to produce Charles Giffard, who had sheltered the Earl during his flight from Wigan to Worcester a few days earlier. So began Charles' week in the hands of the knot of midland recusants, with their priests' holes and their long traditions of concealing hunted guests. The Giffards, their dependents the Penderels, John Whitgreave of Moseley Hall, and the priest Huddleston showed even greater resource and courage (for there was more at stake) than were normal in recusant history. How much the experience influenced Charles' later attitude to the Catholics, one can only speculate. It is certain that the hours in rain-soaked copses, in the barn at Madely, in the priests' hole at Moseley, and not least with Colonel Carlos in the Boscobel oak, must have taught the King valuable lessons about the dangers besetting the fugitive agents of an underground movement; lessons which explain his subsequent reluctance to do more than expostulate mildly from the Continent when his friends at home seemed overcautious. The dangers were not imaginary. Before Charles left Moseley on September 9 both Boscobel and Whiteladies had been searched, with threats to the inhabitants. There was a tense moment when the soldiers came to Moseley itself while the King was there; somehow Whitgreave diverted them from searching the place. Francis Yates, Giffard's servant, was soon to be executed for refusing to betray Charles' movements, and the same dangers, as well as the temptations of £1,000 reward, confronted all who were in the secret.

After the Giffards and the Penderels came the interlude with the

Lanes, the ride to Bristol with Mistress Jane, and the four days at Abbots Leigh. Most of his helpers so far had been people who, although Royalist in sympathy, had not been and were not to be particularly active in conspiracy. But for almost a month after leaving Abbots Leigh, Charles was sheltered and conveyed from place to place by the leaders of the Western Association, which thus achieved posthumous justification. Hertford's man Edward Kirton gave the King a night's lodging at Castle Cary. Giles Strangways sent him £100 in gold, "protesting it was all he had," or at any rate all he could lay hands on, because his father kept a tight rein on the family purse. For three weeks the lion's share of responsibility was borne by Francis Wyndham at Trent, in south Somerset. When the King left Trent this too was arranged by men of the Western Association. Wilmot, Charles' reckless, cheerful, inseparable companion, rode over to Salisbury one late September day and put up at the King's Arms, where the host was a stout Royalist. He enlisted Dr. Humphrey Henchman, a deprived canon of the cathedral, and two of the founders of the Association, John Coventry and Robert Phelips of Montacute. Phelips received Wilmot without enthusiasm, distrusting his Presbyterian connections, but his reserve vanished when he learned the identity of the person for whom Wilmot was asking assistance, and the next day he set off to Southampton to hire a ship. Failing in this, on October 6 Phelips conducted Charles from Trent, where it was felt a longer stay would be dangerous, to Hele, the house of the widow of one of Hyde's cousins.

At Hele began the last act in the escape, and once again it was the Royalists of second rank, rather than the great lords, who made the running. The Earl of Southampton, who lived at Titchfield near Southampton Water, did indeed send to Phelips offering his services when he got wind of the King's presence in the district, but by then the final arrangements had been made. The Seymours were not heard from, but Beauchamp had been released from the Tower on heavy security only a few weeks before, and Charles no doubt felt it politic not to disturb him.[16] The central personality in the final stages was Col. George Gunter, of Racton near Chichester.

16. *CSPD, 1651*, pp. 417, 435.

He and his cousin, Thomas Gunter, took over the search for a vessel, and it was through an acquaintance of theirs, a Chichester merchant named Francis Mansel, and a staunch Royalist as events were to prove, that a ship was at last procured.[17] Mansel traded with France and knew the local skippers well, among them Nicholas Tattersal, whose little brig, the *Surprise,* was retained at Shoreham. And so, after a day spent in counting the stones at Stonehenge, Charles rode over Broadhalfpenny Down, parted from Robert Phelips, and passed through Arundel and Brighthelmstone, to Shoreham and safety. On October 15 he and Wilmot embarked on the *Surprise,* a southern course was set, and the two "broken merchants" fleeing from their creditors were landed the next day at Fécamp.

The courage and resource in defeat shown by Charles II and his loyal adherents were impressive. They should not, however, obscure the fact that the Royalist cause was in ruins. The romantic legends that swiftly surrounded the "royal miracle" may have helped to keep alive the spirit of resistance, yet for almost two years after Worcester there was not the merest flicker of active hostility to the Commonwealth. And although the King escaped, others were less fortunate. Buckingham, with his usual luck, made his way to France, but Lauderdale, Leslie, Massey, and Derby, to name only the most prominent, were all captured, besides many hundreds of lesser rank. Massey again showed his genius for jail-breaking, but on the day that the King was sailing from Shoreham, the Earl of Derby was executed at Bolton. Two of his officers, Captain Benbow and Sir Timothy Featherstonehaugh, received similar fates, and shiploads of the nameless rank-and-file made human cargoes for Bermuda and Barbados. Before 1651 was out the last Royalist standards in the islands came down. The reduction of the Isle of Man was completed on October 31, Jersey surrendered on December 12, and Guernsey five days later.[18] As the smoke of Worcester cleared away, it disclosed a wintry scene for the Royalists.

17. For George Gunter see *CCC,* pp. 1237–38; for Mansel, E. P. Statham, *History of the Family of Maunsell* (London, 1917–20), 2, 176–200.
18. Gardiner, *C&P,* 2, 59–65, 69.

4. The Nadir of Conspiracy

"THERE IS NO TALKE of Presbiterian nor Royalist at present," the usually sanguine Daniel O'Neill gloomily observed after testing English opinion for himself in March 1653. Pessimism seemed even more justifiable a month later, when Cromwell's expulsion of the Rump failed to provoke even the slightest flicker of Royalist response, and Cavaliers exchanged hopeless reflections on the futility of opposition. "As wise as those are, that would have the king in action," wrote one in a letter that entered the Council's files with ominous speed, "I think it fit for him to lye still, and expect further events"; and there was the legitimate inference that where patience was advisable for the sovereign, it was essential for the subject. The Dutch War, prolonged now for a year, might have been expected to provide a promising climate for sedition, but there was no one to take advantage of it. Langdale suggested an attempt on Newcastle and Tynemouth with Dutch assistance, but his failure to follow it up shows that even influential exiles of his stamp were out of touch with their local supporters. Worcester, indeed, was followed by a much longer period of Royalist quiescence than even the defeats of 1648 and the execution of the King. The cause had collapsed even more disastrously, and the process of revival was correspondingly prolonged.[1]

1. *TSP, 1,* 323. *CClSP, 2,* 149. *NP, 1,* 311. O'Neill's letter is printed in C. H. Firth, "Cromwell and the Expulsion of the Long Parliament," *EHR, 8* (1893), 530.

The disintegration of the Royalist party might have gone even further had the Rump been more astute, or at least more consistent, in its policy. A choice between the elementary alternatives of conciliation and repression confronted every Interregnum regime in dealing with the Royalists. Had the Rump concentrated on the first, it might have induced the habit of conformity among enough Royalists to make the monarchy seem more and more remote, and have whittled away the hard core of conspirators to negligible proportions. Had it consistently followed the second, it might have destroyed Royalism at its roots, in the estates of the landed gentry. Economic discrimination against the Royalists, through Goldsmiths' Hall and the local sequestration committees, was continued by the Commonwealth government, and was indeed intensified by the passage of the Acts of Sale. At the same time, however, the beginnings of an attempt to heal the breach made by the civil war can be detected. Both the Rump and the Barebones Parliament followed half-heartedly a policy of conciliation; in 1654 the Protectorate adopted it with more conviction. But in the nature of things, none of these governments could allow the Royalists, or even the Presbyterians, the same freedom that they granted their own supporters. The result was to drive the Royalists into further plots, which in 1655 convinced Cromwell that "settlement" was out of the question and that the Cavaliers could only be restrained by military repression and new experiments in discriminatory taxation.

Three Acts of Sale were passed in 1651–52. The fact that 780 Royalists, many of them the leaders, suffered confiscation in them might suggest that the party received a crippling blow from which it would be difficult to recover. Actually, the damage was not as serious as at first appears. Compared with those who were sequestered and had to pay composition fines, those subject to forfeiture were only a small proportion of the total of English Royalists. Many of the sufferers were already abroad, where they could contribute only indirectly to conspiracy; others took advantage of the escape clause and compounded. Some obtained relief upon articles of surrender, which often guaranteed the beneficiaries exemption from financial penalties. Even when the estates were sold by the

Drury House Trustees, many of them found their way into the hands of the former owners' friends, relatives, or agents. The victims undoubtedly suffered in the process of buying back their own property, but bankruptcies were rare. As with sequestration and composition, confiscation hit the Royalist of modest means harder than the nobility. Thus although the wealthiest and most influential members of the party retained their ability to resist, they were at the same time restrained by fear of losing their precariously held possessions. Cavaliers of smaller resources, on the other hand, had greater reason to conspire, since they had less to lose and more to regain.[2]

Confiscation was thus less fearsome in practice than it appeared on paper. At the same time, the Rump was moving haltingly toward a general policy of reconciliation with those who would renounce their malignant pasts. The cornerstone of this policy was the Act of Oblivion, passed on February 24, 1652. Many individual exceptions were named, so many that the act's title was seriously inaccurate, and the measure also lost much of its value by the continued insistence on the payment of delinquency fines. Finally, the benefit of the act was confined to those who would take the Engagement, making pardon conditional on a verbal renunciation of Royalism. The act was thus much less friendly than it might have been, although many Cavaliers afterward active in conspiracy had no scruples about taking the Engagement and so claiming its protection.[3] Cromwell, however, took the lead in trying to turn the proclaimed oblivion into a reality. His desire for reconciliation and "settlement" was well known, and there were frequent reports of his anxiety to win over "considerable persons" of the party. He did his best to reduce the list of exceptions, and often intervened on behalf of aggrieved Royalists whose promised exemptions under articles of surrender were being overlooked by officious parliamen-

2. For general discussions of the confiscation policy see Joan Thirsk, "The Sales of Royalist Land during the Interregnum," *Economic History Review,* 2d ser. 5 (1952–53), 188–207; C. H. Firth, "The Royalists under the Protectorate," *EHR,* 52 (1937), 639–40; and Hardacre, *Royalists,* pp. 94–99.

3. Cf. the list in *CCC,* p. 623. For general discussions see Gardiner, *C&P,* 2, 81–82; Hardacre, *Royalists,* pp. 93–94; and Firth, *EHR,* 52, 637.

tary committees.[4] The Act of Oblivion was not the only sign of relaxation. In November 1653 the benefit of legal processes was no longer made conditional upon taking the Engagement. The use of the Anglican liturgy in services connived at by the authorities was also noticeably more frequent than before. Altogether, the atmosphere of these years seemed to foreshadow the ultimate acceptance of former Royalists as citizens with the same privileges as their opponents.[5]

The threat to the solidarity of the party latent in even this limited degree of relaxation was enough to terrify the exiles. Shortly after Worcester, Secretary Nicholas foresaw that the Rump's logical policy would now be one of conciliation, and that this would inevitably encourage increasing Royalist acquiescence in the regime. The next month a steady stream of Cavaliers was reported to be leaving Holland for home. Apart from those excepted in the Act of Oblivion, Royalists arriving in England from abroad were "very well received and kindly used," it was said in May 1652. Among those who returned were some who did so only with the intention of plotting for the King's restoration: men like Sir Richard Willys, Sir Philip Monckton, Edward Villiers, and Edward Grey, all of whom made their peace in England before the end of 1653. But most came back with at least the immediate intention of conforming; Roger L'Estrange, one of the most notable, managed to do so almost to the eve of the Restoration.[6]

The first two years after Worcester were thus ones of comparative relaxation for the Royalist party. The Commonwealth, however, offered nothing constructive to attract the Royalists and moderates, no sign that the revolutionary policies of Independency had been

---

4. *ClSP, 3,* 223–24. *CClSP, 2,* 203–4. *Memoirs of Edmund Ludlow,* ed. C. H. Firth (Oxford, 1894), *1,* 344–45. Abbott, *2,* 515, 572. George Kitchin, *Sir Roger L'Estrange* (London, 1913), pp. 36–37. Robert S. Bosher, *The Making of the Restoration Settlement* (London, 1951), pp. 9–10.

5. Firth and Rait, *2,* 774–75. Bosher, pp. 11–12, 15. *Evelyn,* ed. de Beer, *3,* 61 ff.

6. *NP, 1,* 268, 278, 296. *ClSP, 3,* 81. *CClSP, 2,* 139. *Notes and Queries,* 12th ser. *10* (1922), 123. *The Monckton Papers,* ed. Edward Peacock, Philobiblon Society (London, 1884), pp. 160–61. Kitchin, pp. 37–41.

abandoned; and without such assurances conservatives could never
be really pacified. Furthermore, the Rump refused to end the
sequestration system. Although many individual estates were discharged under the Act of Oblivion, there was no general discharge,
and it was not until the more tolerant Protectorate was established
that the system was allowed to wither away. The concessions were
undeniable, but as one Cavalier remarked, "these are not universall
civillitys." In spite of the common tendency toward conformity
(the Royalist clergy set some striking examples), in spite of its
leaderless, disorganized, and discouraged condition, the King's
party precariously survived.[7] Its survival, however, would be of
little consequence if the King's Council abroad continued to be-
little its importance. Fortunately for the Cavaliers it did not do so,
for the Council was drastically reorganized. The King's return to
Paris in October 1651 was followed by the disappearance of Jermyn
and the Louvre gang from the inner circle (they were still on the
fringe, talking volubly), and their replacement by Hyde, Ormond,
and Nicholas. The opportunist obsession with the Scots was replaced by a policy less immediately promising but more consistent
with principle, of primary reliance on the Cavaliers. It was a long
time, however, before the new councilors struck much of a response; and for a long time they scarcely expected one.

One reason for the long delay in the revival of the English Royalists' spirits was the slowness of their recognition of the change at
court. The transition in Paris was not a painless one, and it had
significant repercussions in England. In France and Holland the
Old Royalists, the Louvre interest, and Rupert's Swordsmen continued their public displays of quarrelsome intrigue, and often
actively encouraged it among their followers in England. Early in
1652 an unlikely accusation of treason against Secretary Long led
to his removal from the court. Whatever Long's failings, the affair
set a bad precedent. In July 1653 a combination of politics and
personalities brought together Long, an obscure clerk named
Massonett, and the much more dangerous Sir Richard Grenville,

7. Clarendon MS 46, fol. 71. On the clergy see Bosher, pp. 14–18, 23–24,
27–28.

in a coalition to destroy Hyde by the same tactics: a mischievous charge of treasonable correspondence with Cromwell. The allegation was quickly laughed out of the Council, but there were those who continued to whisper that where there was smoke there must also be some fire. With Berkeley, Jermyn, Lord Keeper Herbert, and the restless Gerard all working to undermine him, it is small wonder that Hyde's own agent, Edward Villiers, should have been worried by the campaign of defamatory rumors he encountered in England.[8] Another disturbing symptom of uneasiness was the widespread readiness to believe Commonwealth-inspired stories of the King's frivolity and extravagance, many holding that "to contribute to any supply for his Majesty were but to maintain luxury," and repeatedly advising his removal from France in the interests of both morality and retrenchment. Charles, no doubt, lived as indulgently as circumstances allowed, but the picture of spendthrift profligacy supposedly enjoyed by the almost bankrupt exiles was an absurd fiction.[9]

Defeat and disunity were not the only factors recommending inactivity in these dark days after Worcester. Always in the background lurked the menace of the Council of State and its espionage system. Directed until 1653 by Scot and Bishop, intelligence in that year passed finally into the watchful care of John Thurloe. Genius had replaced mere competence, and for the Royalists the change brought increasing realization of the hazards of conspiracy. Although Thurloe did not obtain full control of the Post Office until 1655, from the first he kept his experts in interception and deciphering busily employed. The most notable was Isaac Dorislaus, son of the assassinated diplomat. Dorislaus had a room adjoining the foreign letter office, and even that experienced professional John Wildman paid admiring tribute to his skill in recognizing hands and seals. Dorislaus' only weakness was his crude method of opening letters. He "had a salary for that purpose," Samuel Mor-

8. Clarendon, *History*, Bk. XIII, §§ 122–27; XIV, §§ 63–77. *TSP*, 2, 19, 162 (cipher in Appendix, D). See also Scott, *King in Exile*, pp. 429–62, 470–76.
9. Clarendon, *History*, Bk. XIV, § 82. *ClSP, 3*, 243. Cl. MS 45, fols. 483–84. *NP, 2*, 14. *TSP, 1*, 393; *2*, 19, 64, 71 (cipher in Appendix, D).

land recalled, "but, alas, understood no better ways than to cut
letters open with a penknife, and then drop wax under." [10] Besides
Thurloe's supervision of the mails, there were his spies to contend
with. Months after Worcester the exiles were still deploring the
damage done to the party's morale by Coke's treachery, and for the
half-hearted the incident provided the most cogent of excuses for
doing nothing. Although after 1651 Coke's work was done, he was
not the only informer to be feared. Isaac Birkenhead was still at
large. In June 1653 he was reported to have collected a group of
"poore credulous Cavaliers" by a promise of money, and then to
have denounced them to the government. Scot and Thurloe were
always ready to encourage these and other informers with suitable
financial inducements, and besides the normal intelligence appro-
priations, special payments were sometimes voted. Posthumous
Priestman, an obscure Lincolnshire Royalist who played false, was
given £10 in December 1651, for example, and another award of
£20 was made to the anonymous discloser of a plot in the West a
year later.[11]

The tasks of both Scot and Thurloe were made easier by the
chronic inability of many exiles to control their tongues. Although
the Council was often said to have spies at the highest level among
Charles II's advisers, carelessness rather than treason was the real
danger. Scot certainly had his agents in Paris, but their tasks would
have been difficult had not their victims been ready to talk with
unwise freedom. A certain "N.N." was the most regular correspondent; another was an Irish priest named Creely. The worst
example of misplaced confidence was the case of that expert in intrigue Joseph Bampfield. A former colonel in the King's army,
Bampfield had done useful service during the war as a Royalist spy
in London, and had assisted the Duke of York's escape from St.
James' in 1648. He was in high favor at the Louvre for his glib
attachment to the Presbyterian alliance, and was able to collect
large quantities of useful information after his arrival in Paris in

10. HMC, *Buccleuch*, *2*, Pt. I, 50. See also "A Brief Discourse," *EHR, 13*,
530–31.

11. *NP, 1,* 290. *CClSP, 2,* 218 (MS 45, fol. 487). *CCC,* p. 1965. *CSPD, 1651–52,*
pp. 487, 584. SPDI, *95,* fols. 192, 203. There is an undated intelligence report
from Priestman in Add. MS 4159, fol. 121. See also *TSP, 5,* 533–34.

September 1653, information which he systematically transmitted to Scot and Thurloe. Bampfield's relations with Thurloe were soon an open secret, but in spite of repeated warnings the Louvre faction obstinately continued to trust him.[12] The pipeline of information flowed all too freely, swollen with irresponsible chatter about the missions of secret agents on their way to England; and with papers left behind in Jersey at its surrender, when Secretary Long had ineptly omitted to arrange for the recovery of a trunk containing his confidential documents. There was in fact good reason for the anxiety felt by Royalists in England; even Hyde, who thought them "too apt to excuse their own omissions upon the imaginary crimes of others," admitted that thoughtless gossip was an important factor in the party's general feebleness.[13]

Few signs of concerted Royalist action can therefore be detected between Worcester and the summer of 1653. The only tasks that the disorganized party could reasonably be expected to undertake were the same preliminaries that had suggested themselves in 1649: first, to provide the exiles with reliable intelligence of English affairs; second, to send money to reduce the King's dependence on the French and to keep his leading councilors alive. As early as January 1652 Secretary Nicholas was charged with the task of finding an English intelligencer. Even this routine activity seemed to involve too many risks for those in England. There was a delay of several months before Nicholas could find a correspondent, and this proved to be the least of his worries. A professional intelligencer employed by the Dutch was secured, but this economical arrangement fell through in March 1653, when the States of Holland decided to dispense with his services. More complications followed, and Nicholas was able to find an alternative means of paying the scribe only after the greatest of difficulties. Eventually weekly letters of intelligence, erratically supplementing the printed newsbooks, rewarded the Secretary's persistence; but their author's frequent complaints that his salary was in arrears, and his shrill

---

12. *CSPD, 1651*, pp. 311, 362; *1651–52*, p. 2. "Scot's Account," *EHR, 12*, 119. *TSP, 1*, 263, 267. *CClSP, 2*, 241, 255. *NP, 2*, 23. For Bampfield see *DNB*.

13. *ClSP, 3*, 52, 192, 203. HMC, *Pepys*, pp. 294–307; Stowe MS (BM), 184, fols. 189–233. Add. MS 37,047, fols. 204–7.

demands for money to "tavern-treat" his backstairs informants, were depressing signs of his employers' embarrassments. The observations of O'Neill and other occasional visitors to England provided only an irregular and haphazard substitute.[14]

Intelligence was a business that concerned only a handful of Royalists; the collection of money made demands on the loyalty of all who had any to spare. The need for money, it need hardly be said, was pressing. The King managed to live precariously upon the charity of his reluctant French relatives, while his advisers were reduced to almost ludicrous poverty (unless, like Jermyn, they possessed unusual private reserves). There was little to spare for the expenses of emissaries whose journeys to and from England were essential if an effective organization was to be rebuilt. None realized the need more keenly than the exiles, and in January 1652 the faithful Nicholas was entrusted with the duty of opening the channels of supply. Six months later not a penny had been received from England, and the dispatch of a personal agent, the "wise and witty" young William Coventry, was equally unproductive. Neither Hyde nor Nicholas had much confidence in him (they had little time for trimmers), there were the usual complaints of careless talk, and by March 1653 only one "not very considerable" sum had been received from England.[15]

More successful in arousing the English Royalists from their financial stupor was Henry Seymour, brother of the Western Association's former agent, kinsman of the mighty Hertford, and a close personal associate of the King himself. Seymour's connections, and his experience in a number of delicate missions during and after the civil war, were good qualifications for a financial agent. In the interval between the destruction of Royalist hopes at Worcester and their revival in the summer of 1654, Seymour undertook several hazardous missions to England. The first was the least successful. Seymour left Paris in the early summer of 1652, but was arrested in England on information evidently given to the authori-

14. *ClSP*, *3*, 43, 55, 120–27, 142, 153, 166–68, 171, 174, 190–94, 222. *CClSP*, *2*, 182–286 passim (Cl. MSS 45, 46). *NP*, *1*, 290, 316; *2*, 14–17, 61.

15. *ClSP*, *3*, 43, 86, 102, 153. *NP*, *1*, 301, 309. There is an example of a financial agent's credentials, dating from this period, in Add. MS 38,091, fol. 114.

ties by the former Comptroller of the Queen's Household, Sir Henry Wood. He was soon released on parole, but Nicholas reported that his arrest had "so retarded his business for the K. as that he shall not be able to get any money for the K. till Christmas, and much less than he expected." According to Bampfield, Seymour succeeded in raising £1,000 which he brought over to Paris at some time in the first half of 1653. Later in the same year, Seymour was interrupted in his duties by a serious illness during a visit to the West. In December he reported to Hyde on his financial activities in two letters, one of which fell into Thurloe's hands. In spite of rumors that he had been seen in Paris that same December, Seymour in fact seems to have stayed in England until the spring of 1654, when he was at last able to visit Paris openly on an official pass. The accounts which Seymour presented to the King at this time are interesting evidence of the scale of Royalist fund-raising. The King's receipt acknowledges the collection of £1,920 during Seymour's two recent missions; hardly an impressive total.[16]

A complete account of the other Royalist agents who collected money for Charles II would be neither possible nor profitable. John Ashburnham was implicated by a series of intercepted letters in 1654; in June he was sent to the Tower with his brother William, on a charge of having assisted Charles with money. The adventurous James Halsall, the brother of one of Ascham's murderers, afterward asserted under examination that he had dispatched £3,000 to the King between 1653 and March 1655; but this may have been an attempt to mislead his captors, for the accounts he presented at court that June show an excess of expenditure over receipts, all disposed of to other agents in England. Others who contributed directly to the King in this period include Sir Richard Willys and a "Mr. Jeffreys" who was thanked for a gift of £500 in November 1653. It is unlikely that these were the only contributions, but in no case is it possible to account for any large sum with certainty.[17]

16. *ClSP*, *3*, 70, 203, 209, 241. *CClSP*, *2*, 360–61. *NP*, *1*, 314–15; *2*, 33. *TSP*, *1*, 624 (letter to "Francis Edwards," evidently from Seymour), 645 (original in Seymour's hand). Add. MS 37,047, fols. 219, 240. For Seymour see *DNB*.
17. *TSP*, *1*, 649 ("Henry Hart" letter, in Willys' hand); *2*, 159, 161–62, 312,

Most of our knowledge of the work of Royalist financial agents has to be extracted from the deliberate obscurities, the "parcels of gloves," "pounds of tobacco," and the rest of the mercantile jargon used in letters easily open to interception. With such fragmentary evidence, and in the face of conflicting contemporary statements, no accurate estimate of the total amount contributed is possible. Bampfield gave the annual return as between £14,000 and £15,000, the Protector's *Declaration* in October 1655 suggested "many thousand pounds a year." On the Royalist side, the querulous Hatton with characteristic exaggeration spoke of £30,000 "within the space of some monthes"; John Ashburnham more realistically put the figure as low as £1,000 a year. Bearing in mind the only accurately documented contribution, Seymour's £1,920, it is unsafe to put the total higher than a few thousands a year. The majority of Royalists were in no condition, and so soon after Worcester in no mood, to contribute. Individual peers found as much difficulty as the King himself. Lord Hatton's steward, racking his brains for expedients in 1653, had "not lefte one freind untryed that hath mony," but none would lend. Even though bankruptcy and ruin may not have been as common as disgruntled Cavaliers afterward liked to recall, there was little to spare for a defeated monarch idling, it was fondly supposed, in Parisian luxury. Henry Seymour, indeed, brought the advice of the two most prominent Royalist peers, Hertford and Southampton, that as long as Charles remained in France nothing would induce his followers to supply him.[18]

In describing the efforts of the financial agents we have advanced as far as the early summer of 1654, the time of Seymour's visit to Paris. We must now retrace our steps to the year before, to observe the first flickerings of a more dangerous kind of conspiracy: renewed attempts to stir up armed opposition to the Commonwealth, to subvert garrisons and seize ports and bases. For almost two years after Worcester traces of active plotting are negligible. Then

321–22 ("Dab" is Ashburnham); *4*, 645. *CClSP, 2*, 282; *3*, 41 (MS 50, fol. 72). *The Protectorate of Oliver Cromwell*, ed. Robert Vaughan (London, 1838), *1*, 10.

18. *TSP, 2*, 511; *3*, 548. *A Declaration of His Highness by the Advice of His Council* (October 31, 1655), p. 16. *NP, 3*, 122. Add. MS 29,550, fol. 198. Clarendon, *History*, Bk. XIV, § 82.

around the middle of 1653 signs of greater determination gradually begin to shine through the obscurities of intercepted Royalist correspondence. As the rule of the Saints replaced the rule of the Rump, as the base of popular support for the Commonwealth grew correspondingly narrow, so the temptation increased to think that the revolution had run its course to the high-water mark of extremism, and that the moderate majority of the nation needed only the signal of a successful military coup to rise irresistibly on the King's behalf. The reckless adventurers who formed the raw material of the uncoordinated conspiracies of 1653–54 were, of course, incapable of such long-range speculation, but they were undoubtedly encouraged by the obvious possibilities that followed the meeting of the Barebones Parliament. Daniel O'Neill's pessimistic conclusion, quoted at the opening of this chapter, thus represents Royalist morale at its nadir. In the months that followed, the political instability in England gave increasing hopes of better things. "Never," Nicholas' intelligencer wrote in June 1653, "was so fitt a season nor so ripe a disposition to change." [19]

The West, as in 1649, led the Royalist revival. Projects to seize the Dorset seaports of Weymouth, Portland, and Poole had several times troubled the government during the years before Worcester. At Poole, a plan to subvert the garrison continued to smolder even after the King's defeat. In August 1653 the plot was discovered to be part of a wider design embracing other western ports, and extending as far afield as Portsmouth. The principal agent in the affair was Robert Phelips of Montacute, the same leader of the old Western Association who had played a notable part in the royal escape after Worcester. Phelips was in Paris early in 1653, angling for a place in the Duke of Gloucester's household. Failing in this, he returned to England in July, determined to repair his fortunes and spectacularly strengthen his claim to Charles' gratitude: by hoisting the flag of rebellion. Within a few days of his arrival in London Phelips began a regular correspondence with Hyde's secretary Edgeman, and he also made contact with a number of Royalists in London. Among these were another Somerset man, Nicholas Dowthwaite of Enmore near Bridgwater, Richard Thornbury of

19. Cl. MS 45, fol. 483.

Compton in Wiltshire, and Capt. Thomas Gardiner, who had an estate at West Ham and was the brother-in-law of no less a personage than Col. Robert Overton. Dowthwaite seems to have been Phelips' principal confidant. He had served under Hopton in the civil war but managed to avoid taking the Engagement, and was now a clerk of the common pleas in Clifford's Inn. After his arrest, Phelips admitted having had "some rambling discourse" about the strength of Portsmouth with these and other acquaintances; conversations which cannot have been innocent, as Phelips thought it necessary before Dowthwaite's examination to whisper him "some directions how to answere about Portsmouth." Nothing is known, however, about the precise intentions of the plotters at Portsmouth, and Thurloe's investigations drew only blank denials from the suspects.[20]

Further west, at Poole, the evidence is more plentiful. As far back as the summer of 1651 a group of Royalists there had sent an agent to the Continent to enlist the support of Lord Hopton in a plan to surprise the castle and declare for Charles II. The local leaders were two merchants named George Thompson and John St. Barbe, and Dr. Kinninmond, Lady Beauchamp's chaplain. Hopton was approached through his old officer Col. Walter Slingsby, who had been confined successively at Pendennis and Exeter since January 1650. The distintegration of the party after Worcester put a temporary damper on the Poole Royalists' hopes, yet the more optimistic of them did not forget the plan entirely, for the same individuals were associated in much the same project when it was uncovered two years later. The Poole design seems to have been revived before Phelips returned to England, during the winter of 1652–53, when secret meetings began at the King's Arms in Salisbury, a long-established nest of conspirators. Kinninmond, St. Barbe, Thompson, and other members of the Poole group were present, as were Gardiner and Dowthwaite. Activity continued in the West. In Dorset and Somerset a certain Major Fry, otherwise unidentified, was believed to be a principal agent. He and some

20. See below, n. 21, for full documentation of this account of the western plot. For Dowthwaite see *CCC*, p. 2312, and *TSP*, *1*, 409; for Thornbury, ibid., *3*, 308; for Gardiner, ibid., *6*, 447–48, and *CCC*, pp. 1431, 2365.

other impoverished malcontents had enlisted men to surprise Poole, and although it was said that Fry had had no contact with the exiles in France, ten suspects at Dorchester confessed the contrary, and admitted that they had received commissions from Charles II.

The first hint of official knowledge of the plot came even before Phelips' arrival in England early in July, when the Portsmouth authorities were warned of the recent arrival of sixteen suspicious characters at Rye. More sinister evidence of Thurloe's vigilance is to be seen in the emergence of an informer, the merchant Thompson, when the first arrests were made in August—a pattern of events that was depressingly familiar. For a reward of £130 Thompson made a complete disclosure of the plot. The Council of State reacted with vigorous precautions. On August 8 the western authorities were instructed to round up suspects; further measures the next day included decisions to strengthen the Tower and to set up a High Court of Justice; and before the end of the month orders had gone out to dismantle the weak fortifications at Poole, Weymouth, and Portland, in case they should be seized by insurgent Cavaliers. The arrest and examination of Phelips and Dowthwaite on the 12th was followed by that of many less prominent suspects in both London and the West, and the seizure of the estates of those few who possessed any. Phelips was thought sufficiently dangerous to be questioned by Cromwell and Sir Anthony Ashley Cooper, but in spite of a skillful mixture of flattery and threats, he persisted in a bland denial of having done anything seditious.

The direction taken by Cromwell's interrogation implies suspicions that the plot extended beyond the few western counties in which most of the arrests were concentrated. Among other questions, Phelips was asked what he knew of two influential northern Royalists, Lord Belasyse and Sir Philip Musgrave. The latter was arrested on suspicion, but as his release followed immediately it is unlikely that he was really implicated. The Council was also worried by the possibility of a Royalist intrigue with the Levellers, at a time when Lilburne's trial was arousing dangerous popular excitement, but no specific charges could be produced. Official nervousness was further expressed in discussions about strengthening the North Wales defenses, and in instructions to local commanders to prevent alarming gatherings like a recent bear-baiting near Warwick. The Council's caution was exaggerated. The western plot was the work of an insignificant fringe of local extremists and aroused no answering response from the rest of the party. It is important only because it draws attention to a slight revival of Royalist morale in the summer of 1653, and because it is the first instance after Worcester of active conspiracy by more than a handful of individuals. Without the participation of men of substance, and lacking previous preparation to such an extent that even Hyde did not know what was intended, it was aptly described as an "extravagant attempt" even before Phelips was arrested. No move had been made to obtain Dutch cooperation, and Charles II had neither allies nor forces of his own with which to mount a supporting invasion. Phelips soon escaped from the Tower and went again into exile, leaving Dowthwaite in confinement until March 1654. In the West, all but a few of the most dangerous suspects were discharged in October 1653, and the rest in the following June. The western plot had made little noise, and it died even more quietly than it had begun.[21]

The year 1653 ended, however, on a slightly more hopeful note for the Royalists, even though the affair which gave them encouragement was on the most minute and insignificant scale. Conspiracy was again afoot beneath the surface, but outwardly complete quiet descended on the party for three months after the discovery of the western plot. Then in November 1653 Col. Edward Wogan

21. A paper about the earlier history of the Poole conspiracy is in Egerton MS 2542, fols. 3–4. The events of 1653 are reconstructed from the following: *TSP, 1,* 366–67, 408–9 (the letters signed "Peter Richardson" are in Phelips' hand); *6,* 492. *CSPD, 1653–54,* pp. 3, 79, 82, 86–87, 95, 102, 106, 110–12, 165, 171, 202, 251, 432, 434, 455; *1654,* p. 162. *ClSP, 3,* 191. *CClSP, 2,* 236, 243. Phelips' examination in Cl. MS 46, fols. 182–83, is quoted in part in L. F. Brown, *The First Earl of Shaftesbury* (New York, 1933), pp. 56–57. See also Rawlinson MSS (Bodleian), A 5, 68; 6, 214; 12, 71. There are newspaper references in *A Perfect Account,* No. 141; *Mercurius Politicus,* No. 171; *Severall Proceedings,* Nos. 203–6; *The Faithful Scout,* Nos. 125, 130. As always, the newsbooks contain some inaccuracies. In reports of the plot the chaplain is spelled "Kenningman" or "Kynningman"; I think Henry Kinninmond, a canon of Salisbury after the Restoration, is a reasonable identification: see Joseph Foster, *Alumni Oxonienses . . . 1500–1714* (Oxford, 1891–92), p. 857.

slipped secretly into London to raise men and join the Scottish
Royalists in arms under Glencairn. Wogan was a reckless young
adventurer, typical of so many who swarmed about the exiled King.
He fought for the Parliament under Ireton in the first civil war,
for the King under Hamilton in the second. He had been in Ireland, at Worcester, and had been kicking his heels in Paris ever
since. Brushing aside the Chancellor's objections—reason, Hyde
sneered, was "a talent that did not abound in him"—Wogan eventually obtained the King's sanction, and armed with royal letters of
credence he reached London unmolested. There he enlisted
twenty-one men, and the party set out for the north, splitting into
small groups to avoid detection. A few more recruits came in as
Wogan traveled through the northern counties, but it was still a
small company which reached Scotland and joined the Highland-
ers. For once Thurloe's intelligence was at fault, for the Council
was informed that Lancashire was the intended route and the local
justices were warned accordingly; instead, Wogan rode through
Yorkshire and Durham. Wogan's good fortune was short-lived, for
within a month of joining Glencairn he was killed in a skirmish.
The whole affair was romantically improbable.[22]

Trivial or no, Wogan's exploit had its cheerful aspects; as one
observer commented, it gave the "drooping Malignants" a little
life.[23] If nothing else, it had some small publicity value, and like
the western conspiracy it showed that a minority of obscure Royalists with only their lives to lose were prepared to accept the risks of
violence. On the other hand, the direction of Wogan's march has a
negative significance. With the Highlands in open rebellion, many
of the King's party were still thinking of Scotland as the most hopeful scene of action. Wogan's venture might serve as an example for
similar projects, but little more could be expected of it. However,
in December 1653 the "drooping Malignants" badly needed something to revive them, and although neither Phelips nor Wogan
had succeeded in arousing more than a few of the wilder spirits,

22. The fullest account of Wogan's career is by Sir Frederick Maurice,
The Adventures of Edward Wogan (London, 1945). See chap. 8 for the 1653
exploit.
23. Cl. MS 47, fol. 150.

their exploits showed that the party was not entirely dead. More important was the fact, unknown to all but a few, that progress was at last beginning toward the construction of an organization that promised opposition of a far more serious and prolonged nature. By the end of 1653 a central committee to direct such an organization was already in being. Its name was the Sealed Knot.

5. *The Sealed Knot*

THE SEALED KNOT, whose fortunes we shall trace through its nearly six years of troubled existence, succeeded from the first in wrapping itself in obscurity. The precise date of its foundation, the names of its members, the nature of its objectives, and the degree to which it actually was able to direct the planning of Royalist conspiracy in England—all these have been matters of considerable doubt and controversy to both the Knot's own contemporaries and later historians. It is the purpose of this chapter to explore some of the problems surrounding the Knot's foundation, its membership, and its early activities.

While much is uncertain about the origin of the Sealed Knot, it is at least clear that it came into existence during the latter half of 1653, while the Parliament of Saints was alarming the conservatives by the dangerously hectic pace of its legislation, and while the Royalists were reflecting resignedly on the failure of the western plot, or drinking perfunctory toasts to Wogan's little band. According to Bampfield, the Knot emerged after two separate missions to Charles II, by Sir Gilbert Talbot and Robert Phelips. Through these two, the Old Royalists assured the King "that if he woulde retyre to his first principles," (in other words abandon the Scots-Presbyterian alliance), "and intruste the secret management of his affayres to such hands aboute him, as his frends might securely confide in, they would adventure both theyr lives and fortunes for his

73

recovery." This, said Bampfield, was at some time early in 1653, but in this he is supported by no other evidence. The mention of Talbot, however, sounds like an echo of his proposal in 1649 that some such committee should be appointed. Clarendon, years later, explained that the Knot received the royal approval after its members had already begun to associate together, and had sent "an express of their own number" to the King. Nothing is known of the timing of this move, or the name of the agent involved; but it is worth noting that in November 1653 a gentleman came to Paris from England and was important enough to have three secret interviews with Charles. The incident was shrouded in mystery, and Hyde was evasive when he reported it to Nicholas; it is possible that it had some connection with the foundation of the Sealed Knot.[1]

It is unlikely that the Knot was formed much before November 1653, as in that month the absence of any central organization in England was deplored by a Royalist agent who had recently arrived there. This was Major Nicholas Armorer, a bearded and ruddy-faced Northcountryman, once Governor of the High Ercall garrison, now employed in the Princess Royal's household. He was to be one of the most persistent of the underground workers in the King's cause, with an infinite capacity for hairbreadth escapes and dangerous cloak-and-dagger exploits. Armorer wrote to Secretary Nicholas on November 14, requesting the King to "fix on one or two of the most prudent" of the English Royalists to manage his secret affairs, and claiming that most of those he had spoken with joined in this appeal. From Nicholas' reply it is clear that he at least knew of no officially accredited committee in England at this date.[2]

Three months later such a committee certainly did exist. A letter

1. *TSP*, 2, 511. Clarendon, *Con.*, § 23. *ClSP*, *3*, 209. Gossip identified the mysterious visitor as Henry Seymour, but evidently incorrectly: *NP*, 2, 33.

2. *NP*, 2, 22, 30; Add. MS 4180, fol. 104. For Armorer see *LBM*, p. 8 n., and Richard Symonds, *Diary of the Marches of the Royal Army during the Great Civil War*, ed. C. E. Long, Camden Society (London, 1859), pp. 172, 249, 256. He was evidently one of the Armorers of Belford, Northumberland: see Edward Bateson et al., *A History of Northumberland* (Newcastle, 1893–1940), *1*, 278, 388–91. There is a description of Armorer in 1655, aged about thirty-five, in *TSP*, *3*, 164.

of Hyde's agent Edward Villiers, dated February 2, 1654, contains the first indisputable reference to its activities. "The sealed knott," Villiers informed Hyde, "still meete, with an intention to designe somewhat for [the King] his service." [3] Villiers' language implies that meetings had been in progress for some appreciable time, and that Armorer may have been speaking from ignorance when he reported to Nicholas in November. A more likely explanation, however, is that the Sealed Knot came into being during the intervening period, shortly before the end of 1653. On November 27 Charles sent letters to three of the Knot's future members, perhaps intended as written credentials accompanying verbal requests to join the new association. The three letters, to Lord Belasyse, Sir Richard Willys, and Col. John Russell, are couched in the usual jargon of Royalist intrigue, but their general tenor is unmistakeable: the King is resolved to "make another venture in trade," needs the advice of the three recipients, and wishes them to consult together to that end. The formation of the Knot can thus be dated reasonably exactly: between November 1653 and February 1654, and probably in the former month.[4]

The membership of the Sealed Knot can be described with more

3. *TSP*, 2, 64 (cipher in Appendix, D).

4. *CClSP*, 2, 282 (MS 47, fol. 120); to L. B[elasyse], S. R. W[illys], and J. R[ussell]: see Appendix, D. There is much confusion in previous accounts of the formation of the Sealed Knot. The standard version, Gardiner's, is inaccurate and misleading. Gardiner states that there had been an earlier committee, and that about the end of 1653 "its members declined to meddle further with the projects of the exiled court, and their place had been taken by a body of more energetic Royalists who styled themselves the 'Sealed Knot.'" (*C&P*, *3*, 117). This is based on a letter from Sir Miles Hobart dated February 22, no year (*CClSP*, 2, 318; MS 48, fol. 5), which Gardiner supposes belongs to the year 1654. In fact, as internal evidence clearly shows (allusions to Cromwell's speech to the Lord Mayor, Skippon's command of the militia, etc.), the letter's correct date is February 22, 1654, O.S., or March 4, 1655, N.S. It is misplaced in the *Calendar;* Macray must have been misled by Hyde's letter to Hobart on May 1, 1654, acknowledging the receipt of one from Hobart dated the 23d of some unspecified month: *CClSP*, 2, 345. Unless Hyde's "23" is a slip of the pen, it cannot be a reply to the letter quoted by Gardiner, and one would naturally assume it to be a reply to one dated April 23. In Hobart's letter of March 4, 1655, the references to a conflict of opinion among the Royalists relate to the breach between the Knot and the recently formed "Action party," with which Hobart in 1655 was associated. Abbott, *3*, 195–96, is only the latest of several writers to follow Gardiner's error.

precision, although confusion has often arisen when historians have accepted the statements of uninformed contemporaries at face value. Whatever Royalists not in the secret may have thought, there is indisputable evidence that the Knot had six members, and six only: Lords Belasyse and Loughborough, Sir William Compton, Cols. John Russell and Edward Villiers, and Sir Richard Willys.[5] Some of them fell away after the disasters of 1655, but although the Knot acquired a secretary (the post changed hands in 1656), and later a regular messenger to and from the exiled Court, no new members were added before its authority was superseded in 1659. Villiers is the only one whose appointment cannot be precisely dated, but he had evidently taken a principal part in its establishment. He had gone to England in the summer of 1652 and had begun a correspondence with Hyde early the next year. Thurloe later received intelligence that Villiers had made a trip to Paris during 1653, and the language of the King's letter to Belasyse contains a faint implication that Villiers was himself the bearer of it. Perhaps Villiers was the mysterious visitor to Paris in November 1653; if so, the secret was well kept. Belasyse, Willys, and Russell, as already mentioned, were evidently invited to take part by the King's letters of November 27; Loughborough was accredited by a letter sent on February 11, 1654; and Compton was asked to join in the following May.[6]

A brief digression into the earlier careers of these six influential Royalists should do much to indicate the section of the party whose views the Sealed Knot might be expected to reflect and on whose behalf it was primarily intended to act. "There had been," Clarendon tells us, "six or eight persons of general good and confessed reputation, and who of all who were then left alive had had the

5. Carte MS (Bodleian) 194, fol. 43 (see Appendix, E); Add. MS 41,202 A, fol. 19.

6. *ClSP, 3,* 81. *CClSP, 2,* 282, 307–8, 315, 363. Cl. MS 45, fols. 11, 32, 94, 102, 136. *TSP, 2,* 64, 70 (cipher in Appendix, D); *3,* 459. Many of the confusions over the Knot's membership are derived from Royalist writers after 1660. For example, Baker, p. 658, omits Villiers and Loughborough but includes the Earl of Oxford and Sir John Grenville. David Lloyd, *Memoires of the Lives . . . of Those . . . Personages That Suffered . . . from 1637 to 1660* (London, 1668), p. 358, also includes Oxford and omits Villiers, Willys, and Loughborough.

most eminent charges in the war, and executed them with great courage and discretion; so that few men could with any reasonable pretence refuse to receive orders from them, or to serve under their commands . . . some of them having, beside their experience in war, very considerable fortunes of their own to lose, and were relations to the greatest families in England." [7] "The most eminent charges in the war," and "relations to the greatest families in England"—the two phrases between them describe all six members of the Knot.

Belasyse was the second son of Thomas, first Lord Fauconberg, and had been raised to the peerage for his services in the civil war. Although a younger son, his estates in Yorkshire and the neighboring counties, and those of his wife in Hertfordshire, were extensive enough to make him a man of substance. He sat in both Parliaments of 1640 for the family borough of Thirsk, and like his father and elder brother Henry took the King's side in the civil war. His nephew Thomas, on the other hand, who succeeded to the Fauconberg title in 1653, conformed peaceably to the Protectorate, and in 1657 married Cromwell's daughter Mary. Belasyse was also related to Fairfax and Lambert, and was thus more fortunately placed in case of official disfavor than were some of his associates. Another interesting feature of his membership of the Sealed Knot is the fact that he was the only Roman Catholic among the six. His inclusion gave the Knot at least a chance of maintaining contact with the northern Catholics, a cohesive group with the usual recusant tradition of secret activity.

In spite of a certain propensity to dueling, for which he was imprisoned in 1657, Belasyse possessed useful qualities of leadership. Clarendon was impressed with him: "a person of great interest . . . and of exemplar industry and courage." His military experience was extensive. He raised and led several regiments of horse and foot, fought at many of the chief engagements from Edgehill to Naseby, and was wounded in the attack on Bristol in July 1643. Early the next year he took over the command in Yorkshire, where he was defeated by his relatives Lambert and Fairfax at Bradford and Selby respectively. After ten months as a prisoner Belasyse was

7. Clarendon, *Con.*, § 23.

exchanged and succeeded Lichfield as commander of the horse-guards in September 1645. A month later he was made Governor of Newark, where he remained until the surrender. For some time after the war's end he lived at Worlaby, his Lincolnshire house, until forced to leave "by some jealousies which the Committee of Lincoln had of his retaining so many poor cavalier officers about him." He moved to London, compounded, and then joined the émigré stream to the Continent. Service under Condé at the siege of Mardyke, discussions with the Venetians about a recruiting scheme, an audience with the Pope—such were some of Belasyse's activities in the two years following the surrender. In 1648 he was designed to have been Newcastle's General of horse in Yorkshire, but before he arrived Preston had been fought and lost. Eventually, in 1650, Belasyse returned to England, to suffer another spell of imprisonment during the troubled summer of 1651.[8]

Loughborough, the other peer in the Sealed Knot, was even better connected than Belasyse, and his military record was in no way inferior. Second son of the fifth Earl of Huntingdon, he was, like Belasyse, ennobled only during the war; but the prestige of the Hastings family in the Midlands outweighed even that of the Belasyses further north. Apart from Loughborough, none of them took much part in the fighting. The fifth Earl was old and impoverished, and confined himself to some small financial contributions to the royal coffers early in the war. Loughborough's brother Ferdinando, who succeeded as sixth Earl in 1643, originally accepted a commission in the parliamentary army but immediately placed himself on the retired list and relapsed into neutrality. Loughborough's vigor in the royal service more than compensated for his relatives' coolness. He published the King's Commission

8. For general accounts of Belasyse's career see *BIHR*, *4*, 48–49, where the inaccurate *DNB* entry is rewritten; G.E.C., *Peerage;* Keeler, p. 104; J. Gillow, *Literary and Biographical History . . . of the English Catholics* (London, 1885–1902), *1*, 178–79; and the biographical fragment by his secretary, Joshua Moore, in HMC, *Ormonde,* new ser. 2, 376–99. Details of his finances are in *CCC*, pp. 1338–39, and Harleian MS (BM) 991, p. 29. For his civil war career see Clarendon, *History*, Bk. VI, § 62 n.; VII, § 121 n., 400; IX, § 129, 131; X, § 34; also Gardiner, *Civil War*, *1*, 396; *2*, 356, 360; and Maurice Ashley, *Cromwell's Generals* (London, 1954), p. 100. For his arrest in 1651 see *CSPD, 1651,* pp. 137, 150, 417.

Fig. 1. JOHN, LORD BELASYSE.
From the miniature by Samuel Cooper.
Victoria and Albert Museum, Crown Copyright.

of Array at Leicester in June 1642, raised and led a troop of horse at Edgehill, and in 1643 was made Colonel General of the royal forces in Leicestershire. His most important service during the war was his successful defense of his father's house at Ashby-de-la-Zouch. From this stronghold Loughborough was a constant thorn in the enemy's side, interrupting communications between London and the North, and raiding supply-trains. In the spring of 1644 he attacked Nottingham and distinguished himself in the relief of Newark. A year later he joined Charles I before Leicester, and was made governor of the town after its capture. Loughborough held out at Ashby until February 1646. In the second civil war he was in charge of the commissariat at Colchester; after the defeat he was imprisoned at Windsor, escaping to Rotterdam the night before the King's execution. Loughborough remained in Holland until late in 1652, although his agents operated in the Midlands during the conspiracy of 1650–51, and he was designed to command the region when it rose to support the Scots invasion. The Hastings name and Loughborough's military reputation between them fully account for his inclusion in the Sealed Knot.[9]

The third member to be considered, Sir William Compton, was another whose position in the Knot could be explained by family connections and services in the civil war. He also possessed a combination of charm and integrity which impressed even Cromwell. His death in 1663 inspired Pepys to one of his most glowing eulogies: "One of the worthyest men and best officers of State now in England . . . of the best temper, valour, abilities of mind, integrity, birth, fine person, and diligence of any one man he hath left behind him in the three kingdoms." In 1653 Compton was a young man of twenty-eight. Ten years before he had fought at Hopton Heath when his father, the second Earl of Northampton, was killed, and ever since he and his brothers had wholeheartedly supported the royal cause. In 1644 he was Governor of Banbury, brilliantly sustaining a thirteen-week siege against heavy odds until relieved

9. The *DNB* life is adequate. See also *CCC*, pp. 1746, 3029–30; Clarendon, *History*, Bk. V, § 417; VI, §§ 274–75; HMC, *Hastings*, 2, intro., pp. vi–ix, and 84–140; Eliot Warburton, *Memoirs of Prince Rupert and the Cavaliers* (London, 1849), 2, 96–97; and H. N. Bell, *The Huntingdon Peerage*, London, 1821.

by his elder brother James. Compton's youth prevented advancement beyond the rank of a garrison commander in the first civil war, but in 1648 he took part in the Kent rising, and was a Major General at Colchester.

What the Hastings family was to Royalism in Leicestershire, the Comptons were in Northampton, and they were also powerful in Warwickshire, where lay one of their great houses, Compton Wynyates. Whereas Belasyse had ties with important parliamentarians and Loughborough a neutralist brother, Compton came of a family whose Cavalier sympathies were undiluted. Northampton had not followed the common practice, lamented by Clarendon, of those who "warily distributed their family to both sides." James, the new Earl, fought as valiantly as any of the peers; another brother, Sir Charles, helped to defend Banbury and remained an active Royalist in the 1650's, and only Henry, the future Bishop of London, who was abroad during most of the Interregnum, did not participate in Royalist plotting. Prudence obviously dictated that the younger brother should run the direct risks of conspiracy rather than the Earl himself, whose discovery might penalize the family fortunes, heavily encumbered with debts as they already were. In 1651 Sir William married the widowed Lady Alington, sister of Sir Lionel Tollemache, and thereby became brother-in-law to the influential Countess of Dysart. Although too young to have reached the highest military rank, Compton was thus an excellent choice on the essential grounds of personality and birth.[10]

After Compton, it is appropriate to rank John Russell as the fourth member of the Sealed Knot, for he came of a family as powerful and more wealthy than any we have mentioned. He was the third son of the great Francis Russell, fourth Earl of Bedford, the "wise earl," whose death in 1641 had deprived the opposition of one of its ablest leaders. Whether by accident or design, Bedford's sons divided their allegiance. John Russell sat for Tavistock

10. There are brief accounts of Compton's life in *DNB,* and *Collins's Peerage of England,* ed. Sir E. Brydges (London, 1812), *3,* 243–46. See also *CCC,* pp. 261, 1246–51, 1444, 1831, 3272; Clarendon, *History,* Bk. VI, §§ 99, 280–84; VIII, §§ 148, 152; *Diary of Samuel Pepys,* ed. H. B. Wheatley (London, 1904–05), *3,* 286–87; G.E.C., *Peerage, 1,* 107; E. D. H. Tollemache, *The Tollemaches of Helmingham and Ham* (Ipswich, 1949), p. 56.

in the Long Parliament, and when the crisis came he supported the King. His brother William, the fifth Earl, flirted with both sides and twice turned his coat. He was General of the parliamentary horse at Edgehill, deserted to the King in the spring of 1643 and fought for him at Newbury, and then returned to Parliament in the following winter. The increasing extremism of the Army and the Independents soon drove Bedford into retirement, and he lived inconspicuously at Woburn throughout the 1650's. In spite of his brother's vacillations, John Russell's aristocratic connections were beyond question. Among his brothers-in-law were the parliamentarian Lords Brooke and Grey of Wark, the turncoat Earl of Carlisle, and the Royalist Lords Bristol and Newport of High Ercall. He was himself a man of considerable means, with estates at Shingay, Cambridgeshire. In the civil war, Russell commanded Prince Rupert's blue-coated regiment of foot, was prominent at the storming of Leicester in May 1645, was wounded at Naseby two weeks later, and was in the Oxford garrison before its surrender. His inclusion in the Knot strengthened the group's contacts with an important bloc of neutral opinion, committed in 1653 to neither side.[11]

The fifth member of the Sealed Knot has already appeared in this narrative through his part in its formation. Edward Villiers was born in 1620, the fourth son of Sir Edward Villiers, the first Duke of Buckingham's half-brother. The Villiers clan was at the heart of a veritable network of family relationships. Edward's three brothers succeeded in turn to the title of Viscount Grandison; William, the oldest, had been killed at Bristol in 1643, and the title at this time was held by the second brother, John, who had been in the Tower since Worcester. Besides being a cousin of the second Duke of Buckingham (perhaps no real recommendation to the confidence of Hyde and the Old Royalists), Villiers was nephew to Lord Purbeck, and to the Countess of Denbigh. The Countess' son, the second Earl, was one of the few peers to give open support to the Commonwealth, and had been a member of the Council of

11. *DNB;* Keeler, p. 329; J. H. Wiffen, *Historical Memoirs of the House of Russell* (London, 1833), 2, 127–30, 154–60; *Symonds' Diary,* pp. 165, 180; *CCC,* pp. 1208–9.

State until 1651. Villiers was also closely related to another aristocratic house, the Howards, Earls of Suffolk, who had followed a more neutral course. Villiers' younger sister married James, the third Earl, a lukewarm parliamentarian who had narrowly escaped impeachment in 1647; Edward himself married Frances Howard, the Earl's sister. More significant was the fact that he was distantly related to Hyde, whose first wife, Anne Ayliffe, was another of Villiers' cousins. Hyde had a high opinion of Villiers, commending his "diligence and dexterity" and addressing him familiarly as "honest Ned."

Villiers had not attained high rank in the civil war, but like Russell he had risen to a colonelcy. He served against the Scots in 1640, was wounded at Newbury in 1643, and was often employed to carry important confidential dispatches. In 1645 he served at Newark under Sir Richard Willys, beginning a friendship that lasted at least until just before the Restoration. After the end of the first civil war Villiers was soon in trouble with Parliament, on suspicion of complicity in a plot to promote the Duke of York's escape, but was released after examination by a committee of the House of Lords. He took no part in the second civil war, and evidently went abroad in 1649, where he stayed until the middle of 1652. Villiers was not a man of property, in spite of his connections; when he compounded in 1649 his fine amounted to only the token sum of £1. Hard-working, loyal, and self-effacing, he labored longer and probably harder than any of his colleagues to make the Sealed Knot a success. Some years later he made some stupid errors of judgment, but in 1653 he was well entrenched in Hyde's confidence.[12]

12. There are brief notices of Villiers in *DNB; Collins,* ed. Brydges, *3,* 790; and *LBM,* p. 21 n. His family connections can be traced from the above, and from Lister, *1,* 10 n. For his life before and during the civil war see Edward Peacock, *Army Lists of the Roundheads and Cavaliers* (London, 1874), p. 77; Clarendon, *History,* Bk. V, §§ 378–80; Warburton, *2,* 424; Sir Edward Walker, *Historical Discourses* (London, 1705), p. 37; *CSPD, 1645–47,* p. 214; *Symonds' Diary,* pp. 179, 271; *CJ, 4,* 483; *LJ, 8,* 217, 222–23, 234; *CCC,* p. 1608; and Add. MS 18,982, fol. 49. The plot to assist York's escape is mentioned in *LJ, 8,* 622–38; see also *NP, 1,* 77, 131. For Villiers' return to England in 1652 and correspondence with Hyde see above, pp. 75–76. He may have been the "Mr. Villers" summoned before the Council of State in June 1652: *CSPD, 1651–52,* p. 298.

Sir Richard Willys, the sixth and last member of the Knot, was the only one who had no strong qualifications on grounds of birth or fortune. He came of a family of Cambridgeshire "mere" gentry, and like all his associates in the Knot he was a younger son; he was born in 1614, the second son of Richard Willys of Fen Ditton. He was educated at St. John's School in Hertford, matriculated at Christ's College, Cambridge, in 1631, and was admitted to Gray's Inn the same year. Service in the Netherlands, a traditional part of the education of a gentleman, followed his Cambridge days. He fought for the Dutch as an ensign of foot, and in 1637 played a notable part in repulsing a Spanish sally at the siege of Breda. The gathering war clouds at home soon brought him back to England. He served in the futile campaigns against the Scots in 1639 and 1640, and in the two following years was a member of Charles I's guard at Whitehall and Hampton Court.

The outbreak of the civil war opened the way to promotion. Victory in a minor skirmish in Warwickshire earned him a knighthood in October 1642; he then served as a colonel of horse under Edward Villiers' oldest brother, Lord Grandison. In October 1643 he was in Cheshire with the rank of Major General of horse, and early in 1644 was taken prisoner in a night raid on the Royalist camp at Ellesmere. He was already a person of sufficient importance to merit at least two efforts to obtain his release by exchange. The first of these, in August 1644, the Commons rejected "for some urgent reasons," but the second was successful, and Willys returned to the Royalist ranks at Oxford in October. He was then sent to join Rupert's army around Bristol and quickly won the Prince's confidence by his ability as a cavalry commander. Soon afterward he received his first important command, when he was made Governor of Newark and Colonel General of the royal forces in the counties of Nottingham, Lincoln, and Rutland.

Willys' command at Newark ended in a controversy which brought him for the first time into the foreground of national affairs, throws considerable light on his character, and may be of some relevance to the affairs of the Sealed Knot nearly ten years later. In October 1645 the King arrived at Newark, where he was soon joined by Willys' patron Rupert, now in disgrace following the surrender of Bristol. Willys, who had received the King only at the gates of Newark, tactlessly demonstrated his confidence in the Prince by meeting him with an escort at two miles' distance; and it is not surprising that Charles, already dissatisfied with the Governor's inability to restrain his troops from plunder and to cooperate with the local Royalist commissioners, should have taken this as a token of defiance. A partial reconciliation between King and nephew, and a declaration clearing Rupert of disloyalty at Bristol, did not end the tension. Willys was replaced as Governor by Belasyse, and was offered instead Belasyse's old post as commander of the horseguards. Nominally this was a promotion, but in the circumstances it carried for Willys a strong sense of being kicked upstairs and was correctly interpreted by the whole Rupert faction as a further move against them. An angry and undignified scene followed, in which Willys demanded to know the source of the accusations against him, Rupert and Gerard were openly insubordinate, and all the pent-up frustration of the recent defeats received a damagingly public airing. There was a bitter outcome: Rupert, Gerard, Willys, and some other officers, including Edward Villiers, temporarily withdrew from the royal service. Although Willys acted thoughtlessly at Newark, his language and demeanor before the King were at least more restrained than some of his superiors'; it is hard to see why in after years he should have denounced the accepted version of the scene as "a feigned formed lie." He had, however, shown the soldier's characteristic sensitivity and readiness to take offense when his honor and reputation were involved. Whereas Rupert and Gerard regarded Lord Digby as the author of their misfortunes, Willys concentrated his hostility on Belasyse, whom he challenged to a duel, and although Charles prohibited any such frivolity, the grievance against Belasyse seems to have rankled.

In spite of the quarrel at Newark, Willys did not leave the country, and in the spring of 1646 he made his peace with the King. On April 3 he was admitted to the royal presence, received a full pardon and a baronetcy into the bargain, and was one of the commissioners appointed to negotiate the surrender of Oxford. After the unhappy conclusion of the war, Willys went into exile, traveled for the most part in Italy, and it was not until the summer of 1652 that he returned to his native Cambridgeshire. Willys' selection as a member of the Knot can best be explained as the result of his military experience, a general belief in his integrity and willingness to run risks, and his close friendship with Edward Villiers. But he was a poor man, and his family connections were not impressive. His position in the new organization was from the first a unique one.[13]

Certain significant generalizations are suggested by this survey of the careers of the six members of the Sealed Knot. In the first place they were all younger sons. The risks of conspiracy were too great, and the consequences of failure too serious to be accepted directly by the heads of the great noble families who continued to look forward to Charles II's restoration. Belasyse, Compton, and Russell were wealthy men, but their leadership of the Royalist underground movement did not involve the danger of reprisals against their families. Much of the history of Royalist plotting might indeed be written as a conspiracy of younger sons. Another interesting point is the Sealed Knot's unbalanced geographical distribution. For a national committee there was a curious preponderance of East Anglian members, and the West and South of England were entirely unrepresented. Three of the members lived in Cambridgeshire: Compton at Linton, Russell at Shingay, Willys at Fen Ditton; Villiers was a frequent visitor to the region; [14] and Belasyse had local connections through his first wife's family, the Botelers of Watton Woodhall, Hertfordshire. Their territorial influence was not as restricted as this might imply, but even admitting their widespread family ties, the Knot's members do seem to have been drawn from a strikingly restricted area.

To take a more constructive view, only Willys among the six lacked the prestige of an aristocratic name. The Knot in fact was sensibly designed to make use of the remaining influence and patronage of the nobility, and its ultimate failure only reflects the

13. This account of Willys is based on my "Sir Richard Willys and Secretary Thurloe," *EHR*, *69* (1954), 373–76. Besides the authorities there cited see John and J. A. Venn, *Alumni Cantabrigienses*, Pt. I (Cambridge, 1922–27), *4*, 422; Gardiner, *Civil War*, *1*, 346; *2*, 346, 356–59; *The Pythouse Papers*, ed. William A. Day (London, 1879), pp. 66, 70; and *CJ*, *3*, 614.

14. Brodrick MS 1, fols. 22, 90.

temporary disturbance which the recent revolution had created in the social hierarchy. Even if circumstances made it virtually impossible to overthrow the Protectorate by a general rising, it was important that whatever action was practicable should be directed by the Cavalier gentry's natural leaders. At the same time, the caution, or as some thought the temporizing behavior, of most of the nobility, might be stimulated into action if the great lords were persuaded that the underground movement was headed not by reckless firebrands but by men of quality like themselves; men who would permit a demonstration against the government only after the most careful planning, and when it had a reasonable chance of success. Moderate leadership of this kind such a group as the Knot might be expected to provide. Fulfilling most of the necessary conditions, it could thus begin its work with high hopes. "There was no well-affected person in England," Clarendon thought, "who at that time would not willingly receive advice and direction from most of those persons." [15]

Although the six members named were the only ones officially accredited by the King, they were not prohibited from seeking the advice of other prominent Royalists. Instructions sent from the King in May 1654 empowered them to "admitt such persons into ther number whome they thinke, and at such tymes as they thinke necessary." [16] There is no record of any seventh person receiving the King's commission as a full member, but the authorization to seek outside advice probably accounts for occasional rumors that others were included. A certain "Mr. Symson" (it is impossible to identify him with certainty) had some knowledge of the Knot's activities in the spring of 1654, but it appears from later correspondence that he was an emissary appointed to maintain contact between the Knot and a group of northcountry Royalists, not an actual member. [17] Another Royalist sometimes believed to have been in the Sealed

15. *Con.*, § 23.
16. *CCISP*, 2, 356 (MS 48, fol. 215).
17. *CCISP*, 2, 357, 361, 363. "Symson" may have been Thomas Paulden of Wakefield. "Symson's" hand in Cl. MS 48, fol. 240 appears to be the same as that of the agent "Plant" in 1656: ibid., 55, fols. 176, 217; 56, fol. 17. "Plant" was the brother of "Grig," who was Gregory Paulden: *CCISP*, 4, 175, 286. For the Pauldens see *DNB*, and above, p. 9.

Knot was Sir Philip Musgrave, an active man in the northern border counties ever since the first civil war; the evidence, however, is slender. Rumors that Sir Humphrey Bennett (leader of the Hampshire Royalists in 1650) and the Presbyterian Lord Willoughby were involved are equally unsubstantial.[18] Lord Beauchamp, the former leader of the Western Association, would probably have been invited to join, but early in 1654 he died. This was "an unspeakable loss," Hyde wrote gloomily, and "left all the business of the West without any order." [19] The six members originally named were, then, the only ones.

Having settled the Knot's membership, it is necessary to examine its policy and program. When the new leaders sent their messenger to the King in Paris, Clarendon tells us, they declared

> "That if they were approved and qualified by his majesty, they would by joint advice intend the care of his majesty's service; and as they would not engage in any absurd and desperate attempt, but use all their credit and authority to prevent and discountenance the same, so they would take the first rational opportunity, which they expected from the divisions and animosities which daily grew and appeared in the army, to draw their friends and old soldiers who were ready to receive their commands together, and try the utmost that could be done, with the loss or hazard of their lives." . . . And therefore they made it their humble suit, "that this secret correspondence might be carried on, and known to none but to the marquis of Ormond and to the chancellor; and that if any other councils were set on foot in England by the activity of particular persons, who too frequently with great zeal and little animadversion embarked themselves in impossible undertakings, his majesty upon advertisement thereof would first communicate the motives or pretences which would be offered to him, to them; and then they would find opportunity to confer with some sober men of that fraternity . . . and thereupon they would present their opinion to his majesty."

18. *CCISP*, 2, 335. *TSP*, 3, 64, 592.
19. HMC, *12th Report*, Appendix 9, pp. 48–49. *ClSP*, 3, 238. *CCISP*, 2, 167, 331, 359–60. *NP*, 2, 66.

The King, Clarendon continues, "consented to all they proposed; and the cyphers and correspondence were committed to the chancellor, in whose hands, with the privity only of the marquis of Ormond, all the intelligence with England . . . was intrusted." [20]

Several essential points emerge from this statement of intentions. The most important is that the Sealed Knot was the chosen instrument of the Hyde-Ormond group at Court, and embraced its policy of reliance upon the Old Royalists, without entangling alliances or compromises of principle. Hyde and the Old Royalists inevitably looked to each other for support in their hostility to the Presbyterian alliance and in their rejection of the adolescent heroics of the Swordsmen. Whether Hyde deliberately promoted the formation of the Knot through the efforts of Edward Villiers and his other agents, or whether the Knot came together independently and then named Hyde and Ormond as its friends at Court, the conclusion as to its function must be the same. The fact that it was the only group possessing Charles II's commission enabled the Chancellor, in theory at least, to maintain direct control over high-level conspiracy in England.

To say that the Old Royalists trusted Hyde and approved of his influence over the King does not mean that this confidence was universal. There were always those who would listen to foolish rumors of Hyde's alleged correspondence with Cromwell, or would blame him for the King's protracted stay in Paris; and both the Louvre interest and Rupert's Swordsmen tried hard to undermine him by working on their friends in England. Villiers was often depressed by the constant factionalism. On March 13, 1654, he reported: "I finde the great mistrust is of poor [Hyde], and consequently of his correspondent [Villiers] here." Rupert, Gerard, and their friends immediately recognized the Knot as an instrument of the Chancellor, and tried to dissuade its members from acting. Loughborough, Villiers warned, had "a wise caution sent him to have a care who he deales withall." The "wise caution" evidently came from Lord Keeper Herbert, another of Rupert's faction, who according to another Royalist agent had advised Loughborough "not to meddle in this businesse"—in other words to stay out of

20. *Con.,* § 23.

the Knot. The author of this piece of information accused Rupert of having disclosed the secret of the Knot's existence to Herbert, and concluded, "I hope care will bee taken that the P. know noe more of us." So great was the suspicion of Rupert that Villiers argued that the friendship between the Prince and Russell was a possible objection against the latter's inclusion in the Knot. Willys' old admiration for Rupert, on the other hand, seems to have been forgotten.[21]

There was another exhibition of dissatisfaction with Hyde when the Yorkshire agent Charles Davison came to Paris in April 1654. Davison, it seems, was a minister, who had been tutor to Sir George Savile, afterward the great Marquis of Halifax. He was involved in the Rainsborough murder at Pontefract in 1648, and for the rest of his life was an energetic conspirator. On this mission Davison tried to avoid all dealings with Hyde, who recounted the incident to Nicholas with asperity. When the King made Davison present himself to the Chancellor, he "desired to be excused, that he was limited, and that though he knew I was trusted by some, yet there were others who would not willingly have me privy to what should be resolved." The King made short work of Davison's objections, but the affair was nonetheless disturbing. Hyde attributed Davison's obstinacy to the influence of his Catholic rival Langdale; it also showed the sinister hand of Rupert, for Davison would have preferred to deal with the King through Holder, the Prince's secretary, rather than through Hyde.[22]

In spite of these occasional rumblings, the Royalists behind the Sealed Knot were in general united in opposition to the factions confronting Hyde in Paris. For the policies of Hyde and the Knot we must return to the passage already quoted from Clarendon. First, the committee was to have sole authority to supervise Royalist plotting in England, including designs initiated by others. Second, it was to discourage "absurd and desperate attempts" and "impossible undertakings." Third, and in the last analysis the real justification for its existence, it was to prepare for a general rising,

21. *CCISP*, 2, 307–8, 361 (MS 48, fol. 240). *TSP*, 2, 162 (cipher in Appendix, D).

22. *ClSP*, 3, 235, 238. *CCISP*, 2, 335. For Davison see ibid., 4, 69; *TSP*, 3, 264; and Heath, p. 700.

whenever political conditions offered a reasonable chance of success. These three objectives, with some others, are all present in the instructions sent from the King to the Sealed Knot in April and May 1654. The instructions begin by expressing the King's complete confidence in the Knot's members, promising that "he hath and will cause them to be informed of all designs in all places." The second paragraph has already been quoted, giving the Knot authority to recruit new associates at its own discretion. Thirdly, it was suggested that one member be appointed to negotiate with outsiders; an elementary safety precaution, to reduce the risks for the other members, and to convince people that strict secrecy was being observed. The fourth point authorized the Knot to name local commanders for the eventual rising; the King promised to assume personal command, with his brother York as Lieutenant General. The fifth paragraph empowered the Knot to raise money to pay the expenses of the conspiracy. Certain guiding principles for planning the general rising were outlined in the sixth paragraph; a "rationall designe" to seize London was suggested, but this was to be only part of as widespread a rising as possible. Finally, the Knot was authorized to negotiate with Roman Catholics, Presbyterians, and all former enemies except actual regicides. Charles promised to perform "whatsoever you shall undertake for me to the [Roman Catholics] or to [the Presbyterians] well knowinge that you can tell what I am able to pay ether of them." [23]

The extent to which the Sealed Knot was able to translate these wide powers of leadership into preparations for action in these early days is not easy to determine. Even without the setbacks caused by the reckless behavior of others, successful planning was bound to be slow and dangerous. The Knot could meet only intermittently, and its members were often dispersed in the country. When they did meet, it was apparently usually in London, where several gatherings were held early in 1654. They were not always well attended. Villiers twice reported that he had recently been away from London, and on March 6 only he and Loughborough were in town; the others were not expected until Easter week. The result was that

23. *CCISP*, 2, 344, 356, 363 (MS 48, fols. 157, 215, 244; cipher in Appendix, D).

decisions often had to be deferred: "Symson" for instance was unable to report his negotiations to the King until "the result of the next meeting when Sr. R. Willis comes to Towne." [24]

Little is known about the activities of the Knot's members during their frequent absences in the country. It would be reasonable to suppose that they used them to mend the party's fences, to enlist their "friends and old soldiers," but no records have survived. Fortunately the Sealed Knot was able to use agents of lower rank, ordered by the King to put themselves at its disposal. One such was the anonymous "Symson," but not much is known of his proceedings. The efforts of Nicholas Armorer, a similar case, are better documented. Armorer had left The Hague in October 1653, armed with a cipher for correspondence with Secretary Nicholas and with royal approval for his offer to promote the King's business in the North and the west Midlands, where his family and military connections respectively were located. Hyde was at first somewhat skeptical of Armorer's influence, but soon recognized him as a useful agent and instructed him to cooperate fully with the Sealed Knot. After leaving London early in 1654, Armorer went first to the scene of his old military exploits on the Welsh border. He found the Shropshire Royalists reasonably confident. Two of the most prominent men there, Sir Vincent Corbet of Moreton Corbet, and Col. Richard Scriven of Frodesley, assured him that there were good hopes of successful attempts on Shrewsbury and Ludlow; Armorer left a local agent to keep the business alive while he continued his journey. In Yorkshire he was befriended by that devoted Royalist Sir Henry Slingsby of Redhouse, who lent him £100. The Yorkshire Cavaliers talked enthusiastically of a design against Hull, which had been one of the subjects of Charles Davison's mission to Paris. Another of Armorer's friends in the North was Col. Edward Grey, half-brother to the parliamentarian Lord Grey of Wark. He was chiefly interested in a plot to seize Tynemouth; he also worked with Armorer in London and was sufficiently important for Secretary Nicholas to write to him several times during the year. Although Armorer was not directly employed by the Sealed Knot, his activities in this period were ultimately under its author-

24. *TSP*, 2, 19, 64, 143. *CCISP*, 2, 361 (MS 48, fol. 240).

ity. Armorer, however, was entirely pragmatic and soon showed that he was willing to place his talents at the disposal of other leaders if circumstances made it necessary.[25]

Although the information supplied by Thurloe's spies cannot always be taken at face value, at least it suggests that in the first half of 1654 a fair number of Royalists were plotting under the auspices of the Sealed Knot. In an elaborate, confused account of the Royalist party's projects which Bampfield presented to Thurloe later in the year, several clues are to be found. Bampfield recalled that there had been a significant intensification of conspiracy during the previous spring, and that many secret agents had crossed the channel at about that time; no doubt he had been given full details of the visits of Davison, Henry Seymour, and others by his friends in the Louvre. According to Bampfield, the chief centers of the rising were the West and North, and he correctly named Armorer as one of the principal agents involved. In an apparent echo of Grey's design on Tynemouth, Bampfield warned that Newcastle was the object of a planned attack from the sea; men were to be landed "in some of the colliers ships . . . whoe, they say, doe nowe pass Tinmouth castle withoute either examination or searche." Bampfield identified Portsmouth as another center of the conspiracy, and denounced Henry Seymour as one of those engaged in rebuilding Royalist organization in the West. It is certainly true that Seymour was not merely a financial agent. When he brought his accounts to Paris in May 1654, he also made suggestions for the choice of local commanders in the western counties: among them Sir John Arundell, Sir Hugh Pollard, and Sir John Grenville. Seymour's advice produced a number of letters from the King to stir the western leaders into action.[26]

25. *ClSP, 3,* 201, 225, 229, 234–35, 237. *CClSP, 2,* 259, 334–36, 340, 350 (endorsed as from Armorer, MS 48, fol. 184), 363 (MS 48, fol. 245, deciphered in Appendix, A). *NP, 2,* 22, 30, 66. Egerton MS 2556, fol. 17. *TSP, 2,* 244 (letter to "Mr. Grapley"; cipher in Appendix, C). For Corbet see Augusta E. Corbet, *The Family of Corbet* (London, n.d.), *2,* 321–39, and *CCC,* pp. 1370–71; for Scriven, ibid., p. 1859; and for Grey, *Records of the Committees for Compounding etc., with Delinquent Royalists in Durham and Northumberland,* ed. R. Welford, Surtees Society, 111 (1905), pp. 215–17.

26. *TSP, 2,* 510–12. *CClSP, 2,* 359–62; the letter to "H.S." noted on p. 362 is actually to "H.P"[ollard]: MS 48, fol. 242.

The last point in the King's original instructions to the Knot, to make approaches to former enemies, was an obvious preliminary to any open demonstration against the government. The increasing dissatisfaction of many Presbyterians with the extremism of the Army and the Independent minority, the breach between Cromwell and the Commonwealth republicans in 1653, and the general unpopularity of Cromwellian military rule in spite of its professed moderation—all this kept a Royalist-Presbyterian alliance within the bounds of possibility. Such an alliance was only possible, however, on Royalist terms; concessions would merely invite a repetition of the abstentions of 1651. The basis of Hyde's policy, as we have seen, was to resist compromise, and to wait until the logic of events, the necessary contradictions of a regime supported only by the Army while it paid lip service to the traditional English liberties and the Good Old Cause, drove the moderate majority of the nation back to its traditional allegiance. Remembering all this, it is interesting that in April 1654 the King gave the Sealed Knot a blank cheque to make whatever promises it saw fit to old members of the parliamentary parties. The breadth of this power to negotiate is the strongest possible indication of Hyde's confidence that the Knot shared his views on the inadvisability of concessions. The important phrase in the instructions is the one that expresses the King's conviction "that you can tell what I am able to pay ether of them." The Knot was thus in a position to derive what profit it could from opposition to the Protectorate in other, non-Royalist, groups.

Little seems to have been done in this direction in 1654, although Bampfield asserted that the Royalists hoped to win over "some considerable person of the English army." This idea had been in the air ever since the summer of 1653, when both Fairfax and Lambert were mentioned as possible candidates for the role eventually to be played by Monck.[27] In spite of Belasyse's connections with the two Yorkshire generals, no definite approach was made by the Knot. As for Monck himself, his potential value to the cause he had deserted only in 1648 was already well realized by the Royalist leaders, but the idea of winning him over did not go be-

27. HMC, *Ormonde*, new ser. *I*, 293–94. Cl. MS 45, fol. 383.

yond mere speculation. In February 1654 Willys, his old comrade of the Flanders wars, was asked if he thought Monck would be responsive, but nothing came of it.[28] Although Belasyse did nothing with Fairfax and Lambert, he was concerned in approaches to other leading parliamentarians in the North. One of these was the republican Col. Robert Overton, commander of the Hull garrison, whose Leveller sympathies were well known. Belasyse and the northern Royalists had great hopes of Hull; in April 1654 a letter from the King to Overton, promising a full pardon in return for his support, was sent for Belasyse to deliver. At this point, however, silence descends upon the approach.[29]

It is no more certain that the Knot made any serious approach to the civilian Presbyterians, as it was empowered to do. The best known of the Presbyterians who had already come over to the Royalist side was the former Vice-Admiral, Lord Willoughby of Parham, now returned from Barbados. As early as 1648 Willoughby had abandoned the insistence on limitations on the monarchy's powers that distinguished his party from the Cavaliers; in 1654 he was still one of the few not to demand definite concessions. In spite of this compliance, there is no evidence that the Sealed Knot ever followed up the letter dispatched by the King to Willoughby in April 1654, asking for his and his friends' support.[30] Neither is there any sign that the Knot negotiated seriously with the Roman Catholics, in spite of the presence of the recusant Belasyse in its ranks. Perhaps the Knot thought it unnecessary, that the Catholics would inevitably prefer the Royalist side as the lesser evil. If so, this was to ignore the frequent and well-founded rumors of talks between prominent Catholics and agents of the government. The evidence of the Sealed Knot's activities in 1654 is only fragmentary, but what exists gives the impression that its efforts to make conversions among former enemies, or among doubtful allies like the Catholics, were at the best half-hearted.

There is, in any seditious organization, a wide gap between hopes and achievements. To bring into being a central committee is one

28. Cl. MS 47, fol. 330 (cipher in Appendix, D).
29. *CCISP*, 2, 344–45 (cipher in Appendix, D).
30. Clarendon, *History*, Bk. XI, § 35. *CCISP*, 2, 336, 345.

thing; to ensure that its authority is accepted by the restless schemers in the rank and file, is quite another. The first step in constructing a national network of conspiracy had been taken; and in future there would be less excuse for isolated and ill-prepared ventures of the kind that had landed Robert Phelips in jail in August 1653. Nevertheless, important as this was, it was only a first step. Little real progress toward planning the desired general rising was made in the first six months of the Knot's existence. It is possible to argue that Hyde's policy of avoiding concessions to the Presbyterians and relying on the Royalists alone to initiate a rebellion made it necessary to delay action until the stability provided by the Protectorate was shown to be illusory. Yet Hyde knew that many English Royalists were impatient, and could not permanently be restrained. His problem was to promote conditions in which the moderates would support, or at least not actively oppose, a rebellion. Meanwhile, through the Sealed Knot, Hyde could try to control the hotheads and satisfy their demands for action, by providing evidence of responsible preparations. The danger was that the planning might arouse expectations which would push the Knot into violent action before it was ready, or provoke demands for its supersession if it refused to act.

To sum up, the Knot is important for three reasons: it was the only accredited body working for Charles II in England, with at least the promise of exclusive direction of his affairs; its members represented an important body of moderate Royalist opinion; and its existence establishes the connection between this group (the Old Royalists of birth and property) and Hyde's party at Court. But in spite of the high hopes attending its foundation, by June 1654 it had scarcely begun to do the job for which it had been created. Already it showed signs of the overcautious patience which was to be its chief characteristic in later years, and was to exasperate many of its nominal subordinates. It is not surprising, therefore, that other organized groups soon emerged within the Royalist party, aiming at stirring the Knot to greater energy, or even at supplanting it altogether. The summer of 1654 was the crisis of Royalist organization in England. If the Knot could survive the disturbing consequences of the rival designs that were bound to appear—if it could sustain its authority and achieve solid results in the face of the challenges to its leadership that were inherent in the party's divided condition—then it might hope to translate its official powers of command into the reality of action. It was unable to do so for a number of reasons. The principal one was the Gerard plot.

6. Impossible Undertakings

THE SEALED KNOT, it will be recalled, had received Charles II's explicit authority to supervise, and if necessary discourage, the independent designs of "particular persons." However important the preparations for an insurrection, the Knot's most pressing and most difficult function was the negative one of keeping its more reckless colleagues out of trouble. Many Royalists, gradually recovering their confidence as the memory of previous defeats faded, were restive and willing to grasp at straws like the futile minor conspiracies which disturbed the year 1654. The necessary conditions of secrecy; the hazards of communication; and the absence of coherent local organizations: all made it difficult for the Knot's authority to become widely known among the rank and file of the party. The Knot was thus unable to keep its finger on all the "impossible undertakings" promoted by the lunatic fringe, especially when these were deliberately fomented by Hyde's rivals abroad. The most dangerous instance of a combination of interference from Paris with ill-timed and irresponsible behavior by the hotheads in England was provided by the Gerard plot. This unfortunate and idiotic project led to the execution of two of its adherents, and the transportation or imprisonment of many others. It was, furthermore, the principal cause of the Sealed Knot's withdrawal from active conspiracy in the summer of 1654.

The Gerard plot was a long time maturing. It narrowly escaped

97

being stillborn in February, when a number of its insignificant recruits were arrested; but unhappily for the Knot, Thurloe (perhaps intentionally) did not make a clean sweep of the suspects, and the project was allowed to smolder for another three months. The February arrests followed certain seditious meetings which began several weeks before the establishment of the Knot, and came to light at the Ship Tavern in Old Bailey in February 1654. It has often been assumed that this trivial and elementary affair was managed by the Sealed Knot, with the implication that the Knot was at first committed to such half-baked and irresponsible schemes.[1] Actually the Knot was not even remotely connected with the Ship Tavern conspiracy, which was an entirely independent design, planned and supported by the Gerard faction. The only shred of evidence to connect the Knot with the Ship Tavern fiasco is the fact that the latter was said to have been managed by a "Grand Council," a body which had only the most superficial resemblance to the Sealed Knot. According to the informers who betrayed the plot, the "Grand Council" kept carefully in the background, but some of its members were known. Among them were Lords Byron and Loughborough, Sir Thomas Armstrong, Colonel Francis Lovelace, and Sir Thomas Sandys—except the last-named, all prominent Cavaliers with long records of opposition to the Parliament. Loughborough is the only one who was actually a member of the Knot, and he, like the others, was connected with the Ship Tavern group only by the vaguest rumors. Thurloe appears to have had little confidence in his informants; although reported to have fled after the plot's discovery, Loughborough was soon able to clear himself by an appearance before the Council.[2]

The real ringleaders of the Ship Tavern plot were persons of much less eminence than the members of the mythical "Grand Council." Its principal contrivers were Roger Whitley, who had been a busy conspirator in the days before Worcester, and another

1. For example, Gardiner, *C&P*, *3*, 116–17; Scott, *Travels of the King*, p. 55; Abbott, *3*, 195–96.

2. *TSP*, *2*, 95–96, 114–16. *Cromwelliana*, pp. 134–35. For Armstrong and Byron see below, pp. 112–14; for Lovelace, *DNB*. Sandys was presumably the son of Sir Edwin of Northborne, Kent; see Keeler, p. 333, and Foster, *Al. Oxon.*, p. 1310.

Royalist from North Wales, Capt. Richard Dutton. Whitley was a brother-in-law of Lord Gerard, and a cousin named John Gerard also took part in the meetings. It is unnecessary to look further than the Gerard clique for the origin of the Ship Tavern conspiracy, and this alone makes it unlikely that the Knot would have had anything to do with it. Rumors that the Gerard interest had a design on foot had already reached Hyde. Nicholas wrote warningly in December 1653: "I hear Ld. Keeper [Herbert] and Lord Gerard are tempering some Business in England, wherein they make use of . . . a Brother in law of Ld. Gerard's . . . [who] is, I hear, now in France about it." After the affair's ignominious discovery and collapse it was strongly criticized by Nicholas Armorer, who complained that it had hampered his own mission. The conspiracy was in fact inspired by the jealous rivalry to Hyde of Gerard, Herbert, and their friends, with Prince Rupert hovering in the background—a deliberate effort to wrest control of the movement in England out of Hyde's hands. "I wonder not now at the ridiculousness of the late-discovered plot," wrote one of Ashburnham's correspondents, ". . . since you tell me by whose conception and direction it was." So far from being the work of the Sealed Knot, the Ship Tavern plot serves only to demonstrate the existence of rival groups in England, keenly affected by the antagonism among the exiles.[3]

The design itself can be quickly summarized. It began when meetings of obscure firebrands were held in a number of London hostelries during November 1653. There was more tippling and billiard-playing than intelligent preparation, and although Dutton was sent to raise support in the provinces, and Whitley to obtain the King's approval, few of the plotters would even contribute to their expenses. The objective was to foment an apprentice riot and seize London as a preliminary to a general rising. In spite of Dutton's journeyings, no progress was made toward enlisting men out-

3. *ClSP, 3,* 207. *CClSP, 2,* 335 (MS 48, fol. 119), 361. *TSP, 2,* 162 (unsigned intercepted letter, also Villiers to Hyde; cipher in Appendix, D), 183. Add. MS 4180, fol. 110. A minute by Hyde on the draft of the King's letter to Loughborough, February 11, 1654 (*CClSP, 2,* 315), requesting haste because "somewhat of moment is in design," has no bearing on the Ship Tavern conspiracy. The letter makes it clear that Sealed Knot business is under discussion.

side the capital, and there were no signs of disaffection except, for some unexplained reason, at Gainsborough in Lincolnshire. Apart from Whitley and Dutton, the only two conspirators who were anything but nonentities were Thomas Bunce, son of the Presbyterian Alderman, and Dr. Thomas Ross, who took an active part in conspiracy later in the 1650's. Suspicions that the plot was nothing but a "Fanfara," fomented by "coy ducks" were well founded. Roger Cotes, who made the first disclosures on February 16, had been involved in the intrigue since the previous November 1. On the 15th Cotes agreed to pay £10 toward Whitley's forthcoming journey to France; the next day he received £12 from Thurloe. Further installments were forthcoming as the plot proceeded, and a bonus of £50 afterward. Thurloe handled the affair with his usual finesse, but it was too trivial to allow his genius full scope. None of the principal suspects was brought to trial, and all, including the troublesome Dutton, were released before the end of the year.[4]

The second Gerard plot was much more serious. It burst into the newsbooks late in May 1654, and for the next month was the chief source of public excitement. Soon after the imprisonment of Dutton and his cohorts there had arrived in Paris Thomas Henshaw, a deserter from Condé's forces in Guienne and formerly a Commonwealth spy in the Low Countries.[5] With Henshaw were his half-brother John Wiseman, also a deserter from Condé, and Col. John Fitzjames, another adventurer who had been in the Commonwealth's service. They established contact with Rupert and Gerard, and recounted a scheme for the assassination of the Protector. Whitley and John Gerard, who had left England after the Ship Tavern affair, were also in the circle, and the result was a revival of the Swordsmens' project. After some preliminary soundings,

4. *A Treasonable Plot Discovered;* and *A Full and Perfect Relation of the Great Plot* (both February 1654): the former is the more accurate. *TSP*, 2, 95–96, 105, 114–16; Rawl. MSS A 11, p. 311; A 328, p. 155. HMC, *5th Report*, Appendix, p. 192. SPDI, 95, fols. 192–93, 286, 289, 291. *CSPD, 1653–54*, pp. 407, 418, 449; *1654*, pp. 440, 449. For Ross see *DNB*. Gardiner's suggested identification of Roger Cotes as the member of the Barebones Parliament (*C&P, 3*, 116 n.) is not a very likely one: some contemporary comment would surely have been forthcoming if this had been the case.

5. Not the Thomas Henshaw, member of the Royal Society, as stated in *DNB;* see *BIHR, 13*, 114.

Henshaw and John Gerard proceeded to London (Fitzjames was drowned on the way), where they circulated a proclamation offering £500 reward for the killing of "a certaine Mechanick fellow by name Oliver Cromwell." Plans were laid to surprise the guards in the various London garrisons. Henshaw, who was optimistically said to have enlisted 700 men, was responsible for the horseguard at the Mews; John Gerard was to look after Whitehall; a certain Colonel Deane commanded a party which was to fall on the foot at St. James'; and a diversionary attack was planned against Ingoldsby's regiment in Southwark. A Kentish officer, Col. Charles Finch, had charge of a projected rising of young bloods in the City, and two kinsmen of the Gerards, Francis and Somerset Fox, were busy stirring up the apprentices. A blind clergyman, Dr. Edward Hudson, engaged two of the Whitehall guards. But the Gerard conspirators were not an impressive collection. Peter Vowell, an Islington schoolmaster, was a "sober, honest, discreet man," but even this modest tribute could be applied to few of his fellows. Apprentices, debtors from the Fleet, a butcher, an apothecary, an unknown surgeon—nearly all of them emerged briefly from anonymous obscurity and were soon relegated to it again.

The central feature of the plot was the assassination of Cromwell. He was to be ambushed on Saturday, May 13, as he traveled from Whitehall to Hampton Court. A last-minute change of plan, in which the Protector went by boat to Chelsea instead of the whole way by coach, upset the conspirators' dispositions. One of them was standing on Millbank as Cromwell went by, "slenderly guarded," but the chance was missed. A postponement to the following weekend proved disastrous. The Gerards planned to surprise Cromwell in chapel at Whitehall on the 21st, but in the intervening week the whole story was revealed. John Gerard and five others were arrested on the fateful Sunday, and most of their associates were in custody within a few more days. No accurate estimate of the total number of arrests is possible; it is unlikely to have been as high as the 500 mentioned by the Venetian ambassador in a report to his government. Henshaw escaped to the Continent, and was soon loudly asserting that the whole plot was a malicious invention of Cromwell's "mercenary hired witnesses." Once again the government showed moderation, considering the violence of the design. Examples were made of John Gerard and Vowell, who were executed on July 10 after trial by the inevitable High Court of Justice; the only others to suffer anything more serious than confinement were the Fox brothers and a certain Thomas Saunders, who after a year's delay were transported to Barbados.

The parallels between the two Gerard plots are striking but hardly surprising, considering their common origin. In the Gerard plot, as in the February affair, *agents provocateurs* were probably at work. Henshaw was widely suspected, and in retaliation accused one Joseph Alexander of being the guilty party. One of those who blamed Henshaw was John Minors, of Lambeth; a "John Mynors" received £15 in intelligence money from Thurloe in July and August, although this may have been merely a reward for the assistance he gave the authorities when an escaped prisoner was recaptured. Another possible source of Thurloe's prior knowledge of the plot is the clergyman Francis Corker, at this time a schoolmaster and in the next few years a most voluble informer; John Hippon, one of the disaffected soldiers, was his brother-in-law. Among these complaints and accusations the identity of the betrayer of the Gerard plot probably lies concealed. The freedom with which many suspects talked under interrogation shows that Thurloe had little difficulty in unraveling it once the first arrests were made. The Gerard plotters would undoubtedly have done better to have taken the advice of the potential recruit who told one of them to "hold his tongue, and not to meddle with state-matters." [6]

More important than the Gerard plot itself were the conse-

6. The official report on the plot, *A True Account of the Late Bloody and Inhumane Conspiracy against His Highness the Lord Protector* (October 1654), is reprinted in *Harleian Miscellany*, ed. W. Oldys and T. Park (London, 1808–13), *10*, 210–51, and an extract in *OPH*, *20*, 294–96. Many of the depositions in this document can be found, with some others, in *TSP*, *2*, 322–84. Other reports of the plot are in *A True Relation of the Great Plot* (May 1654); *Mercurius Politicus*, Nos. 206–8; and *The Weekly Intelligencer*, Nos. 243–44 (some of the preceding printed in *Cromwelliana*, pp. 142–47). See also Vaughan, *1*, 4, 8, 10; *TSP*, *2*, 503; *3*, 453; *CClSP*, *2*, 387–88; SPDI, 95, fols. 192, 208, 212, 315; Steele, *Proclamations*, *1*, 366–67. The most detailed modern accounts are by Gardiner, *C&P*, *3*, 139–49, and Scott, *King in Exile*, pp. 422–27; there are also frequent references in Abbott, *3*, 293–352.

quences it brought for the Royalist party at large. The discovery of the clique of disreputable scoundrels and adventurers associated in Gerard's harebrained scheme was immediately followed by the imprisonment of Royalists far more useful to the cause, the majority of whom had not the slightest knowledge of the plot. The brothers John and William Ashburnham, two of the most influential men in Sussex, were both imprisoned in the fortnight after the uncovering of the plot. Henry Seymour was another to feel the strong arm of the law, although in his case, if the exiles' gossip is to be believed, the fault was his own foolhardiness.[7] These were all valuable men, but even more serious than their arrests was the impact of the assassination scare upon the fortunes of the Sealed Knot. Although one of the suspects muttered something about a second-hand report that Sir Richard Willys had threatened to kill Cromwell with his own hand, there is no authentic evidence of the remotest association between any of the Knot's members and their incompetent rivals. Innocence, however, did not protect them. Both Willys and Edward Villiers were swept up in the wave of arrests early in June.[8] This not only disrupted the meetings of the Sealed Knot, but also had two more profound and long-lasting effects.

In the first place, it revived the old hostility between Willys and Belasyse. Clarendon's memory of events in the 1650's sometimes failed him, but there is no reason to think that he invented the story, to which he gives considerable prominence, of a personal feud which crippled the Knot: "Two of these principal persons fell out, and had a fatal quarrel . . . the animosities grew suddenly irreconcilable, and if not divided the affections of the whole knot, at least interrupted or suspended their constant intercourse and confidence in each other." Clarendon names no names, nor does he explain the occasion of the quarrel; but there are enough clues from other sources to suggest that Willys and Belasyse were the participants, and the Gerard plot the precipitating cause. One of Thurloe's spies later reported that when Willys was arrested in June 1654, he suspected Belasyse of having betrayed him to Lam-

7. *TSP*, 2, 321. *CSPD*, *1654*, pp. 273–74. *ClSP*, 3, 246. *NP*, 2, 100–1, 124–25.
8. *CSPD*, *1654*, p. 436. *Cromwelliana*, p. 143.

bert, and again challenged him to a duel. Villiers, Willys' closest friend, was also involved in the dispute. In October the King asked Lord Maynard to "take the case of honest [Villiers] to hearte, and use all the interest I have with your frend, to perswade him to a perfecte reconciliacon with him." Maynard's friend may have been his brother-in-law Compton, but it is also possible that it was Belasyse. Further proof that there was an outbreak of faction in the Knot exists in a memorandum it sent to the King during the following winter, assuring him "that the Divisions amongst themselves was look'd into." [9]

The second of the Sealed Knot's responses to the Gerard plot was more clear-cut. Charles II and Hyde had given the Knot full powers; the plot showed that they were incapable of restraining the "absurd and desperate attempts" that it was the Knot's immediate purpose to discourage; and they had not, as promised, warned the Knot that there were other designs on foot. Hyde at once tried to reassure the Knot of the King's good faith. Behind the commercial jargon of Charles' letter to Villiers on July 6 is a clear indication of what was at stake: "Mr. Westbury [Villiers]. I finde that the late raysinge the prizes upon our wares, for which ther was not the least derection from me, hath so disturbed the markett, that our commodityes may ly to longe on our handes." The letter goes on to urge Villiers to continue his efforts, and to report the attitude of his colleagues. The need for reassurance was all the more pressing as other groups of Royalists emerged with plans for a general rising on lines much closer to those of the Knot than the wild ideas of Gerard and his friends; behind these new projects were men of substance and prestige, men who ought logically to have accepted the Knot's leadership. Any lapse in the Knot's activities, however temporary, would certainly provoke the kind of division which it was Hyde's constant preoccupation to avoid.[10]

The King's letter was carried to England by John Stephens, formerly one of Ormond's officers, and an unnamed companion, who were sent to work for unity among the English Royalists, and

9. Clarendon, *Con.*, § 25. *CSPD, 1655*, p. 212. *CCISP, 2*, 404; *3*, 4 (MS 49, fols. 80, 267; ciphers in Appendix, D, E).
10. *CCISP, 2*, 384 (MS 48, fol. 328; cipher in Appendix, D).

to press them to speedy action. Besides the letter to "Mr. Westbury," they must also have been given verbal instructions to discover the Sealed Knot's intentions. On August 11 Stephens made his report, in a letter that is important enough to deserve extensive quotation. In spite of an optimistic conclusion based on discussions with Royalists outside the Knot, the dismal meaning behind the confused punctuation is plain enough:

> Wee delivered Mr. Wesburies letter; and find him, and his Comrades for the present, have resolved, noe farther to agitate yor. busines; they'r become soe shy, and wary; that they refuse to receve prepotitions from any others. Wee understand they have latly writ to you: tis possible, what was writ, was to the best of there Knowlege; however wee humbly desire you would not bee anywhite dishartned, to which onely purpose wee give you the troble of this. . . . Wee are confident you will juge the Mater, both in condition and forwardnes beyond what you could have expected, this not beinge onely our sence, but the opinion of many of yor eminet, and best freinds.[11]

In this letter is to be found the real significance of the Gerard plot. So far from the split between the Sealed Knot and its more venturesome associates being the product of the events of early 1655, as most historians have supposed,[12] it was in fact the outcome of the Gerard plot in the previous summer. The Knot, angry at the Gerards' irresponsibility and disrupted by the quarrel within its own ranks, retreated into its shell, and the leadership passed by default into other hands. The successors were more considerable, more solid than the Gerard gang; but they were self-appointed, and they lacked the clear authorization possessed by the Sealed Knot. The preparations of this new group were, however, being set

11. Carte MS 131, fol. 173; calendared in *CClSP, 3,* 411. See also ibid., *2,* 384–85 (cipher in Appendix, D).

12. For example, Gardiner, *C&P, 3,* 276, and Firth, "Cromwell and the Insurrection of 1655," *EHR, 3,* (1888), 333. In his *The Last Years of the Protectorate* (London, 1909), *1,* 27, Firth contradicts himself and says with equal inaccuracy that it was the Knot that "managed the abortive insurrection of 1655."

forward enthusiastically even before news of the Knot's defection reached the King. When Robert Walters, a Yorkshireman and one of the new organization's principal agents, was asked a year later "if the aprehendinge of Gerrard and others wear nott a discouragement to them," he at once replied, "noe, they concern'd them nott." [13] We must now examine more closely the origins, composition, and aims of this rival group of leaders; for convenience we shall label the new organization the "Action party."

The Action party did not, of course, appear miraculously out of nothingness at the precise moment of the Knot's withdrawal. Its origins may possibly go back to Charles Davison's mission to Paris in April 1654. Davison was sent, it will be recalled, by a group of northern Royalists hostile to Hyde. In the following month a certain Major John Scott of Nottingham arrived in Paris, bearing for the King's consideration a similar paper but one more friendly to Hyde and the Sealed Knot. The document begins tactfully enough by suggesting that the King again thank Belasyse and Villiers for their services. The second paragraph reveals its independent origin: "And because his Maties. affaires depend as much upon Speed as any other part of the designe, that the Sealed Cabinett may bee pressed as suddenly as possible to come to a resolution how and when it must bee executed." The inference is clear that the Knot was already regarded in some circles as excessively cautious. The paper goes on to outline a series of topics for the Knot's consideration, and appears to have been used as a basis for some of the royal instructions of May 12. The mission of the Nottingham agent thus shows that in May 1654 the midland and northern Royalists by whom he was employed were still ready to trust the Sealed Knot, even if they wished to stimulate it into more positive action.[14]

By July the situation had changed completely. Although nothing was yet known at Court of the Knot's abdication, rumors of it must for some time have been rife in England. On July 6 Charles II was at Mons, where he was presented with an important set of proposals from certain English Royalists, brought by Col. John Stephens. The paper embodying them is headed "A particular account of or.

13. *TSP*, 3, 723. For Walters see *CCC*, p. 2922.
14. *CCISP*, 2, 355 (MS 48, fol. 212), 356, 363.

busines and desires," and its contents clearly show that the foundations of a new organization had already been laid. The opening sentence is one that could hardly have been used by the Sealed Knot: "First tis beleved by the Kings freinds, both in England and Ireland, his Matie. hath sum designes to Act, in his dominions." It goes on to emphasize the need for swift action, and to suggest that "if his Maty. have other designes now in England that sum meanes maybe used that wee may ajust ourselves with them." The document concludes with a request for a commission formally expressing the King's confidence. This communication, and Stephens' verbal explanations, were sufficiently disturbing for the Court, Clarendon records, "to make a day's stay at Mons, to despatch those gentlemen, who were very well known, and worthy to be trusted." The Action party was not only in existence, it was now recognized and conducting negotiations with the King.[15]

Stephens' "Particular Account" outlines the plans of the Action party in some detail, but it is more intelligible if examined in conjunction with a second memorandum, delivered to the King at Aachen by Nicholas Armorer in late August.[16] The most obvious difference of policy between the Sealed Knot and the Action party lies in the latter's greater emphasis on securing the help of Presbyterians and disgruntled Army officers; in the phrase "Devisyons in the Rebells Councell aboute successyon" all the Royalists' vague

15. Clarendon, *History,* Bk. XIV, §§ 99–100. *CClSP,* 2, 383 (MS 48, fols. 326–27): previous writers all seem to have ascribed this document to the Sealed Knot. Firth (*EHR, 3,* 325) quotes it in conjunction with the King's instructions of the previous May. Gardiner, *C&P, 3,* 271, and Eva Scott, *The Travels of the King* (London, 1907), p. 56, also fail to indicate the significance of its origin.

16. *CClSP, 2,* 440 (MS 48, fol. 305). Firth suggests June (*EHR, 3,* 325 n.), but August is more likely. It appears to be Hyde's notes of a verbal report, and bears his endorsement, "Account by N. Armo." Later in the year Hyde stated "I never spake word with Mr. Armorer in my life till I saw him at Aken" (Cl. MS 49, fol. 153); the Court was at Aachen from mid-August until the end of September. On August 29 Armorer was reported to have arrived at Aachen within the previous week: *TSP, 2,* 568. Armorer's memorandum is probably the one mentioned by Stephens on August 11: "By the next post, our friend shalbe with you; hee will make you a trew relatione, and sum fresh proposalls." (Carte MS 131, fol. 173). On September 12 the King thanks Stephens for the "accounte of the debts" sent by "Mr. Alton" [Armorer]: *CClSP, 2,* 392 (MS 49, fol. 35).

hopes of detaching a Lambert, a Monck, or an Overton are implied. The Action party proposed a general pardon to all who returned to their allegiance, and advised much more concrete advances to the Presbyterians than any the Knot had made. Letters were asked for Fairfax's brother-in-law Henry Arthington, and for the Cheshire leader, Sir George Booth. Other prominent Presbyterians were named as possible supporters: Lord Willoughby, the Cornish Lord Robartes, and that stout citizen of London Major General Richard Browne. As for military plans, the two papers list strategic centers in all parts of the country, and the names of commanders responsible for their capture. In the North, Hull, York, Tynemouth, and Carlisle; in the Midlands, Shrewsbury, Ludlow, Warwick, and Nottingham; Denbigh castle in North Wales; the naval magazine at Sandwich in Kent; and in the West, Pendennis and Plymouth: such were the garrisons to which the Action party's hopes were directed. Strong local associations would begin the rising. Arms were said to have been provided for 1,500 men in the Northwest, where 300 horse were also in readiness; Surrey, Sussex, and Kent each promised 500 horse; Shropshire made similar offers for forces to surprise Ludlow. A supporting invasion from abroad by 2,000 foot was suggested, but not made an absolute condition, and a simultaneous disturbance was planned in Ireland. Conceding that Stephens and Armorer brought the most optimistic presentation of the Action party's hopes, it is clear that their memoranda embodied the results of more ambitious preparation than anything yet undertaken by the Sealed Knot. The stress on the Presbyterians and Army malcontents, and the requests for foreign and Irish assistance, showed some political realism.

The proposals identify some of the local leaders of the Action party, in the form of notations added to the castles and garrisons earmarked for capture: Sir Philip Musgrave for Carlisle, Edward Grey for Tynemouth, Richard Scriven for Shrewsbury, for example. The two papers do not, however, tell us the names of the directors of the new association at the center. Armorer's memorandum begins, to be sure, with the names of eighteen persons to whom no particular regional responsibilities are assigned; but as they include members of the Sealed Knot like Villiers and Loughborough, and agents of secondary rank like Stephens and Scott, they are not likely to have been the members of a central committee. Eighteen would in any case have been too large a number to operate with secrecy and efficiency. It is not even certain that there was a formally organized committee at all. Stephens was reported to have told one of Thurloe's informants that there was "a Counsell, sittinge in London, but he had tooke an oath never to reveale them," and the spy Manning gave similar warnings; but this is not conclusive. If a central committee did exist, it was not officially accredited; Ormond makes this plain in a reference to the Sealed Knot, "in whom only there is any known authority from the King." [17] However, the new association must have been headed by a recognizable group of self-appointed leaders, with enough unity to send messengers on behalf of the whole party to the exiled Court, to fix and then repeatedly postpone the day for a general rising, and to exercise a rudimentary control over planning and coordinating the whole conspiracy.

To speak with certainty of the identity of the Action party's leaders, we have to look ahead to the eve of the rising. In February 1655 the Earl of Rochester and Daniel O'Neill were sent to England to assume temporary command. They were instructed, before deciding to sanction the proposed action, to confer with five prominent members of the Action party in London, and it is a reasonable supposition that these five were at least part of the group's high command. They were Sir Thomas Peyton, Sir Humphrey Bennett, Edward Grey, Richard Thornhill, and John Weston; [18] all had been directly named in the plans reported by Armorer during the previous August. A sixth, Sir Thomas Armstrong, although not mentioned in the instructions, spoke with O'Neill in circumstances which suggest that he was at least as important as the other five. An examination of the careers of these leaders of the Action party provides a useful basis of comparison between the new association and the Sealed Knot. Three of them have already figured in this

17. *ClSP, 3,* 265. *TSP, 3,* 355, 428. Rawl. MS A 42, p. 192; from internal evidence this seems to be derived from Robert Werden, not, as the Catalogue suggests, from John Stephens.
18. *CClSP, 3,* 19.

narrative. Sir Humphrey Bennett and Richard Thornhill had headed the Royalist organizations in their respective counties of Hampshire and Kent in 1650; Grey, who had returned to England in June 1652 after a spell of wandering in Europe, was an active associate of Armorer in the spring of 1654. They were men of roughly the same caliber and social position: impoverished country gentry with respectable civil war records. Little is known of Grey's personal qualities, but Bennett was incorrigibly unrealistic, and Dorothy Osborne contemptuously dismisses Thornhill as a drunkard, "the veryest beast that ever was." [19]

Sir Thomas Peyton, at this time in his early forties, lived at Knowlton in Kent. He sat for Sandwich in the two Parliaments of 1640, where he showed his Royalist sympathies from the first; but opportunities for action in Kent were limited, and it was not until 1644 that he was expelled from the House and held under restraint in London. His estates were sequestered, adding to the financial embarrassments which, even before the war, echoed as a perpetual refrain in his correspondence. Occupied as he was in Parliament and in prison, Peyton thus took little part in the first civil war. More active in 1648, he was imprisoned after the Kent rising, and again in 1651. Amid all these distractions, Peyton's house still seems to have been a cheerful place. In July 1654 his sister-in-law, Dorothy Osborne, found Knowlton "soe strangly Crowded with Company that I am weary as a dog," and its inhabitants appeared oblivious to either domestic or political worries: "Wee goe abroad all day and Play all night, and say our Prayers when wee have time." This compulsive gaiety, Dorothy suspected, was not at all congenial to Sir Thomas: "as contreary to his humor as darkenesse is to light." Peyton lacked imagination and the dynamic spark necessary to win adherents to an unsuccessful cause, but he was a hard worker and exhibited throughout his career as a conspirator a refreshing and single-minded devotion. Like so many of his party, his view of politics was a personal one. Dorothy Osborne shows her usual insight. Her brother-in-law, she says, is "as easily gained wth compliance

19. *The Letters of Dorothy Osborne to William Temple,* ed. G. C. Moore Smith (Oxford, 1928), p. 177.

and good usage as any body I know, but by noe other way; when hee is roughly dealt with hee is like mee ten times the worse fort." [20]

John Weston was yet another country gentleman of middle rank. He came of a family of Surrey recusants, the son of Sir Richard Weston of Sutton. Although not politically prominent, the Surrey Westons were wealthy and more than capable of keeping their heads above water. When Sir Richard died in 1652, he left unfinished an ambitious project for building a canal and locks to improve the navigability of the River Wey, in which he had invested heavily. The Westons were improving landlords of the new type, interested in irrigation, crop rotation, and the development of new strains of grass and clover; Sir Richard's *Discours of Husbandrie* was an important work in the field of progressive agriculture. John Weston fought for the King at Brentford, was taken prisoner at Colchester in 1648, and suffered another spell of confinement in the threatening days of 1651. He lost his estates in 1652, in the second Act of Sale, but when his father died that same year he inherited a share of the canal scheme. The canal was finished late in 1653 and at first was reasonably successful; later it involved the family in expensive litigation, which swallowed up most of the profits. At the time of the Action party's formation, however, John Weston seemed to have good prospects of recovering from the loss of his estates, and of being able to provide powerful financial backing for the Royalist designs. His wife also brought wealth into the family, although the sale of her Gatton estate in 1654 may be a sign that the canal was already running into trouble. Weston's presence in the Action party enabled the new group to keep in touch with the Roman Catholics. Like Belasyse in the Sealed Knot, however,

20. For brief accounts of Peyton's career see Keeler, pp. 304–5; and *The Journal of Sir Simonds D'Ewes*, ed. Willson H. Coates (New Haven, Conn., 1942), intro., pp. xxxviii–xli. Much of his personal and family correspondence is printed in *The Oxinden Letters 1607–1642*, ed. D. Gardiner (London, 1933), and *The Oxinden and Peyton Letters 1642–1670,* ed. D. Gardiner, London, 1937. There are also many unpublished letters in Add. MSS 28,003 and 44,846–48. See also *Osborne Letters*, especially pp. 89–90, 169–82. Details of his composition are in *CCC*, pp. 459, 864. For his activities in 1651 see *CSPD, 1651*, pp. 174, 203.

Weston's position probably depended more upon his wealth and local influence than on his religion.[21]

These five leaders of the Action party were all men of the same stature: country gentlemen of strong local but relatively minor national prestige. Sir Thomas Armstrong, the sixth, is a remarkable exception, for his family connections were nonexistent and his territorial holdings, of recent origin, confined to Ireland. He was a Low Countries soldier of fortune (he was a cornet of horse at Nijmwegen in 1633), and for a Royalist leader his origins were curiously obscure. Armstrong's civil war experience was limited to the fighting in Ireland. He held the post of Quartermaster General of horse in 1640, was knighted, given estates near Dublin, and sat in the Irish Parliament in 1647. Three years later, after being forced to surrender Trim to Cromwell's forces, he went to the Isle of Man, where defeat again caught up with him. In 1651 he gave up Castle Rushen, one of the island's principal strongholds, and obtained the benefit of articles of surrender, which enabled him to live in England. It is doubtful if Armstrong possessed many qualities of political leadership. Ormond regarded him as an efficient officer, but his lack of powerful connections made him a poor choice for a position of authority. He was a close friend of John Weston (their names are nearly always linked in the conspiracies of the 1650's) and this may explain his inclusion in Armorer's list of leaders.[22]

Before summarizing the general impressions of the Action party's leadership suggested by these six examples, a few words on its most prominent local leaders are not out of place. Owing to the informal nature of the Action party's authority, no clear distinction can be drawn between national and local commanders; there were several other well-known Royalists almost as important as the six named, most of whose work was done outside London. Instances could be given from all the chief centers of conspiracy; for convenience one each from the West, the Midlands, and the North will suffice.

21. *DNB* ("Weston, Sir Richard, 1591–1652"). See also *CCC*, pp. 252, 2170–72, 2291–94; Firth and Rait, *2*, 592; *CJ*, *7*, 686; VCH, *Surrey*, *1*, 422–23, 426; *2*, 247; *3*, 198, 348, 358, 386; and Frederic Harrison, *Annals of an Old Manor House* (London, 1893), pp. 97–111.

22. *BIHR*, *22*, 65–67, replaces the inaccurate *DNB* article, in which Armstrong is confused with his son.

Among the Action party's supporters in the West were two old stalwarts of the Western Association, Sir Hugh Pollard of King's Nympton, and Colonel Richard Arundell of Trerice. These were the men to whom Jonathan Trelawney, sent over with instructions for Rochester in February 1655, was directed. Prominent as were Pollard and Arundell, however, there was another western adherent whose connections and abilities far outweighed their own. Sir John Grenville, son of Sir Bevil of Kilkhampton, represented one of the stoutest and most famous of all Cornish families. The high courage of the Grenvilles burned fiercely in the youthful Sir John, inspired by memories of a dozen battles in the West and by the tragic Cornish charge at Lansdowne, when Sir Bevil fell mortally wounded in the moment of victory. The son was worthy of a great tradition. He played a valiant part in the second battle of Newbury, where he was severely wounded, and in many nameless actions in Cornwall. In 1646 he attended the Prince in the Scilly Isles, and followed Charles on his travels to Jersey and eventually to Paris. For two years, from 1649 until the summer of 1651, he held the important command of Governor of Scilly. Grenville's ardent Cornish loyalty, the prestige of his name, and his comparative freedom under the Articles of Scilly, in both person and estate, made him an automatic choice to assume the leadership of the King's party in the peninsula.[23]

In the Midlands the most prominent advocate of militancy in 1654 was Lord Byron, one of the few peers who can be even remotely associated with the Action party. As Sir Richard Byron he had played a not inconspicuous part in the civil war, had been Governor of Newark before Sir Richard Willys, and had succeeded his better-known brother John as second Lord Byron in 1652. His movements after the end of the civil war are obscure, but in 1654 he was still living at Newstead, the family seat in Nottinghamshire. Logically enough, Nottingham was proposed as his responsibility

23. The *DNB* account of Grenville is adequate. See also Roger Granville, *History of the Granville Family* (Exeter, 1895), pp. 241–350, where there are some details of his movements in 1654. For his privileges under the Articles of Scilly see *CCC*, pp. 2853–54; and *CJ, 6*, 603. For his part in the conspiracy see *TSP, 2*, 691 (cipher in Appendix, D); *3*, 182; *CClSP, 2*, 359–62, 440 (MS 48, fols. 242, 305); and Egerton MS 2556, fols. 19–20.

in Armorer's account of the Action party plans. He was afterward reported to have told Rochester that "he was very much pleased his county had so much confidence in his little carcase as to choose him for their leader." [24] That experienced Cavalier Sir Philip Musgrave can serve as our example from the North. Thurloe's spies were sufficiently impressed by Musgrave to name him as a member of the central committee, and as he was a man of reputation this is not on the face of it unlikely. There is no evidence, however, that Musgrave spent any considerable time in London during 1654, so it is as a provincial leader that he deserves attention. In John Stephens' account, Musgrave was said to have collected arms for 1,500 men, and to be ready to appear with 300 horse; according to Armorer he was assigned his old garrison at Carlisle in the projected rising. Musgrave had played a notable part in arousing his neighbors in 1648, and would have every reason to suppose that he could do the same again.[25]

It is important to make some general evaluation of the status and quality of the Action party's leaders, for only in this way can a fair comparison between the new body and the Sealed Knot be made. The country gentry and their dependents might be expected to support whichever branch of the leadership could make its authority most effective, and it is thus in the central command that the differences between them emerge. The Sealed Knot's members had two principal recommendations: rank and military reputation. The cumulative impression of nine of the Action party's most prominent men is that the new group compared unfavorably with the Knot on both counts. Grenville at Scilly, Musgrave at Carlisle, Byron at Newark, and Bennett at Newbury had all held military posts of consequence; but none had the experience of command possessed by Belasyse, Loughborough, and Willys. Both Grey and Byron were men of noble blood, though Byron's peerage was a new

24. Byron is briefly noticed in *DNB,* in the article on his brother. For his activities in the civil war see also Lucy Hutchinson, *Memoirs of the Life of Colonel Hutchinson,* ed. C. H. Firth, London, 1906. He can be followed in 1654–55 in *TSP,* 2, 96; *3,* 395, 722; *CSPD, 1655,* p. 213; *Cromwelliana,* p. 153; Rawl. MS A 42, p. 193; Cl. MS 48, fol. 305.

25. *CClSP,* 2, 383, 400 (cipher in Appendix, C), 440 (MS 48, fol. 305). *TSP, 3,* 592; *4,* 562.

creation; nowhere in their families are to be found aristocratic names like Compton, Russell, and Villiers. It is true that the names of Grenville, Musgrave, and Byron need not suffer in comparison with any in respect of *local* influence in their several parts of England. The point, however, is not that local interest was lacking in the Action party, but rather that it was not directed by men of national stature. Finally, although the Action party was not controlled by any of the opposition factions at Court, as Gerard's had been, neither was it intimately connected with Hyde and Ormond, the dominant figures in the King's Council. Both of these deficiencies, of powerful coordinated authority at home and of efficient liaison with the court, were to have serious results.

By midsummer 1654 the Action party was in existence and beginning the dangerous and complicated process of preparing for a general rising, which it hoped to launch early in the following year. The enlistment of men, appointment of officers, collection of arms, and all the other multifarious business of conspiracy, must have kept its leaders busy in the eight or nine months before the insurrection. Agents like Stephens, Armorer, and James Halsall crossed and recrossed the channel to carry orders and commissions. In England obscure adventurers of the same type flitted surreptitiously from place to place, maintaining tenuous communication between the various regions and playing a desperate game of hide-and-seek with the authorities. Ardent country gentlemen visited their friends and neighbors and sought quietly to inspire them with their own determination. But to reduce the bewildering details of Royalist conspiracy in the later months of 1654 to an orderly narrative would be impossible; the local conspiracies can be more effectively discussed when we reach the rising itself.

A more useful approach to the Action party's activities is by way of its efforts on the national level, particularly its attempt to create a broader front of resistance by negotiation with other opposition groups. By the middle of 1654 a large reservoir of disaffection existed among the politically articulate minority of the nation. A few Presbyterian moderates—like John Glynne, who entered the Protector's service at about this time—were being reconciled to Cromwell as a savior of society; but the majority could not forget the long sequence of illegalities that had continued since Pride's Purge. The meeting of Parliament in September provided an opportunity for Presbyterian opposition to raise its head: along with Heselrige, Bradshaw, and the Commonwealth republicans a number of Presbyterians found their way to Westminster, in spite of the government's powers of electoral manipulation. The refusal of both Presbyterians and Commonwealthmen to accept the "Recognition" (of Parliament's inability to alter the Instrument of Government), and their consequent exclusion from the House, widened the divisions. It was clearly the Action party's first duty to derive what profit it could from the situation, making the most of the opportunity for an alliance between Royalists and supporters of limited monarchy.

The most energetic of the Presbyterians who had already made the great decision to cooperate was Francis, Lord Willoughby of Parham. As early as 1644 Willoughby had feared the revolutionary consequences of limited rebellion: "Nobility and gentry are going down apace," he gloomily told the Earl of Denbigh. Subsequent experience cannot have done much to alter Willoughby's opinion: impeachment in 1647, a naval interlude with the Royalists in the second civil war, and then the unsuccessful defense of Barbados. Back in England, Willoughby was soon in touch with Royalist friends, at least by the end of 1653. The first definite overture to him seems to have been in April 1654, but little came of it while the direction of affairs was in the hands of the Sealed Knot. The Action party's suggestion that Willoughby be approached had more positive results. A royal letter expressed satisfaction at the news, brought "by your frend Nic.," that he was favorably inclined to the idea of action. Clearer evidence of Willoughby's intentions was forthcoming when he wrote to the King in September. Charles in reply encouraged him to play whatever part he chose in the design, and to try to interest Major General Browne and the great Fairfax. All seemed set fair, but as the autumn wore on, the temper of Willoughby and his friends began to cool. By October 24 the King was expressing some anxiety, stressing that a "conference" between Willoughby and an unnamed Royalist agent was "absolutely necessary" and that the business could not be managed, as Willoughby desired, by secret correspondence. The Presbyterians were beginning to hedge, and Willoughby remained elusive until the very eve of the rising. On December 29 Edward Grey reported that he "had not ye good fortune to see [Willoughby] all the time he was in Town though we had severall appointments"; and in February 1655 news came that the Presbyterians were disinclined to act. Armorer was hastily dispatched with a letter urging Willoughby to appear, whatever the circumstances. In London at about this time Daniel O'Neill found him "not very forward to meddle"; but thanks partly to Armorer's arguments he was eventually persuaded to support the action, and to promise that Browne and Sir William Waller would do so too.[26]

How much these assurances were worth is uncertain. O'Neill spoke of the difficulty of winning Presbyterian support without positive concessions to their point of view. They were still, he regretted, talking about a "Declaration," presumably like the one they had demanded two years before, with engagements for future government, liberty of conscience (no doubt for Presbyterians only), and the exclusion of obnoxious advisers from the royal councils. O'Neill's dislike of "such nonsensicall conceipts" merely echoes the pervasive distrust felt by nearly all the King's friends for Presbyterian support, on anything but the most uncompromisingly Royalist terms. This was in line with Hyde's refusal to dilute the party's principles; but failure to state the terms on which the Presbyterians would be acceptable was certainly one reason for their aloofness in 1655. The majority held aloof, but it is clear that Willoughby was not the only one implicated in the plotting that preceded the March rising. Browne and Waller, the two Presbyterian generals, certainly connived at the design, and there were many rumors that their attitudes had been more than noncommittal. The Wiltshire magnate Alexander Popham was later said to have admitted that he and Waller had been in touch with the Cavaliers early in 1655, and "Waller spoke with [Rochester] in Aldersgate Street, and also with Daniel Oneale severall tymes." That influential Cheshire family the Booths was more deeply in-

26. *CCISP*, 2, 280, 345, 389 (MS 49, fol. 22), 402, 413–14; *3*, 5 (MS 49, fol. 275: cipher in Appendix, C), 19–20. *NP*, 2, 32, 218–21.

volved. Charles II wrote asking for the young Sir George's support in September 1654, evidently without result. However, Sir George's uncle, Col. John Booth, was as active as he had been four years earlier. John Booth was in London shortly before the day of action to discuss plans with Rochester and O'Neill (James Halsall admitted this at his examination); O'Neill then sent him down to Cheshire, to supervise attempts on Chester and Liverpool. The small group of Presbyterians who had come over in 1648 and 1651 seem therefore to have shown as much (or as little) interest in the conspiracy of 1654–55 as most of the Royalist gentry.[27]

The attitude of the majority of the moderates, the neutrals of the Preston and Worcester campaigns, was less encouraging. Towering high above all the others who had abandoned the parliamentary cause in favor of retirement was the great Fairfax. The Lord General had remained faithful to his command in the second civil war but resigned in 1650, when his conscience refused to swallow preventive war against the Scots. His authority was still so great and the reports of his disaffection in 1654–55 so frequent that his case deserves special attention for its own sake. Rochester and O'Neill were both confident of his support; rumors of his involvement were widespread in the North and among the exiles; finally, Fairfax was believed to have enticed Rochester to England with extravagant promises, only to betray the whole design to Cromwell. The Yorkshire agent Robert Walters, who was in a good position to hear the gossip, complained that the General "promised them 100 men and other assistance, but . . . did them noe good." Historians have been at one with Fairfax's biographer in discounting all these as nothing more than "idle reports." [28]

The facts, obscure and contradictory as they are, point to Royalist contact if not with Fairfax himself at least with people fairly close to him. One of the Action party's original suggestions, it will

27. *NP*, 2, 218–22. *CClSP*, 2, 211. *TSP*, 3, 315, 345, 677; 4, 245. Rawl. MSS A 41, p. 577; A 42, pp. 191–92. The attitude of the Presbyterian leaders in 1655 is discussed by Gardiner, *C&P*, 3, 281–82. For Browne and Sir George Booth see *DNB*; for Popham, Bates Harbin, pp. 167–69.

28. C. R. Markham, *Life of the Great Lord Fairfax* (London, 1870), p. 370. See also M. A. Gibb, *The Lord General* (London, 1938), p. 236. Examples of rumors of Fairfax's disaffection can be found in *NP*, 2, 219–22; *TSP*, 3, 186, 230, 302, 312, 355, 358, 723; HMC, *Ormonde*, new ser. 1, 316; *CClSP*, 3, 28–29.

be recalled, was that the King write to the General's brother-in-law, Henry Arthington. The letter was duly sent on July 6, 1654, containing Charles' hopeful promise that in the event of their adherence, Arthington's friends would find "that I have forgotten all that hath bene done amisse." [29] Arthington refused even to receive the overture; yet negotiations with Fairfax's friends were carried on through various other intermediaries. Among the mass of Hyde's correspondence dealing with preparations for the rising is the draft of a royal letter (dated September 26, 1654) to Sir Philip Monckton of Howden, Yorkshire, an ardent Royalist who had commanded the defeated forces at Willoughby in 1648. It is a perplexing document:

I have receaved yours of the 14 of [September], and am sorry that ther should be any pawse in the redempcon of the morgage of [Hull], which I hope yett will be compassed in time; but I should be more sorry that it should in any degree depende upon Mr. Blake's consent, for though I will do whatsoever is in my power to compounde with him . . . yett I would not that the other should miscarry, upon any obstinacy of his: nor is it possible that I can imploy [the Duke of Buckingham] in that businesse for many reasons, therfore some other more fitt person must be founde to cast up that accounte, which is very easy, if Mr. Blake hath any minde to make an end of the sute by a reference, and if he or his frendes still insiste on [Buckingham], you must conclude that they intende nothinge really, and proceede accordingly; and it is no good signe, that A[rthington] would not receave the accounte that was sent to him, . . . it would much satisfy me, to heare that [Lord Belasyse] had bene fully conferred with in that and the other whole businesse: . . . I suppose [Sir Marmaduke Langdale] may come in good time, but nothinge should be differred for that.[30]

29. *CClSP*, 2, 383–84 (MS 48, fol. 328). For Arthington see A. Gooder, *Parliamentary Representation of the County of York,* Yorks. Archaeological Society Record Series (1935–38), 2, 73–74.

30. *CClSP*, 2, 399–400 (MS 49, fol. 64; cipher in Appendix, C). Musgrave is the other "Sir P.M." in the endorsement.

The central problem of the letter is the identity of "Mr. Blake." From internal evidence it is hard to resist the conclusion that the pseudonym conceals Fairfax himself. The letter is written in the cipher used by Nicolas Armorer, but unfortunately the only existing key does not include "Mr. Blake." The pseudonyms in this cipher generally begin with the same initial letter as the deciphered surname, but this rule was not followed in later additions: "Blake" might be an allusion to Fairfax's well-known nickname "Black Tom." There are, moreover, some stronger reasons for this identification. In the first place, the letter deals exclusively with affairs in Yorkshire: a plot against Hull, to which the advice of Monckton, Belasyse (who was related to Fairfax), and Langdale would be relevant. Secondly, the unsuccessful approach to Arthington obviously refers to the latter's refusal to act as an intermediary between the Royalists and Fairfax. Finally, the use of Buckingham strongly suggests an overture to Fairfax. Ever since 1653 there had been rumors of the irrepressible Duke's desire to marry the General's daughter, and contact between the two men had developed because of Fairfax's share of the forfeited Buckingham estates. Buckingham was later said to have complained that Fairfax had promised to engage, "provided that the transactions between his Matie and him might pass through the Dukes hands, which request beeing refused his lordship quitted." This report was denied by Secretary Nicholas, who admitted, however, that "some 3rd person might [have] proposed that the D. might be a fitt man to treate between the K. and that lord." [31] There is no other Yorkshire personage to whom Buckingham was likely to have been thought a suitable intermediary; thus the identification of "Blake" with Fairfax seems irresistible.

What then does the King's letter to Monckton prove? It shows that Monckton and perhaps other Yorkshire Royalists were hoping to approach Fairfax through his future son-in-law, and that the King, although eager for Black Tom's support, was unwilling to

31. *NP*, 2, 335 and n. *TSP*, *1*, 688. On Buckingham's relations with Fairfax see Markham, p. 364, and Winifred, Lady Burghclere, *George Villiers, Second Duke of Buckingham* (London, 1903), p. 78. Early reports of their association are in *TSP*, *1*, 306; *CSPD*, *1652–53*, p. 436; HMC, *Ormonde*, new ser. *1*, 293.

employ the unreliable Duke. Furthermore, the suggestion that Buckingham would be an acceptable intermediary seems to have come originally from Fairfax or his associates; the phrase "if he or his frendes still insiste" on Buckingham implies nothing less. Monckton's part in the overture is supported by his own memoirs. Writing of Fairfax, Sir Philip recalls: "His house being within ten miles of my fathers, I often proposed it to the Kings agents after I was returned from banishment, that if I had commission to him from the king, the one to desire him, the other to empower him to command the kingdom, I would doe by him as Joyce did by the king at Holmby, bring him to any rendezvous they would appoint." [32] The Holmby allusion might suggest that Monckton was thinking of kidnapping Fairfax; but the rest of the passage contradicts it, and if he did have any such idea it was not discussed at the time. The memoirs consistently exaggerate Monckton's importance in Interregnum politics; but we have the evidence of the King's letter to support them in this case. Monckton helped obtain the submission of York to Fairfax and Monck in January 1660; but in 1654 he evidently needed Buckingham's assistance before he could reach the General's ear. Buckingham's attempt to play the leading role came to nothing, but he may have been right in asserting that Black Tom would receive overtures from no one else.

Monckton and Buckingham were not the only Royalists who tried to break through the wall of evasive neutrality surrounding Fairfax. Willoughby was asked to see what he could do in October 1654. A month later the King wrote to Fairfax in terms which make it clear that no definite bargain had been struck. Sir Henry Slingsby was said to have delivered a letter from Charles to Lady Fairfax; and another Yorkshireman, Col. Robert Brandling, boasted "to have bene an instrument to Sr Thom. Fairefax." Langdale, who heard about this, denounced Brandling as "a very knave," (he had in fact at one time fought for Parliament), but admitted "there are others imployed in somethinge of that kinde that are honest." [33]

32. *Monckton Papers,* p. 43.
33. *NP, 3,* 68. *CClSP, 2,* 402 ("Mr. Fowle" is Fairfax: cf. *NP, 2,* 218), 426; *3,* 59. For Brandling see *Yorks. Archaeological Journal, 23* (1915), 353; and *CSPD, 1657–58,* p. 80.

Although there is no evidence that Fairfax ever took the risk of receiving Royalist advances at first hand, several efforts were obviously made to enlist him during the Action party's period of operation. Some of these approaches may have elicited a cautious response from his friends, although how near those friends were to the General it is impossible to say. The negotiations appear to have broken down partly because of the King's well-founded suspicion of Buckingham, partly, no doubt, because of Fairfax's unwillingness to commit himself to a venture whose outcome was, to put it mildly, uncertain. At the same time, there is not a shred of evidence that Fairfax betrayed Rochester or any other Royalist. He was an honorable man, but his behavior in the months before the Restoration shows that he would act only in what he took to be the interest of domestic peace. This, in 1654–55, would require formally correct relations with the Protectorate; although to guard against future changes Fairfax might wish to befriend the man whose estates he would be held accountable for in the event of a restoration. The conduct of both Fairfax and Buckingham shows plainly that this mutual insurance determined their attitudes to each other. If the March rising had shown signs of prospering, Fairfax might well have been less equivocal. But Royalist success was unlikely; if it came, there would still be time to leave the fence on which he, like so many others, was still sitting. Meanwhile, the cultivated retirement of Nun Appleton could remain undisturbed.[34]

In spite of the greater energy shown by the Action party, their attempts to interest the Presbyterians in the projected rebellion met with little more success than those of the Sealed Knot. Fairfax's attitude was characteristic of the moderates, and only with men like Willoughby, Browne, and John Booth did the Action party find it possible to establish even the beginnings of agreement. Contact with other segments of the opposition to Cromwell presents a similar story. These attempts to stir up "Devisyons in the Rebells Councell" were, however, pursued with sufficient vigor to merit our attention. The later months of 1654 were full of ominous murmurings within the republican and Leveller opposition. The dislike of old Commonwealthmen like Scot and Heselrige for the whole basis

34. Fairfax's attitude is discussed at length in Markham, pp. 376–83.

of the Protectorate was shared by many politically minded Army officers, and led more than one into seditious associations with John Wildman and his friends. Opposition of this kind came into the open in the petition of the "Three Colonels" in October 1654; and in the seamens' petition sponsored by the republican Vice-Admiral Lawson in the same month. Wildman and Sexby were doing their best to disaffect units of the Army in which they had influence, and Robert Overton was providing a focus of discontent in Scotland. There was, in fact, plenty of explosive material to encourage Royalist hopes that they would be helped by mutinies in Cromwell's Army, and by the support, however contradictory to principle, of what was left of the Levellers.[35]

"All that was reasonable in the general contrivance of insurrection," Clarendon tells us, ". . . was founded upon a supposition of the division and faction in the army." [36] Although much of the evidence for Royalist collaboration with the Levellers and Army malcontents lies in the unsupported statements of the government, there are enough clues in contemporary correspondence and the depositions of suspects under examination to show that the hope of combined action was not entirely the figment of Thurloe's fertile brain. One Royalist who was on familiar terms with the leading Levellers was Col. Henry Bishop, of Henfield, Sussex. Bishop, a close friend of Wildman, later boasted that he and two other members of the Action party "had a commission from Charles Stuart to treat with the Levelling party." Shortly before the March rising, Bishop was in touch with Wildman and other Levellers in Sussex, and he also assisted Sexby to escape from England after the Army plot fell through.[37]

Bishop's two associates in the supposed commission were John Weston and Col. Christopher Gardiner, of Croydon. Gardiner,

35. On Army and Leveller disaffection, October 1654–February 1655, see Gardiner, *C&P*, *3*, 211–17, 226–32, 269–70; and Maurice Ashley, *John Wildman, Plotter and Postmaster* (London, 1947), pp. 86–93.

36. *History*, Bk. XIV, § 133.

37. *TSP*, *4*, 161, 344; *6*, 830; *7*, 98. *NP*, *2*, 348. For Bishop see *CCC*, p. 1518, and Ashley, *Wildman*, passim. On p. 86 Mr. Ashley seems to confuse him with Capt. George Bishop, formerly Scot's assistant, who was now an active enemy of Cromwell.

one of Thurloe's agents reported, visited Cologne in November 1654, accompanied by an emissary from the Army. It may well have been this mission which inspired Hyde's hope on the 21st "that the army will begin the business for us." In London, Edward Grey was also engaged in talks with the disaffected soldiers, and as late as December 29 was still optimistic about the outcome: "Mr. Archer [the Army] is well," he told Armorer, "I have bene dayly with his freind and am just now going to mete againe." The arrest of Overton and his accomplices frightened the potential mutineers, and on January 19 Weston and Gardiner announced the breakdown of negotiations: "Thay have busines of theire owne, which thay would leave thyne for." When the rising occurred in March, many of the rebels were unaware that the talks had failed. Penruddock, Wagstaffe, and several of their followers all expected help from this quarter.[38] Although no agreement was reached, it is curious that the arrest of the leading Levellers coincided so nearly with the date, February 13, originally set for the Royalist insurrection. It is also interesting that the Levellers should have chosen the same meeting places, Salisbury Plain and Marston Moor, at which the Cavaliers gathered in March.[39] The most likely explanation of the coincidence is that from such men as Bishop, Gardiner, and Grey, the Levellers heard enough about the Action party's intentions to try to profit from a simultaneous rising. There was, clearly, no plan of combined action.

As in the Army, so in the Navy: such contact as occurred between the Royalists and the republican officers was without result. As early as 1652 Hyde had hoped for support in the Fleet, perhaps encouraged by memories of 1648. Nothing was done during the Dutch War; and it was only when naval discontent came to a head in

38. *TSP, 3,* 64, 182, 315, 344, 401. *ClSP, 3,* 259, 265–66. *CClSP, 3,* 5 (MS 49, fol. 275; cipher in Appendix, C), 9 (MS 49, fols. 304–6; "Brerely" is Weston), 11–12 (MS 49, fol. 321). *NP, 2,* 306–7. Egerton MS 2535, fol. 113. Clarendon, *Con.,* § 26. For Gardiner, not to be confused with Robert and Thomas of that name, see VCH, *Surrey, 4,* 222; HMC, *7th Report,* Appendix, p. 686; and *CSPD, 1660–61,* pp. 104, 600–1.

39. Ashley, *Wildman,* p. 93, is right in saying that the Leveller plot was not "arranged in collaboration" with the Royalists. He underestimates, however, the extent of the negotiations between the two groups. Each must have known the other's intentions.

October 1654 that any definite steps were taken. Clarendon asserts that Penn and Venables, the commanders of Cromwell's "Western design," offered their services to the King before the expedition set sail. This is unlikely, but overtures evidently were made by the Action party to disaffected elements in the Fleet; whether before or after the circulation of Lawson's petition it is impossible to say. Long before Christmas, when the Fleet left for the West Indies, the sailors' grievances had been stilled by generous advances of pay, and the opportunity was past. The Sealed Knot, once more in operation, was widely blamed for the failure; the result, the Action party complained, of the Knot's "continued coldness and backwardness to action." One last effort was made in February 1655: an approach to Lawson, after the Hispaniola expedition was well on its way. The King wrote to Lawson and to the Governor of Plymouth; Sir John Grenville and Sir Hugh Pollard were also believed to be involved in it. It was too late. The outbreak of discontent in the Fleet during the previous autumn had been the critical time; now, with both Blake's and Penn's squadrons away from home waters, there was nothing the Action party could do.[40]

With the exception of a small Presbyterian minority which had committed itself in 1648 and 1651, the opposition groups to which the Action party made advances before the March rising displayed much the same reaction. The overtures were not always discouraged, but only the most optimistic Cavalier could see any immediate prospect of overthrowing Oliver Cromwell; Presbyterians and old soldiers of the New Model were neither optimistic nor Cavaliers. Even those Presbyterians who in theory regarded a restoration of limited monarchy with favor could see little point in an inevitably unsuccessful challenge to the overwhelming might of the Protectorate. Public opinion, so far as it mattered, seemed to prefer giving Cromwell's conservative dictatorship a trial. If stability and civil peace were not secured by this, only then was there any likelihood of united action cutting across the lines of past alle-

40. *CISP, 3,* 86, 265. *CCISP, 3,* 11, 17. *TSP, 3,* 182. *NP, 3,* 178. Clarendon, *History,* Bk. XV, § 6. *Barwick,* pp. 185–86, supports the story of Venables' offer, adding some improbable details. For a general discussion see Gardiner, *C&P, 3,* 214–17.

giance. The Action party's failure to organize a rising that would be more than a merely Royalist venture is therefore hardly surprising. The attempt is interesting as an instructive contrast to the wariness of the Sealed Knot. A more dangerous threat to the Protectorate lay in the wide ramifications of the Action party's plotting among the Royalists themselves. Too much suspicion and bad blood divided them from their open enemies of only a few years before, however intense their common hatred of Cromwell. In 1655 the Cavalier party was left to fight alone.

7. Penruddock's Rising

THE INSURRECTION OF MARCH 1655 was the one occasion between the end of the first civil war and the Restoration in which the Royalists attempted a rebellion by themselves. Hamilton in 1648, Charles II three years later, and Booth in 1659 all expected strong Presbyterian as well as Cavalier support; the plot of 1655 was the only one in which the Royalists were without allies. This was not for want of trying; but the final result of the Action party's advances to the men of the center and left, a few vague assurances from conservative Presbyterians like Willoughby, did not dilute the overwhelmingly Royalist nature of the movement. Most Royalists welcomed their isolation. Free from compromising entanglements, they could now try the risky but exhilarating experiment to see if Cavalier enthusiasm could succeed where intricate policy had failed.[1]

This absence of embarrassing allies promised the Royalists at least one important possible advantage: the opportunity of operat-

1. The most thorough treatment of the March rising is in the three articles by Firth, *EHR, 3,* 323–50; *4,* 313–38, and 525–35. Gardiner's shorter account is in *C&P, 3,* 276–95. For an excellent modern version, concentrating on the Wiltshire rising, see A. H. Woolrych, *Penruddock's Rising 1655,* Historical Association Publications, gen. ser., G 29, London, 1955. Fuller details of Penruddock's venture are given by W. W. Ravenhill, "Records of the Rising in the West," *Wiltshire Archaeological and Natural History Magazine, 13* (1872), 119–88, 252–73; *14* (1874), 38–67; *15* (1875), 1–41.

ing under a unified command. Unfortunately the opportunity was wasted. The rivalry between the Sealed Knot and the Action party returned to bedevil the leadership in the critical months before the rising. Before the autumn of 1654 was over the Sealed Knot resumed its meetings. In the absence of directions to the contrary from the King, there was nothing to prevent it. Villiers and Willys were both released from prison before the end of August. The latter's quarrel with Belasyse may have delayed matters, but before the end of October an agent was sent to Cologne to announce the Knot's resurrection. Charles at once signified his approval, and explained that he had applied to "new Councell" only when he heard of the Knot's "sicknesse," and that even then he had "resorted to none but those who were before recommended" by the Knot itself. The old power of leadership was revived, and nothing was said to imply that the Action party was exempt from the Knot's supreme direction. Nevertheless, the "olde Lawyer" was gently prodded toward a more positive attitude. If the Knot thought its present organization inadequate, Charles suggested that some "younger Councellour" might be appointed, to provide greater vigor and coordination.[2]

The Sealed Knot's response to this note of urgency was to appoint a secretary. William Rumbold, the scribe selected, was a Leicestershire man of modest origins, now in his early forties. Before the war he had been a clerk in the Great Wardrobe, and he attended Charles I in this capacity until after Naseby. He then went into exile, joined his merchant brother Henry in Spain, and returned to England at some time in 1649. As secretary, Rumbold was primarily responsible for conducting the Knot's correspondence with the King and Hyde, but he was more than a mere scribe and was expected to play a responsible part in preparing for the rising. The passage of so much business through his hands was too much for poor Rumbold, and early in 1655 the Knot complained that it exposed him to unnecessary dangers, "since unadvisedly all people were addresse to him." Rumbold, the Knot explained, was not intended to be responsible "for the contrivance of the whole, but as he understood how others proceeded he would contribute his best

2. *CClSP*, 2, 413 (MS 49, fol. 115).

endeavours to it." Operating through a covering address "at Mr. Townsends house on Puddle Wharfe Hill neare to the Wardrobe," he was soon busily sending and receiving reports on the conspiracy. When more important issues were at stake, however, his superiors in the Knot preferred to speak for themselves.[3]

Important issues were soon at stake, and they showed that the reorganization had not changed the Sealed Knot's outlook. While Bennett, Grey, and the other Action party leaders were raising the exiles' hopes of speedy and successful action, the Knot was composing, on December 3, a "most melancholique accounte" of the situation, dismissing its rivals' promises as illusions. As if to justify the Knot's dismal forebodings, Charles' reply, which anxiously attempted to counter this pessimism, fell into Thurloe's hands. As the day of action approached, two conflicting voices of the Royalist party, the one advising immediate action, the other caution, continued to besiege the King's ears. Action party supporters expressed bitter resentment at the dampening intrusion of Villiers and his friends. John Weston denounced them as "powerfull obstructors," and Charles Davison, regretting that he had ever been referred to them, complained that they gave "little advise." [4]

Equally threatening from the Royalist point of view were the signs of the government's vigilance that were already much in evidence before the end of 1654. In the last fortnight of the year, in response to the increasing tension in Parliament and to the hints of Royalist and Leveller conspiracy that were already reaching Thurloe, extensive military precautions were taken. Troops were fetched from Ireland, the Tower garrison increased to 1,200 men, regiments were brought into London and placed on a footing of immediate preparedness, and artillery became ominously conspicuous at Whitehall.[5] Worse was to follow. On January 1, 1655, an important

3. *CClSP*, 2, 427; 3, 4 (MS 49, fol. 267), 16. Rawl. MS A 21, pp. 466–69. Carte MS 194, fol. 43; see Appendix, E. For Rumbold see *DNB*, and Sir Horace Rumbold, "Notes on the History of the Family of Rumbold," *TRHS*, new ser. 6 (1892), 145–65. In this account Henry Rumbold says that William was in the Knot's service as early as 1653. There is no other evidence for this.

4. *CClSP*, 3, 3–4, 9–10 (MS 49, fols. 306, 308. "Brerely" is Weston; "Dowcett" is Davison). *TSP*, 3, 76.

5. Gardiner, *C&P*, 3, 233. Firth, *EHR*, 3, 341–42. Abbott, 3, 549–50, 556–57, 559. Woolrych, p. 13.

section of the Action party's organization, concerned with the collection and distribution of arms for the midland rebellion, was uncovered by Thurloe's officers. A series of arrests cleaned up the arms distributors, brought a number of other prominent Royalists into custody, and gave the authorities their first clear knowledge of the extensive sweep of the design.

The central figure in the arms affair was the returned Virginian exile, Major Henry Norwood. He had been arrested on suspicion of complicity in the Gerard plot in 1654, but cannot have been long in prison. Norwood had been using his colonial connections as a cover for dealings with the London gunsmiths, buying quantities of pistols and carbines for "Virginia" through two English merchants trading from Amsterdam. He had also supplied Sir Henry Littleton, the new High Sheriff of Worcestershire, with forty pairs of pistols, throwing in twenty-nine saddles and a score of carbines for good measure. The Midlands carriers did good business in December 1654. The crates sent down to Littleton from London were accompanied by large hampers containing "bottles of wine" for Sir John Packington; other mysterious cases went to Walter Vernon, of Stokely Park in Staffordshire, Edmund Browne, of Bentley in Derbyshire, and Sir Robert Shirley in Leicestershire (an agent of his, Rowland Thomas, was Norwood's principal assistant). The conclusion was inescapable: the existence of a dangerous group busily providing the midland Royalists with the means to fight.[6]

The arrest of the arms conspirators early in January was the crisis of the Action party's existence, and the essential first step in Thurloe's investigation of the design. Among others arrested at this time was one of the Action party's high command, Richard Thornhill. Norwood was found to be of enough importance to warrant personal examination by Cromwell himself, and considerable pressure was also applied to Rowland Thomas, but as Thurloe remembered it, "he proved a peremptory fellow, and would not confess." Two Royalists from North Wales were more cooperative. Nicholas

6. *TSP*, *3*, 65–108, 129–30, 210–11, 283, 662; *4*, 485. Rawl. MSS A 22, p. 1; A 33, p. 612. *CSPD, 1655*, pp. 238, 575. *CClSP*, *3*, 2 (MS 49, fol. 258; in Norwood's hand. Cipher in Appendix, C).

Bagenall, a wealthy Anglesey recusant, and his kinsman Nicholas Bayly, the son of the former Bishop of Bangor, were persuaded to make full confessions in return for Cromwell's pardon. Fortunately their interests were entirely local, and Stephens was the only member of the organization they had met. Another shattering blow fell on February 6, when three more of the leaders, Sir Humphrey Bennett, Colonel Grey, and John Weston, joined Thornhill in captivity, along with an agent named James Read, and Christopher Gardiner, who had been involved in the talks with the Army malcontents. Gardiner was taken at his house near Croydon, where he had stored arms at the White Hart Inn, while in Read's chamber were found a useful collection of pistols and a letter from the King to Colonel Grey. Of the Action party's leaders in London, only Peyton and Armstrong now remained at large. It was, Ormond gloomily observed, a "considerable defeat." [7]

Before the roundup, the Action party had reached a final decision on the date of the rising and had sent Thomas Ross to Cologne for Charles II's approval. On January 19 Weston and Charles Davison both wrote announcing a postponement by a week, from February 6 to 13, presumably to allow time for Ross to reach Cologne and return with instructions. The fatal division within the Royalist party had long demanded a choice of policy at the highest level: a decision by the King himself. It could now be avoided no longer. Ross reached Cologne shortly before the end of January, and his reception exceeded anything he could have hoped for. Charles, fretting at the frustrating idleness of exile, had recently made wild threats "to serve against the Portugalls in the Indyes, or to serve the Venetians against the Turkes." Although refusing to give any positive direction to the Sealed Knot to act against its own collective judgment, the King authorized Ross'

7. *Clarke Papers,* ed. C. H. Firth, Camden Soc. (London, 1891–1901), *3,* 17–24. *Diary of Thomas Burton,* ed. J. T. Rutt (London, 1828), *4,* 301–5. *TSP, 3,* 125, 127. Rawl. MSS A 34, p. 567; A 42, p. 192. *CClSP, 2,* 384 (MS 48, fol. 329); *3,* 16, 21. *Cromwelliana,* p. 152. *Mercurius Politicus,* Nos. 243–44. *A New and Further Discovery of Another Great and Bloody Plot* (February 1655), pp. 5–8. *Declaration of His Highness* (October 1655), p. 26. For Bagenall and Bayly see *Ludlow's Memoirs,* ed. Firth, *1,* 401–2 n.

friends to go ahead, and sent the messenger back with the news that the appointed commander, Charles' friend Rochester, would follow in a few days.[8]

The selection of Rochester for this assignment was not made on the spur of the moment. Charles had promised the Knot in May 1654 that he would have "no Generall but himselfe, nor Lt. Ge. but his Brother the Duke of Yorke," but the commission drafted for York at about that time was clearly intended for the general of an army in the field, not of a rising of conspirators. Rochester was named Field Marshal General "to command next and immediatly under Us and Our said most deare Brother" on September 15, 1654. His brief experience of the conditions of conspiracy during the escape from Worcester must have counted in his favor; his military record and his reputation for sympathy to the Presbyterians were also good recommendations in the circumstances of 1654. His notorious lack of judgment, love of debauchery (Clarendon says he was "inspired" in the pursuit of it), and irresolution in moments of crisis were temporarily forgotten. At least he "never drank when he was within distance of an enemy." He was still at Cologne on January 28 but had left—ostensibly on a mission to Denmark, actually on the first stage of his journey to England—by February 2.[9]

While Ross was speaking so confidently at Cologne, James Halsall was making a hasty journey from England to urge the contrary view, as the messenger of the Sealed Knot. A letter from Edward Villiers on behalf of the Knot stressed the futility of the Action party's plan: "Understanding they have sent to you for your approbation of a day for rising (which they already here have agreed on), we thought itt very undutifull not to represent to yor Matie the dangerousness of ye consequence of itt. . . . We looke on the rising of your party but to the distroying of themselves." Unfortunately for the Knot, Halsall was held up for six days by contrary winds, and he reached the Continent too late to alter Charles' de-

8. *ClSP*, *3*, 265–66. *CClSP*, *3*, 4 (MS 49, fols. 265–66), 9–10.

9. *CClSP*, *2*, 356 (MS 48, fol. 215); *3*, 14. Clarendon, *History*, Bk. VIII, § 169. Add. MS 15,856, fols. 46, 50–52: Rochester's name has been erased from the draft, but is still legible. The date of the commission shows that Clarendon's account, quoted by Firth, *EHR*, *3*, 336–37, is inaccurate.

cision. The paths of the two messengers crossed at Antwerp—Halsall on his way to Cologne, Ross returning to England. Ormond was also in the town, waiting to see if events would make his presence necessary in England, and heard both sides of the argument dramatically presented.[10]

There remained only one chance of repairing the party's unity: a last appeal to the Knot. With this in mind, Ormond sent that "infallible subtle" negotiator Daniel O'Neill to Cologne to explain the situation. Meanwhile, in England there was yet another postponement, to March 8. O'Neill found Charles II still unwilling to order the Knot to act against its better judgment. It is impossible not to sympathize with the King's reluctance to commit his supporters to a military adventure in which they had no confidence. On the other hand, this was war, and an army whose officers disagree has a right to expect clear directions from its commander. However vividly he remembered the oak tree, that commander was Charles himself. On February 8 O'Neill was sent off to London with the King's final, and ambiguous, message to the Knot: "Nor can it be reasonable for me to hinder them from moovinge, who believe themselves ready for it, and undone if they do not, and yett I cannot looke for any greate successe, if whilst they stirr, you sitt still." But the King still balked at imposing his will on the Knot: "It is as unreasonable that any positive commaunde of myne, should obliege you to an action derectly contrary to your judgement, and inclinacons." O'Neill, the bearer of this equivocal advice, was also instructed to mediate between the two groups, to make every effort to persuade the Knot to change its mind, and to sanction or postpone the rising, according to his and Rochester's assessment of the situation.[11]

O'Neill wasted no time. Accompanied by the indefatigable Nicholas Armorer, he reached Dunkirk on February 11, and took ship for Dover. The Royalists had a man there on whom they could rely in the key post of Clerk of the Passage; a certain Robert Day, who had connived at the comings and goings of more than one

10. *CClSP, 3,* 11 (MS 49, fol. 315), 16. The Knot's letter and Ormond's report are printed in *EHR, 3,* 333–35.

11. *ClSP, 3,* 265–66. *CClSP, 3,* 16 (MS 49, fol. 340; in full in *EHR, 3,* 336). *TSP, 4,* 245.

Royalist emissary during the previous months. This time, however, Day's efforts were inadequate and O'Neill and Armorer found themselves in jail in Dover castle. Armorer got away by sticking to his assumed identity of "Mr. Wright," an innocent merchant going to visit his family at Newcastle. The port commissioners could find nothing against him, Day duly engaged for his good behavior, and a harassed deputy-governor was soon defending himself against Thurloe's wrath for losing so valuable a catch. O'Neill had neither Armorer's bravado nor as good a story, and remained in captivity until the 22d, when he escaped by more direct methods and took the road for London.[12]

Rochester, meanwhile, was choosing the slower but safer crossing by way of Margate. The Dunkirk taverns seem to have been much to his taste, and to have given him many "hours of good fellowship," through "a great part of the day and night," as Clarendon moralized severely. However, the delay gave him the roisterous company of Sir Joseph Wagstaffe, who was also at Dunkirk awaiting an opportunity of crossing to join in the stirring events which the whole world knew to be impending. Wagstaffe was a soldier of fortune who had fought in the French service and for the Parliament under Essex, and had eventually become a Major General under Maurice in the West. The "great companionableness in his nature" (we have Clarendon's word for it) was all that was needed to endear him to the convivial Rochester. The Earl and his new-found friend sailed from Dunkirk on February 19, and reached London only a few hours after O'Neill.[13]

The prospects of a successful action, dark already when O'Neill and Rochester left Cologne, were even darker by the time they arrived in London. Although the port authorities, particularly at Dover, continued to make ridiculous blunders and to allow a steady stream of suspicious travelers to get through, they had been suffi-

12. *CClSP*, *3*, 21, 23. *TSP*, *3*, 137–38, 162, 164. Rawl. MS A 22, p. 107. Day's position is discussed by Gardiner, *C&P*, *3*, 279, and Firth, *EHR*, *3*, 343–44. That Day was a Royalist agent is proved, I think, by the presence of his name in a cipher key used by the exiles: Egerton MS 2550, fol. 83. Halsall records in his accounts payments to "a friend at Dover": Cl. MS 50, fol. 72.

13. *NP*, *2*, 205. *TSP*, *3*, 344, 349, 429. *CSPD, 1655–56*, p. 47. Clarendon, *History*, Bk. XIV, §§ 127, 131. *CClSP*, *3*, 22–23.

ciently alerted to detain a number of minor figures. A personal exposition by Cromwell of both the Royalist and Leveller plots was given to the Lord Mayor and Common Council of London on February 13, and was accompanied by another elaborate set of precautions. These included the publication of a new militia commission for the City, the confiscation of horses and private stores of powder, more troop movements, and the usual suspension of horse-racing and other dangerous gatherings. Although the reports from George Bishop at Bristol were deliberately alarmist, Thurloe did not entirely ignore his stories about meetings of Cavaliers and green-ribboned Levellers there; he sent an officer to investigate. Sir Ralph Skipwith was arrested in Norfolk, and further north, at Tynemouth, a watchful eye was kept on the best-known of the suspicious characters of the locality. It was the same story in North Wales, and indeed throughout the whole country there was an air of ominous confidence on the part of the authorities.[14]

The situation was worst in the West. There was a serious breakdown of communication in Wiltshire and Somerset, where several of the conspirators who had previously received orders to rendezvous at Salisbury on February 13 were not warned of the postponement. Several in Somerset left their homes and made their way to Salisbury; Col. Walter Slingsby, Hugh Smyth of Long Ashton, and a number of others gathered there on Monday, February 12. News reached them that the action was off and they dispersed, but not before the damage was done. Stories soon circulated in the city of the appearance of people in "young Tarquin's cullours," and on the 24th a certain Jasper Gill laid an information with the commander of the Bristol garrison. Slingsby and some Royalists of lesser importance were promptly arrested. Smyth vanished, but his stepfather, Col. Thomas Piggott, was taken. Another prisoner, John Stradling of Chedzoy, made a full confession and identified the real leaders of the conspiracy in Somerset. These, he said, were two of the Wyndhams: Colonel Francis of Trent, Charles II's protector after Worcester, and his uncle, Sir Hugh of Pilsdon, who were to

14. Abbott, *3*, 617–24. Gardiner, *C&P*, *3*, 278. Firth, *EHR*, *3*, 342–43. See also *TSP*, *3*, 138, 154, 161, 164–72, 177–80; *Severall Proceedings*, No. 282; Steele, *Proclamations*, *1*, 367.

command an attack on Taunton. There is no direct corroboration
of this from other sources, but it is likely enough; the Wyndhams
were active men, and there were few other Cavaliers in the county
with anything like their prestige. The Wyndhams disappeared with
guilty speed, but both were soon rounded up. A final point in
Stradling's deposition was that Sir John Grenville, the biggest man
in the Cornish plot, had recently left London for the West; by the
beginning of March he was in confinement at Exeter. Such were the
disastrous consequences of the failure to notify the Somerset Royalists of the change of plan.[15]

News of these happenings in the West cannot have reached
Rochester and O'Neill until some days after their arrival in the
capital. There was, even so, sufficient cause for pessimism. The disruption of the Action party's central command; the lukewarmness
of Willoughby and his Presbyterian allies; and the downright hostility of the Sealed Knot: all pointed to a logical decision to call the
action off, and live to fight another day. O'Neill almost reached this
sensible conclusion, but at the critical moment his subtlety deserted
him and he allowed himself to be over-ruled by Sir Thomas Armstrong. The great decision taken, O'Neill sent Armorer to persuade
Willoughby to give a definite engagement. This, with the pressure
applied to Waller and John Booth by Rochester, had the desired
effect. The handful of Presbyterian Royalists once more changed
their tune, announced that they would support the action, and
permitted Willoughby to be sent down to Lincolnshire to await the
day. O'Neill's misguided enthusiasm also made an impression on
the less promising material of the Sealed Knot. The King's letter
of February 8 had of course placed the members under a strong
moral obligation to fall into line. Sir William Compton promised
that his partners would give all the assistance in their power, though
still with the gloomy reservation that "they beleeved little good
would be don."

The arrival of Rochester, airily displaying his commission,
strengthened the hand of those who could see no room to draw

15. *TSP, 3,* 162, 176–77, 181–83, 191–92, 295, 397. For Smyth see John
Collinson, *History and Antiquities of the County of Somerset* (Bath, 1791), *2*,
293.

Fig. 2. SIR WILLIAM COMPTON.
From the portrait by Sir Peter Lely at Ham House.

back at the brink of rebellion. In the five days of his stay in London a survey of intelligence from the principal centers of conspiracy convinced the two leaders that further hesitation would be unpardonable. Only in Kent, where unusually heavy troop concentrations were reported, did it seem advisable to make an indefinite postponement. On Tuesday February 27, Rochester left for Yorkshire, relying on the hopeful stories of Fairfax's promised appearance to make this the decisive battleground. Armorer went with him, and Royalist agents streamed away from the capital to their respective scenes of action: Wagstaffe to the West, Willoughby to Lincolnshire, John Booth to Cheshire, and Halsall to Lancashire. Among the few who remained in London was Daniel O'Neill. The nine days after Rochester slipped away to the North must have sorely tried his patience, but when the fateful day came, on Thursday March 8, he was sufficiently composed to write an optimistic report on the present state of affairs for the edification of the King. Waiting in still undisturbed incognito at Middelburg near Flushing (he had left Cologne quietly on February 14 to be ready to make a dash to England), Charles must have received it as a welcome end to depressing delays and unfulfilled expectations. But in conspiracy, as in war, there is often a regrettable gap between promise and performance.[16]

The March rising was planned on a regional basis, nominally through local associations similar to those of 1650. These varied considerably in strength and effectiveness of organization: in some areas the preparations were nonexistent; in others, notably the Northeast, they were surprisingly thorough. There were, broadly speaking, six regional conspiracies, each capable of acting independently but each in contact with one or more of the others. The most important in the Action party's original plan was the one which included London and the home counties; but this was smashed by the arrests and troop movements in January. Compared with the Presbyterian design of 1650–51, little headway had been made among the citizens. Thanks to the Knot's influence, the eastern counties produced no more disturbance. The fenlands had been simmering with discontent since the summer of 1653, when

16. *NP*, *2*, 217–22. *TSP*, *4*, 245. Rawl. MS A 42, pp. 191–92.

there had been demonstrations against the Earl of Bedford's drain-
age schemes, but the Knot derived no visible profit from it. The
Action party showed some interest in using bases in Norfolk to
clear the way for the much-desired invading forces. Armorer's
memorandum named Lynn as an important target, and the same
paper included a list of Norfolk gentry whose support was anticipated, many of them survivors of the affair in December 1650. The
King was no longer willing to employ Thomas Blague, who had
managed that dismal failure. Instead, two Norfolk gentlemen in
exile offered their services, and were eventually sent into the
county. These were Sir William Denny, the Royalist son of a
former Recorder of Norwich, and Sir Miles Hobart of Plumstead,
a parliamentarian who had changed sides in 1648. When Hobart
reached Norfolk, he was kept out of the inner circle by the Knot's
friends. He refused to be put off, and by the beginning of March
was able to report that the plot was now "setled in more hopefull
handes." The revival of the Knot meant, however, that the area was
even more exposed to conflicting orders than was the rest of the
country. There was, therefore, no perceptible movement in the
fens.[17]

The situation in the Northeast offers a complete contrast. Of all
the regional conspiracies this one had the most intensive preparation, and the best hope of success on March 8. The main effort was
planned against three strategically important centers: Newcastle
with its port of Tynemouth, Hull, and York. Much depended on
the intentions of Fairfax, whose adherence would doubtless have
been the signal for a massive appearance of the moderates. His attitude, as we have seen, was maddeningly uncertain, but there were
enough rumors to convince the optimists. Another Yorkshire mag-

17. *TSP, 1,* 358. *CSPD, 1653–54,* p. 114. *ClSP, 3,* 247–48. *CClSP, 2,* 318 (MS
48, fol. 5; misdated in *Calendar:* see above, p. 75 n. 4), 345. Cl. MSS 48, fol.
305; 49, fol. 345. *NP, 2,* 69, 105. Add. MS 15,856, fol. 45 (commissions to
"M.H."). Rawl. MS A 21, p. 386. Hyde and Nicholas had an agent at Ely
who used the name "John Appleton": *TSP, 2,* 468, 645; *3,* 457. Rawl. MS A
21, pp. 332–33. Carte MS 194, fol. 72 (Appleton's cipher). For Hobart see
CCC, pp. 1646, 2322–24; and *The Knyvett Letters 1620–1644,* ed. B. Schofield,
Norfolk Record Society, 20 (1949), pp. 93 n., 139 and n. For Denny, ibid., pp.
115, 127; G.E.C., *Baronetage, 2,* 81; and *CCC,* p. 115.

nate who might have been almost as useful as Fairfax, was the Roman Catholic Sir Marmaduke Langdale, exiled in Holland. The Action party had asked for him to be sent into Yorkshire to assist them, but the suggestion had a cold reception from Hyde and the Council.[18]

In spite of Fairfax's equivocation and Langdale's absence, by the early months of 1655 Royalist preparations in Yorkshire, Durham, and Northumberland were well advanced. The efforts of Armorer, Davison, and their associates eventually produced a recognizable organization, capable of holding meetings of representatives of the three counties. Considerable sums of money were distributed. Major Thomas Carnaby, the most active of the Northumberland agents, said that it cost the Yorkshire gentry £25 a week to maintain a messenger service to and from London. Some of the necessary funds came from the exiles' scanty treasury. Marmaduke Darcy, the brother of Lord Darcy and another assiduous promoter of the northern plot, was paid £1,000 some time after July 1654, and Robert Walters received £300 when he visited Cologne in the autumn; after his return to England, an informer noted, he had "greate store of money and gold by him." [19]

The men who carried on the northern conspiracy were, as in all such affairs, of two kinds. Most easily recognizable are the lesser agents, who enlisted men, distributed commissions, collected arms and horses, maintained communications with London and the exiles, and generally obeyed orders. Behind them were the men of wealth and rank, landowners accustomed to local leadership; these made the real decisions, but usually kept discreetly in the background. Men like Armorer and Davison were characteristic of the first kind; so were Robert Walters and Carnaby. Walters several times traveled to London with Armorer to confer with the Action

18. *CClSP*, 2, 335–36, 363, 383, 392, 399 (cipher in Appendix, C). *CSPD, 1655*, pp. 216, 221. *NP*, 3, 12, 88. Egerton MS 2535, fols. 109, 122.

19. *TSP*, 3, 336, 722. Add. MS 4156, fols. 168–69. Cl. MSS 49, fol. 345; 50, fol. 72. For Marmaduke Darcy see *Archaeologia, 35,* 338 n.; and W. W. Bean, *Parliamentary Representation of the Six Northern Counties* (Hull, 1890), p. 1012. Thomas Carnaby is hard to place in any of the branches of this Royalist family. He may have been the one who fought at Naseby, and was killed at York in 1665: Bateson et al., *Northumberland, 10,* 408.

party leaders there, and at Cologne in September he was supplied with letters and commissions for the Yorkshire gentry. Marmaduke Darcy was also hard at work in the North that same autumn; he too went to Cologne in January, and was with Rochester in London a month later, traveling down to Yorkshire ahead of his commander. It is not so easy to identify the men behind these lesser figures. Sir Philip Monckton was undoubtedly one of them in the early stages, but some time before the rising he seems to have lost interest; if he maintained his supervision of affairs at Hull and York he covered up his tracks successfully. One of those behind Walters was Sir Richard Mauleverer of Allerton Mauleverer, the Royalist son of a regicide and brother-in-law of Thomas Scot; another was Sir William Ingram of Little Cattal. Rochester made his headquarters at Ingram's house for three days before the rising, and from there, it was said, he "solicited people very strongly, and threatened some." [20]

The outcome of the northeastern conspiracy was pathetically, or comically, feeble, according to taste and viewpoint. In spite of the rumors of seditious infection there during the previous weeks, on March 8 Hull preserved an undisturbed calm.[21] Near York there was more activity. Mauleverer gave a great supper for his tenants, and his and Walters' efforts produced a gathering of some 150 horsemen on Marston Moor. Rochester was there to lead them against York, where the gates were supposed to be open in readiness. Many of the local gentry had their horses saddled, but most waited for signs of real success before they committed themselves. Sir John Mallory of Studley was conveniently ill (possibly a diplomatic illness, but we must be charitable as he died before the year was out); he sent his cousin and a few men, however. Lord Darcy, Marmaduke's brother, also managed to send assistance without appearing in person. It is interesting how many of the most heavily engaged suspects lived only a few miles from the scene—Ingram at Little Cattal, Richard Hutton at Goldsborough, Mauleverer at Allerton,

20. *Burton, 1,* 230–31. *TSP,* 2, 585; *3,* 78, 336, 353, 722–23; *4,* 438. Clarendon, *History,* Bk. XIV, § 130. *CCISP, 2,* 395, 399–400, 413; *3,* 4. Cl. MS 49, fol. 345. Add. MS 4156, fol. 166. *CSPD, 1655,* pp. 215–16. *Perfect Proceedings,* No. 287. For Mauleverer see *DNB,* and *CCC,* p. 2030; for Ingram, Joseph Foster, *Pedigrees of the County Families of Yorkshire* (London, 1874), Vol. 1.
21. *TSP, 3,* 148, 182, 239–40; *4,* 132. *CCISP, 3,* 14, 17.

Walters at Little Ouseburn: their houses form a semicircle strad-
dling the York-Knaresborough road to the west of the moor. Robert
Brandling at Leathley, Sir Henry Slingsby at Scriven, and Sir
Jordan Crosland at Newby Hall lived only a few more miles distant. The Marston Moor rendezvous was in fact a very local gathering of neighbors, by no means representative of the wider circle of
Yorkshire Royalists who had been connected with the plot in its
earlier stages. It was a far cry from the army of 1,500 which Walters
had promised.

There was obviously little point in pressing home the attack on
York. In the darkness Rochester completely failed to establish control over his men. The rebels panicked immediately, mistaking the
cries of passing travelers lost in the night for the shouts of advancing soldiers. Walter Strickland, a younger son of the recusant Sir
Robert Strickland of Thornton Briggs, lost his head completely,
and his precipitate departure set an infectious example. In his headlong flight from the moor, Strickland met Duke Darcy on his way
there; he was a little late, but at least he had fifty men with him.
Darcy went ahead to survey the scene for himself, but most of his
followers took Strickland's advice and fled too. Darcy's late arrival
suggests that the party on the moor would have done well to wait a
little longer. They were, Walters admitted, already discouraged by
several postponements, and their spirits were not equal to a long
night in the place where eleven years before the Royalist cause in
the North had foundered in the few short hours of a summer evening. "Strangely frightned with their owne shaddows," Cromwell's
local commander reported, they went home to bed, leaving several
cartloads of arms forlornly abandoned on the moor, and quantities
of individual weapons scattered among the heather. Mauleverer
was captured in Cheshire ten days later, but broke out after a week
in jail and escaped to London and the Continent. Robert Walters
got away to London, but was run down at Gravesend when escaping
to Rotterdam in July. Rochester and Armorer also fled south in
disguise, but many of the others who had assembled on Marston
Moor were rounded up as soon as they reached home.[22]

22. *TSP*, *3*, 226–27, 240, 273, 344, 530, 722–23; *4*, 393. Vaughan, *1*, 146–48.
Clarke Papers, *3*, 27, 30–31. *NP*, *2*, 322, 327. *CSPD*, *1655*, pp. 213, 215–16.
SPDI, 102, fol. 231. *Perfect Proceedings*, No. 285. *Faithful Scout*, Nos. 218–

It was the same story at Newcastle and Tynemouth, where in the enforced absence of Edward Grey, Major Carnaby had been responsible for the preparations. On the night of March 8 an ambitious plan for a triple assault on Newcastle evaporated because of the indecision and ineptitude of the few conspirators who appeared. On paper the scheme looked impressive. Three troops of horse were to assemble: one to the north at Duddoe, near Morpeth; another to the west in Tynedale; a third to the south at Gateshead. A party inside Newcastle would open the gates to the advancing horsemen, and join them in seizing the city. The leaders were not the most powerful men in the county, but were nonetheless solid and respectable. The commander at Duddoe was Henry Widdrington of Ritton, one of a family well distributed between both sides. In Tynedale the leader was to be William Delaval, Grey's cousin by marriage and the son of Sir John Delaval of Dissington. The Gateshead party was led by Sir Francis Anderson, an influential but indebted Newcastle coal-owner, who had fought as a colonel in the first civil war. The fifth column within the city was directed by Col. William Strother of Kirknewton, a Cavalier son-in-law of "Six Bottle" Mark Shaftoe, the convivial Recorder of Newcastle. To supplement Carnaby's activities in rounding up supporters, there had been frequent meetings to advance the plot in Tynemouth, and the necessary money, it was said, was being provided by Royalist citizens.

When the 8th came, all this was shown to be so much wishful thinking. The Tynemouth garrison had recently been reinforced from Scotland, and the authorities were wide-awake. Carnaby was still hopeful, but Strother's brother-in-law, Col. John Salkeld, exhibited an attitude typical of many when he advised waiting to see what happened in other parts of the country before they committed themselves. Nothing came of either Anderson's or Delaval's parties, and only about seventy men arrived during the evening to join Henry Widdrington at Duddoe. They had been invited, one of

19. *Perfect Diurnal*, No. 275. Clarendon, *History*, Bk. XIV, § 135. For Crosland see *Yorks. Archaeological Journal*, *23*, 357; for Mallory, Keeler, pp. 264–65; for Strickland, Daniel Scott, *The Stricklands of Sizergh Castle* (Kendal, 1908), pp. 143–49, 161–62.

them said, to attend a "wedding and head-washing," but it was not a very convivial gathering. The "guests" waited dispiritedly for several hours, until at about eleven o'clock Carnaby brought the news that "a great Fleete of shipps" had come into the Tyne, and that it would be better to disperse. Before midnight the Duddoe rendezvous had vanished into the night. There were a few rumors of further Royalist gatherings in the next few days, but effectively the rising in the North was over before it had even begun.[23]

The midland Royalists achieved no more on March 8 than those in the North, and the region shows no sign of anything like the same unity of command. In the south Midlands, Royalist hopes were concentrated on Warwick castle and Worcester, where Lord Windsor and Col. Samuel Sandys were the leaders. Windsor had fought in the war and compounded, but in the 1650's he was less interested in politics than in a scheme to build locks in the River Salwarpe. Sandys had played an outstanding part in the first civil war, and was imprisoned in 1651. Neither he nor Windsor showed much energy this time. There were reports that Sandys was in London in the autumn to meet with Sir John Packington, Norwood, and other dangerous characters in a chamber "neare the waterside," but whatever progress had been made in Worcestershire came to nothing with the arrest of Norwood, Packington, and the Littletons in January 1655. There were a few meetings of Cavaliers in the county in March, but no disturbances. In Gloucestershire there were vague hopes of Lord Chandos, but he died in February 1655, and his successor, his brother, was inactive. Warwick was another disappointment. The Action party's promise that the castle would be secured was not followed by any evidence of preparations. Major Creed, the local Army commander, sent a troop of horse to disperse a football match near the town on

23. *TSP*, *3*, 186, 207–8, 216, 222–23, 228, 230, 262, 336. Add. MS 4156, fols. 164–69. Biographical references as follows: Anderson, *Durham and Northumberland Compositions*, pp. 101–5; Bateson et al., *Northumberland*, *11*, 304. Delaval, ibid., *9*, 170–72; *CSPD, 1655–56*, p. 219. Salkeld, Bateson et al., *Northumberland*, *2*, 130–44. Strother ("Strudder"), ibid., *11*, 134; *13*, 364–65; *Newcastle Society of Antiquaries, Proceedings*, 3d ser. *10* (1921–22), 22, 60; *Durham and Northumberland Compositions*, p. 347. Widdrington, ibid., pp. 376–77.

March 8, and he interrupted a race meeting at Brackley, twenty miles to the southeast, by the same means. If gatherings for football and racing were the best they could do, the Royalists of the south Midlands can scarcely be said to have participated in the rebellion.[24]

The chief man in the Royalist organization in Leicestershire and Staffordshire was Sir Robert Shirley, of Staunton Harold in the former county. Shirley was a young man of twenty-five, too young to have fought in the wars but old enough to have been in trouble in 1648 and 1650, and rash enough to have attempted to evict some of his tenants for supporting Parliament. He was well-connected and wealthy, having inherited a large share of the estates of his uncle, the puritan Earl of Essex. Shirley had not been in direct contact with the exiles before the rising, but Daniel O'Neill mentioned him as one from whom a "good example" was expected. According to one of Thurloe's informants, Shirley was head of a Royalist association in his area; he also "undertooke for Horse & foot & had contributed of his fortune." Rowland Thomas, Norwood's assistant, had been in his employment at Staunton Harold, appeared there briefly in December 1654, and sent a consignment of arms to Mr. Lovett, Shirley's tenant. The Staunton Harold steward's accounts record considerable expenditure for entertainment in December 1654 and again in the following March. The results of all this were negligible, for there was no visible movement in the area on March 8. Shirley's Cavalier neighbors waited placidly on events in other quarters.[25]

The underground movement in Nottinghamshire produced a little more excitement, although here again the outcome was only a repetition of events at Duddoe and Marston Moor. The real leader of the Nottingham Royalists, Lord Byron, took care to stay away from danger, and what little credit there was for organizing a rising in the county goes to other, more energetic men. The most

24. *CCISP*, 2, 383, 392–93 (cipher in Appendix, C). Cl. MS 48, fol. 305. *TSP*, *3*, 212–13; *4*, 485. For Windsor and Sandys see *DNB; LBM*, p. 19 nn.; and *CSPD*, *1651*, pp. 157, 203. For Chandos, above, p. 35, and C. H. Firth, *The House of Lords during the Civil War* (London, 1910), pp. 233–34.

25. E. P. Shirley, *Stemmata Shirleiana* (2d ed. London, 1873), pp. 142–59, especially p. 146. *NP*, 2, 218. *TSP*, *3*, 89, 95. Rawl. MS A 42, pp. 191–92.

interesting of them was Sir George Savile, the future Marquis of Halifax. In 1655 Savile had not matured into the dignified apostle of moderation that he was afterward to become: a few years later Evelyn still thought him "a little too prompt, and daring." He was too young to have served in the civil wars, but his father had fought resolutely under Newcastle, and his mother's passionate loyalism had been the inspiration of notable Royalist resistances at Sheffield and Pontefract. Besides his mother's example, it is tempting to attribute some of Savile's enthusiasm to the influence of his old tutor, Charles Davison, who was deeply involved in this area. Rufford Abbey, the Savile seat in Sherwood, sheltered many Royalist agents before the rising, and according to one of the servants arms were stored there under a false floor. Another center of conspiracy was Thurgarton, between Rufford and Nottingham, where the substantial Sir Roger Cooper and his sons held a series of surreptitious meetings during the same period. Among the Coopers' visitors were Major John Scott; Gregory and Thomas Paulden, two of Lady Savile's old heroes of Pontefract; Penistone Whalley, the Royalist nephew of Cromwell's colonel; and Anthony Gilby of Everton, in later years Andrew Marvell's colleague as MP for Hull.

Rufford was the scene of the main rendezvous of the Nottingham Royalists on the night of the 8th. Savile was discreetly absent in London, but nearly forty horses were kept saddled all night, one of the servants rode madly through the countryside rounding up supporters, and during the evening John Cooper arrived with a cartload of arms. He told the servants, aptly as it turned out, that "he could not tell what they must do with these things." William Coventry, Savile's uncle, arrived post haste from London, where he had been plotting with Norwood and others of the Action party. Davison was also much in evidence. Altogether some 200 men collected on the green near the abbey, but there was much confusion and indecision. The conspirators waited without instructions until a rumor spread that the design in Yorkshire had been abandoned and that they were betrayed: Penistone Whalley, who had not appeared, was suspected. The meeting immediately broke up in disorder. Some threw their arms into a pond, but one of the cooler heads persuaded them not to dispose of the whole cartload, and its contents were found a few days later in a barn. Cromwell's local commander was happy to find "none but broken marchants" in the business, but he contrived to run Cecil Cooper and Major Scott to earth within a few days. The others escaped for the time being, some to London, some into hiding within the county; Gilby's wife took the precaution of concealing the silver in case the soldiers came.[26]

The affair on the Welsh border had a depressingly similar conclusion. The original plan had been for the Cheshire and Shropshire Royalists to seize the most important towns and garrisons: Chester, Shrewsbury, Ludlow, Denbigh. The groundwork was laid by Nicholas Armorer in the spring of 1654, in his talks with Sir Vincent Corbet and Colonel Scriven. Another important man whose support was required was Francis, Lord Newport of High Ercall. His attitude, as in 1651, was doubtful; but his brother Andrew was active, and Armorer, who was well known at High Ercall through his wartime governorship, passed on his assurances of loyalty in August 1654. In the end Lord Newport followed the example of the other Royalist peers and did not embroil himself; he was seen, however, at some suspicious hunting parties in February and early March. Sir Vincent Corbet seems to have lost his earlier enthusiasm, and was conveniently absent from the district on March 8. Scriven was still engaged, but the Shrewsbury command had now passed to Sir Thomas Harris of Boreatton, a young man of twenty-six. Harris had been enlisting supporters as far back as the summer of 1654, and in the final stages he showed energy and determination. He collected arms and horses, bullied neighbors into promising to turn out, and sheltered agents from London. After Harris, the most active local officer was Sir Arthur Blayney of Tregynon, Montgomery, a survivor of the Harlech garrison, the last to surren-

26. *TSP, 3,* 222, 228–29, 240–42, 263–64; *4,* 484, 598–99; *7,* 263–64, 301–3. Cl. MS 49, fol. 258. *Perfect Proceedings,* No. 285. *Perfect Diurnal,* No. 276. See also Wood, *Notts. in the Civil War,* pp. 166–69, and H. C. Foxcroft, *Life and Letters of Sir George Savile, Bart. First Marquis of Halifax* (London, 1898), *1,* 23–25. Foxcroft suggests that Coventry may have been at Rufford to keep his nephew out of trouble, but this is unlikely in view of Coventry's earlier contact with the London conspirators. For the Coopers see *LBM,* p. 16 n., and *CCC,* pp. 1324–25. For Gilby, ibid., p. 2632, and *LBM,* p. 169 n. Evelyn's comment on Savile is in *Evelyn,* ed. de Beer, *3,* 337.

der at the end of the first civil war. Blayney's responsibility was an attempt on Chirk castle: a likely target even though its owner, old Sir Thomas Myddelton, had disappointed the invaders of 1651. According to rumor, Myddelton's son promised to open the castle gates, and to join the rising if it prospered. Another of Harris' lieutenants, Ralph Kynaston of Pentrehelin, had the job of raising men for the attack on Shrewsbury.

Nothing happened at Ludlow, but the Shrewsbury conspirators were probably closer to immediate success on March 8 than any of the Royalists elsewhere. Mackworth, the Governor, had only twenty men under his command, and although a troop of horse was being sent from Hereford to reinforce him and a militia regiment being raised in Shropshire, Mackworth could not count on them until the last minute. Meanwhile, Kynaston was enlisting the disaffected riff-raff of the district, using a Llandrinio alehouse as his headquarters. The original plan for the surprise of Shrewsbury had the merit of simplicity. Six conspirators, two of them disguised as women, were to enter the castle during the afternoon on the pretext of sight-seeing, and then seize the gatehouse while their friends rushed from nearby taverns to support them. This scheme was abandoned the day before it was to be effected, when Mackworth received a modest reinforcement of fifty of the local militia. It was now necessary to rely on a concerted attack by the combined forces of Harris and Kynaston. On the 8th, Harris, Scriven, and the other leaders made final plans at Boreatton, and Kynaston's troop assembled at Llanymynech near the Montgomery border, on the usual thin pretext of a wedding party.

Mackworth had already been given general warning from London, and during the morning he received detailed information of the local plot. He sent twenty men to Boreatton to arrest Harris; they made a rich haul of arms which Harris had recently acquired from London, and found a score of horses ready saddled in the stables. Mackworth also sent hasty warning to Myddelton at Chirk, and alerted the local forces to prevent Kynaston and the Montgomery men advancing into Shropshire. Blayney galloped off to warn Kynaston, who "thereupon dissrobed himselfe putting off his bootes cloak & armes & put on his night cappe." In spite of this undignified haste, Kynaston at least retained enough presence of mind to pass the word around that the design was abandoned. The Llanymynech gathering, perhaps eighty strong at the time the alarm was given, rapidly dispersed. Mackworth's troop of horse arrived from Hereford during the uproar, and Myddelton cleared himself with the government by announcing his intention of defending Chirk.[27]

Lancashire was yet another county that was undisturbed. James Halsall's brother Edward, the Ascham assassin, had been nursing a plot against Liverpool, but it was frustrated in January by the arrival of the troops from Ireland.[28] In Cheshire there was much talk, but no action. The leaders were the Presbyterian John Booth, Col. Randal Egerton of Betley, Staffordshire, and Col. Robert Werden; the plan, a vague scheme to seize Chester castle. Werden's presence ought to have been sufficient warning to the others to keep away from it. A few years earlier, Thomas Scot had regarded him as one of his most valuable informers, because of his close connections with the Duke of York. Although the other Royalists knew nothing definite about this, they guessed enough to have a healthy distrust of Werden. It is just possible that Werden was a sincere Royalist all along, and that he entered Scot's service only to mislead him and to secure his own position so that he could go on conspiring. If so, it was at the cost of losing the confidence of many of his fellow Cavaliers. His conduct after the rising suggests, as we shall see, that he gave far more information than would have been necessary if his motives had been entirely pure.

The design against Chester castle was first promoted by John Stephens when he passed through the city after his visit to Mons. Later there were meetings of the local Royalists to advance it, including one at an alehouse near Betley, attended by Egerton, Sir

27. *CCISP*, 2, 335–36, 383 (MS 48, fols. 122, 326), 392 (cipher in Appendix, C). Cl. MS 48, fol. 305. *TSP*, 3, 202, 207–11, 214–20, 226, 229–30, 244–45, 267–72, 282–91, 316–21, 340–42, 353–55, 676–78; Rawl. MS A 12, pp. 448–51. For the Newports see *DNB;* Keeler, pp. 284–85; Clarendon, *History*, Bk. VI, § 66; and *Shropshire Archaeological Society, Transactions*, 2d ser. *12* (1900), 1–38. For Blayney, ibid., 3d ser. *10* (1910), 91 n. For Harris, *CCC*, p. 2027, and G.E.C., *Baronetage, 1,* 216.

28. *CCISP, 3,* 16.

Thomas Armstrong's son, and Sir Robert Shirley. John Booth was in London when O'Neill and Rochester were there, but returned to Chester a few days before the rising. He found much confusion among the conspirators. Werden was pessimistic, and suggested that the decision to rise was premature. Booth's reply bears the stamp of desperation: "It could not be helped, soe many in ye work were ingaged yt it would be discovered." The "many," it might be noted, did not include Booth's nephew, Sir George, or any other leading Presbyterians. On March 4 Booth and Werden sent a few men to reconnoiter the castle; they found unusually strong guards posted, and no hope of a surprise. At the very place selected for putting up a ladder, they heard a sentinel "walk and cough." Werden was "very much startled" at this, and sent them to try again, but all they could hear was the tramp of the sentries' feet in the darkness. On the 5th the plot was called off. The Chester Royalists went home and uneasily awaited the summons of the investigating authorities. With Werden in their midst it was not likely to be long delayed. He was arrested and examined at Chester, but Scot quickly moved Thurloe for his release. It was granted, and Werden immediately went off on a secret mission to Holland, obviously with Thurloe's connivance. At some time either before or just after this journey he was examined about the business at Chester, and as Scot had forecast, proved to be quite forthcoming. Although his relations with Thurloe were less intimate than they had been with Scot, a year later he was still corresponding with him, passing on a letter from another Royalist. It is not surprising that the Cheshire Cavaliers made such a poor showing.[29]

Compared with all these instances of futility and betrayal, the rising in the West Country, however miserable its outcome, at least produced the firing of a few shots. Even here, though, the disturbance made by Penruddock, Wagstaffe, and their little troop during

---

29. *CSPD, 1655*, pp. 328, 597. *ClSP, 3*, 246. *CClSP, 2*, 218, 361; *3*, 152. *NP, 2*, 218, 222, 294–95, 307. *TSP, 3*, 216–17, 223, 337, 344, 348, 350, 359, 429, 676–77, 682, 701; *4*, 10, 245, 315–16, 574. "Scot's Account," *EHR, 12*, 119. *DNB* (Werden). Firth's estimate of Werden (*EHR, 4*, 531–32) is too generous. The case against him is strengthened if the detailed information in Rawl. MS A 42, pp. 191–93, comes from Werden, as it almost certainly does. The Catalogue for no apparent reason identifies the source as Stephens.

three days of hard riding, was a ridiculous shadow of the Action party's ambitious preliminary design. The original intention was a resurrection of something like the Western Association. Beauchamp, its former leader, was dead, and his father Hertford too old and wary to commit himself, but even without the Seymours there were plenty of hands willing to grasp the leadership. In Devon and Cornwall, Grenville, Pollard, and the Arundells had their plan to secure Pendennis castle and Plymouth. Much was also expected from the Wyndhams in Somerset, but their arrest and that of Grenville after the premature disclosure of the Somerset design in February, seriously restricted the area of possible action. In the end the three counties played almost no part in the Penruddock affair.[30]

The region around Salisbury provides a notable contrast. In both Wiltshire and Dorset there were the usual Cavalier stirrings in the months before the rising. With a national organization to support them, they aroused a far wider circle than the handful who had been drawn into Phelips' feeble venture in 1653. Some of Phelips' old friends were still active, among them Richard Thornbury of Compton Chamberlayne. More prominent, and the real leader in Wiltshire, was Thornbury's neighbor, who has given his name to the rising. Col. John Penruddock was a country gentleman of moderate estate; a serious and sober man, responsible enough to draw up a statement of his liabilities four months before the rebellion, to hope that "God will so bless me that I shall be able to go through this great trouble," and to be quietly aware of the consequences of failure. The other Wiltshire leaders included Hugh Grove of Chisenbury, and Col. Thomas Mompesson of Salisbury. Both were men of substance, though hardly of the first rank: typical of the class to which the Action party's desperate loyalism had most appeal. The most energetic of the lesser agents was Richard Pile, the King's surgeon and a former agent of the Western Association. In the autumn of 1654, under the direction of Secretary Nicholas, he was enlisting supporters for the rising, and John Chase, an apothecary in Covent Garden, provided him with a convenient London headquarters. Pile was thus the Wiltshire party's main

30. For the few signs of activity see *CSPD, 1655*, pp. 237–38; *CClSP, 3*, 17, 19, 314.

channel of communication with the leaders in London and abroad.[31]

Preparations in Wiltshire and Dorset went merrily forward during the winter. There were meetings at Compton Chamberlayne, and at the King's Arms in Salisbury, where the Royalist host, Henry Hewitt, was tenant to Mompesson's father. Local gentry held week-long hunting parties, and as a prying official noted in January, the Cavaliers "kept great christmases after the usuall time with sets of fidlers." There was the strong presumption that the music and the jollification had a seditious accompaniment. The Wiltshire plot seemed so promising that O'Neill and Rochester decided to supply Penruddock with an experienced military adviser. Wagstaffe was duly sent down to take charge of what seemed a well-founded scheme to march into Hampshire on March 8, and make a descent on Winchester, where the judges of assize, an attractive symbol of the Protector's hateful authority, would be in session. The news that a troop of horse had arrived in Winchester induced a mood of greater caution; but as the judges were moving to the less strongly defended Salisbury to begin the assizes on Monday the 12th, it was enough to change only the location and timing of the plan. Sir Henry Moore of Fawley was to lead a diversionary attack on a detachment of horse at Marlborough; as this was the only other military force nearer than Bristol, Wagstaffe and Penruddock had a reasonable chance of being able to assemble their party undisturbed.[32]

And so, three days late and at only one of the half-dozen projected centers, the Royalist rising began. During Sunday night and in the small hours of Monday morning, three parties of horse joined forces a few miles west of Salisbury and rode into the city before daybreak. Salisbury awoke to find itself in the hands of a gang of rebels: jubilant Royalists in the market place, guards at every inn, horses being commandeered, and prisoners celebrating their re-

31. *TSP*, *3*, 343–44, 401, 429. *CSPD*, *1655*, p. 99. Egerton MS 2556, fols. 19–21. Penruddock as quoted by Woolrych, p. 12.

32. *TSP*, *3*, 122, 295, 315, 330, 630. For the details of the Wiltshire rising I have generally followed Mr. Woolrych's pamphlet. For Hewitt see *Wilts. Archaeological Magazine*, *26* (1892), 366; for Moore, G.E.C., *Baronetage*, *2*, 19, and *CCC*, p. 2984.

lease from jail by enlisting under their deliverers. The High Sheriff and the judges were arrested in their beds, and only Penruddock's intervention saved them from being hanged without further argument. However, the Sheriff received some rough treatment when he refused to proclaim Charles II. The proclamation was made by one of the rebels, and the others spent the early morning happily enough: burning the judges' commissions, arming the jailbirds, and trying not very successfully to obtain recruits from the more respectable townspeople. About eight o'clock Wagstaffe led his forces out of the city, taking the Sheriff, still in his nightshirt, as a hostage.

Wagstaffe now had about 400 men, divided into three troops under Penruddock, Grove, and a Surrey gentleman named Francis Jones. The next move was a sweep through Dorset and the counties to the west, to rally more recruits to the colors, and to keep away from the Cromwellian forces that would inevitably come scurrying from Chichester and Bristol once the news was out. These tactics were not entirely unintelligent, but Wagstaffe's chances would have been improved if he had waited long enough for supporters from the northern part of the county to reach him. Sir Henry Moore, for example, had been meeting with Lord Sandys and some others at Ludgershall, fifteen miles northeast of Salisbury, on the usual excuse of a hunting party. The projected attack on the army detachment at Marlborough had to be given up, but Moore's men might have joined Penruddock if they had had time. Wagstaffe's hasty exit from Salisbury was indeed a principal cause of the shortage of recruits; as Clarendon complained, those from the east of the city "being angry for their leaving Salisbury, would not follow, but scattered themselves." [33]

The end was inevitable. The rebels' march quickly became a flight from forces closing in on all sides. News of the rising had reached London on Monday night, and Cromwell immediately sent Disbrowe to take command as Major General of the West. By the time Disbrowe arrived, Boteler had marched his horse from Bristol to Salisbury, and set off in pursuit of Wagstaffe. Meanwhile, militia forces were taking the field at Exeter, Bristol, and Taunton, where

33. Clarendon, *History*, Bk. XIV, § 134. *TSP*, *3*, 309, 315, 648–49.

only an absurd dispute over precedence prevented an overwhelming force taking Wagstaffe in the flank. On Wednesday, March 14, while Wagstaffe's dwindling company plodded wearily into Devonshire, a troop under Capt. Unton Croke set out from Exeter to intercept. Croke had only sixty men, but they were enough. Wagstaffe halted for the night at South Molton, on the edge of Exmoor, a few miles from the house of the leader of the conspiracy in Devon, Sir Hugh Pollard of King's Nympton. If Wagstaffe expected last-minute assistance from Pollard, he was disappointed. Croke reached South Molton about ten o'clock, and the last flickerings of the Action party's general rising were extinguished in some desultory street fighting. There were few casualties in the darkness, none of them fatal, and Penruddock quickly put an end to it by accepting Croke's offer of quarter. Wagstaffe had already slipped away into the night.

Before continuing with an outline of the dismal aftermath of the March rising, it is worth interrupting the narrative for a brief discussion of the reasons for this pathetic record of failure and disaster. It is, of course, easy to see that even if the rising had been perfectly planned and executed, the conditions of 1655 would still have made success by an isolated Royalist party unattainable. Left-wing opposition to Cromwell in the Army, rumblings of discontent from republicans both in and out of Parliament, and the sullen neutrality of the Presbyterians were not enough to counterbalance the general acquiescence in the Protectorate's promise of stability. All this may be true; yet it is still relevant to inquire why the affair collapsed so ignominiously. The chorus of angry recriminations, the assiduous search for scapegoats, and the multitude of excuses offered by the survivors show that Royalists both in England and abroad took a lively interest in the question and were hopeful of drawing useful lessons for the future.

The most obvious conclusion is that the Royalists were entirely incompetent in both strategy and tactics. "The truth is," said Clarendon of Penruddock's venture, "they did nothing resolutely after their first action." Yet compared with the others, Penruddock's was an elaborate military operation. For a general rising, the Action party's preparations were disastrously inadequate.

Liaison between the widely separated centers of conspiracy frequently broke down. The premature assembly in Wiltshire shows that news of even such an important decision as a change of date could somehow fail to reach the rank and file. There were bewildering uncertainties and duplications of command. The agent Richard Hopton later reported that in the West "manie were disordered" by this, and Sir Miles Hobart, the Norfolk leader, made similar complaints. Thanks no doubt to the Sealed Knot, conditions were particularly bad in this area: Thomas Ross heard that in Norfolk "the principal persons were only instructed by public rumour." In spite of the Action party's determination to move quickly, there had been several postponements: Wagstaffe and Armorer both agreed with Robert Walters that this explained many of the defections.[34] Finally, the limited financial resources available not only meant that important business was often left undone but also led to many acrimonious complaints by agents who were not paid. Poor James Halsall, who was supposed to look after the other agents' financial needs, inevitably aroused much criticism. Among other cases, we find Edward Grey grumbling about Halsall's tightfistedness in December 1654. With so many hungry mouths to fill, the lot of a Royalist financial agent was not a happy one.[35]

Against this background of disorganization and incompetence must be set the solid strength and efficiency of the government's countermeasures. Although the information given by spies like Bampfield was neither complete nor accurate, Thurloe showed his usual skill in evaluating it, and in deciding that Royalist action was probable in the early part of the year. Through his agents in the London underworld, Thurloe broke into Norwood's armscollecting gang, and from that moment the unraveling of the conspiracy required only time and patience. The Royalists were never famous for their security precautions; in a mass conspiracy absolute secrecy was impossible. There was a half-hearted attempt in the early stages to see that each plotter should know the names of only

34. Clarendon, *History*, Bk. XIV, § 134. *TSP*, *3*, 723. *CSPD*, *1655*, pp. 245–46; *1655–56*, p. 133. *NP*, *2*, 251, 260. *CClSP*, *2*, 318 (MS 48, fol. 5); *3*, 122 (MS 51, fol. 228).

35. *NP*, *2*, 327. *CClSP*, *3*, 5 ("Moore" is Halsall). Cl. MS 50, fol. 72.

one or two of his associates, but although admirable in theory, this was rarely followed in practice. When the rising occurred, the government was prepared for it. A few warnings to garrison commanders, a few troop movements and orders to the militia, and it was stamped out before it could come to a head.

This glaring contrast between watchful, intelligent power on the one side and extreme tactical incapacity on the other does not, however, penetrate to the more fundamental reasons for the Royalist failure in March 1655. Two such reasons may be advanced: first, the Action party's failure to enlist the aid of other opposition groups; and second, the fact that nothing like the full strength of the Royalist party was mobilized. To the first point, it may be objected that such a coalition would have contradicted Hyde's policy of watchful waiting, of refusing to compromise to gain allies who must eventually be driven over to the King's side by the logic of events. This is undoubtedly true, and Hyde's resistance to any repetition of the errors of 1648 and 1651 was intelligible, yet it does not alter the fact that it made immediate success, in 1655, impossible. Hyde, the Sealed Knot, and the Action party all agreed that Presbyterian assistance was desirable, and the last-named group made serious efforts to obtain it; yet all refused to offer suitable concessions. Even the limited discussions that were held, Sir George Radcliffe told Ormond, offended many "who were loth to see that the King gives still so much countenance to the Presbyterian interest." [36] The few former Presbyterians like Willoughby and John Booth who took some part in the planning were not enthusiastic, and the majority of their friends remained conspicuously aloof.

The second underlying reason for the March defeats, the Action party's failure to enlist more than a minority of the Cavalier party, was largely a result of the divided command. The Sealed Knot obstructed the preparations until overruled from Cologne at the eleventh hour. The King, indeed, followed the worst possible policy, neither canceling the rising nor ordering the Knot to support it in the firm language that would have been the last hope (and even then a faint one) of obtaining a satisfactory turnout.

36. Carte, *Papers*, 2, 77.

Unfairly, but not surprisingly, the Knot received a large share of the blame for the catastrophe, and distorted memories of its attitude in 1655 long continued to circulate. Four years afterward, John Mordaunt feared that in similar circumstances they would "serve us as they did poor Penrudduc at Salisbury; engage us to rise and then never second us, but sit still, courting their fortune." [37] The result of the Knot's opposition was that the action was confined almost entirely to Royalists of second rank. In spite of Compton's guarded promise to O'Neill, not one of the six members appeared in arms, and there was no visible movement in East Anglia, the chief center of their influence. Belasyse, instead of throwing his weight behind the Yorkshire rising, stayed quietly in London and was arrested on March 9.[38] The Knot's aristocratic friends and relatives also stood still; the fact that many peers were arrested during the summer is no proof of their complicity in March. Lord Byron, one of the few peers who can be remotely connected with the Action party leaders, was nowhere in evidence on March 8. A few other noblemen, such as Lords Herbert and Newport in Shropshire, Windsor in Worcestershire, and Sandys in Hampshire, were present at suspicious hunting parties at about the time of the rising, but all managed to avoid committing themselves. The men of wealth and power took the Knot's advice and awaited events.

There is nothing surprising in this wariness by the great lords. The counsel sent to the King by Hertford and Southampton two years before, "to sit still, and expect a reasonable revolution, without making any unadvised attempt," still represented the general opinion.[39] The melancholy Southampton had not even been mentioned in the Action party's correspondence. Hertford was a greater disappointment: more had been expected of him in spite of Beauchamp's recent death. Penruddock and his Wiltshire friends were well aware of the importance of a firm assurance of support from the head of the Seymour clan, and in the winter before the rising there were busy negotiations with people in Hertford's immediate circle. The go-betweens included Henry Seymour; Penruddock's

37. HMC, *10th Report*, Appendix 6, p. 210.
38. *Perfect Proceedings*, No. 285. *NP*, 2, 243.
39. Clarendon, *Con.*, § 22.

uncle, Stephen Bowman; and Hertford's chaplain, who was often seen at Compton Chamberlayne. The Wiltshire leaders were all glibly confident of Hertford's adherence; but it was wishful thinking. Hertford confined his relations with Penruddock to the indirect contacts of members of his household. The Seymours might cautiously encourage the design from a distance, but without their open appearance the Wiltshire rebels could hardly claim to have enrolled the real strength of Cavalier sentiment in the county. The absence of "considerable men," "men of condition," was widely lamented as news of the debacle trickled through to the Continent.[40]

The abstention of the Royalist lords was made even more serious by the continued repercussions of the factious squabbles at the exiled Court. Memories of the petty interventions of the Louvre and the Swordsmen formed part of the standard repertoire of excuses for fugitives like Wagstaffe and Armorer. Several important exiles were excluded from the plot. Sir John Marlay, the former Governor of Newcastle, was refused a share in the preparations and was understandably furious with Hyde in consequence. The worst example of Court interference was the ban on Langdale's employment. No doubt Hyde's desire to avoid the appearance of a Catholic design was realistic; but Langdale's influence in Yorkshire was thought by many to outweigh objections to his religion. Langdale's absence "made many fail to come to the rendezvous," Manning told Thurloe; and a Royalist officer agreed that "a great part of the late misfortune was by not imploying him." [41]

Many of those who did appear at the head of the rising were lacking not only in prestige and interest but also in character and ability. Rochester, for all his good nature, was not universally popular, and his Presbyterian inclinations were widely criticized. The talents of his convivial friend Wagstaffe were also better suited

40. *CClSP*, *2*, 440; Seymour's postscript obviously alludes to Hertford. *TSP*, *3*, 295, 315, 330, 344, 428. *NP*, *2*, 243, 253. For the Bowmans see *Notes and Queries*, *196* (1951), 56–59; and *Wilts. Archaeological Magazine*, *26*, 347.

41. *NP*, *3*, 12, 88. *CClSP*, *2*, 424, 435; *3*, 7. Egerton MS 2535, fols. 109, 122. *CSPD*, *1655*, pp. 216, 221, 245–46. For Marlay see Bean, *Northern MP's*, p. 586.

to the tavern than the battlefield. Few of the Action party's leaders were men of real stature, and they included at least one drunkard (Thornhill), and one reckless adventurer (Armstrong). Petty jealousies between local leaders contributed to the party's ineffectiveness. In the West, Sir John Grenville had his local enemies, inspired partly by envy at his having saved his estates on the Articles of Scilly. Sir Miles Hobart, the chief agent in Norfolk, was denounced for being "devoted to his ease and a soft kinde of life." [42]

Leadership, morale, unity, organization—all these were factors at least partly under the Royalists' control, and on which they might have made a better showing. Yet the inescapable conclusion remains that in March 1655 the general opinion of the nation, even of many secretly attached to the cause of monarchy, preferred stability to further bloodshed. Out of the many who gave vague assurances of sympathy, only a tiny fraction appeared on the day of battle. Although the Sealed Knot must bear some responsibility for the divided command, it was right to oppose an ill-prepared and premature attempt, which was bound to make the situation of the whole party worse than ever. There were many who blamed the Action party for its rashness. John Ashburnham was of the opinion "that had they sate still one yeare or twoe, [the King] had undoubtedly come to the crowne." [43] The disaster proved, if it proved anything, that Langdale was right in his contention that only a coalition of opposition parties in England or the introduction of a foreign army could restore Charles II. A worse setback for Hyde and his reliance upon the Old Royalists alone could scarcely be imagined. "You would hardly credit how severely the miscarriage of ye busyness reflects upon Sir E.H.," commented Peter Mews (with some satisfaction, for he disliked Hyde). To one of Hyde's much older enemies, Thurloe's pensioner Bampfield, much the same thought occurred: "And here is an end of all mr. Chan's well-conducted designes; and for the present must be a suspension of others." [44] The Royalist party had once more collapsed in ruins.

42. *NP*, *2*, 219, 251, 267. Egerton MS 2535, fol. 48. Carte, *Papers*, *2*, 77. *CClSP*, *3*, 43. *CSPD*, *1655–56*, p. 133.

43. *TSP*, *3*, 548; cf. Clarendon, *Con.*, § 28.

44. *NP*, *2*, 267; *3*, 54. Egerton MS 2535, fol. 110. *ClSP*, *3*, 277. *TSP*, *3*, 87. For Mews' relations with Hyde see *NP*, *2*, 175–76.

8. The Major Generals

"THIS MONTH HETHERTO hath been very full of rumors of warrs," Dr. Brian Duppa noted at the end of March 1655. "Every tongue hath been full of them, and every eare hath been open to receave them; but as farr as I see," he went on unconcernedly, "they vanish as vapors use to do . . . about this time of the year." [1] The Bishop's refusal to be agitated by the rising's depressing outcome was shared by many Royalists not normally capable of his philosophic detachment. Unfortunately for the passive majority (Duppa's friend Sir Justinian among them), it soon became clear that innocence in March provided no exemption from the punitive measures of a government determined to visit the sins of the activists upon the whole party. The roundup of the rising's ringleaders in the spring was followed by sweeping arrests during the summer, as further evidence of the Royalists' attachment to conspiracy was accumulated by Thurloe. Then came the highest point of Cromwellian military rule: the establishment of the Major Generals and the new militia, and the discriminatory taxation by which Royalists alone were made to pay for them.

The vigilant efficiency of the new system made concerted Royalist action out of the question. The only valid policy was to lie low and hope for better days, but as usual there were many who had not the patience or the imagination to do so. Illusory short cuts like the

1. *Duppa-Isham Corr.,* p. 110.

Leveller alliance and the murder of the Protector were eagerly canvassed. Even Hyde and Ormond, who had previously dismissed assassination as unacceptable, were now discussing it as a rational alternative to mass conspiracy, and encouraging its protagonists to risk their necks. Apart from such cloak-and-dagger escapades, there was little to be done while the leaders of the Royalist party were either in prison or subjected to close supervision by the Major Generals.

The arrests occurred in two stages. In the first, which occupied March and April, the authorities were mainly concerned with those directly implicated in the rising. Many of the leaders were taken on March 8 or the day following. Others, including Peyton and Armstrong, were picked up in the course of the next month. Disbrowe, in charge of operations in the West, sent up a list of 139 prisoners: he had added a good many suspects to those taken in arms at South Molton, but had been restrained in dealing with "the meaner sort" by the shortage of jail accommodation.[2] The government at first displayed comparative leniency. Although many suspects were kept in prison without trial, it was only in the West that blood was shed. The expedient of an emergency High Court of Justice had been the general rule for dealing with seditious outbreaks under both the Commonwealth and the Protectorate. This time, however, the formality of trial by jury was retained. Two Commissions of Oyer and Terminer were issued for the western and northern counties, and if verdicts favorable to the state could be secured only by packing the juries with the "honest and well-affected," that was nothing unusual in the seventeenth century. In the western circuit, thirty-eight of Disbrowe's prisoners were sentenced to death, but less than fifteen, including Penruddock and Grove, were executed. Some of those acquitted were held in jail, and many were later transported to Barbados. Other, more prominent prisoners were also sentenced to transportation: Edward Grey, Christopher Gardiner, and Rowland Thomas among them. Grey's sentence was relaxed on the plea of ill health, and Gardiner and Thomas were back in Europe before

2. For the arrests in March and April see the newspapers for those months (and selections in *Cromwelliana*, pp. 152–53); also *Clarke Papers*, *3*, 27–43, and *TSP*, *3*, 208 ff.

the end of 1656, gazing wistfully across the water at Dover cliffs. The northern commission soon ran into difficulties. The circuit judges had doubts about the constitutionality of Cromwell's treason ordinance and had to be dismissed. Their successors imposed a few fines for riot or misdemeanor, and released most of the prisoners on bail.[3]

Some of the leaders, meanwhile, had eluded Thurloe's net. The most melodramatic escape was, characteristically, that of the carefree Rochester. Accompanied by the faithful Armorer and two servants, and with the aid of his usual good luck and timing, the beaten commander headed for London through a countryside teeming with eager Protectorate officials. At Aylesbury he and Armorer found a tolerable inn—Rochester "departed very unwillingly from all places where there was good eating and drinking"— but their rustic disguises were not convincing. An inquisitive magistrate, appropriately named Henn, was soon at the inn seeking explanations, and they were committed to the care of the constable and the innkeeper. In the magistrate's absence, Rochester bribed the innkeeper, and during the night the fugitives trotted off down the London road. The affair exhibits the charmingly Dogberrian character of the Aylesbury police authorities. Rochester next tried the old escape route of 1651, going into Sussex and finding Gunter and Francis Mansel once again ready to oblige with a ship. It leaked, and Rochester had to wait in London for a few more weeks. Eventually, in June, both he and Armorer reached The Hague, where Daniel O'Neill had already arrived. Wagstaffe followed, to Antwerp, a month later.[4]

By this time the second phase of the arrests had begun. Behind this abrupt reversal of his previous search for "settlement" was the Protector's increasing conviction that the Cavaliers were irreconcilable, that safety lay only in repression, and that the puritan commonwealth could be established only by reliance on the Army. The

3. Gardiner, *C&P*, *3*, 291–92, 298–99, 308–9, 338–39. Woolrych, pp. 21–22. *TSP*, *3*, 453–54; *4*, 39; *7*, 639. *Burton*, *4*, 255–62. Bell, 2, 138–39. HMC, *7th Report*, Appendix, p. 117.

4. Clarendon, *History*, Bk. XIV, §§ 135–36. *TSP*, *1*, 695; *3*, 281–82, 335–39, 659; *7*, 109. *CSPD*, *1655*, pp. 212, 245. HMC, *Ormonde*, new ser. *1*, 318. *CClSP*, *3*, 36. *NP*, 2, 327–28. Egerton MS 2535, fols. 161, 281.

162   *Royalist Conspiracy*

Royalists had been offered the chance of conformity; to Cromwell's olive branch they had responded with rebellion. To distinguish between active and inactive Royalists in such circumstances would be academic: the evidence collected by the Secretary of State showed that all but a negligible minority of Royalists sympathized with the conspirators, even if they did not aid and abet them. Only the fringes of the Royalist network, it seemed, had been exposed when its more extravagant members came to grief with Penruddock.

The information on which this thesis depended came from Thurloe's usual variety of sources: Bampfield, Barkstead's gleanings among the Tower prisoners, agents abroad. One recent acquisition in this last category was the Scotsman Sir John Henderson, who had had an earlier understanding with Cromwell in 1650 but had apparently allowed it to lapse. Henderson came to London to report to Thurloe in November 1654 and in the following March, and was well rewarded on both occasions. He sent a good deal of information of variable quality from Cologne during 1655, much of it obtained from Charles II's untrustworthy Latin Secretary, Peter Massonett.[5] Henderson, however, was of small importance compared with another of Thurloe's new agents: Henry Manning, one of the most dangerous of all the renegades who made spying a profession. Manning was a young man of Roman Catholic family, brought up in the Marquis of Worcester's household. He was wounded, and his father and brother killed, fighting for Charles I. Lack of money drove him out of England, and early in 1655 he came to Cologne, armed with a glib tongue and some impressive (but forged) credentials. He soon made himself acceptable with the good fellows of the Court, Rochester in particular being "ravished" by his conversation. From Rochester and other drinking companions Manning picked up enough gossip about the English Royalists for many months of paid correspondence with Thurloe. His first letter, on March 3, 1655, at once established his value by containing the first exact news Thurloe had received of the King's where-

5. Nickolls, p. 21. *TSP, 1*, 242; *2*, 466–68, 610, 690; *3*, 198, 492–93. Rawl. MS A 24, p. 66. *CCISP, 2*, 240, 381; *3*, 13–16, 22, 29. *NP, 2*, 17. Abbott, *3*, 421–22. SPDI, 95, fols. 192, 227; 102, fol. 204.

abouts since his disappearance from Cologne. Manning's subsequent reports were not always as accurate, but when fact and gossip failed, his fertile imagination was quite capable of inventing his material. He once gave a graphic and detailed account of a Council meeting, complete with whispered conferences between the King and Hyde—a performance the more impressive because it was entirely fictional.[6]

It was through this mixture of fact and fantasy that Cromwell and Thurloe were convinced that fresh trouble was brewing. This was the repeated burden of Manning's letters: the leaders, especially in the Midlands, were only waiting for the present storm to subside. On May 14 he announced that the assassination of the Protector was being seriously discussed. This warning must have reached Thurloe at about the same time as information from a certain Richard Hannam, which seemed to corroborate it. According to Hannam, a group of exiles, including Thomas Howard and the wife of Sir Richard Page, were planning to kill Cromwell with a "stone-bowe made after a very extraordinary manner, & would shoot a bullet of Carbine bignesse about 40 yards with an incredible strength."[7] There was probably no truth in the story, but after Manning's reports Thurloe was taking no chances. On May 21 there was a great search in the Covent Garden district, which Manning had identified as the center of the subversive underworld. This brought in, among others, Lord Byron and the Sealed Knot's secretary, William Rumbold, and it marks the real beginning of the process of securing the leaders, potential or actual, of the entire Royalist party. In June the roundup continued. Early in the month the Earl of Lindsey, Lord Lovelace, and the young Lord Falkland were among a number of leading Cavaliers arrested in Oxfordshire. On the 9th the purge spread back to London: Lord Newport of High Ercall, his brother Andrew, the Presbyterian

6. Clarendon, *History*, Bk. XIV, §§ 138–46. See also Scott, *Travels of the King*, pp. 140–53. Gardiner (*C&P, 3,* 311 and n.) is wrong in saying that Manning's first letter contains no intelligence. Besides the news of the King, it includes aspersions on the Dover authorities and the names of several Royalist agents: *TSP, 3,* 190.

7. *TSP, 3,* 340, 358–59, 384, 428–29. *CClSP, 3,* 37–38 (MS 50, fols. 57–58). There is another paper relating to this scheme in Rawl. MS A 34, pp. 27–29.

Willoughby, and Henry Seymour were the most important of those secured. The London prisons were soon crowded with suspects, and many more were held at provincial centers like Lynn, Exeter, and Worcester. By the end of the summer there were few Cavaliers of any note outside the clutches of Thurloe's officers. The returns, as usual, are incomplete, so no accurate estimate of the total number of arrests is possible; but it must have run into hundreds.[8]

The Sealed Knot's inaction did not save its members from the fate of many other opponents of the insurrection. Belasyse made no effort to escape arrest; after his detention in London in March he returned to Yorkshire, and was again arrested in June. The recent disasters, and perhaps the quarrel with Willys, seem to have destroyed his will to resist. In February 1656 he went abroad, having obtained a pass through his kinsman Lambert, and did not return to England until March 1657. Compton spent the summer away from his Cambridgeshire home. In June he heard that a party of horse had been at the house, and seeing no advantage in resisting the inevitable he got his brother-in-law Tollemache to tell Cromwell that he was in London, and surrendered voluntarily. Willys was imprisoned at Lynn in the same month, Russell and Villiers in London. Loughborough may have escaped—his name does not appear in any extant list of prisoners—but his personal good fortune, if such it was, did not affect the Knot's collapse in the welter of arrests. Ignored and discredited, the Knot again passed out of existence, and there were few who lamented its demise.[9]

With both the Knot and the Action party out of commission, the broken and disorganized remnant of the Royalist party could offer no resistance to the new military regime. The vast majority of the leaders were already secured before the Major Generals took office. Under the "Orders for securing the peace of the Commonwealth,"

8. *TSP, 3,* 521, 537. Rawl. MSS A 27, p. 383; A 34, p. 901. *Clarke Papers, 3,* 43. *CSPD, 1655,* pp. 204, 588. See also newspapers for May 21 to August 30; Gardiner, *C&P, 3,* 311–13; *Duppa-Isham Corr.,* pp. 111–12; and Verney, *Memoirs, 3,* 232–41, 247–48.

9. *Perfect Proceedings,* Nos. 285, 296, 301. *TSP, 3,* 587, 697. *NP, 2,* 243. *CSPD, 1655–56,* p. 578. Add. MS 34,015, fol. 58. *Notes and Queries,* 12th ser. *10* (1922), 123.

their supervision now became the new officials' principal duty.[10]
By this document the Cavaliers were divided into three categories:
those guilty of subversive activity since the establishment of the
Protectorate, who were to be imprisoned or banished, and sequestered; those against whom recent sedition could not be proved, but
who still showed themselves "by their words or actions" to be convinced Royalists, who were to be imprisoned or banished, retaining
their estates; and those who had merely been guilty of delinquency
in the civil wars, who were to be assessed for the Decimation Tax.
With these rules to guide them, the Major Generals could now
release all but the most irreconcilable, who would be included in
the first two categories, taking security for their good behavior.
Those with the most active consciences (Sir Ralph Verney, for example) were reluctant to bind themselves by promises affecting
their future actions, and so were the longest detained. There was,
however, a general discharge of all but the most hardened suspects
before the end of November. Even for those who remained, the
rigors of confinement could sometimes be relaxed, if the right kind
of influence was available. Sir Thomas Peyton was able to make use
of his kinship to Henry Lawrence, President of the Council of
State: in August 1655 he was granted a brief respite from the
Tower, to take the waters at Tunbridge Wells.[11]

Apart from the hard core of prisoners in the Tower, men who
like Peyton were held by order of the Council of State, most of the
Cavaliers were at large again by the end of 1655. They were still
liable to re-arrest under the first and second heads of the "Orders,"
but the Major Generals were allowed plenty of latitude, and not
all of them seriously continued the persecution under the first head.
One who did was Robert Lilburne in Yorkshire. He relentlessly
harried all the leaders of the Marston Moor rendezvous that he

10. A useful study of the system of Major Generals is that by D. W. Rannie,
"Cromwell's Major-Generals," *EHR*, *10* (1895), 471–506. See also Hardacre,
Royalists, pp. 125–31. For the various commissions and instructions see *CSPD,
1655*, passim; *1655–56*, pp. 103–4; Abbott, *3*, 733–34, 839, 844–48; *OPH*, 20,
434–68; *Harleian Miscellany*, *5*, 268; *TSP*, *3*, 486, 701.

11. *CSPD, 1655*, pp. 367–69. *Publicke Intelligencer*, No. 1. Verney, *Memoirs*,
3, 249–53. *Duppa-Isham Corr.*, p. 112 n. Add. MS 44,846.

could lay his hands on (the most notable were Sir Henry Slingsby and Robert Brandling), and in March 1656 confirmed their sentences to indefinite imprisonment and sequestration. In Nottinghamshire Whalley meted out similar treatment to Anthony Gilby, Cecil Cooper, and John Scott. Goffe made a few arrests in Sussex (Henry Bishop was one of the victims), while Worsley initiated but later abandoned proceedings against sixteen suspects in Lancashire. If arrests under the first head were infrequent, those under the second—for "words or actions"—were fewer still. Haynes imprisoned the poet Cleveland at Norwich, Worsley arrested Sir William Neile, and Howard rounded up an unspecified number of suspects at Carlisle. Like the multitude of vagrants and "idle persons" who found their way to prison under the Major Generals' police powers, conspiratorial intentions need not always be ascribed to the victims.[12]

The Royalists' troubles did not end when they came out of jail. The Major Generals were empowered to compel all who had ever been in arms to give in bonds for good behavior, whether they had been imprisoned or not. The enforcement of this provision varied from place to place, but the penalties of forfeiture were an effective brake on any who had violent intentions. A few were goaded into protest or obstruction. The Earl of Southampton was arrested for resisting the order, and Major General Berry had some trouble on this account at Hereford. The bonds were normally limited to a duration of a year or two, but in some cases no definite time limit was imposed. The Earl of Northampton made such a fuss about a bond of this kind that an irate Major General had to arrest him to shut him up.[13] Another persuasive deterrent was the close personal control maintained over the Royalists when at large, by the system of registration outlined in the additional instructions of October 1655. All Royalists as defined by the three heads of the Orders were to obtain the local Major General's permission before they could travel away from home. An office in Fleet Street kept a record of all

12. *TSP*, *4*, 184–85, 213–746 passim; *5*, 33, 185, 187. *CSPD, 1655–56*, pp. 218–19, 317; *1656–57*, pp. 175, 587.

13. *CSPD, 1655*, p. 591; *1655–56*, p. 154. *TSP, 4*, 189, 212, 215, 234, 236, 272, 300, 334–35, 340. For a general discussion see Hardacre, *Royalists*, pp. 128–30.

such changes of address; lists of persons from whom security had been taken; and a file of travelers arriving in London from abroad. How easily these regulations could be avoided it is hard to say. There is no known case of a Royalist being punished for refusing to register, although a few people were reported to Thurloe for not having done so. Most Royalists appear to have conformed peaceably, and the returns record the movements of such active conspirators as Compton, Grenville, Musgrave, and Willys.[14]

While the Major Generals reigned, the Royalists also suffered from many negative restrictions. They were expelled from London by proclamation between July 1655 and the following February, and when the ban was relaxed there were thorough searches in the City for those who had managed to avoid giving security. Special permission was indeed often granted for individuals to stay in London during the prohibition, usually on legal business. At least one well-known Royalist, the Cornishman Jonathan Trelawney, had the temerity to defy the proclamation and appear there openly. Most of the party, however, were more discreet. The restrictions, in spite of their inconsistencies, made conspiracy on the scale of 1654 both physically and psychologically impossible. As Major General Worsley gleefully told Thurloe: "There is hardly a meetinge of three cavaleirs together upon any account, but I am sodainly acquainted with it." [15]

Imprisonment, security, and registration, although repressive enough, were really serious in the long run only for the dedicated adventurers who might have formed the nucleus of a new plot. More damaging for the country gentry at large, and more bitterly resented, was the provision which hit those of wealth and property where it hurt most: in their pockets. Discriminatory taxes levied on defeated enemies were not new in seventeenth-century England; familiarity did not, however, make them easier to bear. Payment, or preferably evasion, of the Decimation Tax became the

14. *CSPD, 1655–56*, p. 129. *TSP, 4*, 293, 742. Add. MSS 19,516, 34,011–17; some of these proceedings of the Major Generals' Office are printed in A. R. Bax, "Suspected Persons in Surrey during the Commonwealth," *Surrey Archaeological Collections, 14* (1899), 164–89.

15. *TSP, 4*, 639. Steele, *Proclamations, 1*, 368, 370. *CSPD, 1655*, pp. 232–33, 395, 594–95, 598–99; *1655–56*, p. 3. Carte, *Papers, 2*, 91–92. *NP, 3*, 37.

overwhelming preoccupation of all but the poorest Royalists during the winter of 1655–56. There were muttered protests, and a few
Cavaliers refused to give particulars of their estates for the assessment. The Earl of Southampton, still obstinate, had to be arrested
before he would comply, and in Lincolnshire Sir John Mounson
was bullied into submission by the quartering of troops in his house.
Rumors of a few other resisters cheered the exiles at The Hague,
but for the most part the Royalists grumbled and paid.[16] The tax
did not weigh equally heavily upon all sections of the party. Exemptions were occasionally granted to those with influence in high
places, which usually meant the nobility. To obtain exemption, a
few Royalists went further than the mild promises not to act against
the state to which they were committed by their bonds. The Cornish Lord Mohun and Sir William Walter of Oxfordshire signed
documents solemnly abjuring the Stuarts and promising to reveal
further plots. Each was allowed to compound for the tax by a lump
sum of £500. Those who succumbed in this way were naturally
unpopular with their former friends: in November 1656 a Cornish
agent described Mohun as a "great enemy." [17]

Considering the relative numbers of the nobility and the rank
and file, only a few lesser Royalists were spared. Discharges were
sometimes given to those who could show that their opposition to
the Parliament had been negligible, and evidence of recent peace-
able behavior was occasionally held to justify exemption. Most
Major Generals received petitions based on this argument with
healthy skepticism. Whalley rejected one from a leading Derbyshire Royalist, John Freschville, with the comment that "at this
time of day you shall have halfe the cavaleeres in England professe
as much as he." In spite of the Major Generals' unanimous opposition, the Council of State was sometimes amenable to individual
petitions. Many Royalists escaped by indirect means, through earlier purchase of their lands by friends and relatives who held them

16. *TSP*, *4*, 190, 208, 234, 240, 324–25, 336–37. *CSPD*, *1655–56*, p. 50. Verney,
Memoirs, *3*, 256–83. *NP*, *3*, 215.

17. *TSP*, *4*, 494, 608–9. *CSPD*, *1655–56*, p. 393. *NP*, *3*, 239. *CClSP*, *3*, 199
(cipher in Appendix, G). For examples of successful applications for exemption see *CSPD*, *1655–56*, pp. 89, 92, 117, 124, 172, 176; *TSP*, *4*, 411, 434, 445,
609.

in trust, thus removing them from the danger of assessment. On the whole, the Major Generals complained, it was the wealthy who escaped payment, but those at the other end of the scale were also exempt. As it happens, the Decimation Tax touched few of the really hardened conspirators, whose estates were mostly below the £100 a year limit. Those liable to the tax, having more to lose, had usually been inclined to prudence.[18]

To determine the full impact of the government of the Major Generals it is necessary to distinguish between long-term and short-term effects. The immediate result was of course to put an absolute stop to united Royalist action. "Wee are asleepe and will continue soe untill you awake us," Richard Pile groaned in the summer of 1656.[19] Yet in the long run the very harshness of the system served to intensify Royalist unity. Not all the Major Generals were blustering tyrants, but there were enough instances of ill-mannered abuse from men like Boteler and Packer for the regime to be remembered only for its overtones of jack-booted militarism. The Protector's Declaration of October 1655 formally renewed the division of the nation into two hostile factions, and to treat the party as irreconcilable was an infallible means of making it so. Hyde pointed out the deduction that all Royalists were bound to draw: "We are without any right or title to any thing we enjoy, and are at your mercy to dispose of us as you please; which is the lowest condition of Traitors." From the republican side, Ludlow denounced both the justice and the expediency of Cromwell's "detestable project." The Royalists were made, he said, "desperate and irreconcilable, they being not able to call any thing their own, whilst by the same rule that he seized one tenth, he might also take away the other nine parts at his pleasure." Indiscriminate punishment hardened Royalist sentiment, and failed to take advantage of the slow change in the party's composition that time was sure to

18. *CSPD, 1655–56*, pp. 212–14, 231–34, 316–18, 338; *1656–57*, pp. 151, 186, 255, 300. *CCC*, p. 1044. *TSP, 4*, 258, 293, 364, 409, 439, 442, 509, 511, 545–46, 550. Rawl. MS A 35, p. 24. For a general discussion see Hardacre, *Royalists*, pp. 125–28.

19. *CCISP, 3*, 220 ("John Cole"). The date of this letter is evidently May 1656: cf. the passages about "Mr. Douce" (the bearer) in Ross' letters to Nicholas, June 2 and July 9, 1656 (*CSPD, 1655–56*, pp. 333, 395).

bring about. Even before Cromwell's death some of those closest to him were convinced that the policy of segregation had been a failure.[20]

All this, however, is to look into the future. To return to more immediate considerations, the repression was completely successful in eliminating whatever danger remained of a repetition of the March rising. In the second half of 1655 and the early months of 1656, Royalist activity was confined to the discussion of futile assassination projects, and more constructively to the old preoccupations of intelligence and financial supplies. Intelligence, although important, was largely a matter of routine. Nicholas Armorer thought he had arranged a correspondence with two "sober and sufficient persons," when he escaped from England in June 1655, but they were not sober or sufficient enough to escape the purge. Roger Whitley, now at Calais, was more fortunate: he was able to forward his correspondent's first report to Cologne in October. By August 1656 he was employing three correspondents in England, paying each of them £100 a year.[21]

For the increasingly desperate exiles, financial assistance was even more important. The unrewarding post of financial agent was assigned to William Rumbold, and his commission was prepared before news of his arrest reached Cologne. Rumbold cheerfully accepted it, but the Tower was not the best place for conducting such business. He had the misfortune to lose £1,000 which Sir Robert Shirley had contributed for the King's service; it was appropriated as payment for a debt allegedly owing by Rumbold's brother. Although Rumbold's commission was not withdrawn, it was necessary to have a financial agent who was less restricted in his movements, and so the experienced James Halsall was sent as a replacement. Halsall duly came to England, only to be arrested in November 1655 for complicity in a plot to murder the Protector. At his examination he asserted, probably truthfully, that he had

20. E.g. Henry Cromwell: *TSP*, 7, 218. See also *A Letter from a True and Lawfull Member of Parliament* (1656), p. 45; cf. *Declaration of His Highness*, p. 38. *Ludlow's Memoirs*, 1, 405.

21. *TSP*, 1, 695. *NP*, 3, 78–79. Egerton MS 2535, fol. 420. *CSPD*, 1656–57, p. 92.

had no success in the financial part of his mission. At last, by the end of 1655, Sir Robert Shirley was given the chief responsibility for the collection of supplies. He too was in the Tower, but seems to have been less constricted by it than was Rumbold; and his wealth, connections, and zealous loyalty were all good qualifications. He met with little encouragement, however, and had to contend with deliberate obstruction as well as with the prevailing apathy. John Cooper, he suspected, had been advising his friends not to subscribe. In July 1656 Shirley reported that he had collected the pathetically small sum of £60, barely enough to cover his messengers' expenses, and to grant £10 to the imprisoned Halsall.[22]

In default of any constructive leadership to unite what remained of the party in England, individual Royalists again took refuge in the idea of cutting the Gordian knot by assassinating the Protector. After the first reports in May that the murder policy was being revived by the exiles, a series of similar warnings reached Thurloe from Henry Manning and other informers.[23] There were actually several different assassination schemes, but none of them embraced more than a handful of Royalists in England, and the inspiration and control usually came from abroad. Only one of the plots got beyond the stage of optimistic discussion. Some, indeed, may have been mere delusions of neurotic informers hopeful of reward, inspired to imaginative imitation by the crop of rumors. Richard Hannam's stone-bow did not come to anything, and the information given by a certain Mr. Greaves on May 23 suffers from a similar lack of corroborative evidence. According to Greaves, Sir Robert Shirley and a number of Cavaliers from the eastern counties were planning to blow up Cromwell, the explosion to be the signal for a new insurrection. Everything we know of Shirley's character makes his participation extremely unlikely.[24]

The disclosures made soon afterward by an interesting adventuress named Diana Gennings were more definite. The lady's ante-

---

22. *CClSP, 3,* 44, 49 (January–April 1656?—see below, p. 185 and n. 12), 89, 111, 142–43, 152, 164, 191–93. *TSP, 4,* 245. Egerton MS 2829, fol. 3 (Rumbold's commission).
23. *TSP, 3,* 429, 591, 617, 659; *4,* 169. Rawl. MS A 26, p. 55.
24. *TSP, 3,* 468. Endorsed as from "M. Greaves": Rawl. MS A 26, p. 312.

cedents are mysterious. She turned up at Antwerp toward the end of May 1655, passing herself off as the widow of a fictitious cousin of the Earl of Derby, recently killed, she said, in a duel. Robert Phelips, with characteristic generosity, took pity on her "afflicted condition," and sheltered her until, to the vast amusement of his friends, she was discovered to be a complete imposter. The Earl of Norwich and the other exiles who regaled each other with the story of Phelips' discomfiture would have found the truth about Lady Gennings less diverting. During her flirtation with Phelips, she overheard much of the gossip of a circle that included Phelips, Major General Massey, the newly returned Rochester, and a "Colonel Brookes," who was none other than Edward Sexby the Leveller. This conglomerate group, Lady Gennings disclosed, agreed to send over four lesser agents to ambush Cromwell on his way to Hampton Court. Sir Francis Vincent, of Stoke D'Abernon, would raise fifty men to cover their retreat, and correspondence about the affair was to be conducted through Chase's in Covent Garden. Armed with this information, Lady Gennings took ship from Dunkirk and reported to Thurloe. The Secretary also acquired a list of prospective adherents of the plot, but does not seem to have taken any special action against them; many had been taken care of earlier in the summer. The plot clearly had no more substantial basis than the ambitious chatter of a few adventurers in the taverns of Antwerp and Brussels.[25]

Only one of the murder plots caused the Protectorate authorities any serious alarm: the business managed by James Halsall, Charles Davison, John Stephens, and the Irishman Richard Talbot, in the autumn of 1655. This was betrayed by Halsall's servant, William Masten. Halsall believed that Masten had received £2,000 for disclosing the plot: he was "very gallant and full of gold." In fact his price was less flattering to Halsall, but it was still temptingly large for a man unused to money. Between November 1655 and the following January, Thurloe's accounts disclose, Masten re-

25. *TSP, 1,* 748–49 (dated by the reference to Talbot and Dongan as traveling companions: cf. *CSPD, 1655,* p. 225). Rawl. MS A 3, pp. 204–5: the list is not endorsed, but the coincidence of many of the names with those in the Gennings information establishes the connection. *NP, 2,* 299–300, 310, 339. For Vincent see G.E.C., *Baronetage, 1,* 158.

ceived £190 in intelligence money. He subsequently served Cromwell as a spy in Spain.[26] Nicholas Armorer's efforts suffered similar frustration to Halsall's. Acting independently, in the late summer of 1655 Armorer sent his servant Thomas Pearce to England, to make yet another attempt on Cromwell's life. Pearce was arrested, and enlisted as an *agent provocateur* to regain his liberty. On Thurloe's instructions, he returned to Antwerp to consult with Armorer, and they went to Cologne together, to interest Hyde and Rochester in the scheme: both, Pearce reported, opposed Cromwell's murder. This is curious, as Hyde knew about the Halsall-Davison affair, and Rochester had been discussing the murder project a few months earlier. Perhaps they regarded a second attempt as an unnecessary complication. Pearce again went to England in November; his cipher and the letters that Armorer wrote in it were soon in Thurloe's possession. But Pearce must have been playing a double game. By the end of January 1656 he was back in the Tower, and in spite of protestations of devotion to the Protector, there he remained until after Cromwell's death.[27]

Insignificant in themselves, the assassination plots demonstrate the helpless desperation felt by many Royalists after the March rising. They raise one important question: the reaction of the leaders in England. Opinion was as divided as it was among the exiles. There were few who had conscientious scruples—Cromwell, ac-

26. The most thorough account of the Halsall-Talbot plot is in Scott, *Travels of the King*, pp. 125–38. An additional point of interest is that Hyde was more than "not ignorant" of the assassination plot (p. 123): he aided and abetted with good advice. See his letter to Davison ("Dowcett"; Egerton MS 2550, fol. 71), on December 13 [1655]: *CClSP*, *3*, 74. A minor correction to Gardiner's account (*C&P*, *4*, 226–27) is that Halsall did not escape from the Tower with Talbot: he was a prisoner until February 1659 (Scott, *Travels of the King*, pp. 136–37). The intelligence payments to Masten are entered in SPDI, 102, fols. 270, 272, 276, 280; 125, fols. 224, 234; 154, fol. 237; and *TSP*, 7, 785.

27. *TSP*, *3*, 573–74 (correct date Jan. 22, 1655/56); *4*, 63 (in Pearce's cipher, evidently his instructions), 68, 206; 7, 598–99. Rawl. MSS A 33, pp. 563–66, 748–57; A 46, pp. 149–50. *NP*, *3*, 85. *CSPD, 1655*, p. 597; *1655–56*, p. 159. *Declaration of His Highness*, p. 18. Cl. MS 93, fol. 132 (Charles II to Crusoe). One interesting point in Pearce's letter to Thurloe (*TSP*, *3*, 573), is that he mentions Dyke and Nelson: both names are prominent in Hannam's information (*CClSP*, *3*, 37–38; Rawl. MS A 39, pp. 27–29).

cording to the crude mental processes of the average Royalist, was a murderer himself, and might legitimately be exposed to retribution—yet the risks and consequences of failure were too great to make the assassination policy worth while for more than an irrational minority. Responsible Royalists unanimously avoided implicating themselves, and were indignant when returned exiles with only their lives to lose brought down fresh severity upon the heads of the whole party. A few went so far as to confide their opposition in the ears of Thurloe's agents: Sir Philip Monckton, for example. He was unable, or unwilling, to name names, but he had heard rumors of the murder plots, and was quick to condemn them. His attitude prompted a hopeful minute by the investigating officer: "I am confident hee may be engaged to be serviceable for the discovery of any intended plott, if not made otherwise usefull." There is no reason to think that Monckton ever made any further disclosures, but his indignation helped to procure his early release when he was arrested under the "Orders for securing the peace of the Commonwealth." [28]

Monckton's ambiguity illustrates the low state of Royalist morale in 1655–56. The manner of the murder plots' discovery is also suggestive. Both Masten and Pearce were poor men, easily bribed or bullied into serving the other side. They were only two of a number of traitors who sold themselves to Thurloe during the same period. None of the other instances approaches Manning's in importance, but they are not without interest. One of the first to make a deal with Thurloe after the March rising was Richard Palmer, a minor official in Charles II's household. He came to England with Rochester and O'Neill, but soon went off the rails. In May he had a conference with an officer of the Council of State, handed over a letter he had received from Cologne, and offered to sell further information. He later served as an intelligencer for George Downing in the Low Countries.[29] John Walters, brother of the Yorkshire agent Robert Walters, also entered Thurloe's service at this time. He was taken in Cheshire after the Marston Moor rendezvous, but escaped

28. Rawl. MS A 37, p. 257. *TSP*, *4*, 498. Cf. Clarendon, *Con.*, § 28.
29. *NP*, *3*, 181, 187. *TSP*, *3*, 190, 339, 358, 425–26, 529; *7*, 150, 167, 182, 272, 398, 502. *CCISP*, *4*, 223. Add. MS 37,047, fol. 9. SPDI, 102, fol. 212.

to London and was not recaptured. In April 1656 he delivered a letter from the King to Sir Henry Slingsby, but only after having it copied by one of Thurloe's officers. He then went off to Antwerp with messages for some of the exiles, wrote a full account of his doings to Thurloe, and handed over more letters after his return to England.[30]

Thurloe's employment of Walters evidently came to an end in August 1656. A more important agent, over a much longer period, was the clergyman Francis Corker, who began his career as a spy in December 1656, if not earlier. Before the civil war Corker had been vicar of Bradford. He fought in the royal army, served as scoutmaster under Langdale, and was in the Pontefract garrison in 1648. According to his own story he was ruined by successive imprisonments and at last settled down as a schoolmaster in Sussex. After he accepted Thurloe's thirty pieces of silver (Samuel Morland said the salary was £400 a year), Corker became one of the government's most prolific sources of information in Sussex and the London area. In an unconvincing defense made when he was imprisoned after the Restoration, Corker claimed that he had entered Thurloe's service only on the understanding that he "would never have a hand in any man's blood," and denied betraying more than four or five persons, three of them by accident. Actually, of all the Royalists who turned traitor, Corker had the fewest scruples about denouncing his comrades; intelligence gushed from him both verbally and in writing. If the evidence of Thurloe's papers had been available in 1660, it is inconceivable that the Council would have allowed Corker to return to his living at Bradford. As it was, he was undeservedly given the benefit of the doubt and restored.[31]

30. *CSPD, 1655*, pp. 213, 215. *CClSP, 3*, 129 (cipher in Appendix, F). *TSP, 3*, 273, 304; *4*, 680; *5*, 147, 176. Rawl. MS A 39, p. 430b. SPDI, 125, fol. 236; 154, fol. 263. There are some obscure letters from Walters, under the pseudonym "Weddall," in *TSP, 5*, 337, 364–65, and Rawl. MS A 41, pp. 498, 536. Possibly the Walters who gave information in December 1655: *TSP, 4*, 299 (endorsed "Memorandum by Walters"; Rawl. MS A 33, p. 220). The letter from Walters in *CSPD, 1655–56*, p. 319, is to Thurloe, not Nicholas: State Papers, Foreign, Flanders, 31, fol. 405.

31. *TSP, 1*, 707–20; *5*, 702–3 (Corker's name is plainly legible in the original, Rawl. MS A 45, p. 171); *6*, 834–35; *7*, 672, 786. Rawl. MSS A 49, p. 275; A 50, p. 274. *CClSP, 4*, 223, 251, 282–83, 418, 488. Corker's defense is printed

The motives of Manning, Corker, and the others we have been discussing were simple: they sold information for cash. There were others more politic, who attempted to secure themselves with Thurloe by making insincere advances, either to protect themselves against imprisonment or to disrupt the government's espionage system. Wildman's friend Henry Bishop comes into this category. He was released from prison during the summer of 1656, possibly after some sort of bargain with Thurloe. On September 23 he wrote to the Secretary vaguely reporting a nebulous visit by a disguised and anonymous person who came to the house while Bishop was out hunting, and conveniently left again before he returned. Thurloe was not likely to be taken in by so transparent an overture. Although some Royalists suspected the contrary, there is no evidence that he ever employed Bishop as a spy, or that he granted him any favors.[32]

Two of James Halsall's associates in his assassination plot adopted similar tactics: Charles Davison, and Richard Talbot's brother Gilbert. Davison was arrested early in 1656 and examined by Cromwell and Thurloe. He at once attempted to save his neck by assuring them that he was willing to spy on his former colleagues. Before anything could be settled, Davison had the bad luck to kill a guard in an unsuccessful attempt to escape, and was detained in prison throughout the rest of 1656. He wrote continually to both the Protector and the Secretary repeating his previous offer. He eventually escaped from prison and resumed his place in the conspiratorial underworld. In the end he was drowned off the Flanders coast just before Cromwell's death, and search among his papers disclosed something of his ambiguous behavior. Although Davison's friendship with Corker may be a suspicious circumstance, there is no evidence of his having followed up his letters with overt acts, or of his having received intelligence money.[33] Gilbert Talbot went further. He returned to the Conti-

in *Retrospective Review*, 2d ser. *1* (1827), 292–95. See also Matthews, *Walker Revised*, p. 391, and intro., p. xxvii.

32. *TSP, 1,* 711; *4,* 673; *5,* 287, 442. *ClSP, 3,* 409.

33. *CClSP, 3,* 172; *4,* 69, 71–72, 77, 251. *CSPD, 1655–56,* p. 226. *Mercurius Politicus,* Nos. 294, 296. *Retrospective Review,* loc. cit. Rawl. MS A 49, p. 275. *TSP, 1,* 713, 718; *4,* 501, 633. The letters attributed to Davison in ibid., *5,*

nent late in 1655, after the failure of the murder plot. He then began a correspondence with Thurloe, promising intelligence in return for money. The King's ministers, touchy about such things since Manning's unmasking, soon heard about it and demanded explanations. Talbot managed to convince them that he was only trying to deceive Thurloe, but although the Secretary refused to pay until more definite information was forthcoming, the correspondence continued. In 1656 Talbot intermittently forwarded quite useful intelligence under a number of pseudonyms, much of it in cipher. In his defense it can only be said that deviousness was a family trait.[34]

We should not make too much of these acrobatic maneuvers by a small minority of adventurers, or of the handful of outright betrayals. The important point about them is that Thurloe's intelligence system was scoring its greatest successes at precisely the time when the Royalist party was at its lowest ebb. The government's repressive measures had been brilliantly effective in preventing an early revival of Royalist confidence. At the beginning of 1656 the correspondents of Hyde and Nicholas were at one in labeling the whole party "much discouraged." "They are so heavily burdened," the Venetian agent reported, "and their fortunes so dilapidated that without money, leaders or support they are better able to grumble than to vindicate themselves." [35]

399, 414, are in a different hand, and the contents suggest a different author; see also Rawl. MS A 41, p. 474. This other "Davisson" (a pseudonym?) received intelligence money on September 16, 1656: SPDI, 154, fols. 229, 288.

34. *ClSP, 3,* 278. *CClSP, 3,* 70, 77–78, 85–86. Carte, *Papers, 2,* 64. Carte MSS 30, fol. 396; 213, fols. 50, 60. *TSP, 4,* 395–96, 592. Rawl. MS A 42, pp. 115–16. See also Scott, *Travels of the King,* pp. 138–39. Talbot uses the pseudonyms "Burford," "le Broise," and "Barton."

35. *CClSP, 3,* 90. *NP, 3,* 192, 246. *Cal. State Papers, Venetian, 30,* 148.

9. The Knot Revived

EVEN THE MAJOR GENERALS could not last forever. A gradual Royalist revival from the Penruddock disaster began tentatively in the spring of 1656, and slowly gathered momentum during the next two years. By the time of Ormond's secret visit to England in 1658 a haphazard network of resistance had been reconstructed. The situation had changed, however, in one significant respect. Bitter experience had now convinced the exiled leaders that the unaided efforts of conspirators in England were insufficient. Throughout 1656 Cromwell was able to cow the opposition with the powerful deterrent of military government. In the elections of the late summer the popular cry "No Swordsman! No Decimator!" exposed the Major Generals' unpopularity, and out of the constitutional readjustment of the following spring emerged a new Cromwellian party of moderation, to replace the now unfashionable militarists. Once more the base of the regime had been broadened. For the exiles the obvious lesson was that internal subversion had failed, and that invasion from abroad by a powerful ally was the only alternative, whatever the political objections. The key to the English Royalists' situation in 1656–57 was, therefore, the alliance that Charles II was able to make with Spain, when Cromwell drifted into war with that crumbling colossus.

The Treaty of Brussels, concluded on April 2, 1656, was an offensive and defensive alliance between Charles and Philip IV. Spain was promised the return of Jamaica and (in a secret clause) the suspension of the penal laws against the English Catholics. In return the Spaniards agreed to provide 6,000 troops for an invasion of England, as soon as a port should be secured by the Royalists for their disembarkation.[1] For the next two years the broad outline of the Royalist design remained unchanged: invasion by a Spanish army and Charles' own Spanish-subsidized regiments, was to coincide with an insurrection by the King's party in England. If possible there was to be a simultaneous rising by Presbyterians and Levellers, or alternatively, since it was doubtful if there really were any Levellers, the assassination of the Protector by some of the handful of conspirators who called themselves by that name. Although no part of this ambitious scheme was ever put into effect, its existence caused Cromwell and Thurloe considerable anxiety, and it provides a constant background to the English Royalists' activities in these years.

Like the Scots alliance six years before, the alignment with Spain was a double-edged weapon. For many Royalists, national and religious prejudices argued just as strongly against an opportunist union with Spanish, and worse still Irish, Catholics, as they had against Scots Presbyterians in 1651. Sir Philip Monckton, already opposed to the assassination policy, was equally unhappy about a Spanish army: his interrogator gained the impression that "he could not be satisfied to joyne wth such but that he & divers others might easilie be engaged to oppose them." [2] This, however, was the attitude of a minority. Moral rectitude was all very well, but recent experience showed only too clearly the hateful consequences of isolation. Most agents agreed that some brilliant initial success, such as an organized foreign army alone could assure, was essential to stir sympathetic neutrals and even Royalists into action. William Rumbold, a good spokesman for those who combined energy with intelligence, repeatedly commended the Brussels treaty on these grounds. The Cornish Royalists, through their agent John Skelton,

1. On the negotiations see Scott, *Travels of the King*, pp. 177–97; Firth, *Protectorate, 1*, 24; Clarendon, *History*, Bk. XV, §§ 18–22. The treaty is in *CCISP, 3*, 109–10; MS 51, fols. 147–54.
2. Rawl. MS A 37, p. 257.

were equally insistent on the need for foreign assistance to convince the waverers. This attitude had its dangers, as Hyde noted with exasperation: "If the King should land tomorrow . . . he will be overpowered as he was at Worcester, whilst all men sit still, and look for the effect of the first battle." [3]

The Spanish alliance thus supplied the cautious majority of Royalists with further arguments for inaction. It did, however, provide some adventurous ones with a chance to show their mettle. One outlet for them was the small army which, in the late summer of 1656, Charles II began recruiting from the Irish regiments formerly in French service, and from the crowd of unemployed English exiles in Flanders. The King had advised his supporters, Thurloe was informed in August, that "as many as were not in bonds shold come to him," and as the autumn passed, a steady stream of Englishmen drifted over to Flanders to join the new regiments. On October 22 Hyde happily told Bristol that within the past few days over forty recruits had come from England, "most or all of them Officers & Gentlemen." One of Thurloe's spies at Bruges was less impressed with their quality: "Diverse runnegadoe English are come . . . to beare company with their king in whoreing, swearing, and drinking his health, as long as their money last, or that hee can give them 6d. per day." In January 1657 another agent wrote that within the past five weeks 250 Englishmen had gone through Flushing on their way to Bruges, and on March 29 there was a report that fifty "young blades" had arrived on the previous day alone. The English government made little effort to stop the exodus, evidently deciding that the fugitives were less dangerous in Flanders, even though they might soon be in action against Cromwell's forces, than they would be kicking their heels in disaffection at home. [4]

However exciting the prospects in Flanders, most Royalists could not permit themselves the luxury of such tempting escapades. For those who stayed at home, the Spanish alliance offered only the

3. *ClSP*, *3*, 364. *CClSP*, *3*, 125, 199 (cipher in Appendix, G), 409; *4*, 22.
4. *TSP*, *5*, 447; *6*, 151. Rawl. MS A 41, p. 578. *CClSP*, *3*, 194 (MS 53, fol. 3), 241. On the Flanders regiments see C. H. Firth, "Royalist and Cromwellian Armies in Flanders, 1657–1662," *TRHS*, new ser. *17* (1903), 67–75; Scott, *Travels of the King*, pp. 219–28, 246–48.

slower hope of liberation after organizing a supporting conspiracy. The King had ordered his friends, Bristol told the Spaniards in November 1656, "not to begynn any action of themselves," but to lay plans for seizing a port and raising diversionary disturbances. The port was the first requirement, but Royalist projects to fall on Hull, Yarmouth, and Portsmouth, among others, never progressed beyond preliminary discussion. Even if the preparations had been more advanced, the Spanish genius for procrastination would still have made action in 1656 impossible. After a series of less excusable delays, the spectacular destruction of their American treasure fleet by Admiral Stayner in December put a stop to thoughts of offensive action.[5] The year 1657 produced much the same disappointing story of postponements. In March the invasion was wisely put off until winter. The Spaniards, as usual, were hopelessly unready, and English opinion was strongly for delay, arguing that Cromwell's anticipated intention to accept the crown would lead to open distractions in the Army. The Protector's refusal and the uneventful dismissal of Lambert frustrated these hopes, throwing Charles II back on the incompetent Spaniards. In September 1657 Hyde announced that for once they were professing "all imaginable alacrity" for the invasion project, and by the end of the year there was a general impression that action at last was imminent.[6] The sequel was disappointing, but before we describe it something must first be said about the revival of conspiracy in the period of the Spanish alliance.

The disintegration of the Royalist party in 1655 was followed by a torrent of well-meant proposals for reconstruction. Only one of these hopeful suggestions came near to penetrating to the fundamental difficulties of organizing a successful underground movement. The author of this exception to the low level of Royalist self-analysis was Sir Robert Shirley, the wealthy Anglican nephew of the puritan Earl of Essex. We have already encountered Shirley as a midland leader in 1655, and as the King's financial agent after

---

5. *TSP*, 5, 273, 407, 500, 512, 572, 578, 694. Rawl. MS A 41, p. 576. *ClSP*, 3, 330. *CClSP*, 3, 142, 148, 152, 177, 192, 198 (MS 53, fol. 25), 205, 213–14.

6. *ClSP*, 3, 326, 330, 366–67. *CClSP*, 3, 210, 224, 250, 252, 369–70. *TSP*, 6, 659. See also Firth, *Protectorate*, 1, 201–3.

Rumbold and Halsall came to grief. In June 1655 Shirley began a lengthy sojourn in the Tower; it gave him time for reflection on past failures, and especially on the lessons of the previous March. From the early part of 1656 until his untimely death in November, Shirley produced a series of interesting proposals for the edification of Charles II and his councilors.[7]

Shirley started from two premises. The first was that past defeats had been the results of Royalist disunity and indiscipline; the second, that loyalty to the Crown was the indispensable complement of loyalty to the bishops and the Church of England. There could be no argument about the first point, and in the second, although there might be some Presbyterian objections, Shirley was expressing a seventeenth-century commonplace, the interdependence of political and religious beliefs. Logic and expediency, he suggested, argued for basing Royalist action on the only nation-wide organization at Charles' disposal, the Anglican clergy. The cohesive discipline of sectaries (in the Army), Presbyterians, and Roman Catholics pointed an obvious contrast: "We only are lost by ourselves, each man to shift for himselfe." The first thing to do, Shirley advised, was to put the Church's house in order. The bishops would be the natural leaders of a reorganized Royalist party, the lower clergy its effective agents: grouped in local associations, they would sustain morale, encourage disciplined obedience, transmit intelligence, and raise the necessary funds.

Shirley's emphasis on ecclesiastical discipline was an expression of his own zealous piety. Among the clergy he sheltered during the persecution were such notable men as Henry Hammond; Gilbert Sheldon, the future Archbishop of Canterbury; Robert Mapletoft and Peter Gunning, afterward Dean and Bishop of Ely respectively. He left money in his will to Sheldon, Gunning, and "orthodoxall and distressed clergie men" in general. He also began, at Staunton Harold, the only Anglican church to be built during the Interregnum.[8] Church-building and sheltering ejected clergy were,

7. Rawl. MS A 33, p. 732. Shirley, p. 147. Shirley's papers are summarized in *CClSP, 3,* 47–49, 127, 142–43, 152, 191–93, 219. His scheme is discussed by Bosher, pp. 30–31. I am unable to account for Scott's statement (*Travels of the King,* p. 243) that it was put into operation.

8. Shirley, pp. 149–58. HMC, *5th Report,* Appendix, p. 369.

however, much easier than conspiracy. Shirley's scheme was ambitious, and in the existing condition of the Church of England, impossible. The clergy had no stomach for conspiracy. In spite of the partial toleration of 1650–55 and the propagandist activity of a distinguished Laudian minority, no central direction was provided. The bishops, indeed, were reluctant to advise their flocks how far they ought to seek accommodation with the regime, and how far to resist openly. The ejected clergy did little beyond helping to preserve the spiritual health of the pious: an important contribution, no doubt, but also one whose value cannot be exactly assessed. Only a few isolated individuals played any significant part in conspiracies promoted by the Royalist party.[9]

Considering the Church's attachment to the sacred cause of Divine Right, the failure of the churchmen to give a lead is to say the least surprising. The most charitable explanation is that the clergy were less politically minded in practice than in theory— especially when the practice was accompanied by physical danger, the uncharitable might add. Few indeed of John Walker's pathetic catalogue of the excluded and sequestered can be numbered among the major heroes of the royal cause. The martyrs Beaumont, executed at Pontefract in February 1649; Thomas Cooper, in the Norfolk rising of December 1650; Peter Vowell in the Gerard plot; and John Hewett in 1658—these are notable exceptions. There were others whose service to Church and King found more active outlets than in ministering spiritual solace to retired country gentlemen, or in the diversions of theological controversy. John Barwick, Guy Carleton, George Hutchinson, and Richard Allestree we have already encountered, or shall encounter, in the course of our study. Yet the highest of callings had its black sheep too. The worst of them, Francis Corker, was one of Thurloe's most diligent spies after the end of 1656: yet he had held the living of Bradford and managed to get himself restored to it after 1660. The position

9. Cf. Bosher, pp. 13–27, 36–44; Matthews, *Walker Revised*, intro., p. xviii. Both of these valuable studies exaggerate the number of clerical agents in Royalist conspiracy. The examples provided by Bosher, although individually accurate, are insufficient evidence for his generalization that "the practice of using the loyal clergy as agents continued unabated." As agents, the Laudian clergy were more "potential" than "actual" (pp. 30–31).

of Charles Davison is more doubtful, but his clerical dignity did not preserve him from some highly ambiguous relations with Thurloe. Doubtless these were no more typical of their order than the Hewetts and the Barwicks; most of the clergy followed the examples of such eminent figures as Sancroft, Sheldon, and Hammond, in maintaining a dignified retirement, broken only by occasional polemical excursions.

Shirley soon found that his ecclesiastical policy was impractical. Two bishops promised their cooperation in October 1656: possibly Duppa of Salisbury and Brownrigg of Exeter, who were said to have taken an obstructive part in negotiations with the Presbyterians during the summer. Shirley's fund-raising efforts were assisted by two London clergymen and by his chaplain, John Heavers, but this was a poor return for his hopes of an integrated church and party.[10] Fortunately, Sir Robert's ideas on Royalist organization were not restricted to his obsession with the duties of the clergy. It may be significant that out of all Shirley's papers, the one that appears to be of latest date contains the least stress on the clergy and most on the appointment of a committee of the laity. In effect, Shirley was suggesting a revival of the Sealed Knot, though he did not call his committee by that name and was well aware of the Knot's weaknesses. He made the obvious point that the body should be properly authorized by the King and composed of men "so qualified with honor that when commands shall issue out no man may thinke it a disparagment to obey." He also stressed the importance of providing the members with the regional responsibilities that had been conspicuously lacking in the Sealed Knot. The committee should have the normal functions of supervising intelligence and the collection of funds, and should be invested with effective disciplinary powers, including the right to administer an oath of secrecy, and to issue "a severe book of marshall discipline." This was perhaps the least practical aspect of Shirley's proposals, for he did

10. *CClSP, 3,* 142–43, 152, 192, 211. Rawl. MS A 41, p. 576. *CSPD, 1660–61,* p. 86. There is no reference to Duppa's part in the Presbyterian talks in the *Duppa-Isham Corr.;* his friendship with the Countesses of Devonshire and Carlisle (p. 71 and n.) may have provided the point of contact. For Heavers see Matthews, *Walker Revised,* p. 36.

nothing to show how these coercive powers were to be used without destroying the organization's essential secrecy.[11]

With this reservation, Shirley's suggestions had much to commend them. There was one serious obstacle to their adoption. To start from fresh beginnings would only be possible if the members of the Sealed Knot could be persuaded that their old commission had lapsed. While Shirley was sending his stream of good advice from the Tower, however, the Knot was already beginning to rise like a blackened phoenix from the ashes of the 1655 conspiracy. Sir Robert's first letters were written at some time between January and April 1656.[12] Before Charles and his Council could reach a decision about his proposals, other letters arrived which indicated that the reconstruction of the Knot was imminent. The leaders in this process of renovation were Edward Villiers and Sir Richard Willys. They wrote to Hyde almost simultaneously—Villiers on April 30, Willys the next day—putting themselves at the Chancellor's disposal. Both were on the defensive against the charges of neglect leveled at the Knot in the previous year. "With the worst misconstructions," Villiers protested, "I can be but looked on as one that hath errd in judgment, not in affection, for were that doubted, my Cristianity is what ought to be called next in question." Willys, excusing his recent silence on the grounds of sickness (and imprisonment, he might have added), complained bitterly "of their hard usage who unjustly have indeavored to lessen me, & my duty, in his esteeme; whose Consernes & service, is dearer to me then my life." [13]

However just the criticisms of the Knot's behavior in 1655, Hyde preferred to rely on his two old correspondents rather than on the

11. Cl. MSS 52, fol. 129; 53, fols. 136–37.

12. *CClSP*, *3*, 47–50. They are dated by the allusions to Halsall's imprisonment and Rumbold's financial difficulties, and by the fact that Toby Barnes, the bearer of at least the first one, was taken at Yarmouth in April on his return to England with the reply: ibid., pp. 89, 111, 127; *TSP*, *5*, 220.

13. *CClSP*, *3*, 36–37, 129 (MSS 50, fol. 51; 51, fols. 275–76). Villiers' letter must be misdated by a year. Any letter of April 30, 1655, would surely allude to the March rising, on which this is silent. The writer says that his letter should arrive at the same time as Honywood ("the Doctor"; cf. ibid., p. 239), who was the bearer of Willys'. Hyde's endorsement to Willys' letter reads "1 May Sr. R.W. & N.V."

younger and untried Shirley. On June 26 Villiers, and on July 3 Willys, acknowledged Hyde's acceptance of their offers, and soon the Knot's new form began to take shape. Willys, who had made several brief visits to London in the spring, was there continuously from mid-June until September 2, and must have been busily engaged in the reorganization.[14] It was interrupted on September 10, when as Villiers described it, there was "a great route of Cavaleeres." Among those secured were Shirley, who was out on bail, Lord Willoughby, and John Russell. Villiers escaped, though his lodgings were searched. The government was suffering one of its spasms of severity: besides the arrests, there was a proclamation ordering all Royalists to leave London, special precautions were taken at the ports, and the issue of passes to leave the country was suspended. Willys was already out of town, and Villiers left immediately, but he spent an unhappy autumn. Early in December he complained that for three months he had been "strangely sought after by Will. Hunt [Cromwell?] (who only pursues me of the Heard now) as pretending to have a particular information against me." Villiers went into hiding to avoid having to give security, and then tried to escape abroad, only to fall ill and have to return from the waterside.[15]

These misfortunes delayed, but did not prevent, the Knot's revival. Willys and Villiers were at first the most active members, employing two subordinates in place of the imprisoned Rumbold: Major Philip Honywood as a courier to and from the exiles, and Alan Brodrick as a combination of secretary and intelligencer. Honywood was a gruff and unpolished soldier, unfitted for positions of command but a good man to face the dangers of conspiracy at its lower levels. He was a younger son of a prolific Kent family,

14. Add. MSS 19,516, fols. 19, 37, 51, 102; 34,014, fols. 28, 30, 36, 61, 72, 85. *TSP*, *5*, 273, 362. *CClSP*, *3*, 143–44. Hyde's endorsement to Villiers' letter actually reads: "From Sr. R.W. Ne. Vi. & P. Ho. by Mr. Dorrell"; i.e. from Willys, Villiers, and Honywood: Cl. MS 52, fol. 58.

15. *CClSP*, *3*, 171, 175, 212–13 (MSS 52, fol. 260; 53, fol. 101). *TSP*, *5*, 398, 407, 555. *CSPD*, *1656–57*, pp. 99–100. *Correspondence of the family of Hatton*, ed. E. M. Thompson, Camden Society (London, 1878), *1*, 14. *Mercurius Politicus*, No. 326. *Publick Intelligencer*, No. 49. Steele, *Proclamations*, *1*, 371. See also Firth, *Protectorate*, *1*, 32; and Scott, *Travels of the King*, p. 244.

and began his career as a naval officer. In the wars against the Scots in 1639–40 he returned to dry land and was a lieutenant in the same regiment as Willys, who had been his friend since boyhood. He reached the rank of major in the civil war, and once more served under Willys at Newark in 1645. Some time after the war's end he migrated to Virginia, but was back in England by May 1653. Although arrested on suspicion of complicity in the Gerard plot in June 1654, he appears to have kept out of trouble in the following year, perhaps because of the absence of any real chance of action in Kent. No doubt it was Honywood's old friendship and military connections with Willys and Villiers that led them to select him for his new employment.[16]

Brodrick, the new secretary, presents an interesting contrast; a good example of the rising Cavalier generation. He was the son of Sir Thomas Brodrick, a gentleman of moderate fortune in Surrey. He was old enough to have been able to fight in the civil war, but he was the oldest son and had the family estates to think about. Instead, he went to Oxford, to Gray's Inn, and then off to Europe in the early 1650's. Through the St. Johns he was one of Ned Villiers' innumerable cousins: apparently it was Villiers' sister, the Countess of Morton, who first aroused his latent Royalism and advised him to seek Hyde's patronage. Brodrick was also well known to Willys, who had met him in Italy. He was capable and intelligent; but he fancied himself as a wit, wrote bad poetry, and was close to such erratic buffoons as Jack Donne, the crack-brained son of the great Dean. Brodrick himself admitted an excessive addiction to good fellowship and a tendency to allow personal antipathies to cloud his judgment; but these were the typical faults of the Cavalier, young or old. The outstanding recommendation for his employment was the fact that he was not a known Royalist and was thus unfettered by the bonds and financial liabilities which provided so many with unanswerable arguments against conspiracy.[17]

16. *CCISP, 3*, 212, 317. For Honywood's career see *Topographer and Genealogist, 1* (1846), 399, 573; *William and Mary Quarterly, 3* (1894–95), 64; *CSPD, 1660–61*, p. 396; Peacock, *Army Lists*, p. 76; *Symonds' Diary*, pp. 249, 271; *TSP, 1*, 240; *Cromwelliana*, p. 143; and M. Hollings, "Thomas Barret: A Study in the Secret History of the Interregnum," *EHR, 43* (1928), 62.

17. This account of Brodrick is based on the following: *Miscellanea Gene-*

The spadework of reconstruction had been done by Willys and Villiers. It remained to be seen whether the other four members of the Knot would resume their old association with it. Two of them, Belasyse and Loughborough, were slow to do so. The former returned to England in March 1657, but it was almost a year before he had any real contact with his colleagues. His antagonism to Willys may have been still smoldering; his nephew's marriage to Mary Cromwell may have made him unwilling to risk the family fortunes when they seemed to be set so fair; he may simply have been involved in his own marital projects. In December 1657 he was said to be wooing Shirley's widow, and a month later he was wounded in a duel by an enraged gentleman whose sister-in-law he was accused of seducing; not until July 1659 did he at last settle on a wealthy widow from Suffolk. Of Loughborough even less was heard. Philip Honywood spoke to him early in April 1657, but if the object was to revive his interest in the Knot, the outcome was negative.[18]

The relations of John Russell and Sir William Compton with their old colleagues were more cheerful. Russell was much in Willys' company in the summer of 1656. He was one of the victims of the September purge, but must have been released by December. He was reluctant to have anything to do with financial matters, but in all other respects, Brodrick declared, "there bee not a more brisk

---

alogica et Heraldica, 2 (1876), 364; *Collins*, ed. Brydges, 8, 460–62; Foster, *Al. Oxon.*, p. 185; Anthony Wood, *Fasti Oxonienses*, ed. P. Bliss (London, 1815–20), 2, 252; Wood, *Athenae Oxonienses*, ed. P. Bliss (London, 1813–20), 3, 808; John Beresford, *Gossip of the Seventeenth and Eighteenth Centuries* (London, 1923), p. 90; *Register of Admissions to Gray's Inn, 1521–1889*, ed. Joseph Foster (London, 1889), p. 236; *Pension Book of Gray's Inn, 1569–1669*, ed. R. J. Fletcher (London, 1901), p. 368; *Evelyn*, ed. de Beer, 4, 59 and n.; *CClSP*, 3, 239; 4, 22, 25. Much of Brodrick's correspondence with Hyde is in Vol. 1 of the Brodrick MSS, supplementing that in the Clarendon MSS; some, but not all, printed in *ClSP, 3*. I am indebted to the Earl of Midleton for permission to consult this volume of the Brodrick MSS. Additional biographical details are in Br. MS 1, fols. 17, 90.

18. Add. MS 34,015, fol. 58. Br. MS 1, fol. 22. *CClSP, 4*, 15. G.E.C., *Peerage*, 2, 89–90. HMC, *5th Report*, Appendix, p. 152. HMC, *Ormonde*, new ser. 2, 397, says that the affronted gentleman was Philip Stanhope. Contemporary references, however, identify him as Philip Howard: *CSPD, 1657–58*, p. 258; *Clarke Papers, 3*, 131. For Loughborough's conversation with Honywood see *ClSP, 3, 335.*

Fig. 3. COLONEL JOHN RUSSELL.
From the portrait by Michael Wright at Ham House.
Victoria and Albert Museum, Crown Copyright.

adventurer [in England]." Compton was named by one of Thurloe's spies as the leader, with Willys, of a dangerous Royalist design in August 1656, but he was still buried in the country in January 1657. A month later Willys suggested that he would make a good treasurer of Royalist funds, but it was only in the early summer that he showed any real application to the King's business.[19]

No commissions for new members of the Sealed Knot were issued during this period of reconstruction. There was a move to bring in Sir Robert Shirley, logically enough after his thorough study of the problems of organization. He preferred, however, to play a lone hand, and before he could be persuaded to reconsider his aloofness he was struck down by smallpox. In November 1656 he died. Brodrick, reporting the news to Hyde, did not sound particularly regretful, and immediately appropriated Shirley's pseudonym, "Mr. Hancock," in his correspondence. By most of the other Royalists Shirley's death was much bewailed. It caused Rumbold "unspeakable greif," and Hyde commented that the "losse at this tyme can not be repayred." [20] There were, then, no formal additions to the Knot after 1656. At least two men, however, were close to it without any specific authority from the King: the former Presbyterian Lord Maynard, and Sir Simon Fanshawe, a brother of Charles II's old secretary.

Maynard, like so many of the peers, had retired from politics after Pride's Purge. He was Compton's brother-in-law, and had been in touch with the Knot before the March rising, but never in an active role. In June 1655 arms were found at his house near Bury St. Edmunds, and he was arrested, remaining under restraint until October. In 1656 Thurloe's spies observed Maynard's intimacy with Willys, and there is plenty of evidence of his association with the Knot in the correspondence of its members.[21] The geo-

19. *CClSP, 3,* 239 (MS 53, fol. 234), 303, 316. *ClSP, 3,* 326. *TSP, 5,* 273. Rawl. MS A 41, pp. 577–79.

20. *CClSP, 3,* 211 (MS 53, fol. 95), 215 (MS 53, fol. 113), 221, 262–63. Cl. MS 59, fol. 327; misplaced, clearly should be dated 1656. Br. MS 1, fol. 17, bears the date November 5, but must be misdated by a month. On December 1, Rumbold reported that Shirley died "friday morning last": *CClSP, 3,* 211.

21. *TSP, 1,* 728; *5,* 273. *ClSP, 3,* 326. *CClSP, 3,* 239 (MS 53, fol. 234), 310 ("Williams"), 336, 340 ("Ld. Ma": MS 55, fols. 210, 233). Br. MS 1, fols. 22, 24. For Maynard see G.E.C., *Peerage;* and *LBM,* p. 19 n. For his activities in 1655

graphical concentration of the Sealed Knot has already been re-marked on. With the disappearance of Belasyse and Loughborough from the circle, this East Anglian preponderance became even stronger. Maynard's estates were in Essex, and Sir Simon Fanshawe, the other new associate, lived at Bayfordbury in Hertfordshire. Like so many of the Sealed Knot's circle, Fanshawe had served under Willys during the war. Since 1646 he had been one of the vast number of sleeping Royalists, but early in 1657 he emerged from inactivity and took part in discussions with members of the Knot. On February 6 Brodrick announced that Fanshawe had been "a partner with us from the beginning, and will hold out as firmly as any in England." Fanshawe's direct association with the Knot was soon interrupted, but his temporary adherence shows its in-creasing tendency to become a merely local organization.[22]

The Sealed Knot's reconstruction did not affect its general out-look of wariness and caution. It consistently procrastinated over the Spanish invasion, always judging that a better opportunity was just around the corner: in February 1657 it was the expectation that Cromwell's vacillations over the crown would provoke a military coup. Hyde received more cheerful news from them in July, but it was a flash in the pan, and before the end of the year he was writing to Willys with asperity: "The little allacrity our freinds shew toward redemption, I wonder at . . . no doubt, this vile good husbandry proceeds from want of action in some few persons . . . But the time hoped drawes near, that all must prepare in plaine English, and be as ready to doe as speake . . . there will be no more left for dissimulation." [23] The warning had little effect on the Knot. Its efforts to organize an insurrection to support the Spanish invasion were characteristically half-hearted. Among the few recorded instances of activity was one in which Brodrick spoke

---

see *TSP, 3,* 574; Rawl. MS A 42, p. 115; *Mercurius Politicus,* No. 263; *Publick Intelligencer,* No. 1; and *The Poetical Works of Sir John Denham,* ed. T. H. Banks (New Haven, Conn., 1928), p. 136. Mr. Banks' suggested identification, however, is off the mark.

22. *ClSP, 3,* 326. Br. MS 1, fol. 24. For Fanshawe see *Memoirs of Ann Lady Fanshawe,* ed. [H. C. Fanshawe] (London, 1907), pp. 309–11.

23. *ClSP, 3,* 326–27. *CClSP, 3,* 335–36. *TSP, 6,* 659 (Hyde to Willys). Br. MS 1, fol. 19.

hopefully of assurances he had received from Wiltshire, but when Hyde pressed him for names he was silent. Willys bestirred himself by enlisting some of his neighbors with the help of another of his old Newark officers, Col. William Rolleston of Kettleburgh, Suffolk. Roger Coke, a grandson of the great jurist, recalled long afterward how he was approached by Rolleston, with news that "the King was making great Preparations to land in England, and that the Cavaliers were intending to rise . . . to assist him: This he assured me he had from Sir Richard Willis." At Rolleston's suggestion, Coke went to London to buy arms, which were secretly conveyed to his house in Suffolk by ship. Two days later the place was searched, and although the arms were not discovered, Coke's father and brother were arrested. Some frustrated arms-collecting in Suffolk and some inflated talk from Wiltshire do not add up to an impressive record.[24]

The most valuable service performed by any of the Sealed Knot in 1657 was that done by Alan Brodrick in the dull business of intelligence. He regularly provided Hyde with useful information about the disposition of the Protectorate's naval and military forces, including in his letters no more than the normal ingredients of rumor and political gossip. There were the usual excitements of conspiracy. Letters miscarried—three in every four by the regular post, Brodrick estimated—and Thurloe's minions broke through the cipher. Then, after a new one was procured, Brodrick had to burn part of it when alarmed by the presence of officers in the next house. The Sealed Knot survived, but precariously.[25]

The Knot's attitude to former enemies had not changed much from the lukewarmness it had displayed in 1654. There is no doubt that some good opportunities of gaining supporters were missed. The Major Generals, Cromwell's short way with the opposition in the Parliament of 1656 when several of the Presbyterian leaders were among those excluded, the moderates' exasperation with a regime that barred them from all but the minor functions of local

24. Br. MS 1, fols. 20, 24. *CCISP*, *3*, 291, 339, 406. *TSP*, *6*, 659 (the "old officer" was Rolleston; see endorsement in Rawl. MS A 56, fol. 56). Roger Coke, *Detection of the Court and State of England* (4th ed. London, 1719), *2*, 61–66. For Rolleston see *CCC*, p. 2071; and *Symonds' Diary*, p. 271.

25. Br. MS 1, fols. 19, 20, 22.

government—all were factors from which the Knot might have profited. It showed an astonishing lack of interest in doing so. Russell had some desultory discussions with the Countess of Devonshire, with Denzil Holles, and with the elusive Alexander Popham. There was also some talk of an approach to Villiers' cousin, the Earl of Denbigh, but none of these overtures were seriously pursued. At a time when Rumbold and Shirley were both tentatively dealing with the Presbyterians (Shirley, indeed, expected considerable support from them if Charles II invaded), the Knot's apathy is hard to defend.[26]

Its advances to the Levellers were little more energetic. After Penruddock's rising, the center of Royalist-Leveller discussions had shifted to Flanders, where Sexby and Richard Overton conducted some complicated negotiations with both the exiles and the Spaniards. Sexby's object—to divert the projected invasion to his own Leveller purposes—sounds fantastic in retrospect. To Hyde and his friends, accustomed by years of exile to seeing England through the blurred haze of conspiracy, the Levellers seemed closer to their own evaluation than they do to us. However, although Hyde was willing to use Sexby, he would make no concessions to him. The Royalist leaders preferred Sexby to concentrate on compassing the Protector's death, leaving the invasion alone. The situation was complicated by the fact that Sexby was no longer working harmoniously with Wildman, the most notable of the Levellers in England, who had secretly entered Thurloe's employment. How far the Leveller leaders represented anyone but themselves is a question that is not hard to answer. Their party was dead from the neck down: a head without a body.[27]

There were a few contacts between Royalists and Levellers in England before the Sealed Knot was involved in them: desultory efforts to disaffect the Fleet and an ill-supported accusation that Sir Thomas Peyton was implicated in Sindercombe's assassination

26. *CClSP, 3,* 152, 156–57, 164–65, 192–93. Rawl. MS A 41, pp. 576–77. Br. MS 1, fol. 17.

27. Gardiner, *C&P, 4,* 223–25, 258–59. Firth, *Protectorate, 1,* 33–39, 113–19. Ashley, *Wildman,* pp. 95–97. Scott, *Travels of the King,* pp. 165–72, 269–70. For reports of mistrust between Sexby and Wildman see *ClSP, 3,* 316–17; *CClSP, 3,* 192; *NP, 4,* 16.

plot.[28] But although Sexby's and Sindercombe's plans were known to a few Royalists, the intricate demonstrations of their ingenuity —the blunderbuss carried in gangster fashion in a viol case, the "strange engines" firing twelve bullets apiece, and the fearsome "firework" which they deposited in Whitehall chapel—all belong to Leveller, not Royalist history. The Knot was more interested in Wildman than in Sexby. He had been in touch with John Weston and Rumbold since March 1656, and in the summer a Leveller Address to the King, with Wildman among the signatories, gave his terms for an alliance: religious toleration, abolition of tithes, restoration of the Long Parliament, and confirmation of the Isle of Wight treaty. One of Wildman's friends was William Howard, the democratic younger son of Lord Howard of Escrick. He had been a soldier in Cromwell's guards, but was dismissed for his opinions early in 1656, visited the King at Bruges, and began a regular correspondence with the Royalists.[29] Howard was responsible for bringing the Knot into the discussions.

In October 1656 Howard suggested that he and Wildman should be "admitted into the Cabala, and secreets of those, whoe are yor. cheife Ministers here," and in January Wildman expressed his own readiness to confer with the King's representatives.[30] Willys and Compton were instructed to meet him, and Compton did so in May. Wildman and the two Royalists were soon jointly employing an agent to look after their affairs, and in July Compton was said to be "abundantly satisfyed" by the negotiations. Wildman, however, was already in Thurloe's pay, and rumors of his duplicity

28. *CClSP, 3,* 90, 114–15, 120–21, 192, 222, 281, 300, 311, 339 ("Shipp" not "Stapp" in MS 50, fol. 230); *4,* 164. *CSPD, 1655–56,* pp. 123, 166, 197, 237. *TSP, 1,* 711, 718; *4,* 299; *5,* 362, 690–94, 710–11. *Burton, 1,* 355–56.

29. *CSPD, 1655–56,* p. 244. *ClSP, 3,* 300. Clarendon, *History,* Bk. XV, §§ 105–31. *CClSP, 3,* 142, 145–46, 152, 167, 174–76, 179, 192.

30. *CClSP, 3,* 196–97 (MS 53, fol. 13), 234–35. The pseudonym for Wildman in Howard's correspondence is "Graves." Howard's letter of January 15, 1657 and the accompanying one from "Graves" are endorsed by Hyde: "15 January M.H. & W. to the Kinge," and "Mr. Graves W. to the K. January." (Cl. MS 53, fols. 211, 213). See also *CClSP, 3,* 335 (MS 55, fol. 203), where Hyde discusses Compton's talks with "Wi.," and p. 340, to Compton, regarding the King's confidence in "Graves." For Howard see *DNB;* Carte, *Papers, 2,* 81; *TSP, 5,* 393; and *NP, 3,* 282.

began to circulate. About midsummer 1657 the participants left London, with the talks becalmed, and on December 10 Willys reported that they had been abandoned. Howard, more sincere than Wildman, also slackened his efforts, upset at the Royalists' failure to pay him for his intrigues. In December he was arrested, and correspondence with the Levellers ceased altogether.[31]

A strange fatality surrounds the efforts of the Sealed Knot in the period between its revival and the end of 1657. John Russell was the only member to be arrested (in the purge of September 1656), but several of the others had narrow escapes. Villiers was reduced to a nervous wreck by the persistence of the pursuit; Brodrick's letters were regularly intercepted, and he had to burn his papers. Honywood was also harrassed in the autumn of 1656, as he told Hyde: "Either by the indiscretion or malice of persons who became privy to my remove, I found so frequent & loud reports concerning my selfe that I judged it safer to seeke shelter." [32] One of the Knot's few efforts to promote a local plot, the affair of the Cokes in Suffolk, came to grief with suspicious promptness after the necessary arms had been bought. These incidents might conceivably be dismissed as part of the normal hazards of conspiracy, but when one adds to them the obstinate futility of the Knot in both conception and execution of policy, the conclusion that the committee's work was being deliberately sabotaged becomes irresistible. The objection that slow, painstaking caution had always been characteristic of the Sealed Knot is answered by documentary proof that there was a traitor in its midst. He has justly been called Thurloe's "masterpiece of corruption," and his name was Sir Richard Willys.

31. *CClSP*, *3*, 216 (MS 53, fol. 120; December 10, 1657, not 1656), 234–35, 303, 316–17, 335 (MS 55, fol. 203), 340–43, 375. Willys' remark on May 7, "I shall take no notice unlesse it be to Sr. Wm. Compton of the King's last commands" (Cl. MS 54, fol. 243) may refer to the King's instructions for meeting Wildman. Macray (*Cal.*, *3*, 303) erroneously identifies "Ashton" as Sir George Lane. The mistake seems to be the result of a misreading of MS 55, fol. 241 (*Cal.*, *3*, 341). See also *ClSP*, *3*, 378. *TSP*, *1*, 708, 711; *6*, 748–49. *CSPD*, *1655–56*, p. 395. For the course of Wildman's relations with the Royalists in 1656–58 see Ashley, *Wildman*, pp. 98–120. Mr. Ashley, however, ignores the talks with the Sealed Knot.

32. Cl. MS 59, fol. 327.

The Willys case will probably never be solved in its entirety.[33] The exact nature and date of his agreement with Thurloe and above all his motives for making it are problems on which we must be content with incomplete and tentative answers. Willys offers a fascinating subject for historical detective analysis, yet the importance of the mystery surrounding him goes deeper than this. As a member of the Sealed Knot, and indeed as one of the two principal architects of its reconstruction, Willys was in a position, if he wished, to make Royalist plotting even more farcically ineffective than it was already. His potential value as a spy far exceeded that of even Bampfield, Manning, and Corker. If he went the whole way in his surrender to Thurloe, the Knot could be written off, except as a mechanism for encompassing the Royalists' own downfall.

It has often been argued that Willys' betrayal began as early as 1654, during his imprisonment as a Gerard plot suspect.[34] There is no real evidence to support this, nor is there any that he became entangled with Thurloe at any time earlier than the late summer of 1656. The first piece of direct evidence against him dates from this period. A Royalist informer with the initials "R.W." had a lengthy conversation with Thurloe either on August 28 or September 3: the Secretary's notes of the interview carry both dates in separate endorsements. This may not have been Willys; it may possibly have been Sir Robert Welsh, a soldier of fortune who had returned to England in the spring, was twice imprisoned, unsuccessfully offered his services to Thurloe, and was employed by the government later in the year.[35] The contents of Thurloe's "Noates of a discorse wth R.W." are, however, more likely to have been available to Willys than to Welsh, a comparative newcomer to conspiracy. In the first place, much of the information is quoted

33. For detailed discussions of the Willys case, see the articles already cited, by M. Hollings and the present writer, in *EHR*, *43*, 33–65; and *69*, 373–87.

34. E.g. J. G. Muddiman, *Notes and Queries*, 12th ser. *10*, 101–2.

35. *TSP*, *4*, 574; *5*, 555, 683. *CSPD*, *1655–56*, p. 579; *1656–57*, pp. 169, 293–97. SPDI, 154, fol. 300. Welsh was imprisoned by the Spaniards from 1657 to 1659: *CClSP*, *3*, 366–67; *ClSP*, *3*, 404; Carte, *Papers*, *2*, 241. For a note on his life see *Evelyn*, ed. de Beer, *3*, 6 n. The notes of Thurloe's interview with "R.W." are in Rawl. MS A 41, pp. 576–79.

as coming from John Russell, Willys' colleague in the Knot; another item from a certain Offley: Willys' brother William was married to an Offley. The remaining sources of the material—Grey, Rumbold, and John Mordaunt—are inconclusive, as Welsh would have had as good a chance of knowing them as Willys. A second feature of the "R.W." interview is that a large proportion, although not all, of its content deals with the activities of Presbyterians rather than Royalists: this was later believed to be Willys' normal practice. Thurloe's interview with "R.W." must be admitted as at least a possible indication that Willys took the fatal step at this time. If the notes are a complete record of the interview, the informer told Thurloe nothing about the revival of the Sealed Knot, contenting himself with an account of Shirley's abortive discussions with the Presbyterians, a petition being prepared by Army malcontents, the King's new regiments in Flanders, and the negotiations with the Spaniards. On the last two subjects Thurloe already had plenty of information.

Willys' movements in the autumn of 1656 can be followed in the register of the Major Generals' Office. He left London for Fen Ditton on September 2, thus avoiding the September purge, and also disposing of the "R.W." interview if that took place on the 3d. He returned to London on November 13 and stayed there until December 12. To this period belong the famous "Barret" letters, which Willys was later supposed to have written to Thurloe under that pseudonym; but they are almost certainly forgeries and so can safely be ignored. However, the dates of Willys' visit to London are important, for they show that he was now engaged in something that he wished to conceal from his friends. On December 1 he wrote to Hyde, asserting that since the beginning of September he had been "confined to utter darkenesse in ye Contrey:" actually for nearly three weeks he had been surreptitiously in London with the permission of the authorities, at a time when Royalists were officially excluded. There can be only one explanation of this deliberate deception. Even if the "R.W." document is ruled out as evidence, the association with Thurloe must date at least from November 1656.[36]

36. Add. MS 19,516, fol. 102, 126. *CClSP*, *3*, 210 (MS 53, fols. 93–94). The

Fig. 4. SIR RICHARD WILLYS.
From the portrait by William Dobson at Newark-on-Trent.

This was not an isolated aberration. Around March or April 1657, Willys afterward admitted, he entered into an understanding with Thurloe:

> It hapn'd that Thurloe had intercepted some letters of Mr. Brodericks and others. Which he supposing to be Sir Richard, Thurloe immediately sent on purpose for him, and strictly examining him to this effect, What he knew of those letters and the persons and matters conteyn'd in them. It being visible that one of ye feighned names often therein specified could meane no other person but himselfe. So having thus shown him the danger of his condition, and spread his nett over him. He began to say that his intention was not to destroy him, if he would be instrumentall for his reconciliation with the king, when time should serve, and that he would absolutely engage not to discover anything without his preacquaintance and leave, and that in the meantime the Royal party should speed the better for him. Which he is very confident has been effected by his management in preserving many of them.[37]

From Willys' point of view, in other words, the understanding was entirely innocent. In return for a little worthless information and a promise to put in a word for Thurloe when the restoration came, the Sealed Knot would be permitted to carry on its activities unmolested. It is superfluous to point out the circumstantial improbability of Willys' defense: Thurloe was hardly likely to have been thinking of safeguarding himself against the return of the Stuarts while the Protectorate was still unassailably established. The important thing is that Willys, already convicted of duplicity a few months before, is here admitting a suspicious agreement with Thurloe in 1657.

Willys was still giving Thurloe useful assistance in December. The arrest of the Cokes in Suffolk has an interesting history. On December 5 Hyde wrote to Willys ordering him to bestir himself,

letter from London on December 10, ascribed by Macray to 1656 (*Cal., 3,* 216), belongs to 1657.

37. *Notes and Queries,* 12th ser. *10,* 123. The dates are O.S.

as the promised invasion was near. He also gave him some specific instructions: "The king desires assoone as tis possible, to finde opportunity to speake with the old officer, and to ingage him . . . to attend any occasion that may offer itselfe in those parts." The "old officer" was Willys' friend Rolleston. That Willys transcribed the letter and provided Thurloe with a copy is clear from Thurloe's endorsement: "H. lettr. to Sr. R. W. 15/5 Dec. 1657. That their bussines is neare. That he should speake wth. Rolston etc." On Christmas Day, Willys had a further interview with Thurloe at which, again to quote the Secretary's notes, it was "Agreed yt an Answer be writt to H. of what Rolston sayth." Thurloe's record of this conversation is immensely valuable, as it is the only certain piece of evidence from which we can judge the kind of information that Willys was giving him. As in the "R.W." discourse, much of it came ultimately from other members of the Sealed Knot. Besides the discussion of Hyde's letter and the approach to Rolleston, Willys mentioned the latest overture to Fairfax, by way of Buckingham and a certain "Mr. Grymes": "This Grymes told to Ned Villers, and he to sir R. Willis." Willys also gave Thurloe some details of the Royalist-Leveller discussions, concealing, however, both his and Compton's direct part in them. This must have caused Thurloe some quiet amusement: Wildman and Willys busily spying on each other, neither realizing that the other was in the Secretary's service, and Willys attempting to disguise his activities from his employer. When William Howard was arrested for the third time in the late summer of 1658, he complained bitterly of having been trepanned by Wildman. His disillusionment would have been complete if he had known that he had been cheated from both sides.[38]

Willys, then, was betraying his trust possibly from September and certainly from November 1656. His relations with Thurloe may have been closer than the surviving evidence implies, and he may have had many meetings with the Secretary or his agents which were not recorded. We know that he was capable of furnishing Thurloe with a copy (apparently accurate) of one of Hyde's

38. *TSP*, *6*, 659 (endorsement in Rawl. MS A 56, fol. 56), 706 (last line misprinted; see *EHR*, *69*, 378–80). *ClSP*, *3*, 408–9.

letters, disclosing that invasion was imminent and enabling Thurloe to arrest the deluded participants in a section of the conspiracy under Willys' immediate direction. On the other hand, there is no proof that he told everything he knew about the Royalists' plans. The Sealed Knot had played little part in preparing for a rising, but its members must have known about the designs of other, more active groups. Willys, in other words, was probably deceiving Thurloe as well as the Sealed Knot, playing the popular game of trying to maintain a footing in both camps: giving the authorities enough information to keep himself out of worse trouble, while at the same time continuing to conspire, and hoping to keep it from Thurloe's knowledge. It was a dangerous occupation, and it brought about the downfall of more than one of its practitioners.

This last reflection suggests a possible clue to Willys' motives. Although he was a poor man, we can discount the supposition that they were merely mercenary.[39] It is more likely that Willys' lapse was a result of the blight of defeatism that produced so many other traitors after the March rising: a resentful conviction that the recklessness of the forward element of the party condemned Royalist plotting to futility, and that the Knot's authority could never be made really effective. The logic of Willys' past no doubt left him psychologically incapable of making a clean break with his Royalist friends; yet if the longed-for restoration seemed beyond the bounds of possibility, what was there to do but protect his personal position? Discouraged and physically broken by recurrent spells of imprisonment, Willys thus took what seemed to him the only way out. There may too have been deeper emotional forces at work, some complicated neurotic expression of personal frustration.[40]

The Sealed Knot had contributed little enough to the planning of Royalist resistance in 1654–55. Thurloe's infiltration of the committee meant that even less could be expected from it in the future. Thurloe may have been aware that Willys was not giving his services unreservedly. However, he made no move to break the

39. Hollings effectively disposes of this point: *EHR, 43,* 51–52.
40. There may have been a streak of instability in the family. Willys' son went out of his mind.

Knot, and one can only suppose it was because he was already convinced of its futility, and regarded it as a positive asset in restraining and dividing the Cavaliers. This would be true even if Willys did not disclose all its activities, and if it should ever become more dangerous, Willys was so deeply in the toils that he could be bullied or deceived into making a cleaner breast of it. The Knot in 1656 and 1657 was thus even less effective than before. Once again its half-hearted and ambivalent leadership was challenged by other Royalist factions. It is time to turn to the emergence of the new "Action party," which at the time that Willys was at once rebuilding and destroying the Knot was appearing from the shadows.

10. The New Action Party

IN 1654 THE SEALED KNOT had failed to satisfy the more militant Royalists, and the result had been the formation of the Action party. A similar, if less clearly defined, group emerged in 1657, and for the same reasons. Once again, it was not discouraged by the exiles. Hyde's problem in 1656–57 was essentially what it had been two years earlier: to persuade the advocates of immediate action to be reasonable and cool-headed, and if possible to put themselves at the disposal of the Sealed Knot, at the same time trying not to dampen their zeal by asking skeptical questions. The Knot did not resume its meetings until near the end of 1656, and when it did, it was as cautious as ever. In the vacuum there developed a new "Action party," out of a chaos of disorganized local conspiracies. By the time Ormond came to London early in 1658 it was already a serious rival to the Knot.

The directors of the second Action party were, for obvious reasons, new men. Most of the former leaders were in prison or had given up in disgust. Hyde maintained a regular correspondence with those in the Tower through William Rumbold, whose brief association with the Sealed Knot had now lapsed completely. Tower or no Tower, Rumbold was strikingly successful in sending and receiving letters without discovery. One of his chief allies was Sir Thomas Peyton. To while away the dreary weeks of confinement Peyton had taken up book-binding, a hobby, one suspects,

affording good opportunities of smuggling seditious papers in and
out of the Tower, hidden in the binding materials. Peyton responded to the King's inquiry about the state of the Bristol defenses, took part in the dissemination of propaganda in the Fleet,
and helped Rumbold dispose of Shirley's secret papers. He was
pessimistic about the prospects of the Spanish invasion and its
attendant rising but would no doubt have loyally supported it if he
had managed to obtain his release. In 1656 he was granted restricted freedom on parole to attend to legal business, but then
came the accusation of complicity in Sindercombe's plot. Peyton
was promptly subjected to such close imprisonment that for two
years nothing more was heard of him.[1]

Two more of the leading men of 1654–55, John Weston and Sir
Thomas Armstrong, were nominally confined to the Gatehouse
prison, but were given frequent spells of liberty on bail. Neither
exercised anything like his old influence in the party. Weston was
still a fervent supporter of the Leveller alliance but overly optimistic about Wildman's good faith. He was ill during the spring
of 1657 but corresponded regularly with the exiles later in the year
and knew all about the increasing ferment of conspiracy in Surrey
and Sussex.[2] Armstrong seems to have recovered his confidence far
less readily, and the exiles heard little from him but complaints of
his desperate poverty. Rumbold let him have £20 out of some
money given to Andrew Newport for the King's service, but this

1. *CClSP, 3,* 134, 192, 211, 221–22. *TSP, 4,* 251; *5,* 690–94, 710–11. *Burton, 1,*
355. On Peyton's life in the Tower see Add. MSS 28,003, fols. 332–468 passim;
44,846 passim; and *Oxinden Letters 1642–70,* pp. 208–22.

2. *TSP, 1,* 712. *CSPD, 1655–56,* pp. 244 (cf. *ClSP, 3,* 289–90), 372; *1656–57,*
p. 17. *CClSP, 3,* 167 (MS 52, fol. 208), 264, 277, 301 (MS 55, fol. 6), 342, 375.
Weston's 1657 letters are in Cl. MSS 53, fols. 37, 45–46, 222–23 (deciphered in
Appendix, B); 54, fol. 325; 67, fol. 330. The first three are wrongly ascribed
to Sir Robert Welsh in *Cal., 3,* 139, 140, 169, and are misplaced by a year;
the last two are not calendared. Weston's second letter bears Ormond's endorsement with the correct year, 1657; no year is given for any of the others,
but they obviously form a series. On August 1 the King acknowledges
Weston's of June 14; Weston then acknowledges the King's on September 13:
MSS 59, fol. 325; 67, fol. 330. "Welsh" is identified as Weston by Ormond's
endorsement of the August 1 letter: "Copy of leters sent by the king to Mr.
Hop. Mr. Wes." See also remarks by Hyde and Ormond about letters to and
from "West": MS 55, fols. 243, 266.

was a mere drop in the bucket. Armstrong was not the only Action party leader to have pecuniary troubles. Richard Dutton and Henry Norwood both had to borrow from their warders to obtain the necessities of life, and even the unsympathetic Council of State could see no choice but to pay their debts for them. Dutton, to avoid further embarrassment, was released in April 1657; Norwood, too dangerous for such leniency, was granted ten shillings a week. Edward Grey, another bankrupt, received similar assistance.[3]

Of the two remaining members of the old Action party's high command, Richard Thornhill resisted payment of the Decimation Tax in January 1656 and was sent back to prison. As a conspirator he was the least active of the clique. Sir Humphrey Bennett was in the Tower until September 1657, when he was released on bail to prepare for a voyage to Surinam. Instead of going to South America, Bennett joined enthusiastically in the rebuilding of Royalist organization in his old area of activity, the counties of Hampshire and Sussex.[4]

For almost two years the activist wing of the Royalist party remained without organized leadership. From all sides there were urgent pleas for the King to commission a new directing body. Shirley's arguments in 1656 were answered only by the revival of an even less effective Sealed Knot. In May 1657 Rumbold emphasized "how necessary it is judged, to have some fit persons here appointed for the manageing of his Matys. affaires." From the already sabotaged Knot the unsuspecting Brodrick joined in with a generous call for unity: "I passionately wish . . . wee might all receiv direction from one Head."[5] The lack of direction was as obvious in the provinces as it was in London. It was in fact out of an uncoordinated series of local conspiracies that the new Action party, in its nebulous way, came into being.

The first of the local designs to assume definite form was one managed by the Hampshire surgeon Dick Pile. Pile seems to have escaped arrest after Penruddock's rising, and in the autumn of 1655

3. *CISP, 3,* 356. *CCISP, 3,* 263–64, 322, 338–39, 346, 374–75, 409. *CSPD, 1656–57,* pp. 276, 291, 330; *1657–58,* p. 108.

4. *NP, 3,* 252. *CSPD, 1656–57,* pp. 17, 330; *1657–58,* pp. 107, 133. On Bennett's activities in Sussex see below, pp. 210–11.

5. *CCISP, 3,* 301, 317–18 (MS 55, fols. 6, 109).

he ambitiously began to lay the groundwork of a new plot in the West. His most important assistants were Col. Thomas Veel, of Alveston near Bristol, and a certain Major William Clayton; both made spectacular claims to influence among the local Royalists. Veel promised to raise 3,000 men at Bristol at three weeks' notice, with arms for 2,000 more, and a force of 1,100 at Gloucester. By March 1656 Veel had glibly increased his potential army to over 6,000. Fortified by such intoxicating promises, Pile was soon writing confidently to his friend Thomas Ross in Paris, his main channel of communication with the Court. For more than three years Pile nursed this project in both London and the West. Where he lived when he was out of town we have no means of knowing, but in the capital he still frequented Chase's, and he also had a covering address at the Mermaid in Bucklersbury, near the house of his father-in-law, the merchant Richard Quiney. There were disturbing fluctuations in the numbers promised by Veel and Clayton, but with this exception the design remained essentially unchanged: Clayton would seize Bristol with the help of men from Shepton Mallet and other Somerset towns, the Gloucestershire militia would be disarmed, the gates of Gloucester opened, and Veel with another strong force, "mal contented tobacco-planters," Pile described them, would enter in triumph. Pile, Veel, and Clayton would win undying glory and a monarch's gratitude. Commissions to command regiments of horse and foot were duly sent to Veel from Bruges in November 1656.

By November 1657 Pile was no longer content with the direction of a provincial conspiracy, and was being passed off to admiring Sussex plotters as "general agent for all England." One of the Sussex group, a minister from Cuckfield named George Hutchinson, recalled the deep, melodramatic gloom of his first meeting with the surgeon. He was brought to London on November 1, 1657, and taken with great stealth to an upstairs room over an apothecary's shop (it may have been John Chase's). His guide "left him there in the dark for about half an hour, and then brought a person to him, which he said was the general agent for all England." It was in fact Dick Pile, who certainly had no reason to think that his position was so exalted. Pile was actually a busy, meddlesome little man, constantly threatening to throw in his hand or leave the country when his advice was ignored: a veritable "Cockescombe," Hyde rightly judged. Pile sought protection in Nicholas' patronage. The Secretary, not surprisingly, was more impressed by Pile's abilities, and decided that he was "very honest and intelligent." Hyde's verdict was nearer the truth.[6]

One of Pile's closest associates was the former parliamentarian Richard Hopton, a younger son of Sir Richard Hopton of Canon Frome, Herefordshire. Hopton was as determined as Pile to have nothing to do with Hyde, and he too placed himself at the disposal of Secretary Nicholas. After some months in Paris, Hopton came to England at the end of April 1656. He was soon with Pile in the provinces, perhaps whipping up Presbyterian support for the Bristol venture. In the spring of 1657 he was operating further north, trying unsuccessfully to disaffect Colonel Mackworth, the Governor of Shrewsbury. In May 1657 he visited the King at Bruges, and was provided with letters for three prominent Presbyterians in England. Immediately after his return he was arrested, and it was only through his friendship with Cromwell's former officer, Robert Huntington, and by a judicious outlay of £300, that he got a speedy release. Hopton seems to have been no more successful than Pile in interesting the more powerful western gentry in the plot.[7]

The turnover of Royalist leaders in the Severn valley had no parallel in the extreme Southwest. The men who had been most prominent in Devon and Cornwall before the March rising were still in control: Sir John Grenville, Sir Hugh Pollard, the Arundells. In this region, indeed, the Action party's organization seems

6. *CSPD, 1655–56*, pp. 49, 69, 80, 122–23, 133, 147, 166, 196–97, 206, 226, 237, 326, 333, 339, 344, 395; *1656–57*, pp. 33, 67. *ClSP, 3,* 289, 299, 366, 373. *CClSP, 3,* 130, 167, 220, 251–52, 286 (MS 54, fol. 205), 291–93, 314–15, 361, 370, 373–74. *TSP, 7,* 77–78, 98. *Archaeologia, 14* (1803), 76–77. For Veel see ibid., 79–83, and *DNB*. For Pile's relation to the Quineys see G. R. French, *Shakspeareana Genealogica* (London, 1869), pp. 394, 566. I am indebted to Mr. A. W. Ashby for this reference.

7. *CSPD, 1655–56*, pp. 123, 166, 206, 237, 263, 326, 333, 395, 576; *1656–57*, pp. 17, 347–48. *CClSP, 3,* 111, 122, 130, 132, 169 (MS 52, fol. 222, deciphered in Appendix, B), 287–88, 301 ("Hopton," not "Honton" in MS 55, fol. 6), 304, 311, 322. *NP, 3,* 264–65, 270. *TSP, 5,* 704. HMC, *Bath, 2,* 118–19 ("Mr. Walton" is Hopton: cf. Cl. MS 55, fol. 128). For Hopton and Huntington see *LBM,* pp. 8 n., 145 n.

to have been unaffected by the disaster—largely because its leaders had not lifted a finger. Grenville was at Stowe in 1656 struggling with his debts and mortgages. The Cornish Royalists' communications with the exiles and the other groups in England were by now in the hands of Capt. John Skelton, an officer "allied to the Grenvilles," who according to Manning, was sent into England late in 1655. On November 4, 1656, he wrote to Hyde from Stowe, and he then returned to the Continent to give a personal account of his mission. The Cornishmen, he said, needed an invading force of at least 500, and preferably 1,000 men, to put the cautious in good heart: "at first most people will stand at Gase, and see how it will goe." Arms for upward of 5,000 men and some field pieces would also be useful, Skelton thought, and if all this could be promised and a week's notice of invasion given, Grenville and his friends could raise an army of over 6,000 within two days of the landing. There were many if's and but's in Skelton's statement, but at least the Cornishmen's request for support from abroad showed greater realism, and their promises more precision, than those of Pile at Bristol. Some degree of organization was restored in the peninsula and the Cornish leaders were soon employing a London agent, Col. Edward Roscarrock, another western Royalist of long standing. Roscarrock was established in London before the end of 1656, keeping in close touch with Sir John Arundell, collecting money for the Cornish design and using Skelton to pass messages to and from the Court.[8]

The most remarkable feature of Royalist conspiracy in the Midlands and the North after the March rising is the revival of Langdale's influence. The men who had managed the plot of 1654–55 were now dispersed: either abroad or in retirement in England; some, like Monckton, disgusted by the exiles' recent opportunism. By September 1656 Hyde seems to have decided that the exclusion of Langdale two years before had been a mistake. After a personal meeting he wrote asking for the names of those Langdale would rely on in any renewed design. It was a clear invi-

8. *TSP, 1,* 711–15; *4,* 101; *5,* 702. Rawl. MS A 1, fol. 274. *NP, 3,* 178. *CSPD, 1656–57,* p. 585. *CClSP, 3,* 199, 210 (cipher in Appendix, G), 374, 408–9 (MS 56, fol. 372). Granville, pp. 335–36.

tation to Langdale to mend his fences, and he was quick to respond. He soon produced a list of his northern friends: Belasyse, Slingsby, Grey, Strother, Carnaby, Sir Francis Anderson, and some others. To revive the Royalist organization beyond the Humber was not, however, a simple matter. The March debacle had been keenly felt in the area where hopes had been highest, and Langdale found that few of his old supporters were willing to risk their necks again. Several of the lesser agents—Scott, John Cooper, the Paulden brothers—were repeatedly sent into England, but little progress was made. Langdale made the mistake of enlisting another of his old clients, Thurloe's spy Francis Corker. Corker was soon handing over Langdale's letters to his employers, and giving them full details of the people on whom he relied.[9]

Langdale's agents did their best. Cooper and Tom Paulden had been imprisoned in the Gatehouse after the March rising but escaped by throwing pepper in the guard's eyes and made their way beyond the seas. In April 1656 Cooper came to England to collect funds in Yorkshire and the Midlands, upsetting Sir Robert Shirley by his competitiveness. After returning to Flanders he attached himself to Langdale and became a regular courier between the English conspirators and the exiles. Scott, banished in 1657 after a long spell of imprisonment, was similarly employed. He arrived at Bruges in June and at once volunteered to return to England. When he got there, Corker's inquisitive eye soon found him out, and Thurloe was duly informed of it. The two Paulden brothers were also at Bruges that June, making a bad impression because Gregory not only had come without money for his return journey but also was £20 in debt. They were sent back to help in raising funds, and found Byron and Belasyse both willing to help.[10] The

9. *CCISP*, *3*, 154, 157, 211–12. HMC, *Var. Coll.*, *2*, 353, 355, 358. *TSP*, *1*, 710, 716–17, 719. Rawl. MS A 1, fol. 274.

10. *CCISP*, *3*, 112–32, 164, 191, 212, 244, 281, 292, 298, 300–12, 321–31, 337, 356. For the identification of "Plant" as Paulden see above, p. 86 n. 17. Cooper's three letters to Armorer in April–May 1656 are wrongly ascribed in the *Calendar* to Abraham Cowley. They are in Cooper's hand (cf. Cl. MS 58, fol. 273), and Armorer specifically mentions having received three from Cooper: *CCISP*, *3*, 130–32. A. H. Nethercot, *Abraham Cowley* (London, 1931), pp. 160–61, accepts them as Cowley's, and prints them in his appendix 6. For Cooper's cipher see my Appendix, F. See also T. Paulden, "Pontefract Castle.

Pauldens were also interested in a design against Hull. In this they relied on Capt. Thomas Gardiner, who had been one of Robert Phelips' little gang in 1653 and was the brother-in-law of the former Governor, Robert Overton. Early in August 1657, however, Gardiner was careless enough to visit a kinswoman employed at Hampton Court, one of the servants of Richard Cromwell's wife. His conduct there, and later at Whitehall, could not fail to arouse comment. He carried two loaded pistols in his pockets, displayed an intense curiosity about the Protector's movements, and asked if he wore a bullet-proof vest. Gardiner's prompt disappearance into the dungeons wrecked the Hull design. The Pauldens continued to frequent the conspiratorial underworld in London, but Gregory was arrested in December. Langdale's efforts to restore the Royalist organization in his counties had come to nothing.[11]

Of all the disjointed conspiracies in 1657, the one in the area around London possessed the nearest approach to a unified command. It is not clear whether there was an official committee; certainly there was nothing with the cohesiveness of the Action party of 1654–55, much less of the Sealed Knot. Nevertheless, certain self-appointed leaders were in the habit of working together, and with men like Pile, Roscarrock, and the Pauldens from the various provincial groups. One of the Sussex conspirators admitted under questioning that John Hewett, the clergyman, told him of "a committee of several persons in the city, who did by order of Charles Stuart manage the whole affair . . . two whereof he said were Sir Humphrey Bennet and himself." [12] However, the problem of Royalist organization in southeast England is better approached by examining separately the three different groups of which it was composed.

Conspiracy near London first raised its head in Surrey. The old leaders of 1654 were not entirely inactive, but only John Weston showed any notable enthusiasm, and he was more interested in the

An Account How it was taken," *Somers Tracts*, ed. Sir W. Scott (London, 1809–15), 7, 8; *TSP*, *1*, 711, 716–17; *4*, 680; *7*, 33–34, 598–99, 622; HMC, *Var. Coll.*, *2*, 354, 358; *Mercurius Politicus*, No. 377; *CSPD*, *1657–58*, p. 549.

11. *CClSP*, *3*, 337, 356. *TSP*, *1*, 711, 715, 719; *6*, 363, 441–42, 447, 492–93; *7*, 598–99. *Retrospective Review*, 2d ser. *1*, 294. HMC, *Var. Coll.*, *2*, 357.

12. *TSP*, *7*, 66. Cf. Corker's reports: ibid., *1*, 707, 709, 712.

negotiations with the Levellers. The rising star in Surrey was the more spectacular John Mordaunt, younger son of the Earl of Peterborough: he had estates at Reigate and had taken part in the county disturbances of 1648. Mordaunt was one of those "new sprung up Cavaliers, such as young gentlemen lately come into their lands and estates," of whom Clarendon speaks; we have seen similar instances in Brodrick and Shirley. The active career of this new leader began soon after he returned to England in May 1656 from a visit to Holland. His mother's Presbyterian connections qualified him as an intermediary between that party and the Royalists: as early as August 1656 he was said to be trying to bring Shirley and Lord Willoughby together. There was some talk of sending him back to Flanders to report on the discussions, but apparently nothing came of it.[13]

Mordaunt's subsequent policy can be observed in these first beginnings: to broaden the base of Royalist conspiracy by enlisting former enemies and neutrals. He began in earnest about Christmas 1656. His first move was an approach to John Stapley, son of Anthony Stapley, the old Sussex regicide and member of the Long Parliament. After his father's death, John Stapley, who was himself a member of Cromwell's Parliament and a deputy lieutenant of the county, began to show signs of repentance. Mordaunt had taken soundings beforehand, Stapley discovered: "He had spoke with sir William Waller therein, and that he had wished him to come to [Stapley] about it, saying that they did nothing, if they did not ingage that gentleman . . . who was, as he said, a moderate man; and many would rise with him, who would not follow the cavalliers." However attractive the neutrals, Mordaunt did not neglect his relations with the Old Royalists of the area. In Surrey he was aligned with men from both factions: the Royalist Sir Francis Vincent, and Col. Adam Browne, son of the Presbyterian Sir Ambrose Browne of Betchworth. In March 1657 Rumbold reported that Mordaunt and his friends hoped to raise four or five hundred

13. Clarendon, *History*, Bk. XV, § 88. *Clarke Papers, 3,* 147. *Surrey Arch. Coll., 14,* 183–84; Add. MS 34,015, fol. 4. Rawl. MS A 41, p. 576. Cl. MS 52, fol. 370. Both *DNB* and M. Coate, *LBM,* intro., omit any account of Mordaunt's activities in 1656.

horse, and John Weston also wrote enthusiastically of Mordaunt's "quality and double interest." This interest extended beyond Surrey and Sussex, for if rumor was correct, Mordaunt was present at Royalist meetings in Buckinghamshire (he had estates in the county), before the end of the year.[14]

While the Surrey Royalists were beginning to organize under Mordaunt, those in Sussex were also stirring. The first signs of life were in the late winter or early spring of 1657, when a group of the hardier Royalists met at the Dolphin in Chichester. Besides the innkeeper, a certain Henry Binstead, they included Col. George Gunter, Major William Smith of Steyning, and George Hutchinson, the Cuckfield minister. The purpose of the discussion was to prepare for action in Sussex in support of the Spanish invasion, which was expected later in the spring. They were in close touch with Henry Bishop, who had known them all for years and had often impressed them with hints about the importance of his Leveller connections. The conspirators agreed to seek definite instructions from Charles II, to be brought by Hartgil Baron, a Wiltshire Royalist who now lived at Croydon and had attached himself to Mordaunt. They may also have been in touch with the King through another of the 1651 circle, the merchant Francis Mansel, who was regularly crossing the channel on the pretext of business in France.

John Stapley, meanwhile, was extending a helping hand. Corker, who had been teaching a "poore schoole" at Bourne and was in the plot with the title of agent for East Sussex, met him at Lewes during the spring. He found Stapley "not only willing but greedy of the imploymt.," moved by a desire for revenge against certain of the local gentry by whom he had been affronted. Stapley told Corker about the preliminaries of the conspiracy: the collection and storage of arms, the appointment of junior officers, and various other details. The plot soon attracted the attention of the leaders in London. Of these, the one most directly concerned was Sir Humphrey Bennett, who plunged into the intrigue immediately after his re-

14. *TSP*, 6, 569; 7, 68, 88. *CClSP*, 3, 169 (MS 52, fol. 222; deciphered in Appendix, B), 263. For Browne see G.E.C., *Baronetage*, 2, 28–29, and Keeler, p. 117; for Stapley, *DNB*.

lease from the Tower in September 1657. Bennett ran the Sussex conspiracy from a headquarters in London; he was soon corresponding with Bishop, Smith, and Gunter, who often went to him for instructions. On one such occasion, Smith and Henry Binstead found Bennett absurdly optimistic about the strength of the forces they could expect to raise in the county. The two Sussex men regarded 300 horse as the maximum, but Bennett was convinced that ten times that figure was within the bounds of possibility. To divide any statement of numbers by ten is a useful rule of thumb in the mathematics of plotting. Unfortunately, Bennett convinced his London friends of the accuracy of his inflated figures, and repeated corrections from Sussex were ignored.[15]

In London during these years we find a complex web of conspiracy, in which it is only possible to disentangle some of the more significant threads. There were three principal factions in the capital: a group of Old Royalists led by Dr. John Hewett; a less patrician group made up largely of merchants and apprentices; and a strong Presbyterian interest, whose chief agent was Richard Hopton. John Hewett, that mellifluous preacher whose sermons had enthralled Evelyn and many another visitor to St. Gregory's by St. Paul's, had been a chaplain at Oxford and with the King's army in the civil war. His ministry at St. Gregory's, where a tolerant Protectorate winked at the celebration of the technically illegal Anglican rites, must have introduced him to some of the more hardened conspirators. His first recorded appearance as a Royalist agent was around April 1657, when he talked to John Stapley about the Sussex plot, and for the next few months he was chiefly engrossed in making sure of Stapley's allegiance. They had repeated meetings, and in the course of them Hewett assured Stapley that he was one of the committee appointed to manage the plot in London. The Sussex design was by no means Hewett's only interest. He tried to stop the Leveller negotiations when Corker inflamed his suspicions of Wildman. He was also involved in the distribution

15. *TSP, 1,* 708–11, 717–19; *7,* 65–66, 77–81, 89, 93–94, 98–99, 109–10. Rawl. MS A 49, fol. 275. *CSPD, 1657–58,* p. 4. *CClSP, 3,* 169 (MS 52, fol. 222; deciphered in Appendix, B), 374. *Retrospective Review,* 2d ser. *1,* 293. Hutchinson may be the one described as of West Grinstead in Foster, *Al. Oxon.,* p. 778. For Baron see *LBM,* p. 1 n.

of commissions in other regions, often gave advice to the provincial agents, and sent others to report to the King. "He himself told me," Corker informed Thurloe, "that on wednesday he did intend to send one Carlton, whom I know, to Ch. Stew." [16]

The mention of Carleton provides a convenient transition to the composition of the second group and the details of the London plot. Guy Carleton, one of the most energetic agents in London at this period, is another exception to the general rule of clerical abstention from active conspiracy. He had been a fellow of Queen's College, Oxford, and as vicar of Bucklebury, Berkshire, he was enough of a conformist to gain the endorsement of the Westminster Assembly. By 1657 all this was past. Carleton had been ejected from his living, and he emerged as the principal organizer of a plot among a group of London citizens, mostly of lesser rank. Carleton's most active associate was Col. William Deane, of Staines, perhaps the same Deane who had been implicated in the Gerard plot. Deane and Carleton enlisted men, appointed officers, and established liaison with other factions both in and outside the capital. Strategic points were selected and men assigned for their capture: 150 men to each of the gates, 200 to London Bridge, 200 to Tower Hill. Street patrols were planned, some of them to be provided by the Surrey Cavaliers. The Guildhall was to be occupied, the Lord Mayor and Major General Skippon secured, and after an initial rising by 2,000 men, support to the extent of 10,000 "by modest computation" was expected.

The most interesting feature of Carleton's memorandum about the plot is its confident expectation of support from the hitherto generally parliamentarian merchant class. Clarendon contends that by this time, "the putting many gentlemen's sons as apprentices into the city, since the beginning of the troubles, had made a great alteration, at least in the general talk of that people." Apprentices were of course invariably against the government on principle, and it is not surprising to find the angry young men of

16. *TSP*, *1*, 708, 711–12; *7*, 65–68, 74, 88–89. Rawl. MS A 49, fol. 275. *CClSP*, *3*, 310–11, 358, 388–89, 396. The information in *Cal.*, *3*, 281 (MS 54, fol. 178) obviously refers to Stapley, derived from Hewett. It is endorsed "Mr. Dau. by Mr. Coope": possibly by Charles Davison, though it is not in his hand. For Hewett see *DNB*.

the capital nearly as hostile to Cromwell in 1657 as they had been to Charles I in 1642. The participation of established merchants in Carleton's project is more striking. Mr. Ascot, a Ludgate Hill draper, contributed to the expenses of one of Carleton's journeys; Mr. Herne, "a stout and active young citizen," had received many promises from his friends; Mr. Bunkley, a Spanish merchant, knew many citizens who were eager to engage. None of these were men from the great merchant houses, but Bunkley's advice shows how Cromwell's war with Spain was beginning to strain the loyalty of at least some of the citizenry. "Upon his knowledge there was not one in a hundred, of all the Spanish and Turky marchants, but stood well affected to your Matie." Commercial opinion was actually far from unanimous in its condemnation of the war, yet even allowing for exaggerations, the trend away from the Protectorate is unmistakeable.[17]

The Royalists' chances of profiting from this discontent were reduced by the incompetence of the leading conspirators. In the first place, they failed to arrange a united front with the Presbyterians; in the second, Carleton and Deane fell out among themselves. Carleton had originally been wisely aware of the importance of an agreement with the Presbyterians. In his first mission to the King he asked for the appointment of a Presbyterian agent to work for a satisfactory union with his own group; Charles named Richard Hopton for the post. When Carleton returned to London, he and Hopton "often discoursed freely together," and Carleton promised that his party would serve under suitably qualified Presbyterian officers. Carleton proposed Major General Browne to command the foot, leaving the cavalry command open. Hopton's friend Robert Huntington was also prominent in the discussions on the Presbyterian side. Eventually, Carleton's Royalists awaited only the fulfillment of the Presbyterians' promises to start the rising. "But," said Carleton, "when we expected present action upon Major Huntington's promise, they flatly by him denied any assistance, their agent [Hopton] alleging that he would meddle no

17. *CClSP*, *3*, 372–73 (MS 56, fols. 146–47). Clarendon, *History*, Bk. XV, § 88. See also Firth, *Protectorate*, *2*, 72–74. For Carleton see *DNB*, and Matthews, *Walker Revised*, p. 68.

more in the business." The Presbyterian defection precipitated the breach between Deane and Carleton. There was already some jealousy between them, Deane having refused to furnish Carleton with a list of his adherents, and when Richard Pile was proposed as arbiter of the quarrel, Carleton would have nothing to do with him. Unfortunately for the Royalists, the ubiquitous Corker was mixed up in it all; and when the final breakdown occurred, Thurloe soon heard about it. There was a meeting at which Hopton told Deane and Carleton that the Presbyterians were not ready. Deane was furious and announced that he would go ahead alone, instead of awaiting further orders from the King, as Carleton wished to do. Soon afterward Deane was arrested at his lodgings, and although he escaped the same day, he disappeared from London. Carleton was left to repair the damage.[18]

Such were the preparations of 1657. The prospects of successful action in 1658 were obviously remote. The new Action party was even more amorphous than its predecessor of 1654: a collection of local conspiracies, coordinated only by the intermittent liaison which each maintained with the exiles. Agents of the stamp of Pile and Hopton were therefore even more lacking in intelligent direction than they had been three years before. The old leaders of the Action party were either in jail or retirement, and conspiracy was almost entirely deprived of the active support of the party's essential foundation, the gentry. The few gentry who were involved, Veel, Gunter, and the rest, were not men of powerful interest. Only in Devon and Cornwall, under Grenville, Pollard, and the Arundells, was there a local organization directed by men of the old caliber. The much desired foreign army still hovered mirage-like above the horizon. But there was little to support it in England,

---

18. *ClSP, 3, 369–70.* Carleton uses the initials "J.H." for the Presbyterian agent, but in his other paper he mentions Hopton by name in the same context. The association of "J.H." with Huntington is further proof that Hopton is intended. See also *CClSP, 3, 372–75; TSP, 1, 709, 711–12, 714;* and Egerton MS 2542, fols. 281–82. In this last paper Deane uses initials for the leading figures. It seems reasonable to identify "D" as Deane, "C" as Carleton, and "D.P." as Pile. Firth, *Protectorate, 2, 73,* misses the point that the trouble was caused by friction between Royalists and Presbyterians.

even if the Spaniards were capable of overcoming their military and administrative lethargy. Actually the Spaniards at the end of 1657 were showing unusual energy—a sudden, unaccustomed desire to live up to their commitments. On September 11 Bristol, Charles II's principal negotiator, announced that Don Juan was setting aside 150,000 crowns to equip the joint expedition. While far short of the Spaniards' original promises, this was enough for a force sufficient to secure a bridgehead. On November 28, Hyde told Rumbold that they would embark 1,000 musketeers no later than mid-January, provided there was assurance of a port in England to receive them, covered by a supporting insurrection.[19]

The assurance was entirely outside the power of Rumbold, or any other Royalist. The government was already displaying its usual vigilance. On December 2 Cromwell warned the authorities at Bristol and Gloucester of imminent danger. On the 7th Brodrick's cousin, Allen Apsley, reported mounting tension in London, and the doubling of the guards there. Philip Honywood arrived in town the same day, after an adventurous crossing. His ship was examined by a naval squadron off Gravesend, and when he reached London he found the Tower prisoners under much closer supervision than usual. On the 17th the Council of State ordered the Lord Mayor and Aldermen to provide extra guards for the City, and took steps to send emergency supplies to various garrisons up and down the country. They were evidently necessary: at Gloucester the militia had only 150 muskets and no pikes. On the night of the 18th there was a general search for Royalist agents in London, and on Christmas Day a roundup of congregations at Anglican services. The indignant John Evelyn was subjected to some "frivolous & insnaring questions" by the investigating officers. Vague rumors of a new plot continued to be the talk of the town. The usual ban on horse-racing was imposed, and before the end of the year orders had gone out for the securing of suspects at various provincial centers. Within a few days the commanders at York and Shrewsbury had made diligent response, and the innocuous Wil-

19. *ClSP, 3,* 367, 377. *CClSP, 3,* 370, 394. See also Firth, *Protectorate, 2,* 53–54.

liam Blundell, under restraint at Liverpool, heard that "there are many such prisoners in divers parts of England." [20]

Once again the situation demanded a decision by the King himself: to continue or postpone the action. On December 16 Jonathan Trelawney arrived at Bruges with sanguine, inflated estimates of the strength of the designs in Sussex and London. "The truth is," Hyde wrote urgently to Ormond, ". . . the conjuncture seems as favourable as can be wished, nor can it ever be presumed that the kinge can be in a greater readynesse then he is at present. . . . Every paper from Englande, wherof one is to you from J. Ashburnham, cryes to hast away, matters cannot be better praepared." Every paper, that is, except those from the wary gentlemen of the Sealed Knot. The Spaniards must have had their suspicions about the divided opinions in England. On December 21 Don Juan suggested that Ormond should go to England to make a last-minute examination of the new Action party's plans. It was a sensible proposal, and Ormond, fretting at the boredom of exile, jumped at it. Hyde's middle-aged objections were overruled, the King approved, and stories were soon being put about that the Marquis was off on a mission to the Imperial Diet, gone to raise troops in the dominions of the Duke of Neuburg; anywhere but England. Ormond did not have to look far for an assistant; Daniel O'Neill with his subtlety and experience in 1655 was conveniently at hand.[21]

Ormond arrived in London on Saturday, January 30, 1658. Nine days of narrow escapes and busy negotiations followed. Thurloe's men made regular searches, and Ormond was never more than one move ahead of his pursuers. Willys was probably responsible both

20. *CClSP, 3*, 397, 399, 406. *TSP, 6*, 727; 7, 598–99. Rawl. MS A 56, fol. 242. *Mercurius Politicus*, No. 399. *Clarke Papers, 3*, 130–31. HMC, *5th Report*, Appendix, pp. 152, 165–66. Abbott, *4*, 678 and n. *Evelyn*, ed. de Beer, *3*, 203–5. *CSPD, 1657–58*, p. 217. *Bibliotheca Gloucestrensis*, ed. John Washbourn (Gloucester, 1825), pp. 419–20. *Cavalier Letters of William Blundell . . . 1620–1698*, ed. Margaret Blundell (London, 1933), pp. 67–68. Blundell's imprisonment is here given as December 1656, but there is obviously confusion over O.S. dates: cf. ibid., pp. 70, 83.

21. Clarendon, *History*, Bk. XV, §§ 84–86; *Con.*, §§ 28–29. *ClSP, 3*, 386. *CClSP, 3*, 404–6. Cl. MSS 56, fol. 351; 57, fol. 43. See also Firth, *Protectorate*, 2, 60–61; Scott, *Travels of the King*, pp. 326–28; and Winifred, Lady Burghclere, *Life of James first Duke of Ormonde* (London, 1912), *1*, 487.

for the pursuit and for Ormond's good luck in evading it. He later admitted that Thurloe and Morland pressed him to betray Ormond, and that he had more than one meeting with them about it. His earlier, allegedly innocent understanding with the Secretary was not innocent at all; and he had as good reason to misrepresent this incident as he had the other one. Carte, Ormond's biographer, believed that Willys regularly informed Cromwell of Ormond's lodgings, but always tipped him off in time for a move to other quarters. Either Ormond was incredibly lucky in his movements or Willys was indeed responsible for the comedy. Thurloe, at all events, was soon hot on Ormond's scent: "I got knowledge of his business, but could not come at his person," he told Henry Cromwell on February 16.[22]

Amid these adventures, Ormond contrived to perform the business of his mission. At first glance, the political situation appeared reasonably favorable. Five days after Ormond's arrival, Cromwell dissolved Parliament with an angry "Let God be judge between you and me." A medley of disgruntled opposition voices, a Spanish fleet in the Flanders ports—the tinder was there, if the Royalists were capable of supplying the match to produce combustion. Ormond soon found, however, that the high promises that had encouraged the exiles evaporated on close inspection. His first conference was with the protagonists of action. Faced with Ormond they at once emerged in their true colors; they "would not be persuaded to declare until the King should be first landed . . . some of them saying, they knew very well the preparations in Flanders were not so forward as I delivered them." Richard Pile's grandiose scheme in Gloucestershire was the biggest disappointment. "I found nothing like a probability that it could be effected, if attempted; nor any disposition in the actors to attempt it, till the King's landing," Ormond reported. As for Hewett and Stapley, Ormond did not even think it worth taking the time to speak with them. The whole affair had been managed by "honest but unskilful

22. For the best general account of Ormond's mission see Thomas Carte, *The Life of James, Duke of Ormond* (Oxford, 1851), *3*, 658–67. For Thurloe's knowledge of it see *Notes and Queries*, 12th ser. *10*, 123; Clarendon, *History*, Bk. XV, § 91; XVI, § 28; *TSP*, *6*, 806.

men." The discussions which some of the new leaders had been having with prominent members of the anti-Cromwellian opposition seemed equally futile. Sir Henry Moore, who had promised to enlist Alexander Popham, wrote confidently to Hyde that he had obtained definite assurances, but they were illusory. Popham would be "no beginer seperat from his Presbiter party," Ormond decided. The influential Col. Richard Norton, a Hampshire Presbyterian of whom much had been heard, was another broken reed. Ormond found that the only way of securing him was through the old puritan magnate Lord Saye and Sele, whose terms were uncompromisingly based on the Isle of Wight treaty; and this to Ormond was not worth discussing. The Levellers were even more useless. Wildman's duplicity was generally admitted, and William Howard was in prison.

Ormond next moved into the more fashionable world of the Sealed Knot. At Russell's lodgings in Bedford Gardens and at Willys' chambers in Gray's Inn, he explored the opinions of the secret committee. Villiers was there, and William Legge, who had not previously been associated with the Knot; but Compton was out of town, nothing was heard of Loughborough, and Belasyse contrived to reach London the day after Ormond left. Those who were present showed even greater coolness than Ormond had observed in the men of lesser rank: coming from the Knot it was at least more consistent. Willys, according to Carte, was "more copious than any other, in setting forth the impediments that lay in the way of an attempt." He was not alone in this opinion, however, and Ormond himself shared the Knot's conclusion that the various projects were distinguished only by their utter lack of realism.[23]

Ormond waited a few days to see what effect the dissolution of Parliament would have, and then finding it was going to be very little, on February 8 he left for France. After his pessimistic verdicts on the regional designs, his general conclusions are remarkable. He found, he told Hyde in his first dispatch, "all the inclinations imaginable" toward a general rising, more "than I could have beleived without the proof of my senses." The ineptitude of indi-

23. Carte, *Ormond*, *3*, 660–62. Carte, *Papers*, *2*, 118–20, 122–23, 125, 129–30. *CClSP*, *4*, 8 (MS 57, fol. 71), 9, 13, 15.

vidual conspirators might be discouraging, but Ormond was certain that all that was needed for the Royalists, and many of the neutrals, to appear in arms, was an initial success. "If the King can but once land at or near Yarmouth, but with the numbers and provisions designed him," Ormond asserted, "that town will be his before it can be succoured." The point was not that there had been any special preparations by the Yarmouth Royalists (though Shirley had once investigated the possibilities of nearby Lovingland), but that Cromwell would be unable to deploy his forces rapidly enough to stop the Spaniards disembarking. A landing at Yarmouth, Ormond insisted, would enable Charles to "gain reputation enough to gather a force sufficient to do (I think) his own business, and (I am sure) the King of Spain's." The essence of Ormond's advice is plain: first the invasion, then the rising.[24]

The final impasse had now been reached. The Spaniards had all along demanded a Royalist rising as a precondition of invasion; the conspirators were now laying down exactly the contrary requirement. There was still time for the Spaniards to change their minds, and Charles, Hyde, and Bristol joined in a chorus of advice that they should do so. It was too late. In February the expedition could have sailed, for the blockading English squadron had been driven off the Flanders coast by the weather. On February 27 Vice-Admiral Goodson arrived off Ostend with twelve frigates, re-established the blockade, and broke up a small fleet of chartered Dutch transports sailing to pick up the Spanish troops. Although the Spaniards still talked hopefully of breaking the blockade, it was impossible, and the exiled leaders recognized as much. On March 20 word was sent to Brodrick for the Knot, and to Mordaunt for the Action party, that the invasion was off. Five days later O'Neill and the other agents who were still in London were recalled.[25]

Nearly eight weeks elapsed between Ormond's departure from London and the arrival of O'Neill's recall notice on April 2. It was

24. Carte, *Papers,* 2, 118, 120–21, 123. For the previous history of the Yarmouth-Lovingland design see *CClSP, 3,* 142, 264; *TSP, 5,* 512; Br. MS 1, fol. 17.

25. Carte, *Papers,* 2, 124–26, 131–32, 135. Bristol's letter on p. 135 is misdated; the original (Cl. MS 57, fol. 202) is dated March 5/15. *ClSP, 3,* 397. *CClSP, 3,* 268; *4,* 31. See also Firth, *Protectorate,* 2, 65–67.

a time of energetic but pointless activity. Agents from the Continent bustled into the country, clamoring for action. Daniel O'Neill stayed in London, "full of negotiations"; perhaps fortunately, he had no written authority from either the King or Ormond.[26] After Ormond's departure O'Neill had several conferences with members of the Knot. His general criticisms are surprising: "I find, either they are very reserved to me, or else they have very little informed themselves of the state of things here; their too cautious dealing has made most of your friends shy of them, and them to trust few; all the design I see they have, is but to get on horseback with their friends and find you out when they can." This mingling of reckless desperation with their usual caution was curiously out of keeping with the Knot's past. That O'Neill was probably right in detecting it is suggested by the contrast between the attitudes of Russell and Villiers. O'Neill approached Russell about a plan to seize Warwick castle. Russell invented a long catalogue of objections, and although in the end he consented to try, O'Neill concluded that little would come of it. Villiers, on the other hand, reported with unusual optimism "that all in whom he hath interest persuade the King's speedy coming." Russell was in the Tower before the end of March, and Villiers, although he claimed to have some "little irons . . . in the fire," hastily left town after a proclamation expelling Cavaliers from the capital. Villiers was mainly distinguished for an absurd suggestion that Charles should marry Cromwell's youngest daughter, the recently widowed Frances Rich. "Indeed Ned Villiers makes a lusty proposition," Hyde commented scornfully, ". . . and if he were in his wits he would believe nothing in nature more impossible." [27]

Villiers may or may not have been out of his mind; other members of the Knot were little more constructive in their intelligence. Belasyse came to London as soon as Ormond was out of the way, engaged in some half-hearted negotiations with the Presbyterian

26. Carte, *Papers*, 2, 132–33. *TSP*, 6, 834. *ClSP*, 3, 388. *CClSP*, 4, 12 ("Horwood" not "Norwood" in MS 57, fol. 123), 18, 36.
27. *ClSP*, 3, 390–91, 396. *CClSP*, 4, 13 (MS 57, fol. 126), 15–16, 18, 29, 34. Steele, *Proclamations*, 1, 373.

Earl of Manchester; he does not seem to have been much concerned about raising his northern neighbors. Compton was in the country during the whole of O'Neill's stay; early in March O'Neill asked him to come to London, but on the 26th he was still in Cambridgeshire. Although Willys kept in touch with O'Neill, he made no pretense of having exerted himself. His letters were little more than laments of his "age & sicknesse," or peevish complaints against people who had tried to cause trouble between him and Brodrick. He soon withdrew to Fen Ditton. Only Brodrick, keeping up communications when the others were driven out of town, was really trying to live up to the Knot's obligations while O'Neill was in London.[28]

O'Neill's relations with the Action party's representatives were more encouraging than those with the Knot but equally fruitless in the end. His negotiations were hampered by the usual difficulties. A week after Ormond left for France, Brodrick reported continued troop movements and the arrest of suspicious persons. On March 3 all Papists and Royalists were ordered to leave London and stay within five miles of their usual residences. On the 11th the authorities at Bristol and Gloucester were again warned to take precautions, and the next day Cromwell harangued the Lord Mayor and Aldermen at Whitehall, telling them of Ormond's recent visit and of the apparently imminent invasion; the sequel was yet another reorganization of the London militia. Although some of the suspects arrested earlier in the provinces were released in the first week of March, they were soon replaced in prison by others; notably in Yorkshire, where Sir Jordan Crosland and Sir Philip Monckton were among those secured at Hull. The Presbyterians Robert Harley and Sir William Waller were summoned before the Council on the 21st, and although the latter was discharged, Harley went to the Tower. Two nights later there was a thorough search in London for Royalists foolhardy enough to defy the proclamation, and a number were taken. Those arrested included John Stapley, and the Bristol agent William Clayton. In this

28. *ClSP*, *3*, 329–30 (1658, not 1657; see *Cal., 4*, 19–20), 390, 392, 395. *CClSP*, *4*, 13, 15, 19–25 (MS 57, fols. 208, 219). Br. MS 1, fol. 90.

last case an _agent provocateur,_ a certain Charles Wheeler, was responsible.[29]

O'Neill, still awaiting news of the Spaniards' plans, contrived to keep the creaking wheels of conspiracy turning. He arranged a meeting with the agents promoting the designs on Bristol, Gloucester, and Shrewsbury and with those managing approaches to opposition magnates like Popham and Denbigh. "The first half hour," he told Hyde, "was spent in venting their discontents against you for the encouragements you gave them to make preparations when you knew you could not come, and Lord Ormond for coming." After a general denunciation of their pettiness, he concluded: "Here is Pyles, he knows as much as you or more. . . . I must confess itt terrifyes me to know soe senceless a creature should know all he does." Suppressing his wrath, on March 25 O'Neill made a tentative proposal to begin the action within twelve days, by which time he hoped to receive final instructions from the King. As in 1655, O'Neill allowed his judgment to be swayed by possibilities rather than certainties. There were even fewer signs of planning than in 1655, but he put his faith in the assurances of a few prominent individuals, and hoped for the best: Hertford in the West; Compton in the area south of the Trent; Byron in Nottingham and Derbyshire; the Newport interest in Shropshire; Sir George Booth in Cheshire; and more improbably, the Earl of Denbigh at Coventry. Commissions were being distributed, but O'Neill must have known that he was wasting his time. The agents for the regional schemes spoke enthusiastically from a distance but always hedged when asked for definite commitments. On March 25 Richard Pile brought the considered verdict of the London plotters. Their answer was monotonously repeated: we will fight, but the rebellion must be begun "somewhere else." The only section of the conspiracy that seemed eager to strike the first blow was the one in Gloucestershire, which Ormond had dismissed as hopeless, and was already betrayed to Cromwell. The Gloucester militia commissioners had even managed to increase their stock of muskets

29. _ClSP, 3,_ 388, 397. _CClSP, 4,_ 18–19, 22, 32, 36. _TSP, 1,_ 713–14; _7,_ 13–14; 97–98, 785. Steele, _Proclamations, 1,_ 373. Abbott, _4,_ 758–61. SPDI, 180, fol. 206. See also Firth, _Protectorate, 2,_ 50–52, 67–69.

to 300. Fortunately for the other Royalists, O'Neill's recall orders came before the twelve days had elapsed.[30]

The most significant result of O'Neill's two months in London was a more determined approach to the Presbyterians. They had provided some earlier recruits—Willoughby, Browne, the Booths, for example—and there were many more who might be won over by minor concessions. These did not include old-line Presbyterians like Saye and Sele, Robartes, and Richard Norton, who stood rigidly by the Isle of Wight terms. Through men like the Earl of Manchester, O'Neill was in touch with both factions. Manchester advised that the extremists should be conciliated by the publication of something "that would join them to the more moderate"; but, O'Neill reported, "he would not undertake to say what it was." The behavior of Colonel Norton during these months illustrates the dangers of even making approaches to the more implacable Presbyterians. Ormond had refused to meet Norton, but other Royalists had been less wary, and Norton must have gained an inkling of the current design from them. His response was to send Thurloe an enigmatic letter, warning of "some intention of trobles to come upon us," declining to mention the grounds of his fears but assuring the Secretary of his loyalty to the Protector. The return of the vague and conditional answer to the Royalist overture, then the move to obtain clearance with the authorities—this seems to have been the typical behavior of the neutral in 1658.[31]

From Manchester's more moderate friends, men like Sir William Waller, there was more to be hoped. These, O'Neill believed, required no real concessions, but "would be contented with what would secure their lives and estates." The discussions between Belasyse and Manchester, from which O'Neill expected much, were slow in getting under way, and in spite of Manchester's moderation Belasyse could not obtain from him anything more than a "general engagement." Mordaunt achieved only the same kind of partial success with Waller. By this time Thurloe was convinced of Waller's

30. *ClSP, 3,* 394–96. *CClSP, 4,* 20–21, 30, 34 (MS 57, fol. 301), 36, 38. Washbourn, pp. 422–23.

31. Carte, *Papers,* 2, 125, 128, 130, 133. *ClSP, 3,* 392. *CClSP, 4,* 9, 17, 29. *TSP, 6,* 856.

complicity in Royalist plotting, but he was unable to produce irrefutable evidence against him; after being questioned by the Protector, Sir William was allowed to go home.[32] Alexander Popham, one of the surviving moderates from the Rump's Council of State, was another subject of discussion. His interest in Wiltshire and Somerset made him indispensable if the western Presbyterians were to be engaged. Early in 1658 the Royalists tried to win him over, but the attempt was not well conducted. Sir Henry Moore, the entrusted agent, gave repeated assurances of Popham's support; his optimistic inaccuracy completely destroyed Ormond's confidence in him. When Ormond tried to enlist John Russell in the affair Moore refused to have anything to do with him, in spite of the fact that Russell was known and trusted by Popham. Eventually, O'Neill sent Russell's brother Edward to Littlecote to ask whether Popham "would admit of Wil. Leg, Sr. Richard Willis and other good officers . . . to assist him to forme his party and to prevent the disorders naturall to insurrections." Before his attitude could be clarified, however, Popham suffered a diplomatic fall from his horse and withdrew to convalesce.[33]

The position of the great Fairfax, an even more desirable recruit from the neutrals, was little changed in 1658 from that of three years before. In September 1657 his daughter Mary had at last married the Duke of Buckingham, producing the usual crop of rumors of Fairfax's inclinations toward the Stuart cause. Buckingham's own loyalty was of course highly questionable, but the Council of State had not forgiven him, and in October 1657 he was arrested for defying their order to stay away from London. A more promising avenue to Fairfax's ear was through his cousin Robert Harley, a Presbyterian-Royalist ever since 1648, who was often at Nun Appleton. Harley played some part in arranging the Buckingham-Fairfax match, and his aunt, Lady Vere, the General's mother-in-law, had also done much to promote it. Harley's presence in Fairfax's household proves nothing, but he was certainly in touch

32. *ClSP, 3,* 388–89, 392–95. *CClSP, 4,* 17–18, 20. *Clarke Papers, 3,* 144–45. *TSP, 7,* 84, 100. Sir William Waller, *Recollections:* appendix to *The Poetry of Anna Matilda* (London, 1788), p. 116.

33. Carte, *Papers, 2,* 122, 125, 129–31. *ClSP, 3,* 393. *CClSP, 4,* 8–9, 20 (MS 57, fol. 260), 29, 36.

with Royalist agents during 1657. Another of Harley's relatives, the Earl of Oxford, had been frequently mentioned as a suitable commander of the Royalist rising, and both Harley and John Denham tried to use him to the Royalists' advantage. In March 1658 O'Neill heard that Denham had "much interest with Lord Oxford unto whome hee is now goeing . . . wth some foolish design from [Buckingham]."

The Buckingham marriage and Harley's presence at Nun Appleton suggest nothing more than the usual unverifiable suspicion that Fairfax may have known more about Royalist intrigues than his public actions seemed to imply. In March 1658 Harley and Oxford were examined by the Council, but provided no clues to the General's position. Willys, who had volunteered information about Fairfax in December, said merely that he was angry at the arrest of Buckingham, and had been heard to complain that since the dissolution of the Long Parliament "there was nothing but shifting and a kind of confusion; and that he knew not but he might chuse by his old commission as generall to appear in armes on behalf of the people of these nations." From the extremely fragmentary evidence it seems unlikely that Fairfax had edged any further toward the Royalists than in 1654; once again, however, it is possible that he did not discourage the approaches of those close to him. Safeguarded by the Buckingham marriage, Fairfax would have little reason either to fear a restoration, or to wish to see the country plunged into bloodshed by an attempt before the time was ripe.[34]

Although none of these overtures to the Presbyterians in the early months of 1658 achieved anything definite, the increased tempo of the discussions is still significant. The Presbyterian feeling for a restoration was rather a tendency than an established policy, but there were signs that the years of neutrality were drawing to an end. The Presbyterians had never abandoned the principle of limited monarchy; but they had learned their lesson in

34. *TSP, 1,* 707, 713; *6,* 124, 616–17, 706; *7,* 20, 66, 79, 84. Rawl. MS A 55, pp. 298–312. *ClSP, 3,* 396. *CClSP, 3,* 167, 318, 373; *4,* 21 (MS 57, fol. 261). See also Firth, *Protectorate, 2,* 56–57; Burghclere, *Buckingham,* pp. 80–93; Markham, pp. 371–73. For Harley and his connections see *LBM,* p. 10 n.; *Letters of the Lady Brilliana Harley,* ed. T. T. Lewis, Camden Society (London, 1854), intro., pp. xii–xiii; and HMC, *Portland, 8,* 8–14.

1648 and 1651 and as long as a Royalist victory still appeared unthinkably distant they would prefer passive acquiescence to the prospect of another civil war, and would still insist on the distasteful Isle of Wight terms as the price of their support. The improvement of Charles II's position by the Spanish alliance encouraged the proposal of more moderate conditions, which however were never clearly defined. Their assimilation with the Old Royalists had as yet scarcely begun, except in isolated instances like that of Willoughby, whose indifference to terms makes it impossible to class him as a Presbyterian at all. It is rather in the changing attitude of Manchester, and perhaps even Popham, that real progress can be measured.

The Presbyterians might offer important possibilities for the future, but for the present we are concerned with the Royalists. The plot investigated by Ormond and O'Neill was undoubtedly underprepared and would have ended in disaster if it had been allowed to proceed. The moral effect of yet another cancellation was none the less unfortunate. The activists were bitterly cast down. Dick Pile, true to form, had already announced that he would wait a fortnight and that if nothing was done he would "endeavour his peace and meddle no more." The postponement, Corker jubilantly told Thurloe, "hath so deaded the hearts of all our party, that hereafter Ch. Stew. will scarce get any to appear for him in England." Fortunately for Charles, it was not quite so bad as this, and the sober majority approved the decision: even Mordaunt admitted that the postponement had received no worse than a mixed reception.[35] This ought to have been the end of the conspiracy of 1658. There were soon even stronger arguments against any further foolish intrigues. A new series of arrests swept more of the Royalist leaders into prison, as well as some, like Sir Justinian Isham, who had not been actively involved. Early in April Willys and Sir William Compton went to join John Russell in the Tower. John Stapley's terrified volubility under examination led to the securing of Hewett, Mordaunt, Sir Humphrey Bennett, and a number of lesser men from Sussex. Before the end of the month Thurloe was in possession of most of the details of the conspiracy in the counties

35. *TSP, 1,* 718. *CClSP, 4,* 34–36. *CSPD, 1657–58,* p. 336.

south of London. Stapley saved his neck by the comprehensiveness of his disclosures, and by an abject appeal for the Protector's pardon. Preparations were soon on foot for the trial of several of the leaders by an emergency High Court of Justice.[36]

The only sensible policy for the Royalists was to lick their wounds and await better days. The Carleton-Deane group, however, persisted in their plans to raise disturbances in London. Deane had recovered from his earlier discontents, Carleton was still distributing commissions and urging on his followers, and a new leader had emerged in the person of Robert Manley, a Turkey merchant from Threadneedle Street. There was the usual round of secret meetings at the Feathers in Cheapside and other popular taverns. Early in May they decided to ignore the defection of their Presbyterian and Cavalier allies, and act alone. Zero hour was set for Saturday night, May 15, at eleven o'clock. Most of the original objectives were still included: to seize London Bridge and the Tower; requisition the arms stored at the Artillery Ground; arrest the Lord Mayor and the sheriffs; obtain additional mounts from the inn stables, funds from the goldsmiths' shops, and recruits from the jails. It was a ridiculous venture, recalling the worst aspects of the Gerards' schemes. Through the assiduous Corker, Thurloe kept pace with the developments and allowed the design to mature until its leaders had been given rope enough to hang themselves. On Friday night, the 14th, Corker gave the final warning, and the full resources of the government went swiftly into action the next morning. The guards were doubled, regiments placed on a footing of immediate preparedness, and the trained bands ordered to assemble. Barkstead's regiment patrolled the streets and searched alehouses for suspects. About forty prisoners were taken, among them Deane and Manley; the latter escaped almost at once, and got away to the Continent. Carleton and a number of other leaders also vanished, but the design was smashed with contemptuous ease.[37]

The pitiful consequences of the London conspiracy burst into

36. *Publick Intelligencer*, Nos. 119, 122. *TSP*, 7, 25, 61–110. *Duppa-Isham Corr.*, pp. 149–51, 158–59. *Notes and Queries*, 12th ser. *10*, 123.

37. *TSP*, *1*, 713, 715; 7, 137–38, 140, 147–48. *CSPD*, *1658–59*, pp. 39–40. *Cromwelliana*, p. 172. *Mercurius Politicus*, Nos. 416, 420. *Clarke Papers*, *3*, 150. See also Firth, *Protectorate*, 2, 74–76.

the limelight after the High Court of Justice had already begun its sessions, and some of the new prisoners were promptly added to the accused. The trials proceeded in three stages: the first, to deal with three of the most prominent prisoners, Hewett, Mordaunt, and Sir Henry Slingsby from Yorkshire; the second, Bennett and two of his lieutenants in Sussex, Henry Mallory and Thomas Woodcock; and the third, seven of the London plotters. The government was not far off the mark in identifying Hewett and Mordaunt as the ringleaders. Slingsby, on the other hand, was merely unlucky, as he had not been intimately connected with the underground movement for some time. His case stands out as one of the worst examples of the distasteful business of "trepanning" during the entire Protectorate. In December 1657 Slingsby was a prisoner at Hull, where he tried to subvert Major Robert Waterhouse, one of the officers of the garrison. Waterhouse reported the matter to his commander, and was instructed to lead Slingsby on until the proofs of his treason were legally complete. The whole process was controlled at every stage by Cromwell and Thurloe, and although such incidents are not uncommon in the history of Royalist conspiracy, this one exhibits the Protector at his most vindictive.[38] Trepanned or no, Slingsby was guilty according to the law; he was executed on June 8. Hewett refused to plead and suffered the same fate. After a chain of fortunate circumstances, Mordaunt was acquitted on the casting vote of the president of the court.[39]

The other trials followed in quick succession, and all were over by the first days of July. The case against Bennett was dropped, Woodcock was acquitted, and Mallory sentenced to death and reprieved. Six of the minor figures from the London plot were sentenced to death: three were executed and three reprieved.[40] It was not a happy ending to the busy efforts of Carleton and his friends, but

38. *TSP*, 6, 777–81, 870; 7, 13–14, 46–47, 65, 98, 111–13, 121–27.

39. For the trials of Hewett, Slingsby, and Mordaunt see Howell, ed., *State Trials*, 5, 871–936; *Mercurius Politicus*, Nos. 417–19; *The Tryals of Sir Henry Slingsby and John Hewet, and John Mordaunt for High Treason, in Westminster Hall*, June 1658; and M. Coate, *LBM*, intro., p. xi.

40. The trials and executions of the second and third groups of prisoners are described in *Mercurius Politicus*, Nos. 420, 423; and *Publick Intelligencer*, No. 133. See also *TSP*, 7, 162–66; Clarendon, *History*, Bk. XV, §§ 95–102; and Firth, *Protectorate*, 2, 76–82.

it might have been worse. The government's intention to deter further conspiracies by making a few bloody examples was only partly successful. Repression, as always, worked both ways, and after a few months of quiescence there was the inevitable hardening of opinion. Recovery, however, was bound to take time. Once again the militant wing of the Royalist party had come to grief.

11. *The Great Trust and Commission*

THE CRUCIAL EVENT of the year 1658 was, ironically, one over which Royalists had no control, often as they had hoped for it. On September 3 Oliver Cromwell died peacefully in his bed, removing the one strong hand capable of reconciling the divergent pressures of puritan militarism and constitutional moderation, on which the Protectorate had been balanced. As if to foreshadow the release of hitherto harnessed political forces, the natural elements had combined in a tumultuous prelude, for the previous week was marked by "the greatest storm of wind that had ever been known . . . which overthrew trees, houses, and made great wrecks at sea." Cromwell was dead, and the Leveller William Howard noted the surge of optimism that fleetingly inspired his enemies, Royalist and republican alike: "All men's hearts (almost quite dead before) are of a sudden wonderfully revived to an expectation of some great change." [1]

The Royalists might rejoice, but for the present this was all the advantage they were likely to derive from the situation. "Contrary to all expectation both at home and abroad, this earthquake was attended with no signal alteration," Clarendon regretted. In some

1. Clarendon, *History,* Bk. XV, § 146. *ClSP, 3,* 407. *Evelyn,* ed. de Beer, *3,* 220 and n. One victim of the storm was the agent Charles Davison, who was washed overboard when outward bound from Antwerp: *CClSP, 4,* 69–72, 77.

respects, indeed, they were worse off than ever. Richard Cromwell, quietly succeeding to the uncrowned monarchy, inherited little of the accumulated hatred that had colored the attitudes of so many to his father. If Richard showed only a reasonable degree of statesmanship he might complete the work of "settlement": win over the neutrals who asked only for stability, and gain something more positive than the resentful acquiescence of the inactive majority of the Royalist party, which Oliver had obtained only by repression. Richard's friendly relations with neutral and even Royalist gentry, cultivated in leisurely Hampshire hunting parties, might make him an even more dangerous enemy than Oliver had been, although for diametrically opposite reasons.[2]

The condition of the Cavalier party at the time of Richard Cromwell's accession is enough to explain the serenity of the transition. The failure in the spring of 1658, the arrests in the early summer, and the severity of the High Court of Justice left the resistance movement in one of its periodic states of confusion and indecision. The Sealed Knot, as usual, was seriously affected. When Willys, Russell, and Compton were released from the Tower in July, Thurloe gave them solemn warning, according to Brodrick, "that if they negotiated after their enlargement they must expect no quarter." The threat had little meaning as far as Willys was concerned, but it succeeded in deterring Russell and Compton. On August 13 Brodrick explained the Knot's position to his patron Hyde: "From the rest of my friends I have no commission of farther intercourse, but Sir Richard Willis hath impowered me to say, that though he hath shared the same hard fortune, he will not . . . be so unmannerly as to withdraw himself from the King's service without his Majesty's leave and your Lordship's knowledge; he only begs that affairs may a little cool and his name be forgot, before your Lordship address to him, being forced to a present retirement from London; and if he be at any time mentioned in Flanders, he desires your Lordship to pass him over with all slightness." [3]

---

2. Clarendon, *History,* Bk. XVI, §§ 1–2. See also Hardacre, *Royalists,* p. 132; and Godfrey Davies, *The Restoration of Charles II 1658–1660* (San Marino, Cal., 1955), pp. 7–8, 15–16.

3. *ClSP, 3,* 406. *CClSP, 4,* 177. HMC, *5th Report,* Appendix, p. 145.

Although Brodrick resumed regular correspondence with Hyde early in October 1658, the interruption of the Knot's activities continued for several more months. Brodrick's letters are not informative; he was mainly concerned about answering reports of his own indiscretions and complaining of the failure of Hyde's letters to reach him. Villiers was the only one of the six to report symptoms of a swing toward the Royalists. The day of Cromwell's death he was visited by "an eminent person" of the Cromwellian party, "who fell into a discourse tending to his Majesty's advantage." Villiers hoped the person would clarify his intentions, but three weeks later he had heard nothing more from him and concluded that it was merely a sign that the Cromwellians scented a crisis and wished to insure themselves against a Stuart restoration. Whenever there was a real possibility of this, Villiers thought, "there will not want those of Cromwell's party that will close with his Majesty." Villiers decided to stay in London through the winter, hoping to resume contact with the same person, but there were no further developments. Little is known about the activities of the other members, who were dispersed in the country. Belasyse had been having desultory discussions with Major General Browne and Fauconberg; in January 1659 the King authorized him to use the family connection to make an overture to Richard Cromwell himself. The Knot seems to have made little effort to influence the elections to Parliament. Brodrick, unhindered by past convictions for delinquency, had some hope of getting in, but it came to nothing.[4]

Hyde must have been accustomed to the Knot's long periods of retirement. More disturbing was the silence of many others who had borne the heat and burden of conspiracy. William Rumbold was released from the Tower at about the time of Cromwell's death and continued his correspondence with the Chancellor, but he was not a man of sufficient weight to do much without assistance. Sir Henry Moore, after a visit to Flanders, also continued to write regularly on the general state of affairs. There is nothing in his letters to suggest that Ormond's scornful assessment of his abilities had been mistaken. Another of the Action party's agents, Edward

4. *ClSP, 3,* 411, 415–16. *CClSP, 4,* 94, 116–18, 130–31, 149.

Roscarrock, was still in touch with his friends in the West after the purge of May and June. According to one of Thurloe's spies, he and John Seymour were still frequenting Chase's in Covent Garden. Among the midland Royalists, John Cooper of Thurgarton was still active, and other agents made surreptitious cross-channel passages: the Oxfordshire Cavalier William Whorwood, Stephens (now Sir John Stephens), and Jonathan Trelawney—all between July and October 1658. But these provide no more than a few exceptions to the general absence of effort by the old mainstays of the Action party in the period of Cromwell's death.[5]

The opening of Parliament in January 1659 presented an opportunity to cultivate a more favorable climate of opinion. Hyde advised Rumbold and Brodrick on the attitude for Royalists to adopt. As many as possible were to seek election, concealing their allegiance, and to combine with other opposition groups against the regime, on general constitutional rather than openly Royalist grounds. In spite of the restrictions, more than a score of Royalists, mostly of Presbyterian background, got in, and in an atmosphere more relaxed than that of 1654 and 1656 many of the King's supporters helped to elect other opposition candidates. With Presbyterians like Browne and Sir George Booth, and newcomers like the young Lord Falkland to second them, the Royalists had a significant party in the House. The expulsion of a few openly Royalist members made no material difference, and those who were left were soon helping the republicans Vane and Heselrige to assail the constitutional fundamentals of the Protectorate.[6]

The meeting of Parliament thus enabled the Royalists to contribute to the general discontents. It also assisted some members of the party more directly: those long imprisoned without trial, who were able to take advantage of the rising opposition to arbitrary government and obtain their liberty. Already in December

5. *TSP*, 7, 221, 255. *CClSP*, 4, 46–153 passim.
6. Davies, *Restoration*, pp. 46–48. Hardacre, *Royalists*, pp. 132–34. E. L. Klotz and G. Davies, "Membership of Richard Cromwell's Parliament," *HLQ*, 6 (1942–43), 219–20. Davies, "The Election of Richard Cromwell's Parliament," *EHR*, 63 (1948), 488–501. The lists of Royalists in these articles are not exhaustive and include some who could better be described as Presbyterians.

1658 the government, anticipating criticism, had begun to discharge some of the prisoners. On January 20 Henry Norwood was released from Jersey, and in February Sir Humphrey Bennett, James Halsall, Gregory Paulden, Robert Harley, and some others were discharged on writs of habeas corpus. On March 10 two stalwarts of the first Action party, Peyton and Sir Thomas Harris, were released on security, the former evidently for a temporary period only. Two weeks later a group of Royalists transported to Barbados after Penruddock's rising had a thorough airing of their grievances in Parliament. The debate was damaging to the government but nothing was done for the petitioners, thanks to Thurloe's successful intervention when Rowland Thomas, Norwood's old associate, presented a similar petition. Finally, anticipating events after the return of the Rump, in June two more of the Action party's former leaders, Sir Thomas Armstrong and John Weston, were also successful in their petitions.[7]

The vital question for conspirators at large concerned the leadership. The Knot's authority was by now a mere fiction, and the failure of 1658 had amply illustrated the consequences of a vacuum in the high command. The chorus of voices calling for a reorganization at the top had been growing in 1657, and its volume swelled during the following year. Mordaunt had originally advised that new powers of command should be exercised by someone sent over from Court, but Ormond's mission had demonstrated the hazards of that, and he offered no suggestions when Hyde invited him to name some alternative from among the nobility in England. Mordaunt's arrest in April 1658 interrupted the discussion, and nothing was done until the period of calm after Richard Cromwell's accession. On November 25 Mordaunt wrote to the King, announcing that he was ready to resume his activities; Charles responded warmly, and Mordaunt was launched on the correspondence which rapidly established him in a position of special authority in England. He promised, as instructed, to communicate exclusively with Hyde, although, never quite sure of the Chancel-

7. *ClSP, 3,* 434. *CClSP, 4,* 116, 148, 178. *CSPD, 1658–59,* pp. 260, 302, 373, 395. *CJ, 7,* 606–7, 614–15, 620, 622, 685–86. *TSP, 7,* 598–99, 605–6, 622–23. *Burton, 4,* 253–73, 301–8.

lor's favor, he actually relied more on Ormond. In February 1659 Mordaunt again proposed that new powers should be granted to supplement or replace those the Sealed Knot was so glaringly failing to employ. This time he made no mention of sending over one of the exiles, and his silence implied that he himself would be the logical choice. On March 1 and 2 Charles II's decision to place full confidence in Mordaunt was signified in two documents. One was a warrant for a viscountcy, the other the "Plenepotentiary or Great Trust and Commission." [8]

The Trust, as it is convenient to call the body brought into being by the new commission, was in its original form merely an attempt to reinvigorate the Knot by giving its members more positive instructions, and by adding Mordaunt to their number. The commission was directed to Mordaunt and five of the old members of the Knot, Villiers being the only one omitted. The response of the wary gentlemen was unanimously unfavorable. Willys, Russell, and Compton could fall back for an excuse on Thurloe's categorical warning of the previous year, and received Mordaunt's repeated overtures with obstinate suspicion. In Compton's case the pretext was fortified by an illness in April; there were some who thought that the real reason was "his greatest illness, his wife." The Knot's effectiveness was further reduced by the fact that Russell and Belasyse were temporarily at odds. Loughborough by this time was completely isolated; he had resisted the malign influence of the Louvre and the Swordsmen five years before, but he was now fatally under the thumb of Mordaunt's mother-in-law, Lady Herbert, the Lord Keeper's widow. This did not bring him any closer to Mordaunt, for the lady detested her son-in-law as cordially as she did the Chancellor.[9]

The Knot rejected the new commission on two grounds: first because it was superfluous, duplicating existing powers; secondly because it involved too close a dependence on the Presbyterians.

8. *CCISP, 4,* 34–35, 113, 127–28, 136. *CISP, 3,* 426–30. *LBM,* p. 2. The texts of the commission and supplementary instructions are in HMC, *10th Report,* Appendix 6, pp. 189–90, and *CISP, 3,* 437–38; abstracts, with names supplied for the ciphers, in *LBM,* pp. 3–4.

9. *LBM,* pp. 3 n., 92 n. *CCISP, 4,* 177–79, 216. *CISP, 3,* 452–53, 463, 470–71, 482, 496. HMC, *10th Report,* Appendix 6, pp. 210, 212.

The "small confidence they have of any Party but our own," was especially directed at the proposed reliance on Major General Browne, who was being voted his arrears and restored to the aldermanic bench by an anti-Cromwellian Parliament. These favors, the Knot argued, would end Browne's flirtation with the Royalists. The Knot's reluctance was anticipated when the commission was drafted. In some supplementary instructions Mordaunt was authorized to recruit the Presbyterian leaders Lord Willoughby, Sir William Waller, and Browne, and the Shropshire Royalist Andrew Newport. The Earl of Oxford, the Presbyterian Major General Massey, and his friend Silas Titus were also noted as being worthy of special confidence.[10] Only Browne and Oxford refused outright. The former, Edward Phillips tells us, was "a Prudent wary man," and he showed it now that Parliament had listened to his complaints. Oxford had a low opinion of Mordaunt, not surprising in one whose friends included Brodrick, Denham, and Sir Allen Apsley, all vehement critics of the new viscount.[11] These abstentions were balanced by the inclusion of several not named in the original instructions. By August 1659 eight persons had joined Mordaunt as members of the Trust: Willoughby, Newport, Sir Thomas Peyton, William Legge, Rumbold, the Earl of Northampton, Sir John Grenville, and a lawyer named Job Charlton. Five more were closely associated with it, although possibly not as full members: Waller, Massey, Titus, Sir George Booth, and the Kentish Royalist Sir John Boys.[12]

We have, therefore, nine certain members and five possibles. Of the nine certainties, only Willoughby and Charlton came of anything but a Royalist past; if we include the possibles six out of

10. *CISP, 3,* 436–38, 445–46.

11. On the attitudes of Browne and Oxford see Baker (ed. 1674), p. 667; *NP, 4,* 115; *CISP, 3,* 539–40, 586; *CCISP, 4,* 178, 243, 294 (Brodrick's "cousin" here mentioned is, I think, Apsley rather than Villiers, and his "great neighbour" must be Oxford; cf. p. 298).

12. The list is compiled from the Trust's letters, reports of its meetings, etc., in *CCISP, 4,* 191–92, 194, 280; *CISP, 3,* 460, 469, 472 (the abstract in *Cal., 4,* 205, is misleading), 483, 488–89, 492, 524–25; HMC, *10th Report,* Appendix 6, pp. 198–99, 206, 208–11; *LBM,* p. 3. According to Phillips (Baker, p. 658), the Presbyterian Arthur Annesley was also a member of the Trust, but I know of no other contemporary evidence for this.

fourteen come into this category. The Trust, clearly, was designed to establish connections with as varied a selection of the opposition as possible: Presbyterians of varying hue like Booth, Willoughby, and Waller; moderates whose only goal was stability, like Charlton; the more respectable survivors of the Action parties, like Peyton, Grenville, and Newport; even, if they would, the hitherto overprudent peers.[13] This inclusiveness had been Mordaunt's policy ever since 1656; he was now able to pursue it more effectively, armed with official recognition. Not that this foretold a return to the damaging compromises of the Scots alliance, for Mordaunt resolutely opposed concessions. "Nothing can secure the Crown that destroys the Mitre": Mordaunt's Cavalier creed, like Hyde's, was an old-fashioned one. But if the Trust was not based on any definite bargain with the Presbyterians and moderates, the fact remains that as individuals it gave them a warm welcome. The participation of men like Willoughby and Waller is remarkable only in that it marks a transition from the restraint of 1655 and even 1658, to a willingness to accept the responsibilities of leadership; both, however, had really been Royalists for years. Perhaps the most interesting recruit was Charlton, a man of the new, trimming generation, unhampered by memories of old wars and stale controversies, recognizing the barrenness of both alternatives to a Stuart restoration: a disintegrating Protectorate, or a minority republic of fanatics.[14]

The wider base of its membership was the Trust's greatest strength compared with the old Knot. Its chief weakness was the inadequate representation of the Royalist nobility, whose interest had been reduced by the war but who were still able to make armed action ineffective if they held aloof, as they had shown in 1655. Northampton is the single exception, but his conduct in the crisis shows that even he did not place his full confidence in the Trust.

13. For Charlton see *DNB;* the account of his early career is incomplete and ignores his apparent loyalty to the Rump before 1653. His father lent money to Charles I, but Charlton himself was regularly named as an Assessment Commissioner during the Commonwealth: Firth and Rait, 2, 299, 467, 475, 664, 673.
14. For Mordaunt's attitude to the Presbyterian terms see *CISP, 3,* 459–60, 592–94; *LBM,* p. 82.

The two immediate causes of the great lords' abstentions were the Knot's hostility and the widespread resentment at Mordaunt's parvenu arrogance and unwillingness to take advice; but underneath can be detected the continued preference of the peers for self-preservation rather than martyrdom. The Trust was stronger than either of the two preceding Action parties; on the other hand, none of its Cavalier members were men of first-rate ability, reputation, or, apart from Northampton, rank. Much would depend on the strongest personality, Mordaunt. "When you have better considered me," he told the King, "you will find me only diligent and honest." Valuable qualities; but it was hardly likely that they would be enough by themselves.[15]

The Trust's commission and two sets of supplementary instructions provide a convenient outline of its objectives. The Trust was empowered to negotiate with former rebels who showed signs of willingness to come over, offering pardon and rewards proportional to services rendered—regicides only excepted. No general commitments were to be made, particularly in regard to confiscated lands. A national rising was to be prepared, and the King would come over to lead it whenever advised to do so; local commanders were to be commissioned in readiness. The Trust was given a free hand in the matter of propaganda, and was left the choice between declaring openly for the King when the rising began or merely announcing its objectives as the restoration of constitutional government and the ancient laws.[16]

On the most important question confronting the Royalists in 1659 the instructions were silent. This was the old choice between waiting for the contradictions in the enemy position to lead to open conflict, in which a Royalist restoration would be accepted as the only alternative to chaos, and the activist policy of hastening the day of liberation by military uprising. Ever since 1654 this had been the real issue between the Knot and its critics; it was now present in a more acute form than ever. In April the Cromwellians and the Army reached the parting of the ways, and the generals

15. *ClSP*, *3*, 443.
16. HMC, *10th Report*, Appendix 6, pp. 189–90. *ClSP*, *3*, 437–38. *LBM*, pp. 3–4. See also Davies, *Restoration*, pp. 125–26.

restored the same Rump that they had expelled so ignominiously in 1653. There were now two discontented Cromwellian groups which the Royalists could exploit: the politicians, and the sympathetic Army officers who were purged from their commands during the summer. The incompatibility of the aims of the remaining Army chiefs, Lambert, Fleetwood, and Disbrowe, with those of the parliamentary republicans led by Heselrige, Vane, and Scot suggested further chances of disruption. There were convincing reasons for following the Knot's advice and sitting still until a bloodless restoration became a logical necessity. Yet the same data could be used to prove the contrary case, as the obvious disintegration of their old enemies increased the more militant Royalists' confidence of success. The republic had never before been so unstable: perhaps it never would be again. Against this it could be urged that the one thing most likely to reunite the parliamentary factions was the old cry of the "Good Old Cause" in danger; armed resistance might defeat its own ends. "For, believe it, my Lord," Hyde was warned by one of his correspondents in England, "not anything can so much conduce to the cementing of the growing divisions here amongst ourselves, as your party but appearing to fall into action against us." [17]

Under Mordaunt's uncompromising direction the Trust preferred to accept the risks of violence. Mordaunt's repeated criticisms of the Knot's pleas for delay are conveniently summarized in his letter to the King on June 10.[18] To wait for a breach between the republicans and the Army, Mordaunt argued, was the height of folly, for the Rump would only be replaced by a far more ruthless and efficient military oligarchy. Meanwhile, although the purge of the unreliable officers might provide another source of discontent, in the long run it would strengthen the Army by putting the regiments in the hands of the fanatics. As long as the disaffected still retained their commands the Royalists could make use of them; the best examples were the forces at Lynn and Shrewsbury, where their

17. *ClSP, 3,* 525. See also Davies, *Restoration,* pp. 123–24.

18. HMC, *10th Report,* Appendix 6, pp. 191–92, dated April 10. The date must be an error; cf. references to the Army purge, Fitch as Lieutenant of the Tower (he was appointed June 10: *CJ, 7,* 679), the chances of a breach between Parliament and Army.

hopes would be ruined if they delayed until friends in the garrisons were removed. The Knot's expectations of support from commanders like Lockhart, Monck, and Mountagu were entirely hypothetical, and if they were to wait until their attitudes had clarified, the present opportunity would be lost. Furthermore, Mordaunt urged, Royalists in favor of immediate action would be discouraged and exposed to unnecessary danger if nothing was done while they were so well prepared. As for the Knot's hope of foreign assistance from France or Spain, this was in any case chimerical until peace was signed between the two crowns, and to most Royalists the idea was repugnant: "a sad cure for an ill disease, when more nobly wee may do it ourselves."

This is not to say that Mordaunt and the Trust did nothing to profit from the difficulties of the Protectorate and—after it was recalled on May 7—the Rump. The existence of a Royalist bloc in Richard Cromwell's Parliament has already been mentioned; among those friendly to Mordaunt it included Charlton, John Grubham Howe, Sir Horatio Townshend, and Booth, all of whom helped foment opposition to the government. Howe was a young lawyer from Gloucestershire: a second son, but he made a good marriage and acquired an estate in Nottinghamshire. He had been in contact with the Royalists, through the Bristol agent William Clayton, since the middle of 1657. Townshend, a prominent man in Norfolk, also was of parliamentarian origins; and he was Fairfax's nephew. Mordaunt helped to inflame the anger of another member, Richard Knightley, at the arrogance of the soldiers. The most ambitious of the Trust's schemes was an attempt to approach Richard Cromwell himself. One obvious avenue to Cromwell had been closed to the Trust by Belasyse's decision not to join. However, the Presbyterian Waller seems to have been in touch with him, and on May 11 Mordaunt reported an attempt to win him over through one of the Royalist Cromwells. The idea was that Richard would order Mountagu's fleet to Dunkirk to pick up Lockhart's regiments and bring them to Portsmouth, where Col. Richard Norton would prepare for their landing; these, assisted by Henry Cromwell's troops in Ireland, would combine with the

Royalists to bring about an agreed restoration. In return, Richard would get £20,000 a year and a title. In spite of the reward, this was expecting a good deal of the timid Protector, and in the end he refused to cooperate. A little later Rumbold hired a ship so that Richard could escape to the Fleet, but again he defaulted.[19]

However promising and important, all these intrigues were merely secondary to the Trust's real task, the organization of a successful rising. In such a rising Presbyterian and Cromwellian help might be valuable but would not deprive the Royalists of their right to dictate the terms of restoration in the event of success. The Trust's schemes bear a general similarity to those of 1658, although rather more of the country was covered, and the presence of a few new leaders, recent recruits to conspiracy, indicates a broader base of support. The home counties made up one association. Mordaunt again played a large part in the preparations, but there was an unfortunate dispute over the command of the whole region. The Earl of Winchelsea, a son-in-law of the powerful Hertford, wanted it, but there were local objections. There had been talk of his restrained complicity in various conspiracies in Kent ever since 1655, but he had not done anything notable; perhaps he was already, as Evelyn described him later, a "prodigious talker." Winchelsea was rebuffed and took no part in the association, either as a regional or as a county commander; there was officially no regional commander at all. There was another association in East Anglia. Designs against strongholds like Ely and Lynn were in the air, the latter as a possible port for the disembarkation of invading forces. Lynn was to be secured through the corruption of one of the officers of the garrison, Capt. James Whitelock, son of the great Bulstrode; in May he was reported to have offered his services to his uncle, Sir Humphrey Bennett. The cooperation of the Sealed Knot and its friends in this area was vital. On June 16 Mordaunt was still opti-

---

19. *CCISP, 4*, 78, 88, 90, 205. *CISP, 3*, 411, 436, 460, 468–69, 477–78. See also Davies, *Restoration*, pp. 48, 60–61, 68, 99. For Howe see *LBM*, p. 9 n.; *Bristol and Gloucestershire Archaeological Society Transactions*, 25 (1902), 268; and W. R. Williams, *Parliamentary History of the County of Gloucester* (Hereford, 1898), p. 58, where it is stated that it was Howe's father who was an MP in 1654 and 1656. For Townshend see *DNB*.

mistically hoping that Willys, Russell, and Compton would be able to "draw a considerable body of gentlemen together." It was a large assumption.

In Southwest England there was no challenge to the old leadership of Grenville, Pollard, and the Arundells. By now there were hopes of adding to them some of the more pliable Presbyterian gentry; and Sir Chichester Wrey, of whom little had been heard since 1650, was said to be active again. A more vocal section of the conspiracy was that centered in Bristol and Gloucester. This was a development of the one whose groundwork had been laid by Dick Pile, Clayton, and Veel three years earlier. All these minor agents were still operating, but the men of whom most was demanded were Massey, John Howe, and Alexander Popham. Popham's willingness to participate was hedged around with the usual conditions—the securing of Bristol and the landing of at least 500 horse from abroad —but he was still trusted in spite of his equivocations in 1658. The Gloucestershire design was supposed to be integrated with those in Oxfordshire under Lord Falkland, and Worcestershire under Charles Littleton, Samuel Sandys, Lord Windsor, and Sir Ralph Clare. In Herefordshire another Old Cavalier, Sir Henry Lingen, was responsible for the preparations. The area surrounding the lower Severn was well covered in the Trust's plans, at least on paper.

The Midlands and the North were patchy. In the south Midlands the Compton interest predominated. Derby and Nottinghamshire were under the Earl of Chesterfield, Lord Byron, John Freschville of Stavely, and Col. Edward Vernon. Byron and Vernon had both been active in 1654–55. Chesterfield was a gay young widower with little time or energy to spare from the charms of Barbara Palmer. Freschville had been Governor of Welbeck in the civil war and retained some connection with the Cavendishes. In Lincolnshire the command was neatly divided between the Presbyterians Willoughby and Rossiter and the Royalists Sir John Mounson and Lord Castleton. No suitable commander appeared for Yorkshire, the result of Belasyse's rejection of the Trust and his nephew's caution; Castleton, however, had married Belasyse's niece, so the family was not entirely unrepresented. In the Northwest, Booth in Cheshire, Sir Thomas Myddelton in North Wales, and Sir Charles Wolseley in Staffordshire gave reason to expect a substantial accession of both Presbyterians and Cromwellians.[20]

This brief recital of the Trust's plans and expectations in the summer of 1659 tells us little, however, about the progress made by its agents. The patterns of local conspiracy will emerge more clearly when the August rising is reached. In the last weeks Mordaunt and his colleagues had enough problems of their own: setting the date; striving to overcome the objections of the Sealed Knot; ensuring that Charles II would be ready to come over at the right moment. Although the Trust was providing more energetic leadership than any of the earlier committees, it was not unanimously supported. As a preliminary to the events leading to the rising, an account of the rival factions is required.

Some of the opposition to the Trust was inspired by Hyde's enemies at court. This was natural enough, for the Trust had now openly replaced the Knot as the organ of his confidence. The agents of Berkeley, Gerard, and all who tended to adhere to the Duke of York, whether of the old "Swordsmen" or the Louvre factions, were still busily disparaging Hyde, and by extension all who supported him in England. One who paid little attention to the Trust was the poet John Denham, generally regarded as a follower of the Louvre, although he himself denied it. In the summer of 1659 Denham was claiming the confidence of a group of Royalist peers, Hertford, Southampton, and Oxford among them; but even Brodrick, who disliked Mordaunt and the Trust with great passion, was unwilling to employ him. The Kent Royalist Philip Froude was another who

20. For the Trust's plans see *CClSP*, *4*, 195–96, 201–3, 205, 227, 233. *ClSP*, *3*, 433, 455, 469–73, 476, 478, 482–83, 490, 505, 509–10, 525. HMC, *10th Report*, Appendix 6, pp. 202–6, 211–12. *NP*, *4*, 98, 114–15, 131, 158–59. Carte, *Papers*, *2*, 173. For a general discussion, Davies, *Restoration*, pp. 128–30. For Winchelsea see *DNB; LBM*, p. 15 n.; *Evelyn*, ed. de Beer, *3*, 537. There are references to his earlier Royalist activities in *CSPD*, *1655*, p. 225; *TSP*, *3*, 330; *7*, 68, 98; Rawl. MSS A 21, p. 499; A 27, p. 383; A 41, p. 576. For Whitelock see *DNB; LBM*, p. 18 n.; and C. H. Firth and G. Davies, *The Regimental History of Cromwell's Army* (Oxford, 1940), pp. 51, 98. For Chesterfield, Mounson, and Wolseley see *DNB*; for Castleton, *CCC*, p. 1151, and G.E.C., *Peerage*; for Freschville, ibid., *5*, 578, *LBM*, p. 23 n., and for his Cavendish connections, HMC, *Portland*, *1*, 253, and *2*, 141, 144.

emphasized Mordaunt's unpopularity and suggested that a rival committee should be set up. William Ashburnham, Russell, Sir Thomas Fanshawe, and Denham, he thought, "men of years and knowledge in the world," could better negotiate with the more responsible people who had no confidence in the Trust.[21]

More tangible than these vague hints of Louvre influence were the suspicions of the Trust harbored by a group on whose behalf Alan Brodrick was corresponding with Hyde after April 1659. The Sealed Knot's decreasing activity enabled him to appear as spokesman for a clique of younger men, mostly his personal friends, who saw little hope of advancing themselves on Mordaunt's coat-tails. On May 4, 1659, Brodrick asked the King for formal recognition of their existence: "I am employed by my Lord Falkland, Mr. Howe, Mr. John Talbot, Ralph Delaval, and many others who intend to rise in Oxfordshire, Gloucester, Warwick and the North, to negotiate for them, and to procure . . . your Majesty's orders." This was not a request for the kind of supreme powers wielded by the Sealed Knot (in fact Brodrick asserted that his engagement with the new group was made with the Knot's express permission), but it was nonetheless an attempt to bypass the Trust. "Though less conversant in affairs" than the Knot, Brodrick told the King, his new friends had "the same sense towards your Majesty, and a great estimation of the Lord Chancellor." Hyde later expressed grave doubts about the discretion of some of Brodrick's friends, but he gave them a qualified recognition, sent preliminary instructions, and eventually a letter from the King. He was careful to stress, however, that they were still to take orders from the Trust.[22]

Some of Brodrick's assertions about his group's influence were absurdly inflated; he followed the practice of including anyone of importance with whom he or any of his friends had been in conversation. Actually the faction was limited to Sir Allen Apsley and Lord Falkland (both cousins of Brodrick), John Talbot in Worcestershire, Ralph Delaval in Northumberland, and a number of lesser men in Wiltshire and South Wales. Among these was a

21. *CCISP*, *4*, 177, 209, 225. *CISP*, *3*, 462, 470–71, 486, 527. For the York faction see Scott, *Travels of the King*, pp. 383–85.

22. *CISP*, *3*, 461–62, 477–78, 517, 519. *CCISP*, *4*, 202, 280. Br. MS 1, fol. 79.

Welshman named Robin Thomas, nephew of the important William Morgan who had been member for Monmouth in Richard Cromwell's Parliament. Hyde judged Thomas ridiculous and indiscreet, although his uncle was a man of greater solidity. More reliable was the Wiltshire leader William Basset, on whose plans Brodrick reported to Hyde on June 8. Delaval, Talbot, and Falkland were all members of the crypto-Royalist group in Richard Cromwell's Parliament. The first-named was head of the Presbyterian family of Seaton Delaval, which had provided the Royalists with a recruit in 1655. Talbot was the son of Sherrington Talbot of Salwarpe, Worcestershire, and related to the Earl of Shrewsbury. Through these friends and kinsmen Brodrick appears at one time or another to have been introduced to a good many former parliamentarians and neutrals of influence; the most notable was the powerful northcountry Cromwellian Sir Charles Howard, with whom Delaval was the usual intermediary.[23]

Brodrick's faction was a small one, but it does not take any deep insight to see that whatever interest it possessed would not be used in favor of Mordaunt and the Trust. The hard core of hostility to Mordaunt consisted of Apsley, Falkland, and Brodrick himself. Apsley had been corresponding with Brodrick ever since the latter entered the the Knot's service in 1656. He was older than his cousin, with considerable military experience, having been a colonel of horse during the war and governor at various times of Exeter and Barnstaple. His jealousy of Mordaunt was contagious: it influenced the Earl of Oxford, whose refusal to collaborate with the Trust could in part be laid at Apsley's door. Falkland was the son of Hyde's friend the second Viscount, but unlike his pious father he was a dissolute young man. In 1659 Brodrick claimed that he was a reformed character, but he was still capable of wild talk on occasions. He had at one time flirted with the Gerard faction, a period of his career to which Brodrick attributed his alleged statement in

23. *CClSP, 4,* 177, 198, 202–3, 212, 225, 233, 269–70, 282. *ClSP, 3,* 461, 477–78, 482, 521–23, 530–33, 536. For Delaval see G.E.C., *Baronetage, 3,* 68–69; Bateson et al., *Northumberland, 9,* 127, 160. For Talbot, *LBM,* p. 22 n.; W. R. Williams, *Parliamentary History of the County of Worcester* (Hereford, 1897), pp. 51–52. For Morgan, *HLQ, 6,* 220. For Basset, below, p. 264.

Westminster Hall "that the Chancellor publickly reproached those who were forward to serve the King, with the name of Penruddockins . . . and said that it would never be well, till a hundred of them were served as Penruddock was." Falkland was obviously no more friendly to the Sealed Knot than to the Trust; but his language about Mordaunt was so vitriolic that Brodrick thought it best to suppress it. In spite of all this, Falkland did at least meet Mordaunt in June to discuss his design in Oxfordshire. Even though ordered to follow the Trust's directions, however, he continued to insist on receiving them only through Brodrick.[24]

Apsley, Oxford, and Falkland all resented Mordaunt's rapid advancement, but their hostility was tame compared with the vendetta between Mordaunt and Brodrick. It is not difficult to account for some degree of jealousy between them. Both were young and ambitious; each regarded the other as his chief obstacle to advancement. It is hard not to sympathize with Brodrick, whose position seemed so secure as long as the Knot was the only entrusted authority but whose value to Hyde was immeasurably diminished by the old committee's disintegration in 1659. Mordaunt's resentment of Brodrick's independence is equally understandable. Confident of the value of his own services, sensitive to criticism, and imputing the worst of motives to those who uttered it, Mordaunt regarded Brodrick as a selfish and destructive interloper, doubly tainted by his association with the Knot, and by his attempt to keep his new faction out of Mordaunt's control.

With all these allowances, the insults exchanged by the two rivals were still deplorable, and Mordaunt was the worse offender. Brodrick's charges against Mordaunt were the standard ones leveled at him by many who resented his upstart arrogance: he was vain, overbearing, ostentatious, and tactless, and presumptuously claimed a position of exclusive command for which he had no authority. Brodrick, on the other hand, according to Mordaunt was jealous, interfering, and debauched; a knave, juggler, papist, Jesuit, parti-

24. *CClSP*, *3*, 239–40, 302; *4*, 167, 200, 203, 216, 233, 243, 269–70, 277, 298. *ClSP*, *3*, 522, 530–32, 536, 539–40. Br. MS 1, fols. 19, 24, 90. For Apsley see *DNB*. For Falkland, Kurt Weber, *Lucius Cary, Second Viscount Falkland* (New York, 1940), pp. 94–95, 314–15; G.E.C., *Peerage*; Wood, *Ath. Oxon.*, *2*, 571; Verney, *Memoirs*, *3*, 16–17; *LBM*, p. 22 n.

san of the Duke of York, and indiscreet nonentity, of whom no one outside the Knot had ever heard. "His indiscretion and vanity is scarce to be expressed," Mordaunt told Hyde, "and great prejudices have already befallen us by them, and lest they may encrease, I think it my duty to inform you he is sadly given to drink, and clearly laid aside by the leading men of the old Knot, whom he has exposed as well as us who act now." There was some truth in the charge of excessive conviviality—Brodrick himself admitted frequenting taverns in the line of duty, and years later Pepys was shocked to hear how he and Apsley had made a drunken scene in the House of Commons—but this does not excuse Mordaunt's more extravagant charges. There was a half-hearted reconciliation about the middle of July 1659, but it did not last long.[25]

More dangerous than the personal hostility of Brodrick and his "New Cavalier" friends was the continued obstructiveness of the Sealed Knot. In the first week of June Mordaunt reported that the new members of the Trust were working harmoniously together, and he was able to describe their local plans in detail. Until the Knot's hesitations could be removed, however, he was disinclined to start the action and invite the King to England. In conference with Mordaunt, some of the Knot seemed compliant, "though by after hands," he complained, "I know they discredit us as much as they can." By the 16th the Trust was optimistic enough to expect the Knot to participate, at least in its East Anglian bailiwick, and the King was urged to come over as a final guarantee of success. The Knot, however, demanded three weeks' notice of the day; this the Trust regarded as dangerously long. Between June 20 and 24, Russell, Compton, and Belasyse were at last willing to meet Mordaunt and the Trust, and Brodrick told Hyde that he was glad of the decision to sanction the rising, as it was important to move before the harvest. The worst of the divisions seemed to have been overcome. Mordaunt made a flying visit to Charles II at Brussels; he had left London by June 24 and was on his way back on the 29th. Although the Trust had still not reached a final decision about the

25. *CClSP, 4, 200* ("Goodrike" is obviously Brodrick), 216, 248–50. *ClSP, 3,* 479, 483–84, 527, 533–35. *LBM,* pp. 27–28. HMC, *10th Report,* Appendix 6, pp. 205, 211. *Pepys, 6,* 103–4.

date of action, Charles agreed to leave for England on July 11. Mordaunt returned to London with Titus to make the last preparations.[26]

The situation had changed in two ways when they reached London. The Sealed Knot had resumed its campaign of dissuasion, and Sir Richard Willys had been publicly accused of treason, in an anonymous placard which appeared at the Exchange and several other places. Willys' treachery had already been disclosed to Charles II by Samuel Morland, Thurloe's assistant, but his delay in sending documentary proof had enabled Charles and Hyde to suspend judgment. Nothing was known of Morland's move in England, but Mordaunt and Titus were told that there were doubts of Willys' integrity when they were at Brussels. Even if the contents were not generally believed, the placard was bound to widen the Royalists' internal divisions. Everyone was suspected for one reason or another, through the influence of wife, mistress, priest, poverty, or lack of conscience, Brodrick remarked. Willys at first blamed the placard on Henry Norwood; others thought Sir Gilbert Gerard responsible. Actually it was the work of an obscure fellow named Paul. Angry words passed between Willys and Norwood's friend Andrew Newport. Meanwhile, Morland was following up his original denunciation by sending the King the required proof, letters allegedly written by Willys to Thurloe; there is good reason to think that Morland forged them. Not until July 18, too late to affect the rising, were orders sent to Willys to come over to Brussels and defend himself.[27]

On July 5 and 6, Mordaunt having returned, the Trust assembled to discuss the situation. Massey arrived with encouraging reports from the West, but the shortage of arms and ammunition made it necessary to seek supplies of both money and equipment abroad. The Knot continued its damaging propaganda, but the most serious development was the news from Ireland, where Henry Crom-

26. HMC, *10th Report*, Appendix 6, pp. 205, 207–8, 210. *CClSP, 4*, 243, 248. *ClSP, 3*, 482–83, 488–90, 506–7, 519–20.

27. HMC, *10th Report*, Appendix 6, p. 210. *NP, 4*, 169–70. *CClSP, 4*, 223, 245, 258, 270, 285, 290. *ClSP, 3*, 518, 526–27, 535–36. *LBM*, p. 32. *Clarke Papers, 4*, 304–6. For the denunciation of Willys see the articles by M. Hollings and the present writer, in *EHR, 43*, 33–65, and *69*, 373–87.

well had submitted to the Rump, ending the possibility of distract-
ing disturbances there. Booth in Cheshire and Howe in Gloucestershire both regarded this as sufficient reason for postponement.
Popham was at his old game of equivocating, his wife refusing to
allow him to see anyone. In these circumstances the Trust advised
Charles II to delay his departure, and John Baron, Hartgil's
brother, was hastily sent to stop him; he reached Brussels just in
time. On the 9th the Trust met again and came to a final decision
on the date of the rising. Mordaunt, Willoughby, Grenville, Massey, Peyton, Newport, and Titus were there, and the Earl of Northampton arrived after the decision was made, but gave his full consent. The Knot, Mordaunt told the King, "were civily desired to be
there, but neither came, nor sent." Only Newport, uneasy at the
shortage of equipment, betrayed any reservations when it was
agreed to rise on Monday, August 1. John Cooper was soon hastening over to Brussels with the news.[28]

There was now no turning back, and in the three weeks that intervened before the rising, a bitter struggle was waged between the
Trust and the Knot. In the last analysis the members of the Knot
declared that they would act, particularly if the ultimate demand
on their loyalty was made by the arrival of the King or the Duke of
York; but as in 1655, their hearts were not in it. Northampton advised the King not to repeat the error of 1655, and to give the Knot
a positive command to appear; but even neglecting Willys' betrayal
it is obvious that nothing could be done to change them. On July
23 Willys delivered an impassioned speech to his friends: "I were
neither Christian nor Englishman, should I encourage or give way
to action, the bloud and miseries considered will ensue." After this
"pious preamble," as Mordaunt described it, Willys gave three reasons for his opposition: the harvest had to be gathered, the action
was "totally presbiterian," and it was managed by "rash, vaine,
giddy people." Brodrick a week earlier had passed on to Hyde another statement of Willys' objections. One, again, was the harvest:
"The generality of peasants will rather work in harvest for 2s or 2s
6d per diem (such is now their price in most counties) than fight

28. HMC, *10th Report*, Appendix 6, pp. 211, 215 (correct date July 6:
LBM, p. 27 n.). *CClSP, 4*, 267–69, 280. *ClSP, 3*, 516–18, 524–25.

for nothing." Another, perhaps more solid, reason for delay was the inaccuracy of many of the Trust's estimates of support. In Willys' own region, the eastern counties, "Sim. Fanshaw's gaiety . . . too far advanced the number of horse, calculating Sir John Watts, Sir John Gore, etc., at twenty; Colonel Roleston, Walden, Nanton, etc., at forty; whom Sir Richard Willis examining particularly, found it in their wishes, not in their power." It was an old story in Royalist conspiracy, and spy or no spy, Willys was right in pointing to its dangers.[29]

The Willys enigma thus remains in 1659 as baffling as ever. On its merits his advice was sound enough. The policy of waiting for the growing hostility of Rump and Army to reach a breaking-point was correct; the rising was likely to cause a temporary closing of the enemy's ranks; the common people, whether for economic or for political reasons, were unlikely to "fight for nothing" against the forbidding strength of the redcoats; and the preparations were incomplete and based on exaggerated promises. The arguments were good, yet we know that Willys had been betraying his trust for nearly three years. How much information he gave the government in the summer of 1659 it is impossible to guess. His patron Thurloe had fallen with Richard Cromwell in May, but Morland, although secretly trying to secure his position with the King, still retained his post in the intelligence department. Willys himself admits being in touch with Thurloe at about this time. Soon after the fall of the Protectorate, according to Willys' defense, "Thurloe sent for him againe, telling him that now he visibly saw that the King could no longer be kept out and that now was the time, he must be beholding to him in the making of his peace." It was an attempt to revive the bargain of 1657, but in the end Thurloe decided that he preferred the Rump to the Royalists. According to Willys, contact was thereupon broken off until the autumn.[30] The question is, therefore, whether Willys transferred his services to Thomas Scot, who was again the leading member of the Council of State's intelligence committee.

29. HMC, *10th Report*, Appendix 6, pp. 212–14. *CClSP*, *4*, 294. *ClSP*, *3*, 526–27. *LBM*, p. 31.
30. *Notes and Queries*, 12th ser. *10*, 123.

Willys' movements in the last weeks before the rising can be followed fairly closely. On July 13 one of the frequent proclamations expelling Royalists from London had been issued, and to stay in the capital Willys needed special exemption. About the 20th he got Brodrick and Russell to approach their friends on the Council of State for this purpose. Instead of following up the overture, Willys entered a bond of £6,000 on the security of himself, his brother Sir Thomas, and a Mr. Browne, for his good behavior, on condition of being granted freedom of movement. Brodrick concluded from the amount of the security and from Willys' abrupt departure immediately afterward that he had abandoned any further part in the conspiracy. On the 29th, however, the Council of State once more summoned him to appear. No details of Willys' interrogation are known, but it can hardly have been coincidence that Brodrick was promptly advised by his Council friend to conceal himself, "the business in agitation being discovered by a person, whom above all others I trusted." On August 1 Brodrick was arrested.[31]

With this exception, Willys does not seem to have performed any particularly valuable services for Scot. He knew all the plans for the rising, however, for they were transmitted to him only a week before it began. By the time he was called before the Council on the 29th most of the essential details of the design were known and precautionary measures were already being taken. In his later account of the Rump's intelligence system Scot recalls inheriting three of Thurloe's agents through Morland, but does not even mention Willys. A payment of £60 to "Mr. Barret" (Willys' alleged pseudonym in the correspondence with Thurloe) may be significant, but the reward is not large enough to suggest any elaborate disclosures. The Council certainly had adequate information about the rising from other sources. Among others on Scot's list are Bampfield and Robert Werden. The nefarious cleric Francis Corker was also continuing his sinful ways: he told one of Scot's colleagues of the date of the rising at least by July 19. Corker had already been denounced to Charles II by Morland, but there had not been time

31. *CISP, 3,* 562–63. *CSPD, 1659–60,* pp. 23, 38, 59. Rawl. MSS A 259, p. 43; C 179, pp. 206, 235, 264.

to warn the local Royalists. In Surrey a Catholic friar by the name of Robin Rookwood gave useful intelligence; Barkstead, the former Lieutenant of the Tower, had his own agents; and spies were busy in Gloucestershire and among the London apprentices. So many people were in the plot that absolute secrecy was as impossible as ever. Whatever Willys' disclosures, there was no shortage of other information on which the Council of State could base its dispositions.[32]

We are, it seems, as far as ever from reaching definite conclusions in the Willys case. There is little doubt that he communicated with the Council (after his relations with Thurloe he could hardly avoid it, especially as Morland was still employed), but apart from the betrayal of Brodrick there is nothing to suggest that Scot found him especially useful. His vociferous opposition to the insurrection can be explained in one of two ways. Willys may still have been loyal at heart and have regretted falling into Thurloe's trap; in this case his advice would be based on a sincere conviction that the rising was bound to end in disaster. On the other hand he may have persisted in his opposition in a spirit of wrecking, to create the maximum confusion, and the fact that his advice was objectively correct may be irrelevant.

As we approach the rising of August 1659, it is clear that the effort to remodel Royalist organization in England had met with only partial success. The continued divisions within the party—the result of the adhesion of new recruits of varying backgrounds, the influence of Hyde's opponents abroad, personal quarrels like that between Mordaunt and Brodrick, and the lingering opposition of the Sealed Knot—still prohibited united action. The Trust, although bringing the Royalists closer to the neutrals and former parliamentarians, was no more successful than either the Knot or the old Action parties in establishing its authority without chal-

32. "Scot's Account," *EHR, 12,* 122–23. *TSP, 7,* 787. Carte, *Papers, 2,* 216. *CSPD, 1659–60,* pp. 58, 207. *Clarke Papers, 4,* 34. *NP, 4,* 159. *ClSP, 3,* 574. *CClSP, 4,* 223, 238, 251, 282–84, 296–97, 302, 329, 351. Bordeaux, the French Ambassador, speaks as if the rising was common knowledge for several days before August 1: F. P. Guizot, *History of Richard Cromwell and the Restoration of Charles II,* tr. A. R. Scoble (London, 1856), *1,* 441–42. For Rookwood see *LBM,* p. 51 n.

lenge. For this Mordaunt's tactlessness could partly be blamed, but it must be conceded that without the support of the aristocracy he faced an insuperable task; the interest of the remaining members of the Trust was not a sufficient compensation. When the commissioners rode out of London in the last days of July the controversy was still unresolved; it would show for how much the Knot's interest counted among the more solid members of the party. "Be assured we strive still against mallice and envy," Mordaunt encouraged his faithful Hartgil Baron, "and if not against treachery, I doubt not but God will blesse us. Farewell." [33]

33. *LBM*, p. 33.

12. Sir George Booth's Rising

THE RISING OF AUGUST 1659, like that of March 1655, is known to history by the name of its most effective leader. The attribution can be defended, for Sir George Booth does deserve to be remembered as the commander of the only serious force that the Royalists collected; and in spite of the contemptuous ease with which Lambert smashed it, a much stronger force than the one led by poor Penruddock. But in both cases the title can be misleading. Booth's appearance at Chester, like Penruddock's at Salisbury, was only part of a wider plan, in which the Rump was to be assaulted by Royalist assemblies from Tunbridge Wells to Warrington, from Sherwood to Stonehenge. The similarities between the two risings are obvious. Each counted on the support of much stronger forces in other areas; each occurred after serious disagreements within the Royalist party. The differences are no less striking. The most obvious one is suggested by the names of the two leaders. Penruddock was an Old Cavalier, Booth a former Presbyterian. The contrast symbolizes the change in Royalist policy after the Trust took over, for whereas the 1655 rising had been almost entirely limited to the Old Royalists, Booth's was as much a Presbyterian as a Royalist rebellion.[1]

1. For brief accounts of the rising see Davies, *Restoration,* pp. 131–41, and J. R. Jones, "Booth's Rising of 1659," *Bulletin of the John Rylands Library,*

If the Royalists' dissensions in 1659 made the outlook little more favorable than in 1655, the general political situation was incomparably more promising. When Penruddock's venture was launched, the Protectorate was at the height of its power and seemed, apart from a little parliamentary grumbling, to have fulfilled its promise of stability and order. In August 1659, on the other hand, the unpopularity of the Rump was boundless. To the passive conservatism of the unpolitical could be added the growing conviction of Presbyterians and neutrals that only a Stuart restoration could save the country from anarchy or from the social and religious revolution threatening from vaguely identified, hence all the more deeply feared, Quakers and Anabaptists. Although most of the Protector's supporters had followed Richard's example in conforming quietly to the Rump, the Royalists had some hopes from Cromwellian officers dismissed in the recent purge. The most notable convert was that reluctant regicide, Col. Richard Ingoldsby. He was approached by the Earl of Northampton some time before Richard Cromwell's fall, but it was only when he lost his regiment that Ingoldsby really showed interest in Royalist overtures. Mordaunt first mentioned receiving assurances from him about the middle of June. On July 26 Ingoldsby promised to try to win over two troops of his old regiment, stationed in Sussex; he and several of his officers actively supported the Royalists during the following eventful week.[2]

Disaffection among Cromwellian officers was not the only symptom of unrest which the Royalists could exploit in August 1659. There were already signs of the Rump's inability to maintain law and order, admonitory danger signals to the propertied classes. Enclosure riots early in the summer in the Forest of Dean and at Enfield, Middlesex suggested two alternative possibilities. In the first place, the government's vigor in suppressing them might goad the rioters into supporting a new uprising, whether Royalist inspired or not; in the second, the gentry might be convinced by their oc-

---

39 (1956–57), 413–43. I am indebted to Basil D. Henning for the latter reference.

2. Carte, *Papers,* 2, 333. *ClSP, 3,* 489, 492. *LBM,* pp. 33–34. For Ingoldsby's position in 1659 see Davies, *Restoration,* pp. 64, 80, 86, 131; and *DNB.*

currence that the Rump was unfit to govern.[3] A more widespread though less clearly defined threat to property was the ominous militancy of the Quakers and other "fanatic" sects. The Quakers, of course, were easily made scapegoats for all possible dangers to the Establishment; but it is a fact that in 1659 they had not yet adopted that passive abstention from politics which was later to be their distinctive characteristic. The unstable conditions of 1659 produced what a recent writer has called "millenarian excitement" among the Quakers; a feeling that some great change impended, in which the godly would be given another chance to govern. The encouraging attitude of Vane and a few other leading politicians seemed to threaten dangerous social experiments. Heselrige and a strong party in the governing oligarchy averted the danger, and by July the wave of Quaker-Anabaptist agitation was receding; but a nebulous Quaker menace could still serve as a useful slogan to unite the Rump's enemies. There was a curious incident at Tiverton on July 14. The town was aroused about midnight by rumors of an imminent massacre by "the Fifth Monarchie Men, Anabaptists and Quakers," and there was a violent commotion, in which the sectaries were fortunate to escape retaliation. Reporting the outbreak, the government print pointed out how easily the Cavaliers could turn this kind of mass hysteria to their own seditious purposes.[4]

The Royalists needed no prompting. As August 1 approached, full use was made of the supposed dangers from the Quakers. In Norfolk a Cavalier gentleman bought saddles and arms on the pretext of defending himself against Quakers and Anabaptists. From Hampshire to Shropshire men were raised to fight against the Quakers, "who had a plot to cut all men's throats." The Presbyterian clergy conscientiously enflamed their congregations to violence. Richard Britten, the minister at Bisley, Gloucestershire, said that "the Anabaptists and Quakers would pull down the light of

3. *CJ, 8,* 648, 670, 708, 721–22, 726. *Mercurius Politicus,* Nos. 578, 579. *CClSP, 4,* 210, 278, 294. *CSPD, 1658–59,* pp. 362–64, 368. Rawl. MS C 179, p. 37.

4. See J. F. Maclear, "Quakerism and the End of the Interregnum," *Church History, 19* (1950), 240–70. The Tiverton affair is reported in *Mercurius Politicus,* No. 580.

the Gospel and the ministry, if a course were not taken with them."
In Lancashire on July 31 the clergy preached on Judges 5:23,
"Curse ye Meroz," and urged their congregations to follow Booth
against the Quakers. "Horrible things" were spoken in the pulpits
all over the county, a shocked parliamentary officer reported. To
pray for the peace of Jerusalem was not enough, Peter Harrison of
Cheadle declaimed; one must fight for it against heretics and sectaries. At Manchester, Henry Newcome's colleague Mr. Stockport
decided "to invite the people to arms upon the score of the Quakers being up." Newcome agreed that the Quakers were "very inso-
lent and troublesome" but was unhappy when Stockport made the
call to arms, denouncing the sectaries "in very unwary expres-
sions." At Rotherston, the next parish to Sir George Booth's, Adam
Martindale was as troubled as Newcome at basing the rebels' case
on "lying and deceit." Most of their brethren were less scrupulous.
The Quakers provided a convenient pretext for a rising that had
other, more positive aims.[5]

The Royalists' readiness to exploit this fear of social disorder was
an important point in their favor. Before the rising began, however, two developments added to their difficulties. The first was the
Council of State's energetic set of countermeasures; the second, the
Sealed Knot's campaign of dissuasion. The Rump from the first had
shown the same interest as the Protectorate in the subject of internal security. It came to power at a time when Royalists were
officially excluded from London, and immediately conducted a
thorough search for Cavalier agents on the night of May 8–9; even
the houses of foreign ambassadors were not spared. On May 22 the
Council of State named a special committee to investigate the activities of some London gunsmiths accused of selling arms to the
disaffected. Two days later a standing committee for intelligence
came into being; Thomas Scot was its most active member. At the
same time special warnings were sent to the local authorities at
Gloucester and Oxford of the dispatch of arms into their regions,

5. *CClSP*, *4*, 304, 356, 371, 376, 381. *CCC*, pp. 749, 3253. *Publick Intelligencer*, No. 187. *Clarke Papers*, *4*, 33. *Autobiography of Henry Newcome*,
ed. R. Parkinson, Chetham Society (Manchester, 1852), *1*, 109. *Life of Adam
Martindale*, ed. R. Parkinson, Chetham Society (Manchester, 1845), p. 137.
For Britten see A. G. Matthews, *Calamy Revised* (Oxford, 1934), p. 76.

and John Howe was questioned on the subject for the second time. Warrants were prepared for the arrest of a number of other Royalist leaders: Massey and Titus, Popham's friend Sir Henry Moore, and Col. Adam Browne, who had been active in Surrey. Massey, Titus, and Moore eluded their pursuers, but Browne was taken.[6]

After this there was a lull, and the Council began to relax its precautions. The first sign of renewed crisis appeared while Mordaunt was on his way back from Brussels. On July 1 horses were seized in London, those belonging to dangerous persons being retained for the service of the state. Three days later *Mercurius Politicus* reported that several suspects were being examined about a Cavalier design, and within a few days a stream of instructions began to flow from the Council. On the 7th the London militia was reconstituted and orders given for the distribution of arms. Then, in quick succession, regiments were brought up to strength, officers ordered to their commands, the artillery at St. James' made fit for service, and troops moved from the North into the Midlands. Householders were required to submit lists of their lodgers, and the horses and arms in their possession; there was the usual prohibition of horse races and other dangerous gatherings; and on the 13th yet another proclamation ordered delinquents out of London. Instructions for local militia forces foreshadowed a general reorganization by an act passed on July 26. Hardly a day passed without additional issues of muskets, pikes, and ammunition from the Tower, and troop movements into key areas like Kent continued. The disaffected troops of horse at Chichester and Lewes were removed, and special precautions taken at Arundel and Chepstow. Road patrols were organized near London, barges watched the Thames, and people traveling without passes were liable to arrest.[7]

Amid all this activity the Royalist leaders did not escape atten-

6. *CJ*, 7, 641–42, 646, 662. Steele, *Proclamations*, *1*, 375. *CSPD, 1658–59*, pp. 343, 352–57. Rawl. MSS A 259, pp. 1–2; C 179, pp. 5–8, 12–13, 24, 40. *CClSP, 4*, 203–4, 210. *Cal. State Papers, Venetian, 32*, 20–21.

7. Rawl. MSS A 134; A 259, pp. 22–42; C 179, pp. 134–257 passim. *CSPD, 1659–60*, pp. 6–7, 10–11, 15–16, 23–48. Firth and Rait, *2*, 1293–98, 1304–5, 1308–42. *CJ*, 7, 705–32. *Mercurius Politicus*, Nos. 577–80. *CClSP, 4*, 260–96. See also Davies, *Restoration*, pp. 115, 131–33.

tion. The arrest of Legge, Andrew Newport, and Mordaunt was ordered on July 14, and although Mordaunt was not taken, the other two were both in custody by the 20th, Newport being kept incommunicado. Grenville, another member of the Trust, appeared before the Council of State on the 23d; he made the most of earlier ill-treatment at the hands of Oliver Cromwell and was released on parole. Meanwhile Sir John Packington and Samuel Sandys had been arrested in Worcestershire by the 22d; the commander of the Bridgnorth garrison was summoning local suspects to appear before him; and among many others, John Howe in Gloucestershire and Thomas Blague in Norfolk were in custody within a few more days. The Council sat "all day and almost all night for a good while together," its president, Bulstrode Whitelock, records, the members sleeping at Whitehall and snatching their meals when they could.[8]

What the government did not do by way of discouragement, the Sealed Knot supplied. Mordaunt later asserted that even on Thursday, July 28, "I could discern nothing, that spoke discontent, or dis-satisfaction from any." That this is not quite accurate is apparent from his letter to Baron on the 26th. Willys' bitter words the previous Saturday, he complained, had been so persuasive that they almost swayed even the faithful Rumbold. Compton had impressed his brother with the objection about the harvest, and Russell had convinced another important personage who had given a positive engagement, Lord Bruce. Mordaunt made a last effort to stem the tide. Although Russell refused to see him, Mordaunt managed to get an assurance that he would re-engage those he had dissuaded. By the week end, however, the Knot's members were again at their destructive work. Stories were spread of Royalists leaving England in disgust, burying their arms, selling their horses, anything to avoid participating in a hopeless action. On Saturday the 30th, Oxford, Bruce, and Northampton were again "taken off," and the

---

8. Rawl. MSS A 134; A 259, pp. 27, 29; C 179, pp. 204, 207, 210, 214–15, 219, 235. *CSPD, 1659–60*, pp. 35, 38, 43. *CClSP, 4*, 294, 296, 300. *ClSP, 3*, 543. *Mercurius Politicus*, No. 580. Whitelock, *4*, 355. *Cal. State Papers, Venetian, 32*, 53. Legge must have been released after questioning—he was at large on the 26th, his re-arrest was ordered on the 29th, and he was in custody by the 31st: *LBM*, p. 31; Rawl. MS C 179, p. 235; *Mercurius Politicus*, No. 581.

Knot sent out messengers with news that the Council of State had penetrated the design and that the rising was abandoned. It was too late to stop Booth, but the advice he received on Sunday the 31st, while the preachers were already thundering in the pulpits, "changed his humour so visibly, that from a chearful temper he was observed to be pensive and sad." It is not difficult to imagine what effect the Knot's advice had on many who were less deeply committed.[9]

The opening stages of the rising were further marred by the premature appearance of conspirators before the appointed day. As early as July 24 the commander of the Oxford garrison heard of a Royalist meeting at Chipping Norton; he sent soldiers to break it up. The next day the Governor of Bristol reported the arrest of Sir Hugh Middleton of Pinbury Park, who had been detected saddling horses. On the 27th the Hereford authorities received intelligence of a gathering at Pembridge, twelve miles away; they sent a party of horse, which followed the trail back to Burghope wood, four miles from Hereford. A few armed prisoners were taken, and the Council of State was sufficiently alarmed to send immediate reinforcements, in the shape of a troop of horse from Gloucester. The investigating officers suspected that Sir Henry Lingen knew something about the affair, but were unable to find definite evidence. Apart from Major Thomas Coningsby, son of the monopolist MP of 1640 Fitzwilliam Coningsby, the other suspects were men of no significance.[10]

More serious, although equally ineffective in the end, were the developments in Gloucestershire. The plot here had been a long time maturing. Its origins go back to 1655, to the early activities of Pile, Hopton, and Clayton. In 1659 Pile and Clayton were again busy in the West: the latter must have been released from the previous summer's imprisonment, and the former must have forgotten his petulant decision to "meddle no more." Thomas Veel was also as active as ever, and Richard Hopton had returned to

9. *LBM*, pp. 31–32, 67. *ClSP, 3*, 552–53, 556, 558–59, 564. Carte, *Papers, 2,* 194–95. For Bruce see *DNB*.

10. *CClSP, 4*, 295–96, 304. *CJ, 7*, 741. *CSPD, 1659–60*, p. 55. *CCC*, pp. 770–71, 2066. *Clarke Papers, 4*, 29–30, 285. *Mercurius Politicus*, No. 581. Rawl. MS C 179, pp. 246–47. For Coningsby see Keeler, pp. 139–40, and *CCC*, pp. 2064–69.

England to conspire. Encouraged by the Forest of Dean riots, Hopton went down there in May to fan the flames, but after this nothing is heard of him.[11]

The Gloucestershire plot depended on the support of three much more powerful figures: Alexander Popham, John Grubham Howe, and Edward Massey. All were former parliamentarians, and only Massey, who arrived in England early in the year, was an open Royalist. Popham by this time had recovered from the fall from his horse, and Massey arranged a meeting with him. He found Popham as maddeningly elusive as ever. He was "very harty and full of zeale for the King, etc., yet came to no perticulars," promising only that he would appear if the Royalists looked like being successful. He also suggested that there was more to be gained by waiting for the inevitable Army-Parliament conflict than by precipitate action. In spite of this cloudy statement, by the middle of May the Royalists were confident that Popham would contribute his powerful interest to the Bristol design. Moore was giving his usual optimistic assurances, Falkland was in the negotiation, and even Mordaunt seemed to be satisfied. Toward the end of June Titus brought more certain news. Popham promised to rise with 20,000 men and seize Bridgwater and Taunton, on condition that Bristol was first secured and that the King land in the West with 500 horse. Without the King, Titus reported, he could promise nothing. The qualifications were crippling: the Gloucestershire men had made their own engagement conditional on Popham's first moving against Bristol. By July 6 Popham was obviously a broken reed; his wife was carefully shielding him from the dangerous influence of Royalist agents. This, however, did not save him from a brief period of restraint in August after arms had been discovered at Littlecote.[12]

11. *NP*, *4*, 74, 97, 114, 131, 158–59. *CClSP*, *4*, 137. *ClSP*, *3*, 509. *CSPD, 1658–59*, p. 310 ("Lipe" is Pile; "Minden" is Massey). HMC, *Bath*, 2, 128, 132–33. A letter from the King dated March 3, 1658, purportedly to Veel, is printed in *Archaeologia*, *14*, 75–76, making it appear that Veel was abroad at that time. The letter is actually to Massey, and the correct date is 1658/59; apparently the same letter as in *CClSP*, *4*, 152.

12. *NP*, *4*, 75, 97–98, 158–59, 179. *ClSP*, *3*, 443, 453, 478, 485, 487, 505, 510, 516–17. *CClSP*, *4*, 203, 312, 323, 330. Carte, *Papers*, 2, 173. *CSPD, 1659–60*, pp. 50, 53, 68.

Howe's part in the conspiracy was less ambiguous than Popham's but not much more productive. Mordaunt, who regarded Howe as the Trust's main supporter in the county, omitted to tell him to work with Massey, and the result was a serious dispute over the Gloucestershire command. Massey had difficulty establishing contact with him in the spring and was soon criticizing Howe's inactivity, frequent absences from the county, and unrealistic promises. Howe was certainly guilty of the common error of faulty multiplication. He originally talked of being able to raise 4,000 men at a few days' notice; Brodrick complained that at the time he had arms for only twenty. To his local supporters Howe went as high as 10,000; Massey thought 1,000 more reasonable. Like Popham, Howe regarded Henry Cromwell's submission as a good enough excuse to delay action. By this time Hyde was trying to end the dispute by defining Howe's powers as subordinate to Massey's, but the letter was not dispatched until July 29, by which time Howe was in custody.[13]

Massey's efforts after his return to England were much more vigorous. He spent some weeks in London picking up the threads, and left for his county about the beginning of May. Apart from a brief visit to London in July he spent the whole summer in the West. His agents distributed commissions and drummed up recruits, and he received particular assistance from the Presbyterian clergy: Blanchard of Wraxhall, Britten of Bisley, Hodges of King's Stanley, and Thatch of Stonehouse were all implicated. In Gloucester, Massey relied on the Mayor and the keeper of the castle, Stephen Halford; a local physician, Robert Fielding, promised to secure one of the gates. A more distinguished supporter in the county was Lord Herbert, son of the Marquis of Worcester, who had married Beauchamp's widow. Herbert had been a Cromwellian, but this aberration ended with Oliver's death. Whatever the outcome, Massey's enthusiasm provides a striking contrast to the cautious maneuvering of Popham and Howe.[14]

13. *CClSP, 4,* 161, 190, 200, 202–3, 217, 233, 237, 297. *ClSP, 3,* 433, 449, 455, 460–61, 464, 478, 509, 517, 527. *NP, 4,* 115–16, 131, 158–59. *CCC,* p. 749. *Mercurius Politicus,* No. 580. *CSPD, 1659–60,* p. 103.

14. *NP, 4,* 74–75, 97–98, 114–15, 158–59. *CClSP, 4,* 203, 242, 291. *ClSP, 3,* 509–10, 524. *CCC,* pp. 748–49. Tanner MS (Bodleian) 51, fol. 140. Two letters

During the last week of July, tension at Gloucester mounted rapidly. The city had been alerted on the 14th, and the Rump's leading agents, Alderman Pury and his son, feverishly raised volunteers. By Monday the 25th, spies had brought news that Massey was lurking nearby, that 500 muskets were hidden in readiness, and that the conspirators would assemble in the city on the pretext of business at the assizes, due to open that day. Another report was that a party of disaffected miners would march from the Forest of Dean, a second group would come from the direction of Stroud, and other, smaller forces would be supported by the fifth column inside Gloucester. No keen intelligence was needed to see that action was imminent: suspicious characters were in motion all over the county. The Purys acted decisively. In the small hours of Sunday the 31st several troops of horse were sent to sweep the surrounding countryside. One of them rounded up Lord Herbert, three of the Veels, and Massey, "with all his fyre workes and other engines of warr." On the Forest side of Severn more conspirators were intercepted at the house of a certain Colonel Berrow. Massey contrived to make one of his characteristic escapes while being brought prisoner to Gloucester through the rainy twilight of Nympsfield Hill. A few days later there was a report that he had been retaken going over a ferry near Bristol, but he was again at liberty early in September, for on the 6th he took ship to the Continent.[15]

Massey's escape did not alter the fact that he had failed, and his failure wrecked the plot throughout the whole county. The most important of the other schemes was for a rendezvous on Lansdowne, the height overlooking Bath where Hopton and Waller

written by unidentified conspirators near Gloucester in July 1659, with some blank commissions issued at Brussels in May, are in the Gloucestershire Record Office: D 225/15, 16. Two of the commissions are printed in *Archaeologia*, *14*, 78–79. For Herbert see *DNB*, and *Evelyn*, ed. de Beer, *3*, 159 n. Fielding was Mayor of Gloucester in 1664: T. D. Fosbrooke, *Original History of the City of Gloucester* (London, 1819), p. 418.

15. *Clarke Papers*, *4*, 34–37, 285–86. *CClSP*, *4*, 296, 308, 313, 364. *ClSP*, *3*, 559. *Mercurius Politicus*, No. 581. *CCC*, pp. 748–49. *NP*, *4*, 178–79. Washbourn, intro., pp. cxxxi, cci. Berrow is presumably John Berrow or Barrow, of Field Court, Awre, a parliamentarian in the civil war: Washbourn, intro., pp. clxxvii–clxxviii, and p. 26; *Visitation of the County of Gloucester*, *1623*, ed. Sir John Maclean and W. C. Heane, Harleian Society (London, 1885), pp. 19–20.

had fought a stout battle in 1643. The man behind it was William Basset, a Royalist whose father had been MP for Bath in the Long Parliament and who was a comparative newcomer to conspiracy. The Lansdowne rendezvous was to be formed by several groups of Royalists converging on the hill before dawn on August 1, after preliminary assemblies at various places near the Gloucester-Somerset border. Around midnight on the Sunday night a score of men collected at Keinton Park, near Bath, including servants of Lord Herbert and of the influential Hungerfords of Cadenham. An hour or so later about forty horsemen met at Basset's house, and both groups were at Lansdowne by dawn, where they were joined by a few others; estimates of the total number range from just over fifty to about 120. Two parties were expected from Bristol, where arms and ammunition had long been in readiness. Col. Thomas Piggott and such prominent citizens as the Lawfords and Major Robert Yeamans were supposed to be in charge. The Lawfords were enlisting men on July 31, but they did not reach Lansdowne. This and the news of Massey's arrest persuaded Basset that the game was up, and he ordered his dejected followers to disperse. Some hid in a nearby wood; the rest went home, providing Colonel Okey and the local magistrates with inviting opportunities for investigation.[16]

All over the West schemes related to Massey's went down like ninepins; some earlier, some later. A projected meeting of Royalists from Dorset and south Wiltshire at Stonehenge had been prepared by Capt. Henry Butler of Hanley, Dorset, and William Chamberlain, a Shaftesbury shopkeeper. They were boastfully confident a few days earlier, but on Saturday July 30 they called it off. Perhaps they had received one of the Sealed Knot's messengers.[17] In Devon and Cornwall the silence was completely unbroken. Grenville and his friends had insisted on two conditions

16. *CCISP, 4*, 110, 141, 225, 296, 308–10, 314–16. *CISP, 3*, 509. *CSPD, 1659–60*, pp. 50, 87. Rawl. MS C 179, pp. 225, 232, 234. For Basset's background see the article on his father, Keeler, p. 100. Both John Lawford and Yeamans were future mayors of Bristol: Latimer, pp. 498–99.

17. For the plot in this region see *CSPD, 1659–60*, pp. 81, 87; *CCISP, 4*, 303, 305–7, 313, 315, 317; Rawl. MS C 179, p. 220; Tanner MS 51, fol. 104. For Butler's earlier activities see *CCC*, p. 1231; *TSP, 3*, 122, 630.

for their participation: that Popham and Howe should seize Bristol and Gloucester, and that the King or the Duke of York should come to lead them in person. Neither condition was fulfilled. One of the old leaders, Sir Charles Trevanion, had already applied for a pass to go abroad, and Richard Arundell had been swept away by Willys' persuasive tongue. The county commissioners collected depositions, which even they admitted were of doubtful value, against some local gentry absent from their homes on August 1; a cache of arms was found at Torrington, and a few suspects secured at Exeter. Of Pollard and his more considerable friends nothing was heard.[18]

Falkland's efforts in Oxfordshire were little more impressive. His differences with Mordaunt did not help matters, and there was yet another dispute over the command; rumors got about that William Legge had tried to claim it. Falkland managed to recruit a few men, apparently without much equipment for them. He had assurances from Sir Francis Henry Lee of Ditchley, stepson to the recently deceased Earl of Rochester; and from Sir Anthony Cope of Hanwell. An Oxford barber named John Wilcox did most of the recruiting in the university town. The Oxford conspirators planned to rendezvous in Oriel garden; meetings had been held in the rooms of the Provost, Robert Say. As early as July 20 Anthony Wood noted the vigilance of the authorities: houses were searched for arms, and horses seized from college stables. On July 31, the eve of the rising, there was a panic during the service at St. Martin's Carfax, when the noise of trumpets calling the troops together outside the Golden Cross coincided with the collapse of part of the tower in a strong wind (it was a stormy day all over the country). There were cries of "murder!" and fears that "the anabaptists and quakers were come to cut their throats." The alarm was exaggerated, for Falkland had already abandoned the plot. His arrest was ordered on August 1; he was in custody at Oxford by the 5th, and a week later was examined at Whitehall and sent to the Tower.[19]

18. Details of the conspiracy in Devon and Cornwall are in *CCISP*, *4*, 186, 250, 258, 263, 276, 306, 319; *ClSP*, *3*, 482, 490, 510, 544; *LBM*, p. 32; *CSPD*, *1659–60*, pp. 36, 100; *CCC*, pp. 763, 1234, 1509, 1652, 1679, 2893, 2980; Rawl. MS C 179, pp. 203, 258, 407.

19. Depositions and other information from Oxford in *CCISP*, *4*, 202, 209, 233, 277, 280–81, 295, 312, 386–91; *ClSP*, *3*, 532, 536; *Clarke Papers*, *4*, 38, 42;

The outcome of the risings near London was equally dismal, in spite of much talk of preparations. The idea was that outbreaks in the surrounding counties would draw the Army away from London and make possible an apprentice rising in the City. To the south, Surrey, Sussex, and Kent were theoretically linked in an association: Kent under Boys and Peyton, Surrey and Sussex under Mordaunt. Dover and Sandwich were to be secured for the landing of whatever men and supplies the exiles could provide. In Sussex, with the assistance of Ingoldsby's officers, Lewes and Chichester would be the main foci. Mordaunt and Legge were supposed to be supervising a design against Windsor, and on the north side of London, Buckingham and Bedfordshire would rise under Col. William Tyringham and Lord Bruce. On paper there was a rough logic in it.[20]

In fact almost nothing happened in Berkshire, Buckingham, and Bedford. According to Mordaunt, Bruce sent word that all was ready in Bedfordshire, but if so he was absurdly unrealistic, and at the end of July Bruce was persuaded by John Russell not to rise. This did not save him from arrest; on August 15 the Council examined him without getting him to admit anything. Tyringham's talk of having 200 horse ready in Buckingham was no more accurate. There had been a few meetings at his and other Cavalier houses in July, but they produced nothing more serious than an indefinite plan for a rendezvous at Thornborough, a few miles east of Buckingham town, for which arms were collected. In spite of positive orders from the Trust, the county Royalists made no move on August 1. Tyringham was soon arrested. As for Legge's design on Windsor, nothing whatever came of it, although the garrison was reinforced and alerted. Further afield, there was a rumor about a meeting on Wantage downs, but it did not materialize, and the commander at Reading, although he did his duty

---

CSPD, 1659–60, pp. 103, 105; *Mercurius Politicus*, No. 583; Rawl. MSS A 134; A 259, p. 71; C 179, p. 246; *Life and Times of Anthony Wood*, ed. Andrew Clark, Oxford Historical Society (Oxford, 1891–1900), *1*, 280–81. For Lee see *Evelyn*, ed. de Beer, *3*, 383 n.; for Cope, G.E.C., *Baronetage*, *1*, 36–37; Wood, *Ath. Oxon.*, *3*, 1270; *4*, 396; for Wilcox, Wood, *Life and Times*, *1*, 385; for Say, Foster, *Al. Oxon.*, p. 1321.

20. *ClSP, 3*, 472, 476, 482, 489–90, 547, 558–59. For Tyringham see *LBM*, p. 23 n.

by searching houses and disarming suspects, admitted that he found no real evidence of a plot.[21]

In spite of the hopes aroused by Ingoldsby's officers, Mordaunt's plans in Surrey and Sussex also came to grief. There were suspicious meetings at various Cavalier houses in Surrey in the last days of July, and recruits were busily enlisted. On Friday, July 29, Mordaunt came down from London and the conspirators began moving toward Redhill, the place of rendezvous. The Council of State had already broken into the design. Following the interception of some letters at Reading, Lady Mary Howard, daughter of the Earl of Berkshire and also one of Mordaunt's cousins, was arrested and examined. On the 30th the Council instructed Major Audley to be at Redhill with his troop by dawn on Monday. While patrolling the Surrey lanes near Reigate on the Sunday, Audley took a number of prisoners: some of Ingoldsby's officers, on their way to Chichester; Edward Penruddock, brother of the unfortunate colonel of 1655; a few apprentices and young men from the Inns of Court; and Col. Adam Browne, innocently returning from church. At nightfall Audley posted his men in adjoining barns and sheds, and at first light they came out to patrol the hill. They found no enemy, for Mordaunt had decided to await better days. Altogether not more than eighty suspects were taken, a far cry from the 500 horse who were supposed to collect at Redhill.[22]

Peyton's plans in Kent also collapsed disastrously. The schemes to seize the ports all evaporated, and the only real show of resistance was a small gathering near Tunbridge Wells, at which a few prisoners were taken. This was attended mainly by young bloods from London, and once again the real leaders were conspicuous by their absence. The Council had been sending reinforcements into Kent ever since July 20; on the 29th the forces near Tunbridge Wells

21. *CClSP, 4,* 198, 216–17, 295, 300, 303, 310, 319, 365, 547. *ClSP, 3,* 478, 490, 553, 556, 558–59. *LBM,* pp. 29, 31, 67. *CSPD, 1659–60,* pp. 77, 102, 112, 125, 138. Rawl. MSS A 259, p. 50; C 179, pp. 251, 255, 272, 292. *Mercurius Politicus,* No. 584. Stowe MS 189, fol. 66.

22. *Clarke Papers, 4,* 28–29, 31, 37, 286–87. *CSPD, 1659–60,* pp. 53–55, 60–61, 87. *CCC,* p. 3255. *Mercurius Politicus,* No. 581. *ClSP, 3,* 559. *CClSP, 4,* 283, 300–2, 305–6, 311, 319, 322, 332, 335–36. Rawl. MSS A 259, pp. 34, 40, 42; C 179, pp. 234, 236, 240, 249, 254–55, 263. See also Coate, *LBM,* intro., pp. xiii–xiv.

were alerted, and Colonel Rich was ordered to be at Blackheath on the Monday morning, to guard against an expected rendezvous. On Sunday Colonel Gibbon energetically scoured the countryside between Tunbridge Wells and Sevenoaks. Some fifty prisoners were taken, and elsewhere in Kent a number of more prominent men were arrested on suspicion. These included Lord Strangford and his steward Thomas Colepeper; others like Sir Edward Hales and Lord Tufton absented themselves when summoned to appear. More suspects were unearthed in London a few days later, but the danger of a serious outbreak in Kent was over before the day of action came. The Council of State recognized the fact: on August 1 a troop of horse was moved from Tunbridge Wells to Chichester, and the Blackheath force ordered to return to its quarters.[23]

Hampshire, vaguely associated with Surrey and Sussex, was no more fruitful. Sir Humphrey Bennett still showed much interest in the county, his friend Edward Grey was said to be involved there, as was another old associate, Sir William Courtenay. A new member of the Hampshire directorate was the 14th Lord De la Warr, a recruit from the parliamentary side. He and one of his dependents, Richard Stanesby of Winchester, attempted to revive Richard Cromwell's flagging spirits. On July 31 they went to Hursley, the house of Richard's father-in-law, and while the godly were at morning service invited the deposed Protector to declare for the King. Richard, it was said, blandly told them that he had already done so, and the delegation could not get a more satisfactory answer out of him. In spite of Richard's exasperating futility, the Hampshire design limped forward. Agents distributed commissions, collected arms (some were stored in De la Warr's house in Winchester), and with the connivance of disaffected militia officers, laid plans for a rendezvous. It all collapsed on Sunday, July 31, when one of De la Warr's grooms deserted and gave information of the plot. De la Warr was soon cornered; he jumped a ditch trying to escape but did not get far, and spent a fortnight in the Tower. Courtenay's

23. *CCISP, 4,* 304, 308, 312, 314, 319, 326, 367. *Clarke Papers, 4,* 29, 31. *CSPD, 1659–60,* pp. 50, 54–55, 61, 68, 87, 100. *Mercurius Politicus,* Nos. 581–82, 584. Rawl. MS C 179, pp. 200, 219–21, 234, 247, 249, 260, 266, 272. For Strangford see G.E.C., *Peerage;* for Colepeper, *DNB.*

arrest was ordered on August 13, and several of the lesser men were soon being interrogated.[24]

In the region between the Thames and the Wash the interest of the Sealed Knot had always predominated. Although there was no clearly defined local organization, there was some cooperation between the several counties, and they formed a rudimentary association. Russell, Willys, Compton, and Villiers all lived in the area, and they had powerful friends. Lord Maynard in Essex, the Fanshawes in Hertfordshire, Fuller's patron Sir Henry Wroth, Brodrick's cousin Apsley, and the sulky Earl of Oxford—here were the men who would determine the fate of the rising in East Anglia. Long before the Knot announced its final veto there were signs that the conspiracy was not well founded. Sir Horatio Townshend undertook to raise Norfolk, but he was not widely trusted and his engagment was conditional on Lynn being secured for the landing of foreign forces. Although James Whitelock's overtures gave some hope of this, talk of disaffection at Lynn died away as the summer passed. Oxford continued to make difficulties in Essex, and both Lord Capel, son of the hero of Colchester, and Sir Henry Felton, a leading Suffolk moderate, resented the Trust's highhandedness. There were, however, some tentative preparations during the summer. Sir Simon Fanshawe, Rolleston, and other officers listed men, with the usual inexactness when it came to counting heads, and there were the normal comings and goings among the Cavalier gentry. An example is an interesting series of meetings at Helmingham, near Ipswich. Sir Lionel Tollemache, who lived there, had hitherto prudently abstained from conspiracy; we may class him as a neutral, though he had been willing to exchange favors with both Commonwealth and Protectorate governments. His wife, the Countess of Dysart, had always been a Royalist (in spite of a suspicious friendship with Cromwell) and had a number of ties with the Sealed Knot. Her husband was related to Compton by marriage, Lord Maynard was her sister's husband, and

24. *CClSP*, *4*, 303, 307, 316, 321, 323–24, 351–52, 355, 362, 369–71, 380, 382. *Clarke Papers*, *4*, 37, 42. *CCC*, pp. 1922, 2095. *CSPD*, *1659–60*, pp. 105, 224. *Mercurius Politicus*, Nos. 583, 584. Rawl. MS A 259, pp. 71, 73, 92. For De la Warr see G.E.C., *Peerage*.

Willys and John Russell were both among her friends. Lady Dysart was at Helmingham early in July, her arrival coinciding with a lavish display of hospitality. Among the frequent guests were Felton and other substantial local Royalists, and on July 8 there was a great dinner for the tenants, at which beer was freely dispensed.[25]

The Knot's opposition wrecked the East Anglian design. There were some last-minute preparations, but to no purpose. Arms were being bought in Norwich at the end of July, and Tollemache spent 28s. 8d. on saddles and other equipment. He waited at Helmingham until August 5, when a messenger arrived from Fakenham, his other house, and he left in what appears to have been a great hurry. Ned Villiers went into Essex and Cambridgeshire, but found the design abandoned. Maynard followed Willys' example by appearing before the Council and engaging not to disturb the peace. The Earl of Oxford ignored the Trust's formal invitation to appear; it evidently followed a standard formula, but he chose to regard its tone as insulting. There were a few arrests: warrants were issued for Sir Thomas Fanshawe and Sir John Watts in Hertfordshire, and Rolleston was among those taken by a patrol in Suffolk. The Knot saved most of its supporters from this inconvenience by preventing the kind of feeble outbreak that gave the authorities pretexts for repression in other regions.[26]

August 1 also passed peacefully in the Midlands. In spite of the Earl of Northampton's last-minute withdrawal, the Comptons had made some slight efforts to interest their neighbors in the plot. At the end of April Sir Justinian Isham received a letter from Sir Charles Compton, one of the Earl's brothers, full of dark injunctions to secrecy. Isham was given an introduction to Lady Mordaunt

25. *CClSP, 4,* 195, 202, 210, 227, 329. *ClSP, 3,* 472, 483, 485, 490, 510–11, 526, 537. *CCC,* pp. 756, 2553–54. *TSP, 3,* 697. E. D. H. Tollemache, *The Tollemaches,* pp. 56–58. Helmingham MSS, Bk. II, 2, 1 (Steward's accounts). I am grateful to Lord Tollemache for permission to use the Helmingham MSS, and for letting me read the typescript "History of the Tollemache Family," by Mary Lady Tollemache, which does much to illuminate the connection between the Knot and Lady Dysart's circle. For Wroth see *DNB.*

26. *ClSP, 3,* 586. *CClSP, 4,* 300, 304, 308, 311–12, 336, 376. *CSPD, 1659–60,* pp. 53, 56, 67. *Mercurius Politicus,* No. 588. *CJ, 7,* 785. Rawl. MS C 179, pp. 247, 269. Helmingham MSS, Bk. II, 2, 1. For Fanshawe see Keeler, p. 172, and *Fanshawe Memoirs,* pp. 293–302.

and told that "the place" was within a mile of Wollaston, near the Comptons' strongholds of Castle Ashby and Grendon. Sir Justinian was no more responsive than usual, but the Comptons had more success with some of their other friends. Mordaunt expected a good appearance from them, and was correspondingly bitter when both the Earl and Sir Charles changed their minds. There was therefore no movement in Northampton, and only a slight ripple in Leicestershire, where about twenty men rose under John Prettyman, a former sheriff of the county, and were duly captured. Byron and his friends in the north Midlands decided to await events.[27]

Little had been done by the Trust to organize the counties beyond the Humber. The system of 1655 had been shattered; Langdale's influence, in spite of a brief revival in 1657, had been only partially restored, and the Trust made no apparent effort to replace it. The Newcastle Royalists had been in difficulties since the summer of 1658, when their former governor, Sir John Marlay, sold himself to Thurloe to ward off the twin diseases of bankruptcy and exile. Marlay probably had little influence over affairs at Newcastle; still, his defection was a bad sign.[28] Mordaunt left it to Hyde to deal with Belasyse, the Knot's local man. The Chancellor wrote to him on June 10, asking him to arouse his friends. Belasyse was in London, and merely offered the leadership to his nephew Fauconberg, whose Cromwellian past did not make him an ideal choice. The Trust showed more interest in Lincolnshire, no doubt through Willoughby's connections. Edward Rossiter was to join Willoughby in rousing the Presbyterians of the county, balanced by Lord Castleton and Sir John Mounson from the Old Royalist side. Willoughby was also involved in the design against Lynn, and there was some talk of Boston as a port for disembarking forces from abroad.[29]

The only activity in Yorkshire and Lincolnshire at the beginning of August was a depressing roundup of suspects. Belasyse was taken at Worlaby, in the company of the Earl of Middlesex, a recent convert engaged by Sir John Grenville. Willoughby afterward gave the

27. *LBM*, pp. 31, 67. *Duppa-Isham Corr.*, pp. 165–66. *ClSP, 3*, 558–59. For Prettyman see *Evelyn*, ed. de Beer, *3*, 73 n.

28. *TSP, 7*, 149–50, 181, 203, 229, 252, 268, 312–13, 333, 346–47, 526, 549, 785. *CClSP, 4*, 142.

29. *ClSP, 3*, 490, 500, 506. *CClSP, 4*, 327–28.

standard excuse for his failure to rise: the absence of any attempt in the adjacent counties and, in particular, the Comptons' defection. It is clear, however, that by the end of July he had lost faith in the plan which he had helped to prepare. The Council of State took a few precautions in the area: moving troops, strengthening garrisons like Hull and Skipton, issuing arms to the local forces. But the real danger lay beyond the Pennines.[30]

Of the two centers of violence near the Welsh border, that in Cheshire and Lancashire was incomparably the more serious. There was, nevertheless, a smaller affair near Shrewsbury, in which Royalists from Shropshire and Worcestershire were involved. There were actually two groups in the latter county, one led by Brodrick's friend John Talbot, the other by Charles Littleton, who had been active in 1655 and was a friend of Andrew Newport, Lord Windsor, and other prominent people. Talbot's party was to move south and support Massey; it came to nothing, and Talbot was arrested early in August. Littleton was more interested in the assault on Shrewsbury, and his accomplices began to assemble toward the end of July. On the 25th, Henry Norwood and Sir Thomas Harris, another of the old leaders of 1655, left London for the scene of action. Littleton's party came together as appointed on Monday August 1, first at the Littleton seat at Hagley near Stourbridge, and then at Hall Close near Bridgnorth; there were said to be about forty-five of them, with colors rolled up and a trumpeter. The little company rode to the Wrekin, the great hill commanding Shrewsbury, cheering themselves by capturing a solitary parliamentary trooper. The commander of the Shrewsbury garrison, Captain Waring, was alarmed by the unwillingness of the town magistrates to take defensive measures; his instinct told him that many people were sympathetic to the rebels and needed only a setback to the Parliament's forces to declare themselves. By now between fifty and sixty strong, Littleton's men met Norwood on the rain-swept

30. *CClSP*, *4*, 275, 301–2, 323, 382, 394, 462. *ClSP*, *3*, 544, 557, 559, 609. *CSPD*, *1659–60*, pp. 75, 116, 118, 127, 162. *Clarke Papers*, *4*, 31. Rawl. MSS A 259, pp. 59–60; C 279, pp. 160, 207, 235, 273, 281. HMC, *Ormonde*, new ser. 2, 397–98. For Middlesex see G.E.C., *Peerage*.

Wrekin. He talked glibly of the massive support that would join them in the morning, but lost his head and was the first to flee during the night. In the morning the rest of the Wrekin party followed his example; a few were captured at Shiffnal, some miles to the east; the rest dispersed.[31]

After this monotonous record of dismal failure, Sir George Booth's area of operations in Lancashire and Cheshire provides a welcome contrast. Three reasons for Booth's success in actually getting into the field can be advanced. His region was the one in which the Council of State had taken the fewest precautions; and the absence of any special vigilance by the local officers enabled Booth to survive the critical first few days, when his adherents might have been frightened off by a strong counteroffensive. A second reason was that the warning messengers sent round by the Knot failed to reach him in time for orders canceling the rising to be issued.[32] Finally, and perhaps most important, Booth received the full support of the clergy, in one of the most tightly organized of all the Presbyterian classes.

The Lancashire clergy's concentration on the Quaker phantom on the day before the rising has already been described. After Meroz had been duly cursed at the afternoon sermon, the drums beat in Warrington, the chief place of rendezvous, and the insurrection began to spread. Booth arrived at Warrington on Monday morning, and supported by the Earl of Derby and other gentry raised the standard of rebellion. Some 500 men collected at Warrington, another 500 at Manchester, and armed men were in motion all over Lancashire and Cheshire. Landlords summoned their tenants to follow them, although the government print may have been right when it sneered that many went reluctantly. Some of

31. *CClSP, 4*, 163–65, 173–74, 202, 233, 273, 280, 294–96, 306, 309, 312–13, 349–50, 356, 360, 395, 407. *ClSP, 3*, 428, 478, 490, 559. *CSPD, 1659–60*, pp. 77, 101, 132, 137. Carte, *Papers, 2*, 227–28. *CCC*, pp. 2027, 2899. *Mercurius Politicus*, No. 582. Rawl. MSS A 134; C 179, p. 204. For Littleton's circle of friends see *Hatton Corr., 1*, 11–19, and for Windsor's role, Add. MS 29,550, fol. 328.

32. Davies, *Restoration*, pp. 134–35, and n. To this it might be added that the messenger was sent to Booth by Bruce, a supporter of the Knot, not by those who knew about Willys' treachery; the latter (Mordaunt, etc.) wished to go on with the rising. See Jones, *John Rylands Library Bulletin, 39*, 436.

the Royalist gentry in north Lancashire held off because Booth and Derby could not give them commissions from the King, but their defection was more than made up for by the numbers further south. Royalist Egertons, parliamentarian Brookes: it seemed that at last the Royalist-Presbyterian alliance was a reality.[33]

From Warrington, Booth's main force moved on Chester. His uncle, John Booth, had been there for several days, and with the help of one of the sheriffs the gates were opened early on the morning of the 2d. The Mayor and about half the corporation took the line of least resistance and supported the rebels, but the city was far from unanimous. "Many of the Citizens . . . seem to embrace Neutrality, and decline both parties," one observer noted. Croxton, commanding the garrison, retreated into the castle, posing a constant threat to Booth's position, which the rebels' shortage of artillery made them powerless to erase. By the end of the first week of the rising, while Lambert was hurrying north to deal with it, Booth's situation was already precarious. He was, however, doing his best to strengthen it by enlarging his area of operations. In spite of the bad weather that hampered movement all over the country, the mustering of men continued. Derby occupied Preston, and Roger Whitley, who had arrived from abroad a few days before the rising, seized Hawarden castle. Booth's Presbyterian friends brought in powerful assistance. Col. Gilbert Ireland occupied Liverpool, and persuaded some of the militia to desert their colors. Warrants were sent out to raise the posse comitatus: twenty men enlisted at Bury on August 8, forty at Bolton the next day. Booth sent two troops of horse to Chirk castle on the Welsh border. They were eagerly received by Sir Thomas Myddelton, who threw himself into the rising with an enthusiasm that contrasts strikingly with his attitude in 1651 and 1655. He sent a trumpeter to invite the militia at Oswestry to come over. They refused, but Myddelton went off to join Booth at Chester, leaving Chirk in Royalist hands. On the way, at Wrexham, he proclaimed Charles II in the market place: "either through dotage . . . or the natural depravity of his

33. *Clarke Papers, 4,* 31–33, 287–88. *Newcome, 1,* 109. *Mercurius Politicus,* Nos. 582–83, 586. *CClSP, 4,* 306, 501.

own heart," Ludlow commented. Within a week a large tract of country between Chirk and Preston was in Booth's hands.[34]

Two important requirements, however, were missing. One was support from other parts of the country: by August 7 Sir George could see the end coming, and told Henry Newcome "how basely he was deserted." The other was agreement between Royalists and Presbyterians on the rising's fundamental objectives. Booth did his best to evade the issue. None of his three declarations mentions the question of monarchy, and although few can have doubted that a successful rising would lead to a restoration, the important question of what the terms would be was left in the air. Booth was careful not to proclaim Charles II, and when the Earl of Derby did so, Booth protested that "it would bee their ruine." Myddelton's enthusiasm caused similar misgivings. Some Presbyterians, like Adam Martindale, held aloof because of the inconsistencies in Booth's professed intentions: a rising to establish Presbyterianism, which at the same time promised liberty of conscience, something Martindale "utterly abhorred." For the Anglican Royalists the Presbyterians would have been unpopular allies at best; they were derisively dismissed as "New Cavaliers, and but younger brothers," and the war as "Bellum Presbiterale." A few withdrew altogether. Henry Bridgeman, a future bishop, said "that he forsooke them at Manchester because he perceived that some of the grandees were cordiall for the king but not for the church." A large group of the Lancashire Royalists, the Roman Catholics, were deliberately excluded from the start.[35]

---

34. *CCC*, pp. 748, 751–52. *Clarke Papers*, *4*, 33. Carte, *Papers*, 2, 196. "A Declaration of Sir George Booth," *Tracts Relating to the Civil War in Cheshire*, ed. J. A. Atkinson, Chetham Society (Manchester, 1909), p. 165. *Newcome*, *1*, 110. *Martindale*, pp. 137–38. HMC, *Portland*, *1*, 684. *Mercurius Politicus*, No. 583. *NP*, *4*, 177. *CClSP*, *4*, 309, 381. Baker, pp. 667–68. *Ludlow's Memoirs*, 2, 108–9. Barwick claims to have converted Myddelton: *Barwick*, pp. 49, 183.

35. *Newcome*, *1*, 110. *Clarke Papers*, *4*, 38. *Mercurius Politicus*, No. 583. *NP*, *4*, 177. Carte, *Papers*, 2, 196. *CClSP*, *4*, 348, 501. *CSPD, 1659–60*, p. 163. *Martindale*, pp. 134–39. *Blundell Letters*, p. 90. For analyses of Booth's declarations see Davies, *Restoration*, pp. 135–37, and Jones, *John Rylands Library Bulletin*, *39*, 438–39. For Bridgeman see *DNB*.

Although no significant risings occurred elsewhere to save Booth from destruction, the news that he was in arms encouraged a few recent converts to the Knot's inaction to revise their opinions. In most cases the leadership was as ineffective as ever. In Yorkshire, according to John Cooper, Fauconberg emerged from his tent after the arrival of the news from Chester. All he did, however, was to pass the word to the Cavaliers through Sir Jordan Crosland that they must wait for further instructions from his Presbyterian allies. When all was ready for an attempt on York, Cooper asserted, Fauconberg arrived early in the day, deferred action for two hours, and left the town. A few more suspects were rounded up in the course of the month, including Langdale's agent Sir Theophilus Gilby, and Robert Walters, who was taken on landing in Lincolnshire. There was a report that Fauconberg had been arrested early in August, but it was not until September 13 that he was brought to London in custody.[36]

The repercussions in Nottingham and Derbyshire were more explosive. In spite of Mordaunt's optimism, it appears that before the original rising things were far from well. Col. John Freschville, responsible for Derbyshire in conjunction with the Stanhopes and Vernons, grumbled about being left in ignorance of the Trust's plans. Byron, at Nottingham, also complained early in June that he had received no commissions, and no notice of the expected date of the rising. The commissions were duly sent, but according to the critical Cooper, Byron again mismanaged things: several rendezvous were planned and countermanded. Eventually, on August 12, Byron acted. With the aid of the Presbyterian Colonel Charles White of Newthorpe, Robert Pierrepont, the young nephew of the Marquis of Dorchester, and a handful of other local gentry, Byron gathered between 80 and 120 horse early in the morning near Sansom wood in Sherwood. The idea seems to have been to attack the militia troop at Southwell, which was not expected to show fight. The militiamen, however, displayed unforeseen courage, and Byron retreated in what Cooper described as "scandalous haste."

36. *CClSP, 4*, 236, 346, 365, 418, 462. *Clarke Papers, 4*, 38. *Mercurius Politicus*, Nos. 586, 588. *CSPD, 1659–60*, pp. 191, 225. *CJ, 7*, 786. Sir Philip Monckton claims to have had men ready in Yorkshire: *Monckton Papers*, p. 24.

About eight o'clock Nottingham was alarmed by men galloping through the streets "in a disorderly and confused manner"; it was Byron's force in headlong flight. They scattered, some toward Leicester, some toward Derby, but not before a man had been killed and prisoners and colors taken. Byron's Cavalier friends had again failed to distinguish themselves.[37]

White, who went on to Derby, found the Presbyterians there more energetic. The local ministers had been stirred by the militant example of their Lancashire brethren. One of them, Robert Seddon of Kirk Langley, had been sent into Lancashire ostensibly to calm the tumults but actually to offer assistance. Henry Newcome heard of the discussions, met Seddon, and was only prevented from going back to Derby with him by his wife's opposition; Newcome always had excellent excuses. The uprising at Derby was thus by no means unprepared. Luke Cranwell, one of the ministers there, was among the first to welcome White, who was also well received by some of the Aldermen. White read Booth's Declaration in the market place, and this produced an immediate uproar, "some crying a King, others a Free Parliament, some both." Many of the merchants closed their shops and joined White, and a handful of militia officers came over. The senior officer in the town, Col. Thomas Saunders, one of the "three colonels" of 1654, attempted to arrest White but was prevented by the mob, and White then invited him to join the rebellion. Saunders managed to avoid committing himself, but there were suspicions that he had connived, putting on a show of resistance merely to cover himself. The local sequestration commissioners were unable to find proof of his misbehavior, but the fact that some months later Saunders had joined several of White's partisans in a campaign of obstruction against them is at least suggestive. Capt. Samuel Doughty, the county treasurer, was more forthright. He shook White by the hand, caused the bells to be rung backward to call in supporters from the coun-

37. There are accounts of the affair in Sherwood in *Mercurius Politicus*, No. 583; *Clarke Papers*, *4*, 43, 45; *Hutchinson Memoirs*, pp. 308–11, 445–46. For a brief summary see Wood, *Notts. in the Civil War*, pp. 176–77. See also *CCISP*, *4*, 325, 417; *CSPD*, *1659–60*, pp. 113, 120; *CCC*, p. 769. For White see Wood, *Notts. in the Civil War*, pp. 32, 132; for Pierrepont, *Hutchinson Memoirs*, pp. 312–13.

tryside, and tried to arrest one of the hostile officers; some said he gave the rebels £4,000, recently collected revenue.[38]

In the towns under Booth's control the news from Derby was received with bonfires and hysterical relief. Unfortunately Booth had no men to spare to send to White's assistance. Major General Egerton made a few tentative maneuvers on the borders of the county, but that was all. The Derbyshire Cavaliers were surprised by White's appearance and did little, which seems inexcusable since Booth had been in arms for almost a fortnight. Col. John Shalcross and Sir Henry Every raised a few men, but the county leaders failed to take the plunge. Chesterfield sent a messenger to Every, but we have no indication what he said. White was not long left unmolested. Lambert was already moving on Chester (he had been held up by floods near Stafford), and on the afternoon of the 12th one of his officers, Colonel Mitchell, rode into Derby to warn the rebels of the consequences of "their base ingratitude to the Parliament, under whom they had such opportunities of gaining estates." Mitchell then withdrew to Uttoxeter, and on Sunday, assisted by parties of horse from Leicester and Nottingham, entered Derby. By now the town was "pale-faced"; there was no resistance, and Mitchell's men were feasted by the magistrates, who joined in proclaiming Booth and his adherents traitors to the state. White, Doughty, and a few others found themselves stranded on the losing side.[39]

Not all of Byron's dispersing party followed White in his brief hour of glory. Some went south into Leicestershire, where there were two minor incidents. The first arose from a rumor that Belvoir castle had been taken by the Royalists. Parliamentary troops came scurrying to the rescue, and near Melton Mowbray some of them collided in the darkness, mistook each other for Cavaliers, and blazed away with their muskets for a few hectic minutes.

---

38. *Mercurius Politicus*, Nos. 583–84. *CSPD, 1659–60*, p. 120. *CCC*, pp. 754–55, 772–73, 3251. *Clarke Papers*, *4*, 45. *Newcome*, *1*, 111. *CClSP*, *4*, 325, 417–18. For Saunders see Firth and Davies, pp. 282–89; for Cranwell and Seddon, Matthews, *Calamy Revised*, pp. 142, 431–32.

39. *Mercurius Politicus*, No. 584. *CCC*, pp. 748, 750–52, 1265, 2449, 3249, 3252. *CClSP*, *4*, 418. *CSPD, 1659–60*, pp. 158, 188, 197. *CJ*, *7*, 786. For Every, see *CCC*, pp. 2448–49; and G.E.C., *Baronetage*, *2*, 85–86.

The other was less comic. A detachment collecting horses for the militia called at Bradgate, the house of the Presbyterian Earl of Stamford, who happens to have been Booth's father-in-law and whose son, Anchitell Grey, later a notable parliamentary reporter, had been involved in the business at Derby. The house was full of arms, and there were about thirty horses in the stables; armed men were also conspicuous—some of them, it was believed, fugitives from Nottingham. One of Ingoldsby's officers, Major Thomas Babington, invited the Rump officers to desert to Stamford's side. To make his meaning clearer, the Earl drank Charles II's health and produced first a blunderbuss and then a banner with the legend "King and Covenant." Stamford's behavior suggests that in August 1659 some even of the Presbyterian grandees would have been willing to commit themselves if encouraged by an early victory. The day after the Bradgate incident, however, the situation began to look less favorable. Stamford's party dispersed, and the Earl came to Leicester to submit to the county commissioners. He had plentiful excuses: it was only a gathering of tenants come to present their grievances, and so on; he was arrested all the same and sent to London for examination.[40]

While all this was happening in the Midlands, Mordaunt was trying again in Surrey, and reviving the scheme for a London rising. Young men at the Inns of Court and their servants provided the horse; the foot was to be made up of apprentices. John Cooper and Ned Villiers were both in London early in August and attempted to contribute to the horse detachments. The commander was originally to have been the Earl of Oxford, but his abstention left it to Col. Thomas Panton, a sporting Cavalier from Ashby-de-la-Zouch, who had been an emissary between the Trust and the Sealed Knot before the rising. The leadership of the Presbyterian citizenry and the apprentices was left, as usual, to Major General Browne. The woodmongering Alderman had been less than responsive in his relations with the Trust, but there were some hopes of his appearance. Browne was directed to present himself to the Council

---

40. *Mercurius Politicus*, Nos. 583–84. *Clarke Papers, 4,* 44. *CSPD, 1659–60,* pp. 113, 120, 125, 164, 166. *CClSP, 4,* 325. For the Greys see *DNB,* and *BIHR, 5,* 55; for Babington, Firth and Davies, pp. 148–55.

on July 29; he ignored the summons, and went underground. There was, however, little sign of enthusiasm. "We are endeavouring to quicken this city," Rumbold told Hyde, ". . . but it hath always been my opinion . . . that there is little to be done here by design amongst the graver sort of people; not but that the apprentices are very apt for commotions." Panton twice named dates for the London rising, and on each occasion countermanded them. The first was on August 9, which the Council of State frustrated by an ominous display of artillery; the second on the 19th, and again the would-be rebels were cowed by a show of force. The guards were tripled, street patrols sent out, and there was a thorough search of the Inns of Court for potential trouble-makers.[41]

Panton's bungling helped to ruin two related plans for risings near London: Mordaunt's in Surrey, and an unprepared attempt in Hertfordshire. The Surrey affair was the more serious. Mordaunt's principal assistants were his cousin Thomas Howard, second son of the Earl of Berkshire; the young Earl of Lichfield, recently come from France; and Charles Bickerstaffe, of Chelsham near Croydon. On Wednesday, August 10, Mordaunt and some of his friends gathered at Tooting to arm and put on their buff coats. A few hours later young fellows from London began to drift into Tooting; about sixteen of them soon collected. At twilight Hartgil Baron met them in a barn and conducted them to Chelsham woods, where they stayed until Saturday the 13th. At about nine that evening Lichfield, Mordaunt, Bickerstaffe, and others to the number of about eighty gathered on Banstead downs, with the intention of attacking the county militia. Sir Francis Vincent was to have joined them from the direction of Leatherhead with another party. When it was discovered that parliamentary troops were approaching, the rendezvous dispersed; it was later believed that Rookwood, the friar, guided the soldiers to the place. Major Audley sent out his usual patrols and netted a few more prisoners; one of them, mistaking Audley's men for Royalists, politely handed over a list of

41. *ClSP, 3*, 547, 557. *CClSP, 4*, 299–300, 317–18, 322–23, 329, 336. *Clarke Papers, 4*, 29, 31, 38, 45–46. *Mercurius Politicus*, Nos. 582–83. *CSPD, 1659–60*, pp. 52, 90, 93, 128, 130. Rawl. MSS A 259, pp. 47, 85, 90; C 179, pp. 240, 248, 401, 404. For Panton see *DNB; LBM*, pp. 31 and n., 32; *TSP, 4*, 661; *CClSP, 4*, 319.

already engaged supporters. By Sunday the 14th, Mordaunt realized that there was no hope. That night he, Lichfield, and Howard dined at Bagshot, at the furthest end of the county. The next day he went to Chertsey and took a barge to London; early in September he sailed for France.[42]

The business in Hertfordshire was even more trivial. On the 18th the Rump's local commander, Boteler, was informed that the Cavaliers intended to rendezvous that night at Sawbridgeworth, the house of Sir Thomas Leventhorpe, near the Suffolk border. Besides Leventhorpe his wife's cousin, young Thomas Fanshawe of Ware Park, was involved, and an improbable rumor had it that the commander was to be one of the Compton brothers. Boteler promptly marched his troop to disperse the gathering. Leventhorpe and his more important friends were warned in time and disappeared, but Boteler took six insignificant prisoners, about a dozen horses, and a good deal of baggage. He also found forty cases of pistols, eight loaded carbines, and enough saddles and bridles to equip a troop of horse. Leventhorpe, Fanshawe, and Sir William Compton were immediately included in the proclamation ordering the leaders of the rising to surrender within a fortnight. Compton had apparently done so even before the proclamation was published, for on August 26 the Cambridge authorities were instructed to send him up to the Council on parole. Leventhorpe and Fanshawe surrendered on September 13 and were sent to the Tower.[43]

The frustration of these diversions was accompanied by the extinction of Booth's last hopes of assistance from abroad. There had been much talk during the summer of transporting Charles II's Flanders regiments, supplemented by Spanish forces or by men supplied by Turenne. The preparations could not, however, have been worse managed. There were the usual difficulties about a port,

42. *CISP, 3,* 548, 557, 559. *CCISP, 4,* 328–29, 331–33. *CSPD, 1659–60,* pp. 113, 207. *Mercurius Politicus,* No. 583. Carte, *Papers, 2,* 216. Coate, *LBM,* intro., pp. xiii–xiv. *CCC,* pp. 3251, 3255. Rawl. MS C 179, p. 115. For Lichfield see *DNB;* for the Bickerstaffe family, VCH, *Surrey, 4,* 273, 290.

43. *Mercurius Politicus,* Nos. 584, 586. *Clarke Papers, 4,* 45–46, 290. *CCC,* pp. 1864, 3248. *CSPD, 1659–60,* pp. 149, 180, 191. Steele, *Proclamations, 1,* 377. For Leventhorpe see G.E.C., *Baronetage, 1,* 196; for Fanshawe, *Fanshawe Memoirs,* pp. 305–8.

money for arms and equipment was lacking, and liaison with the blandly dilatory Spaniards was as ineffective as ever. Nobody was sure whether the ships were available; it would not have mattered, as contrary winds would have kept the expedition in the Flanders ports whatever its state of readiness. The King fulfilled his promise by moving from Brussels to Calais early in August, but Kent had not risen and the news from Chester suggested that a landing in the West was the last hope. Charles accordingly made his way through Normandy to St. Malo; fortunately he was unable to secure a ship in time to join Booth in the field. Meanwhile his brother James, left behind at Calais, seemed to have enticed Turenne into making an offer of effective assistance, but the transportation problem was still unsolved when the news of Booth's last stand reached the Continent.[44]

While the exiles were showing their typical indecision, the sands were running out for the rebels in the North. Hemmed in at Chester, where he had not succeeded in dislodging Croxton from the castle, Booth had no alternative but to die gloriously, and given the state of his men's morale he had little prospect of doing even that. By August 15 Lambert had passed through the Staffordshire floods and was established at Nantwich. The complete collapse of all the other attempted risings enabled the Rump's military power to concentrate on Booth; not its full weight, but enough. Lambert had about 4,500 men, including over 1,000 horse; smaller forces under West in north Lancashire, Robert Lilburne in Yorkshire, and Creed at Shrewsbury were not far away. There was no chance of being able to sustain a siege, and on the 16th Booth decided to come out and fight. He was hampered by having to leave a garrison to contain Croxton in the castle; and Mordaunt later asserted that Booth did not even wait for Derby's Lancashire men to arrive before he gave battle. Even so, Booth's army was not far, if at all, numerically inferior to Lambert's: in morale, discipline, and equipment, however, there was no comparison. On Friday morning, August 19, Roger Whitley, Myddelton's Major General of horse, made contact with Lambert's scouts beyond Winnington

44. Clarendon, *History*, Bk. XIV, §§ 35, 44–45. Scott, *Travels of the King*, pp. 399–407. Coate, *LBM*, intro., p. xiv.

Bridge, the enemy's natural passage over the River Weaver. Whitley gave the alarm and Booth's army drew up in battle array in
front of Northwich, but it was too late to hold the bridge. Lambert's foot drove across it, and the horse, previously restricted by
the hedges of enclosed fields, were now free to do the rest. Booth's
infantry, many of whom, said Mordaunt, "had no match, others no
ball," were safe among the hedges; "the horse trotted away, which is
the civilest term," he added sarcastically. So ended the "battle" of
Winnington Bridge. The victors suffered one fatal casualty, the
losers perhaps thirty or forty.[45]

The towns previously held by Booth were soon reoccupied by
Lambert. Many of the officers at Chester dismissed their men; most
had already left without waiting to be told. Liverpool and Manchester were occupied without resistance: "a sad day . . . when
the soldiers came to town," Henry Newcome groaned. Chirk castle
held on for a few days more, but on the 24th articles of surrender
were signed and all was over. The process of rounding up and examining fugitives went on for many more weeks. Altogether perhaps 700 prisoners were taken, about half of them in the battle. Sir
George himself fled south in disguise, but on the 23d he was captured in female garb at Newport Pagnell. "He acted the Womans
part not so well," the government print airily remarked, as though
offering dramatic criticism. It might indeed have been more appropriate if some of Booth's Royalist colleagues who were supposed to
have risen in other places had been taken in the same disguise.[46]

With no insult to Booth, it was a fitting end to the August rising.
The catalogue of adverse circumstances is overwhelming: the
Sealed Knot's disrupting opposition, the confusion of contradictory
orders, Willys' treachery, Mordaunt's tactless arrogance, the Trust's
reckless decision to go ahead when local Royalist groups were still
unprepared or torn by disagreement, the friction between Cava-

---

45. See the reports in *Cheshire Civil War Tracts*, pp. 167–81; *Clarke Papers,
4,* 289; Carte, *Papers, 2,* 197–99; *ClSP, 3,* 552–55; *CClSP, 4,* 558; Davies,
Restoration, pp. 138–40; and Jones, *John Rylands Library Bulletin, 39,*
441–42.

46. *Mercurius Politicus,* No. 584. *Cheshire Civil War Tracts,* pp. 176–84.
HMC, *Portland, 1,* 684–85. *Clarke Papers, 4,* 47–48, 293. *CSPD, 1659–60,* pp.
157, 192, 219, 224. *CClSP, 4,* 382–83. *Newcome, 1,* 112.

liers and Presbyterians, the lack of coordination and timing, the cautious aloofness of the great lords. "The lords abused us," John Cooper complained, but it was not only the lords. As in every Royalist conspiracy since 1649, those with property or social position to protect refused to commit themselves until a chance of success became a mathematical certainty. Royalist peers like Northampton, who had actively helped to prepare the design, were no more forward when put to the test than judicious neutrals like Popham, who had covered themselves with reservations. Although the Presbyterians were more willing to appear in arms than ever before, and although the rising only advanced beyond futile preliminaries in the one area where the ministers threw their weight behind it, the Royalist alliance with them had not been completed. Nor, in spite of Ingoldsby and his officers, had more than a handful of Cromwellians come over. As usual, the government met the first signs of opposition with the solid military power at its disposal; still, in spite of the recent purge, more than enough for Booth's ill-armed and disorganized levies. How much Willys, now the "Arch-traitor" to his former friends, contributed to the Council's prior knowledge of the plot it is hard to say. Even without him—through spies like Corker and Rookwood, depositions of terrified prisoners, and intercepted Royalist correspondence—the Rump would have been able to take adequate countermeasures.

It is therefore not enough to blame tactical factors like the bad weather or Booth's inexperience for the failure of the August rising. However general the detestation of military government under a Rump oligarchy and however deep-seated the fears of social dislocation by Quakers and sectaries, the concept of restoration by violence was still invalid. Once again the Knot was right and Mordaunt wrong, even though Willys' motives for opposing the action may have been discreditable. Rebellion, as the Knot prophesied, stimulated a momentary closing of the enemy's wavering ranks. The moderates wanted a restoration, if at all, to save society, and society would not be saved by a new civil war; the Earl of Manchester, a good index to moderate thinking, was afraid "of his Majesties restoration by tumult." Until that danger was overcome, people like Manchester would take care not to offend the winning side; although, as the magistrates of Chester and Derby had shown, they would be content enough if the winning side was the King's. The fact that the Army-Rump alliance was short-lived and that it was followed by a period of anarchy indicates how little difference the Booth rising had made. Once more the Royalists were waiting on events; it was the Sealed Knot's policy, and the only paradox is that the Knot was no longer there to direct it. There was also the chance that when the Commonwealth disintegrated, order might be restored by an invading army. It might be one hired in Europe by Charles II; it might be the only disciplined force in the British Isles, in Scotland under a general named George Monck. The dream that Charles could be brought back by his devoted Cavaliers alone had vanished, "under a wench's petticoat." [47]

47. Quotations from *ClSP, 3,* 556; *CClSP, 4,* 355; *LBM,* p. 163.

13. Toward the Restoration

THE ROYALISTS ESCAPED lightly after the Booth rising. There were no Major Generals, no decimation taxes, and although most of the leaders were consigned to jail during the rising or soon afterward, their imprisonment was neither long nor arduous. Revival of the sequestration machinery looked ominous at first but was never effectively administered. The reasons for the Rump's leniency are obvious enough: the regime could not trust even the generals who had restored it. When the breach with the Army occurred in October, the Cavaliers were immediately able to resume their plotting. Royalist policy was now to undermine what was left of the Commonwealth's authority; to contribute to the growing anarchy; and to persuade men of influence that a restoration was inevitable, and that they had better secure themselves in advance. Talk of yet another attempt to rise in arms was never completely stilled, but the arguments for restoration by agreement became more and more compelling as it became more and more likely. In this chapter we shall therefore see the ultimate triumph of the Sealed Knot's policy of restraint, of waiting for the republic to die of its own contradictions.

The most important Royalist leaders had been secured before the end of August 1659, and many others were taken by the middle of September. The London apprentices still talked of an attempt to seize the Tower and release Booth; some of them met on the night of August 26 but found the place too strongly guarded. In spite of its weakness, the Council of State was alive to the danger of renewed outbreaks. The proclamation against delinquents in London was still in force, and on September 1 at least one violator was sent to the Gatehouse. At about this time Dr. Brian Duppa's house at Richmond was searched for suspicious papers. The investigators could find only a couple of mystifying letters on which to exercise their detective skills. One contained a learned disquisition by Isham on the passage of the Israelites through the Red Sea. This, Duppa told Sir Justinian, was carefully studied, on the supposition "that there was some notable Cabala in it, and taking the Red Sea, and the wilderness of Etham, to be as hieroglyphicks relating to som present matters." The cipher was found to be impenetrable—not surprisingly, as there was none.[1]

Both the Rump and the Army committee which succeeded it in October treated their prisoners with moderation. Some of the suspects against whom there was least evidence were released even before Booth was taken. One practical argument for generosity was shortage of accommodation. The Tower, Newgate, and the other jails were soon overcrowded, and suitable buildings like Leadenhall, Gresham College, and Thanet House were full of troops. By the end of September most of the lesser prisoners had been released, as well as some better-known figures like the Earl of Oxford and William Legge. Chesterfield and Fauconberg got out early in October, and after the Committee of Safety took over, the few still in jail were soon let go. The bulk of the remaining lords were discharged on November 2: Northampton, Falkland, Castleton, Herbert, and Belasyse. Sir George Booth was granted bail for reasons of health on December 9 but did not receive complete freedom until February 22, 1660, when the last of the prisoners went home.[2]

1. *Duppa-Isham Corr.,* pp. 171–72. *CClSP, 4,* 346. Rawl. MS A 259, p. 102. A search of Duppa's house was ordered on August 5: *CSPD, 1659–60,* p. 76. It is possible that Duppa was in touch with Royalist plotters before the rising. Miss Coate's identification of him as the "Dr. D." in Mordaunt's letter of July 26 is, however, improbable; Brodrick's friend Dr. John Donne is more likely: *LBM,* p. 32, and cf. *ClSP, 3,* 669.

2. *CClSP, 4,* 365, 385. *CSPD, 1659–60,* pp. 78–245 passim. Rawl. MSS A 134; A 259, pp. 61, 138–55; C 179, pp. 278–79. *Mercurius Politicus,* Nos. 582, 598. Whitelock, *4,* 369, 378.

The resurrection of the sequestration system on August 27 sounded more serious than it really was. Few of the county committees functioned with any efficiency, and there was a notable absence of the old enthusiasm. Some found difficulty in getting the nominated members to serve, and in Lancashire more than one of them was suspected of having supported Booth. Even the more successful committees met with frequent obstruction. At Gloucester witnesses refused to give evidence on oath, and at Derby, Saunders and Doughty, both believed to have encouraged White in August, made it impossible for the commissioners to continue. Young Thomas Veel forcibly ejected the sequestrator from Simondshall in November, adding some abusive taunts about Monck's intentions. Hyde lost some sleep over the possibility that many Royalists might take the line of least resistance and compound, but the ineffectiveness of the local authorities nullified the danger.[3]

Although there were a few fleeting hopes that Booth's defeat might be retrieved by renewed hostilities, it was obvious that people who had not stirred in August talked high in September only because they knew their professions were unlikely to be tested. Mordaunt showed what he thought about the prospects by leaving the country. He landed at Calais on September 7, and it was not until he received news of Lambert's having overthrown the Rump that he returned to London.[4] Meanwhile, in a crescendo of bickering and recrimination, Cavaliers at home and abroad conducted their post-mortem on the rising. Many agreed with John Cooper that it was the fault of the great lords. Barwick, for instance, declared after a visit to the Midlands: "Things are at a stand for want of my Lord Northampton, and would not be much better if he were there; for he hath much lost himself in the hearts of the people." Others, including Edward Villiers, blamed Mordaunt's vanity and ambition. Unseemly personal squabbles received a thorough airing. Robert Werden and Roger Whitley charged each other with misconduct during the fighting under

3. *CCC*, pp. 755, 765, 773, 3248. *LBM*, pp. 69, 85. Carte, *Papers, 2,* 252. See also Davies, *Restoration*, p. 141; and Hardacre, *Royalists*, pp. 135–36.

4. *ClSP, 3,* 548, 566. Carte, *Papers, 2,* 214–15. Coate, *LBM*, intro., pp. xiv–xv.

Booth, and each proceeded to hawk a paper around the country asking his friends to certify to his integrity. Whitley was probably guilty of the common fault of embroidering the value of his services, but certainly of nothing worse. Werden, on the other hand, although he was sequestered and proclaimed traitor, was at his old game of insuring himself with both sides. Thomas Scot remembered his earlier services as an informer and persuaded him to go to Brussels to spy on the Court. By the time Werden went abroad, in December 1659, Scot was out of office, but it seems likely that Werden was equally willing to work for the Committee of Safety. In return for "some special services" they at least took off the sequestration of his wife's estate.[5]

All these disrupting controversies paled into insignificance beside the explosion which followed the release of the charges against Sir Richard Willys. The Knot's attempt to countermand Mordaunt's orders at the start of the rising had been bad enough; as the leaders of the "dissenters," its members would inevitably have been exposed to bitter reproaches after the defeats. What had previously been interpreted as excessive caution, or a sensible opposition to foolhardy recklessness, according to taste, could now be blamed on the malignant influence of one single villain. It seemed, furthermore, a convenient explanation of all the years of futility and failure. If Morland's motive in denouncing Willys had been to spread mutual doubt and suspicion among the Royalists, he had succeeded brilliantly. When Willys was suspected, no one was safe. "Where shall we expect to find faith?" Brodrick lamented, ". . . How shall we trust each other?"[6]

The incident would have been sufficiently damaging even if Willys' guilt had been promptly and universally accepted. What made it worse was the difficulty of convincing Royalists who had so long trusted him, without being able to disclose the evidence. To have done so would have destroyed Morland's ability to perform similar services in the future; and his value to the King was reasonably held to be incalculable by those who could not know

5. *ClSP, 3,* 556–57. *CClSP, 4,* 336, 488, 524, 557–58, 581. Carte, *Papers, 2,* 201, 227. *Barwick,* pp. 475–77, 492. *CCC,* pp. 745, 1155. *CJ, 7,* 754. Steele, *Proclamations, 1,* 377. "Scot's Account," *EHR, 12,* 123. Rawl. MS A 259, p. 141.
6. *ClSP, 3,* 556, 558, 564. *CClSP, 4,* 354, 358. *Barwick,* p. 208.

that his capacity for deception was even greater than Willys'. The other members of the Knot were the most obstinate in their loyalty. Philip Honywood grumbled that it was no new thing to asperse those who refused to follow the lead of "everey braynesick parson." Brodrick was plunged into extreme mental anguish; duty to the King and natural reason were in opposition, he admitted. "The great conviction is his hand," Brodrick reflected, unaware of Morland's genius at forgery, "more unlikely to be counterfeited by another or disguised by himself than any I know." He was eventually persuaded, and on October 21 promised to try to convince his colleagues. This meant only three, for Willys' old enemy Belasyse, and the other peer, Loughborough, were no longer within the circle.[7]

Even more than Brodrick, Compton and Russell received the news that Willys was suspected with horrified disbelief; for years they had suffered and struggled together, and had had no reason to doubt his fidelity. The accusation seemed to reflect on their judgment and integrity almost as much as on Willys', and Compton angrily complained of the slights to which he and his friends were subjected, merely because of loyalty to an old friend condemned without a hearing. They both ignored the King's command to break with Willys, and their obstinacy confirmed Hyde's assumption that they were fatally dominated by the traitor's powerful personality. Of the two, Russell was the more ardent: Willys' "great Champion," Robert Phelips described him. It was not until January 1660 that they reluctantly submitted, and even then Mordaunt suspected that it was only a surface conformity. A month later Willys was still claiming to be on good terms with Russell, and the latter's brother Bedford continued to speak in his favor.[8]

Villiers had already fallen a long way from Hyde's good graces. His ineffectiveness in the Sealed Knot, his absurd proposal that Charles II should marry Cromwell's daughter, and his recent refusal to go to Ireland to negotiate with his friend Lord Broghil

7. *ClSP*, *3*, 562–64. *CClSP*, *4*, 345. Br. MS 1, fols. 28, 33.

8. *ClSP*, *3*, 564, 582, 586, 601–2. *CClSP*, *4*, 435, 520, 559. Carte, *Papers*, *2*, 286. *LBM*, pp. 111, 165. Br. MS 1, fols. 32–33.

had produced in Hyde an attitude of indulgent exasperation. Villiers now made matters worse by espousing the cause of the fallen idol. On December 7 he wrote to Hyde explaining that if Willys knew the charge and the name of his accuser he would come over to justify himself; and that Willys was "rather a seducer than seduced" in his relations with Thurloe. Villiers, Hyde grumbled, was "infected with the passion about Willys," and he repeatedly warned him against still further damaging his sinking reputation by this misplaced loyalty. Eventually, on March 28, 1660, Villiers recognized that he was only involving himself in guilt by association, and complained pathetically that Hyde should have given him clearer warning of the consequences. His steadfast refusal to desert an old comrade does him credit, but Villiers' last remaining claims to the Chancellor's favor had been destroyed.[9]

The members of the Knot were not the only Royalists who stood by Willys. Others in the Knot's circle were equally skeptical. Thomas Chicheley, Willys' neighbor in Cambridgeshire, was expected to require a good deal of convincing. Suspicions that this was an intrigue by Hyde and Mordaunt to destroy a dangerous rival lingered on into the winter. Some of John Heath's correspondents, "considerable persons" too, were not satisfied, and even William Rumbold accepted the accusation only with obvious reservations. More significant was the speed with which Hyde's enemies at Court made common cause with the disgraced man, however scornful they had previously been of the Knot as the Chancellor's tool. Hyde was quick to note it: "My Lord Berkley and his friends are well satisfied in the point, and now magnify him and his friends, who, whilst they were trusted, were never worthy of a good word." The most articulate spokesman for Willys was the Duke of York's agent, Richard Nicolls, who was sent to England by the Duke in August 1659. He arrived too late for the rising but stayed in the country for about two months, doing his best to advance the interests of his patron, which were frequently inimical to Hyde's. Toward the end of September, Nicolls called on Willys' friend Sir Henry Wroth. There, by accident or appointment (Rum-

9. *CClSP, 4,* 448, 472, 485, 542, 559, 563, 582, 621, 658. Br. MS 1, fols. 35, 58, 69.

bold, who reported the incident, suspected the latter), he met Russell and Willys. The accused man complained bitterly of his ill usage, and used all his gifts of persuasion to convince Nicolls of its injustice. Visiting the Earl of Oxford, Nicolls encountered the same arguments. Early in November he went to Brussels, ostensibly employed in a scheme to subvert the Dunkirk garrison. He spent much time denouncing Willys' accusers, and obtained an interview with Hyde on the subject. He was, he said, entrusted by Oxford, Russell, and Compton, three men of such honor and eminence that they deserved to be shown the letters on which they understood Willys to have been convicted. Hyde pointed out that this was unthinkable and gave the standard reasons why all loyal subjects should accept the King's word. Nicolls left the interview "with much civility," but he was soon writing to Mordaunt to repeat his skepticism and to insist on a suspension of judgment. "I am a friend to unity and peace amongst ourselves," he told Mordaunt. The sentiment was unexceptionable, yet the sight of the Duke's partisans lining up with the remnant of the Knot in a campaign for Royalist unity was curious. Although after monotonous repetition a majority of the party accepted the accusation by the end of 1659, the operation cost serious scars and much spent emotion.[10]

These domestic quarrels were overshadowed by more dramatic political changes. As it turned out, there was not much the Royalists could do during this last hectic winter of the Interregnum. They could conduct a vociferous propaganda campaign, they could negotiate with leaders in the various opposition factions. But for the most part they could only watch from the ringside while anarchy increased and their enemies' confusions became worse and worse confounded. On October 13 came the long-threatened crisis, and after a tense day on which bloodshed was narrowly averted, the Rump again found itself in the street. During the ensuing month Monck consolidated his army in Scotland by removing doubtful officers, and made it plain that he intended to

10. *ClSP, 3,* 566, 574, 601–2, 608, 616–17, 681. *CClSP, 4,* 353, 363, 378, 404, 428, 435, 442–43, 445. Carte, *Papers, 2,* 284–87. *LBM,* pp. 86, 111, 113–14. *Barwick,* p. 454. Br. MS 1, fol. 63. For Wroth's earlier connection with the Knot see *CClSP, 4,* 22; *ClSP, 3,* 490. For Nicolls see *DNB.*

restore whatever shred of constitutional authority the Long Parliament possessed. Before he moved over the Tweed, military government in England had collapsed of its own weight. Fleetwood, Lambert, and the grandees lost their hold over their men, and in a situation of increasing hysteria were opposed by a coalition of Presbyterians and Rumpers who seized Portsmouth and raised several regiments against them, by apprentice riots in London, by Lawson's fleet in the Thames, by Fairfax and a conglomerate alliance in Yorkshire which included Royalists and mutinous soldiers, and behind them all Monck, with the only disciplined force left, poised at Coldstream. On Christmas Eve Fleetwood returned the keys to the Speaker and the Rump sat again. How long it would be permitted to sit was a question which only Monck, who marched into England on January 1, could answer.

During this crescendo of anarchy the Trust played a waiting game. Booth's failure had converted Mordaunt to Hyde's opinion that to launch a rebellion without landing troops to support it would invite disaster and once more paper over the cracks of their enemies' divisions. This, Hyde pointed out, was no less true because the Knot had happened to espouse the same policy. Mordaunt agreed and was all the more anxious to obtain the foreign assistance. In the autumn of 1659 he was hoping to get it either from Turenne, with whom discussions were still in progress, or from the English garrison at Dunkirk, which offered some hope of being subverted; most of all, he looked to the Pyrenees negotiations. The King made the long journey to Fuentarabia but found Mazarin and the Spaniards unwilling to commit themselves. Indeed, the conclusion of peace between the two crowns made Charles' position worse than ever, for Spain no longer needed him.[11]

Talk of organizing another rising was, therefore, as futile as ever. Even in London in December the Royalists played only a negligible part. Some of the seething unrest among the apprentices can doubtless be attributed to the survival of Royalist in-

11. See Coate, *LBM*, intro., pp. xv–xvi, and references there cited, especially ibid., pp. 101–2; Scott, *Travels of the King*, chap. 15, and pp. 441–44; F. J. Routledge, *England and the Treaty of the Pyrenees* (Liverpool, 1953), pp. 57–58, 71–79, 86–94.

fluence from the previous summer's intrigues; some to the impact of pamphleteers like Roger L'Estrange and John Evelyn. Much more, however, can be put down to the powerful but negative dislike of military government: the cry was always for a free Parliament. The bloody apprentice riot of December 5, when the troops were pelted with tiles, stones, and lumps of ice, was not directly Royalist-inspired. Some Royalists in the capital were nevertheless inspired to prepare for action. Major General Browne was persuaded to resume nominal command of the apprentices, to assist the ousted Council of State's attempt on the Tower.[12] The design failed when the Army leaders arrested Fitch, the Lieutenant, but Browne's party did not disintegrate. John Cooper soon reported that the apprentices would not be put off longer than the 19th, and that Browne and "all of us" would rise with them. To back up the apprentices, Roger Whitley had thirty or forty men ready; most of them had served with him in Booth's rising.

Unfortunately the apprentices had been dampened by the failure of the Tower scheme, and the Army and its supporters in the City were prepared to use what little authority they possessed. On the 15th an order went out for a general search for arms in boats and wagons, and on the 18th the troops moved swiftly against the conspiracy. Stragglers going to join the rendezvous were arrested, and several larger groups of armed men dispersed, some being taken prisoner. Most of the victims apparently came from Whitley's party. There were the usual cries of betrayal, but the truth was that Browne was induced to abandon the attempt both by Disbrowe's show of force and by the advice of his Presbyterian friends.[13] This disappointment was accompanied by similar failures in the provinces. There were repeated outbreaks of disorder in many places, but again there were more shouts for a free Parliament than for Charles II. In Sussex Colonel Fagge was halted when he tried to raise men to join Whetham and Heselrige at

12. On the apprentice riot and the Tower design see Davies, *Restoration*, pp. 181–83.

13. *Mercurius Politicus*, No. 599. *Clarke Papers*, *4*, 210–11. *Ludlow's Memoirs*, *2*, 174–75. *CClSP*, *4*, 481–82, 488–89, 494, 497, 499. *LBM*, pp. 145–46. *NP*, *4*, 192–93. Guizot, *Richard Cromwell*, *2*, 312. Rawl. MS A 259, p. 158.

Portsmouth. Tumults at Colchester and Bristol and an attempt to seize Taunton castle were all directed against the Committee of Safety rather than for the King. Only in Kent was there any movement by Royalists alone. On Monday morning, the 18th, about a hundred horse under Col. Thomas Colepeper created a disturbance at Greenwich, to support the expected rising in the capital. There were conflicting accounts of what happened, but all agree on the only important point, that the party quickly dispersed. Under neutral or Presbyterian leaders individual Royalists played minor parts in demonstrations in other places: Sir Philip Monckton, for example, gave Fairfax useful assistance at York. There was, however, no general movement commensurate with the strength of Royalist feeling in the country at large.[14]

Meanwhile, even the shakiest government could still make conspirators think twice about appearing in the open. The Committee of Safety had no time to build up its counterintelligence machinery, but Thomas Scot was another matter. In some ways, Brodrick thought, he was more dangerous than Thurloe himself: "Tenn tymes more dilligent in search of pacqets males, etc., pretending very vayngloriously hee will unriddle any cypher that ever was made." Whether Scot was actually more successful in intercepting letters than Thurloe, who was no mean performer at the game, it is hard to say; but in deciphering he was certainly better served. Samuel Morland was still at work, and although he had secretly gone over to the King, he had not abandoned his old habits. As late as March 1660 Brodrick suspected that letters were being intercepted, copied, and indistinguishable duplicates substituted: an old trick of Morland's. Scot's best claim to superiority over Thurloe was in the return of the mathematician John Wallis to official employment. In February 1660 Wallis threw a considerable scare into the Royalist ranks when several letters from Mordaunt, Rumbold, and other members of the Trust were intercepted and deciphered. Hyde at first was skeptical of Wallis' abilities and

14. For the disturbances in Sussex, Essex, and the West see *Mercurius Politicus*, Nos. 598–99; Whitelock, *4*, 378, 380. For the Greenwich affair, *Mercurius Politicus*, No. 599; *CClSP, 4*, 495; *LBM*, p. 144. For Monckton's role in Yorkshire, A. H. Woolrych, "Yorkshire and the Restoration," *Yorks. Archaeological Journal, 39* (1958), 483–507.

assumed that the Council had laid their hands on a cipher key. In spite of Wallis' success with the Naseby documents, all the experts, Hyde thought, were "Mountebanks." When deciphered letters were recovered through the distribution of a few judicious bribes, Hyde admitted that he had underestimated the Savilian Professor.[15]

But if the Royalists were to play any constructive part in events, it would not be enough to corrupt a few Council officers. The Trust would have to be put in order. Some of the original members had dropped out in discouragement. Job Charlton had the lawyer's characteristic lack of interest in the unsuccessful: he had no recorded contact with the Trust after Booth's rising. Lord Willoughby was regularly corresponding with Hyde from the middle of November, and Mordaunt often referred to him in terms of warm commendation; but he too ceased to attend the meetings. In October Mordaunt proposed that two of the recent culprits should be officially expelled: Newport, who had spoken against the rising on July 9, and Northampton, who had made promises and then defaulted. In their places Mordaunt suggested the names of Sir Thomas Peyton and Sir John Grenville, which is puzzling, as both were members already. Possibly Mordaunt felt that all the members needed new commissions. None was sent to Peyton or Grenville, who in January 1660 were both attending meetings without them.[16]

By this time the Trust had been enlarged and given greater control over the Royalists in the counties. Mordaunt's unpopularity made him unfit to handle the negotiations, so the more pliant Grenville was employed. Early in 1660 he was empowered to invite the Earls of Northampton, Chesterfield, and Middlesex and Lords St. John and Belasyse to join the Trust. Northampton swallowed his pride, and Middlesex was the only one to refuse outright. However, Chesterfield's membership soon became purely

15. Br. MS 1, fol. 48. HMC, *Buccleuch*, 2, Pt. I, 49–50. *ClSP*, 3, 665, 694, 699–700. *CClSP*, 4, 550, 561, 568, 571, 580, 598, 631. *Barwick*, pp. 251–52, 500–1, 504–5, 510. Lister, 3, 84. Some of the deciphered letters are in Wallis' letterbook: Add. MS 32,499, fols. 4–13.

16. Carte, *Papers*, 2, 229. *CClSP*, 4, 519, 535. For Willoughby's correspondence with Hyde see ibid., 452–633 passim.

nominal (he had to leave the country after killing his man in a duel), and St. John played no very active role. He was, according to Burnet, "a very crafty politic man," capable of feigning insanity when it suited him; perhaps he was too politic to involve himself too far. Belasyse's acceptance marks the first break in the Sealed Knot's aloofness. He had been friendly with Grenville since before the August rising and was now associated with him in a commission to negotiate with Monck; his willingness to think the worst of Willys may also have helped to bring him round. Another possible new member was the dramatist Sir Robert Howard, a cousin of Mordaunt's. He had been active in Stafford before Booth's rising, and in March 1660 Mordaunt reported that he had joined the Trust. Difficulties intervened, however, and Lady Mordaunt declared that she would not after all deliver the King's letter to him. Apart from his kinship to Mordaunt it is hard to see what special recommendations "Sir Positive At-All" possessed.[17]

The addition of Belasyse and St. John and the return of Northampton gave the Trust a more solid foundation in the Royalist nobility. But for the accident to Chesterfield it would have been even stronger. Changes at the center, however, would add little to the Trust's ability to promote a general rising unless something was done to tighten up the local organizations. Early in 1660 the Trust at last succeeded in arranging the counties in associations, with two commissioned leaders in each county. This was necessary not only for planning the rising that was becoming more and more improbable but also for controlling the more practical tasks of presenting petitions and preparing for elections. The irony is that it came so late; there had been local commanders before, but never any systematic selection. The Trust received definite orders to name local commissioners in the supplementary instructions of January 4, 1660; by February 12 a good part of the work had been completed. It seems superfluous to list more than a selection of

17. CClSP, *4*, 522, 527, 600, 616. ClSP, *3*, 656–57, 709. LBM, pp. 89, 115, 117, 165–66, 169. HMC, *10th Report*, Appendix 6, p. 210. The instructions printed in LBM, pp. 157–60, are calendared under the wrong date, July 29, 1659, in CClSP, *4*, 288. For St. John and Howard see DNB, with additions to the article on the latter in BIHR, *3*, 64–65; and *18*, 95–96.

the Trust's local commissioners. Many of the names are familiar: Peyton in Kent, Henry Butler in Dorset, Robert Phelips in Wiltshire, Samuel Sandys in Worcester, Sir Henry Lingen in Hereford, John Booth in Cheshire, the Earl of Derby in Lancashire, Sir Horatio Townshend in Norfolk, Falkland in Oxfordshire. In a few places there were difficulties. Hampshire was still unsettled, but Hyde was quick to suggest Lord De la Warr and Sir Humphrey Bennett, both of whom had been sent commissions for regiments of horse. Essex, Suffolk, and Bedford had not been filled, but the Earl of Oxford could have the first for the asking, Sir Henry Felton or Lord Hereford the second, and Russell or Lord Bruce the third. Derbyshire had been upset "by reason of the Earl of Chesterfield's misfortune," but Freschville was in London and was the most likely substitute.[18]

The worst conflicts over precedence occurred in Gloucestershire, Shropshire, and Yorkshire. The first we shall discuss later. In Shropshire the Newports were the leading Old Royalists, but early in January a commission had been sent to Sir Thomas Myddelton making him commander-in-chief of North Wales. The question was whether this region included Shropshire, where Myddelton claimed a good interest among the Presbyterians. Eventually the matter was arranged without much hard feeling; perhaps Myddelton was too old to care. Yorkshire was a more thorny problem. The Belasyse interest was pushing Sir Henry Cholmley, a Presbyterian, on the grounds that he would be more acceptable to the Bethells and to Fairfax. This was opposed by the Darcies, who wanted an Old Royalist. To Hyde, deploring "factions and emulations," it appeared quite simple: let Yorkshire unite—Wentworths, Belasyses, Saviles, and the rest—under the Fairfax banner, as they had temporarily done when they supported Monck against Lambert. As in so many local rivalries, however, it was easier said than done.[19]

For London there was a special commission, differing from those sent into the counties in that the commissioners were not

18. *LBM*, p. 158. *ClSP*, *3*, 676–77, 718. *CClSP*, *4*, 536, 549, 558. Lord Windsor seems to have been dissatisfied at being omitted in Worcestershire: Add. MS 29,550, fols. 345–49.

19. *Barwick*, pp. 483–87, 493–94, 507. *ClSP*, *3*, 698, 718. *CClSP*, *4*, 534, 595.

directly subordinate to the Trust, although the two groups were told to cooperate. The events of December, when Browne had not handled things well, had shown the need of a more definite chain of command in London. Meanwhile, the possibility of using the City as a lever to push the Rump into more liberal courses became steadily more obvious. The election of the Court of Common Council on December 21, at the height of the disturbances, strengthened the Royalists' influence, and although the Aldermen were less sympathetic, there were always men like John Robinson and John Langham to urge them along. On January 30 Rumbold reported that he was doing his best to execute the London commission. Richard Ford, a Royalist member of the Common Council, was helping him, and must have been one of the commissioners. The others would no doubt have included Browne (proposed in the instructions to command the Tower), Robinson, Langham, and the Recorder, William Wilde.[20]

Although the instructions of January 4, 1660, contain provisions for the raising of armed men, military preparations were now meaningless except as a last resort. The Trust, indeed, was warned in language reminiscent of the Sealed Knot, "to restraine and suppresse all unseasonable commotions and insurrections." Some of the other points in the instructions were merely matters of routine: the dispatch of messengers, the collection of funds to finance their journeys, and other "emergent occasions." The most active financial agents in this period were the two clergymen, Richard Allestree and John Barwick, the latter assisted by Gregory Paulden and John Cooper. Rumbold, Mordaunt, and some of the other leaders also had supplies of Privy Seals on which to raise money; when they did so, it was not always on very good terms and there was some speculation. As the Restoration approached, financial problems disappeared and Royalist gentry fell over one another to demonstrate their loyalty to a winning cause. Receipts had begun to increase the year before. Barwick sent over a total of £1,728 5s. between April and June 1659; Allestree sent a bill of exchange for

20. *LBM*, pp. 155–56. *Barwick*, pp. 232–36. *ClSP, 3*, 643–44. *CClSP, 4*, 509, 538. On the situation in the City see Davies, *Restoration*, pp. 256–58. For Ford, Robinson, and Langham see *LBM*, pp. 150 n., 163 nn.; for Wilde, *DNB*.

£340 and another £300 from Sir Henry Frederick Thynne: Fauconberg, Bruce, and Sir Thomas Ingram sent a bill for £1,000 in June 1659: altogether the funds pouring into Charles' coffers were on a more opulent scale than in the days when Henry Seymour and Shirley had struggled against the tide of indifference.[21]

Returning to the Trust, the rising star was obviously Grenville. From the command of a remote island garrison and later from the leadership of a rather inactive circle of conspiracy in Cornwall, he had climbed high in the Royalist hierarchy. He had always been an easier man to deal with than Mordaunt, and his aristocratic friends would associate themselves with the Trust only if Grenville was employed. Grenville's greatest asset, however, was the fact that since the end of 1658 he had been engaged in matters so secret that at first even Mordaunt was excluded from them: the overtures to Monck. Grenville was distantly related to him: more important, he had presented the General's brother Nicholas to the living of his own parish, Kilkhampton. The story of Nicholas Monck's visit to his brother's headquarters in August 1659 needs no re-telling. Grenville's part in it was authorized by a commission from the King for himself, his friend Belasyse, and the latter's nephew Fauconberg, sent from Brussels on July 11. At about the same time Grenville was promised a patent for the barony of Bideford: one more sign of the high regard in which he was held at Court. No real headway was made before Monck left Scotland, but the fact that Grenville was entrusted with the talks contributed materially to his importance.[22]

While Grenville's reputation rose, Mordaunt's declined, at any rate in the eyes of Hyde and the more responsible Royalist leaders. Mordaunt was still busy, courageous, indefatigable in the only ways his limited imagination could envisage; but his tactless hand-

21. *ClSP, 3,* 506, 575–76, 649. *CClSP, 4,* 208, 248, 258, 285, 297, 302, 442, 488, 504, 534–655 passim. *Barwick,* pp. 398–508 passim. *TSP, 7,* 646, 658, 667. For Allestree see *DNB*.

22. *ClSP, 3,* 417–21, 516, 543, 618, 621–22. *CClSP, 4,* 119, 128, 162, 258, 263, 268–69, 275–76, 354, 359, 390, 428–29. See also Baker, pp. 669–71, and John Price, "The Mystery and Method of his Majesty's happy Restauration," in *Select Tracts Relating to the Civil Wars in England,* ed. Francis Maseres (London, 1815–26), *1,* 707–29.

ling of his colleagues became increasingly intolerable. Much of his bitterness was no doubt mixed with a desire to put the blame for the August failure on other shoulders. The slightest error was enough to throw him into fury. John Cooper had been sent to the King after the Trust's meeting of July 9, to report the newly agreed date of action and to conduct the King to England. Either the orders were not fully explained or Cooper misunderstood them; at all events, he returned to England alone. It was a serious but in the end fortunate omission, for although Charles' presence would undoubtedly have increased the size of the Royalist turnout, it is exceedingly unlikely that it would have been enough to defeat Lambert. It is hard to say where the blame really lay, but Mordaunt did not help matters by his reproaches. The result was that Cooper was only too happy to pass on to Hyde the mounting evidence of Mordaunt's unpopularity.[23]

Cooper was a new enemy; Alan Brodrick had long been Mordaunt's *bête noir*. Mordaunt put out a half-hearted olive branch in November 1659, but the letter was so arrogantly phrased that Brodrick could be pardoned for ignoring it. The two men continued to abuse each other energetically in their letters to Hyde. Eventually, after the interception and deciphering of Rumbold's letters, Mordaunt surpassed himself. Since the idea of deciphering as a science was absurd, Mordaunt asserted, somebody must have betrayed Rumbold's cipher to the Council of State. The traitor, he triumphantly concluded, was Brodrick. When Brodrick had had to burn his own cipher key some time earlier, Rumbold had lent him his; and Brodrick, Mordaunt recalled, often spent hours with it in his chamber, with only one letter to show for it. Furthermore, Andrew Newport had been solemnly assured by one of the Council of State that Brodrick had been keeping up a regular correspondence with Scot. "I now extremely pity my Lord Chancellor, who will be troubled at the heart for this," Mordaunt ended with savage satisfaction. Hyde made short work of the charge, pointed out that Rumbold's was not the only cipher to have been cracked, and curtly told Mordaunt that there could be

23. *CISP*, *3*, 555, 688. *CClSP*, *4*, 280, 286, 295, 430, 442, 449–50, 523–24, 541. *LBM*, pp. 69–70. Baker, p. 667.

no doubt of Brodrick's integrity. This temporarily stopped Mordaunt's mouth, but not for long: on March 23 Lady Mordaunt informed Hyde with little probability that Brodrick had been slandering Hyde's son. Mordaunt's final efforts must have damaged him in Hyde's opinion far more than they hurt Brodrick.[24]

Mordaunt's treatment of Massey was another matter which offended Hyde, and the Presbyterian General was a more powerful antagonist than either Cooper or Brodrick. The choice of John Howe as the leader in Gloucestershire had already had regrettable consequences. Early in 1660 Mordaunt proceeded to repeat the error when the new commission for the county had to be disposed of. Massey returned to England in January, carrying instructions which clearly destined him for the Gloucestershire command. Mordaunt at once made difficulties, claiming that he could give Massey no commission, as none had been left for him at Calais. Eventually Mordaunt bowed to Hyde's insistence, made a lame defense of his conduct, and promised Massey that it would be put right. This was a deliberate deception, for he told Massey that the only commission Howe had received was the one issued the previous year, when he had already named Howe as the holder of the new commission in a report to Hyde. Massey continued to complain that Mordaunt was obstructing him in every possible way, and that he was mixed up in some discreditable intrigues against Hyde. Even allowing for Massey's indignation, it is undeniable that Mordaunt's behavior was inept and offensive.[25]

These incidents make it plain why Mordaunt was generally regarded as bombastic and presumptuous. They also explain why Mordaunt's relations with Hyde deteriorated early in 1660 into open hostility. Mordaunt had always shown a neurotic sensitivity to criticism. Hyde and the King had repeatedly soothed his wounded pride and assured him that he was not undervalued, but there was a fundamental insecurity in the man which nothing could cure. He was already in a state of extreme nervous irritation when in February 1660 Hyde decided that it was time to mince

24. *LBM*, pp. 114–15. *ClSP*, *3*, 644, 655, 662, 668–69, 675–76, 694, 716. *CClSP*, *4*, 550, 562, 568, 570, 616.

25. *ClSP*, *3*, 646–47, 686. *CClSP*, *4*, 509, 533–34, 541, 543, 556, 570, 573, 583, 614, 621, 678.

no words with him. Mordaunt's worst fault, Hyde thought, was the "strange error spread abroad industriously," that his powers were superior to those of the other commissioners. Reports of this kind were bound to create jealousies, Hyde pointed out, and it was important to correct them before they completely alienated Mordaunt from his followers, and even more from the great men whose confidence was indispensable. Hyde reproved Mordaunt for doing nothing to restrain the untimely enthusiasm of his friends, who contributed to the resentment by exaggerating the new Viscount's services. Hartgil Baron was the worst offender: "They say he says—'The King must owe his Crown to my Lord Mordaunt.' " Baron foolishly dismissed all criticisms as the fantasies of jealous women, who disliked Mordaunt's superiority to their husbands, or of "discontented hectors," enraged by his refusal to listen to their petty projects.[26]

Hyde's anger may have been increased by the knowledge that Mordaunt had recently been mending his fences at the Louvre. He first wrote to Jermyn when he arrived at Calais in September 1659, and although the subject was innocent enough (a request for information of the King's whereabouts), it led to a general improvement of their relations. Jermyn sent a friendly reply, and the two men were soon assiduously cultivating each other. When Hartgil Baron was sent to the King at Fuentarabia early in October he found time to spend a few days in Paris, to pay his patron's respects to the Queen and Jermyn. Mordaunt was himself in Paris a few weeks later. Jermyn went out of his way to offer him ostentatious entertainment; Mordaunt found him "so obliging I cannot express it." In December Jermyn sent him a cipher so that they could correspond more freely. Early in the next year Mordaunt was writing from London to both Jermyn and the Queen; with nothing like the same freedom that he still used to Hyde, Ormond, and Nicholas, it is true, but that he was willing to write at all is significant.[27]

26. *ClSP, 3,* 671, 680, 684–86. *LBM,* p. 164. For some examples of attempts to reassure Mordaunt see ibid., pp. 86, 149, and *ClSP, 3,* 710. For Baron's relations with Mordaunt see *CClSP, 4,* 541; *LBM,* p. 168; and *CSPD, 1659–60,* p. 278.

27. *LBM,* pp. 39, 41, 61–62, 127, 132, 148, 167, 173–74. *CClSP, 4,* 456.

Hyde's criticisms produced a furious outburst. Mordaunt attributed it all to Brodrick's sinister influence, and enlisted the three most active members of the Trust to dispose of the allegation that he claimed exclusive powers: Peyton, Grenville, and Legge. On February 13 they wrote assuring the King that Mordaunt had never pretended to be trusted above the rest. This was true, but it missed the point: the impression that Mordaunt had supreme powers was held outside the Trust, not inside it. For a time Mordaunt's letters to Hyde dwindled to a mere trickle. Instead he chose to write to Secretary Nicholas, usually with complaints about Hyde's lack of appreciation of his services. The quarrel must have been widely known among the Royalists, for it led to reports that Mordaunt had engineered a revival of the old, stale slander that the Chancellor had given intelligence to Thurloe. That anyone should have believed Mordaunt capable of this is enough of a commentary on his reputation for erratic behavior. As the Restoration approached, the breach with Hyde began to be repaired. While it lasted, however, it provided a further display of Mordaunt's morbid sensitivity.[28]

Thus hampered by its leader's frailties, the Trust was far from being a satisfactory instrument for the conduct of the King's affairs in England. Nevertheless, it had been given full powers and Hyde had to make the best of it. This unfortunately did not mean that the Royalists were unanimous in accepting its authority. There was the handful of Sealed Knot diehards. There was also Alan Brodrick, who tried desperately to re-establish the clique for which he had corresponded before Booth's rising. When Brodrick began to rebuild this group in October 1659 he was careful to ask if the Trust's commission was still operative, so that he would not conflict with it; later he was less scrupulous. Early in November he wrote that he was now the confidant of a number of prominent men, recently his fellow prisoners in the Tower. Most of the seven he named quickly lost interest. Belasyse and Northampton joined the Trust; Castleton, Fauconberg, and even his old friend Falkland had little further contact with him; and only the one-time Cromwellians, Lord Herbert and Charles Howard, continued to allow

28. *LBM*, p. 176. Lister, *3*, 96–97. *ClSP, 3*, 677–78. *CClSP, 4*, 565, 570, 626–27, 639, 665–66, 669.

Brodrick to handle their dealings with the Court. Brodrick's other allies were not men of great consequence. The most notable of them was Roger Palmer, who the year before had married Brodrick's interesting cousin, Barbara Villiers. On April 13, 1660, Brodrick asked Hyde to intercede for Palmer with the King, so that something could be done to assist him financially: he had, Brodrick pointed out, great expenses, a slender fortune, and a flighty young wife. Perhaps Brodrick did not realize that Charles already knew a good deal about the Palmers; two months earlier Hyde had been surprised to learn that the King was aware that the lady had been ill with smallpox.[29]

As a last resort in his campaign against Mordaunt, Brodrick moved reluctantly toward the faction headed by John Denham. Before Booth's rising Brodrick had been cool to him as too friendly to both Buckingham and the Louvre, but in January 1660, scenting that Denham's star might be rising, he began to take more interest in him and to speak of his having abandoned the Louvre. "Though I have ever wished [the King's restoration] might be achieved by your own dependents," Brodrick told Hyde, "I must now propose his adoption into that number as the last remedy." In March Brodrick reported that Denham had asked him to attend the meetings of his friends. Hyde showed little enthusiasm for Denham, although he did not directly discourage him. He made sure, indeed, that Denham acknowledged the Trust's authority. Several of the people Denham tried to bring together in February 1660 were members of the shattered Sealed Knot; his claim to have won the confidence of Russell and Compton does not, however, seem to have had much foundation. Belasyse, another of the Knot claimed by Denham, managed to combine an association with both the Trust and Denham's friends. But this is not enough to establish Denham's group as a real successor to the Knot.[30]

29. *ClSP, 3,* 597, 644, 665. *CClSP, 4,* 552, 557, 561, 585, 600, 608, 613, 621–22, 655. Br. MS 1, fols. 28, 33, 38. The King's interest in Barbara in February 1660 certainly suggests that their affair may have begun before the Restoration, and even before the Palmers came to Brussels in April. Barbara's biographers have found no evidence for an earlier visit. See, e. g., G. S. Steinman, *Memoir of Barbara, Duchess of Cleveland* (Oxford, 1871), pp. 21–22, and P. W. Sergeant, *My Lady Castlemaine* (Boston, 1911), pp. 29–30.

30. *ClSP, 3,* 644. *CClSP, 4,* 536, 546, 561, 579, 659. Br. MS 1, fols. 63, 69.

Denham's other friends, with whom he certainly had frequent discussions, included John and William Ashburnham, men of prudentialist rather than activist backgrounds, and two Yorkshire gentlemen, Sir Francis Cobb and Sir Thomas Ingram, Belasyse's brother-in-law. Ingram was currently engaged in negotiations with the Presbyterians through the Earl of Manchester; he was, however, hindered by the lack of the necessary credentials, Hyde having heard that he and the Ashburnhams were close to the Louvre party. At the end of March another old Louvre hand, Sir William Davenant, went off on a visit to Paris. According to Lady Mordaunt, he was sent by Ingram and the Ashburnhams, and if this was true, Denham was doubtless involved in it. Davenant certainly did go to Paris, but Jermyn assured the King that it was a private visit to old friends, with no political significance. Davenant's actual motives were probably to enlist Jermyn's good offices in clearing himself from the King's displeasure after some recent indiscretions. The circumstances surrounding the emergence of Denham's group are vague and confusing; however, it seems that Denham was trying to advance himself by uniting all Royalists who disliked Mordaunt's leadership, whether from the Louvre or the Sealed Knot factions. Such an alliance would have been a curious cave of Adullam.[31]

By the time the Trust was enlarged and given its new instructions, the whole nature of the problem confronting Royalist conspirators had changed. After the distintegration of the Army in October and even more after Monck's arrival in London on February 3, the immediate objective was no longer a general rising but the restoration of the King by agreement. Politics had replaced conspiracy. There were a few more futile outbreaks of violence toward the end of January, notably at Shrewsbury and Bristol, but they were entirely outside the Trust's control, and even less important than those of December.[32] The details of the complicated negotiations that occupied the late winter and spring of 1660 lie

31. *CClSP, 4*, 579–80, 587–88, 599, 616, 622, 625, 637, 651, 672–73. Lister, *3*, 98. Br. MS 1, fol. 69. On Davenant's previous relations with Jermyn see A. H. Nethercot, *Sir William D'Avenant*, Chicago, 1938; the account of Davenant's activities in March 1660 (pp. 341–43) is inaccurate. For Ingram see Keeler, pp. 229–30; for Cobb, *Yorkshire Archaeological Journal, 23*, 355–56.

32. Latimer, pp. 290–91. J. E. Auden, "Shropshire and the Royalist Con-

beyond the scope of this study; all that is necessary is to indicate briefly the Royalists' role in them. The subject can be divided into four: Royalist overtures to the Presbyterians, to other leaders of the Parliament and Army, to the Fleet, and finally to Monck.

The Presbyterians were not a well-defined party, as we have often observed. The influence of leaders like the Earls of Manchester and Bedford, however, was weighty enough, both among those who had already committed themselves to the King and those who had not: the "Presbyterial Republicans," Clarendon calls them. During the last winter an elaborate game was played as the Presbyterians tried to tie Charles at least to the conditions of the Treaty of Newport; while the Royalists tried to secure Presbyterian support without committing themselves to anything. In the uncertain situation of 1659, Hyde had been willing to accept the Presbyterians' essential demands, subject to a saving clause about parliamentary confirmation, trusting Parliament to repudiate them. By the spring he was so convinced of the Presbyterians' disunity that he decided it would be enough to secure prominent individuals, leaving the general question of terms unsettled. As always, the English Royalists supported him in his determination to avoid binding conditions. "Those I doubt not will restore you," Mordaunt told the King, speaking of the Presbyterian lords, "but not so restore you, as your faithfull servants desire." [33]

It was widely believed that the Presbyterian lords had been in correspondence with Monck since the beginning of the turmoil. They were also willing to talk to Royalist agents about the Isle of Wight terms. In November they tried to interest the Marquis of Hertford in them, evidently without success. In January 1660 the Earl of Northampton claimed to have won Manchester's confidence, and a few weeks later proposed him for the post of Lord Treasurer. In March the peers were still meeting regularly at Manchester's house and at Lord Wharton's, using Philip Warwick, a Royalist apostle of conciliation, as their intermediary. Warwick was anxious to meet the Presbyterians half way. In particular he suggested that Charles should confirm the owners of confiscated

---

spiracies," *Shropshire Archaeological Society Transactions*, 3d ser., *10* (1910), 155–56.

33. *LBM*, p. 95. See also Davies, *Restoration*, pp. 295–97, 308–9.

lands in their possessions; a proposal which Mordaunt bitterly denounced with almost Harringtonian arguments. Thus the Presbyterians were unable to win their concessions before Monck got rid of the Rump, and by then it was too late. Part of the trouble was their lack of precision. As Brodrick complained: "Can the King . . . know what they would have, who do not request it?" By the time the Long Parliament dissolved itself Presbyterians on all sides were testifying to their loyalty with or without terms. The example of Willoughby, Massey, and men of their stamp became more and more infectious, and although some, like Sir William Waller, still tried to prevent an unconditional restoration, they were swimming against the tide.[34]

The question of general terms was of less moment in the negotiations with the Army leaders. The distintegration of the Independents meant that there was no single authority to speak for them, and even more than with the Presbyterians the personal approach was essential. Ingoldsby's regiment had already provided some significant converts before Booth's rising. Another regiment officered by Cromwellians, Cochrane's, came back from Dunkirk in August 1659, unpaid and in a high state of disaffection. In January 1660 it was on the point of mutiny at Gloucester, and provided the local Royalists with the chance to do something. They failed to take advantage of it, but there were disturbances both there and at Bristol. Other overtures were made to civilian Cromwellians like Broghil in Ireland, to whom Edward Villiers was at last induced to send a messenger early in March 1660; and Willys' ambiguous negotiations with Thurloe continued.[35]

The most successful Royalist agent in the complicated game of angling for the support of prominent Army men was Dr. John Barwick. One of his earliest converts was Col. Robert Venables, dismissed by Cromwell after his failure in the West Indies. Barwick's

34. *LBM*, pp. 82, 95–96, 178. *CClSP, 4*, 525, 527, 547, 564, 580, 583, 602–3, 622–23. *ClSP, 3*, 629, 664, 670, 680, 705. Carte, *Papers, 2*, 256. Sir Philip Warwick, *Memoires of the Reigne of King Charles I with a Continuation to the Happy Restauration of King Charles II* (London, 1701), pp. 428–29. See also Davies, *Restoration*, pp. 304–5.

35. *CClSP, 4*, 525, 582, 610. Firth and Davies, pp. 685–89. Latimer, pp. 290–91.

story that Venables had decided to serve the King even before the Hispaniola fiasco can be discounted, but there was no doubt of his intentions in 1660. Since his humiliation Venables was a back number, but Barwick had other, more influential, friends. His most useful means of contact with them was John Otway, like Barwick an excluded fellow of St. John's, Cambridge. One of Otway's brothers-in-law, Col. Daniel Redman, was a Cromwellian officer purged by the Rump in Ireland; another, Col. John Clobery, was among Monck's most trusted men. Redman made his peace with the Royalists at about the same time as Ingoldsby. He was removed from his command, but at the beginning of 1660 he was responsible for bringing the Irish brigade over to Fairfax in Yorkshire, although he could not restrain it from issuing a republican declaration. Otway went to Edinburgh to try Clobery as early as July 1659. It was a long time before Clobery would openly give Monck Royalist advice (perhaps his arguments for admitting the secluded members on February 20 can be taken as the first instance), but all along he gave Otway a hearing.[36]

The Cromwellians were a promising field for Royalist intrigue; in the other two main factions, the Rumpers and the military party, there was inevitably less response. Early in 1660 John Evelyn conducted some tepid negotiations with his old schoolfellow, Col. Herbert Morley, the newly appointed Lieutenant of the Tower. He also hoped to gain Morley's kinsman, Col. John Fagge, but they both preferred to wait until Monck declared himself. Massey, Waller, and Robert Harley were all stirring up the soldiers in London in January, and helped to foment the mutiny of February 1.[37] More important, especially if Monck should prove unsound, were the overtures to Fleetwood and Lambert. Fleetwood's flabby incapacity would have made him a recruit of doubtful value; never-

36. *Barwick,* pp. 119–20, 184–90, 195–97, 221–24, 228–29, 431, 434, 451, 473–74. *ClSP, 3,* 723–24. *CClSP, 4,* 201, 208, 456–57, 497, 499, 549–50, 640. *LBM,* pp. 9 and n., 117 and n.

37. *Evelyn,* ed. de Beer, *3,* 235–40, 245. E. S. de Beer, "Evelyn and Colonel Herbert Morley in 1659 and 1660," *Sussex Archaeological Collections, 78* (1937), 177–83. A. H. Nethercot, "New Marginalia by John Evelyn," *HLQ, 1,* (1937–38), 439–46. Baker, pp. 679–80, 694–95. Lister, *3,* 83–84. *CClSP, 4,* 533–34.

theless, before the final breach between Army and Parliament a Royalist named Francis Finch attempted to get at him, through Fleetwood's brother-in-law, Sir John Pettus. Pettus gave encouraging assurances, but it is unlikely that he had any authority for them: Fleetwood invariably agreed with the last speaker. His most infuriating display of vacillation occurred in the hectic days before Christmas, when the Army leaders at last realized their isolation. Willoughby and Browne persuaded Bulstrode Whitelock, who by now had accepted the inevitable, to talk to Fleetwood; Popham and Manchester also knew about the approach. Fleetwood gave Whitelock an encouraging reply, but Vane and Disbrowe immediately bullied him into changing his mind again.[38] Lambert was at once a tougher and more inviting proposition. There was never any real chance of winning him, yet the Royalists' hopes were natural enough. In October 1659 Mordaunt and Lord Hatton thought of promoting a match between one of the royal brothers and Lambert's daughter—a proposition only slightly less ridiculous than Villiers' suggestion that Charles marry Frances Rich. In December Lambert was again being sounded by Royalist agents: Villiers and Philip Warwick were reported to have sent an emissary to him. Eventually, as Barwick feared, Lambert was "bewitched, with an itch of having all," and omitted to secure himself with the King, by either a family or a political alliance.[39]

The Royalists had narrowly missed an important accession of strength from the Fleet at the time of Booth's rising. Correspondence between Edward Mountagu, commanding the English squadron in the Sound, and his Royalist cousin of the same name almost led the Admiral to declare himself. He suspiciously returned to English waters without orders before the end of August, but Booth's defeat compelled him to conceal his intentions. Although removed from his command he still retained much influence among the seamen, and discussions with him continued during the

38. *LBM*, pp. 57, 63, 66, 110. *ClSP*, *3*, 551, 576–77, 635. *CClSP*, *4*, 413–14, 497. Carte, *Papers*, *2*, 228. Whitelock, *4*, 380–83. For Finch and Pettus see *LBM*, p. 57 nn.; and for the latter, *DNB*.

39. *LBM*, pp. 53, 55, 59, 112. *CClSP*, *4*, 359, 428, 450, 467, 485. *ClSP*, *3*, 592. Carte, *Papers*, *2*, 237–38. *CSPD*, *1659–60*, pp. 246–47. See also W. H. Dawson, *Cromwell's Understudy* (London, 1938), chap. 23.

autumn. The principal agent was his kinsman Christopher Hatton. Soon after Mountagu was restored to his command, on February 23, 1660, Hatton found him willing to accept a letter from the King, and he played a notable part in the Restoration.[40] As for Lawson's fleet, here too the Royalists had hopes, but not such strong ones as with Mountagu. Lawson's background was republican, and well to the left at that, but in December 1659 he threw his weight against the military party. The Royalists had been working on him since the autumn, chiefly through Arnold Breames, a Kentish Royalist who received the King's authority in a letter dated October 23. Roger Whitley and John Heath also had their friends among the seamen and junior officers. Breames obtained Lawson's assurance that if there was to be a "single person" he would prefer the King, but that was as far as he would go before the Rump, with Lawson's help, was again restored. At last, on February 11, Breames helped to persuade Lawson to join his interest with those of Monck and the City in favor of the secluded members and a free Parliament. Only one more step was needed. It came a month later when, again at Breames' insistence, Lawson agreed to follow Mountagu's orders. The Fleet had been won without the kind of division and faction that wrecked the Army. No doubt the commanders would have followed Monck's lead in any case; nevertheless, there was general agreement that Breames had at least a share in Lawson's conversion.[41]

And so we come back to Monck. After the fission of the Army in December he alone had the power to make or mar a settlement, for he alone had disciplined military force at his command. Since 1648 the sword had governed, and now it was Monck who controlled it. This absorbing fact made all the other devious negotiations with Presbyterians, Army leaders, and reluctant admirals of only second-

---

40. *LBM*, pp. 6 n., 7 and n. *ClSP*, *3*, 497–98. *CClSP*, *4*, 359, 427, 450, 523, 588, 594, 610, 627. Carte, *Papers*, 2, 202.

41. *ClSP*, *3*, 637, 706. *CClSP*, *4*, 533, 535, 550, 564–65. *LBM*, pp. 89–90, 142–43, 150. *NP*, *4*, 193. *CSPD*, *1659–60*, pp. 308, 333. Carte, *Papers*, 2, 301. Godfrey Davies is wrong in identifying Breames as a naval officer: *Restoration*, p. 302. He was a Royalist who traveled regularly between England and Flanders in the years 1656–58: *CClSP*, *3*, 359 ("Breames," not "Breare" in MS 56, fol. 39); *4*, 61; *NP*, *3*, 250; Add. MSS 19,516, fol. 6; 34,014, fols. 11, 15, 30.

ary importance. Although Monck could move only slowly and in the direction indicated by the current of public opinion, only he could move at all without throwing the country into blood. No one could fathom Monck's mental processes—certainly not the Royalists, many of whom, to the end, feared the worst about his intentions. Many things contributed to Monck's slow passage by way of the restoration of the Rump, the defense of the City, the recall of the secluded members, and finally the dissolution of the Long Parliament, to the day when he summoned Grenville for the fateful interview. He was "the great master and conductor of his own affairs," Warwick insisted; nevertheless, the advice he received from Clobery, Clarges, Morice, and his other confidants cannot have been entirely without effect.[42]

Grenville's commission from the previous July was still in force, and as his two associates, Belasyse and Fauconberg, were not in London, the main responsibility for the approach to Monck devolved on him. Barwick and Otway were authorized to continue their efforts through Clobery, with new urgency when Monck appointed him as one of his London representatives. In January Grenville's hand was strengthened by a clause in the supplementary instructions to the Trust, by which he and Mordaunt were especially empowered to carry on the negotiation. By the time Monck reached London early in February he had had ample time to test the feeling of the country. The spontaneous appearance of declarations by the gentry of the southern and midland counties showed which way the wind was blowing: a free Parliament, often endorsed with arguments almost openly Royalist. Royalists had only a minor part in the addresses, though Barwick helped to revise an early draft of the Northampton one.[43]

While Monck was picking his way carefully in London, clearing one hurdle at a time and probably unwilling to admit to himself the consequences of his actions until there was no retreat, the Royalists could only watch with gnawing anxiety. It was "like the

42. Warwick, p. 420. Cf. Davies, *Restoration*, p. 310.
43. *Barwick*, pp. 228–29, 455, 467, 473–74, 482. *LBM*, p. 160. *ClSP, 3,* 618, 621–22, 663. *CClSP, 4,* 456–57, 499. On the addresses see Davies, *Restoration*, pp. 269–72.

last sceane of some excellent play," Mordaunt remarked, with rare detachment. Grenville and Mordaunt tried to pass on what encouragement they could, through Otway and their other channels; in February they got Richard Ingoldsby to approach the enigma. Monck's actions spoke louder than his words until the Long Parliament at last voted itself out of existence. Until then he managed to avoid seeing Grenville alone, but a night or two after the dissolution Morice arranged the confrontation in his room at St. James'. The King's letter was delivered, and Monck instructed Grenville to "assure his Majesty, that I am now not only ready to obey his Commands, but to sacrifice my Life and Fortune in his Service." Soon Grenville and Mordaunt were hastening to Brussels with the news. Monck had made his own decisions, but it was not unfitting that the two leading members of the Trust should obtain a share of the credit: Mordaunt, ardent and devoted for all his quarrelsome outbursts; Grenville, with his long record of service from the days of Scilly. After Monck opened his mind to Grenville the unconditional Restoration was assured; all that remained was to arrange the details.[44]

44. Davies, *Restoration,* pp. 311–13. M. Coate, "William Morice and the Restoration of Charles II," *EHR, 33* (1918), 367–77. See also *CClSP, 4,* 562; *LBM,* p. 174; Baker, pp. 717–18; Price, *Maseres Tracts, 1,* 784–86.

14. Royalty Restored

IN THE PAGES OF Pepys, Anthony Wood, and others who lived through it, life in England in the spring of 1660 reads like one long, riotous celebration. Between February 11, when Monck announced that he would stand by the City against the Rump, and the King's triumphal entry into London on May 29, the bells, bonfires, and loyal toasts continued uninterruptedly. The King played his expected part. In the Declaration of Breda he promised toleration and conciliation, and referred outstanding questions to a free Parliament; nowhere did he commit himself to any of the Presbyterians' restrictions. In his letters to Monck, the Speaker, the Council of State, and the City he used language of studied moderation and generosity. These documents were brought from Breda by the resplendent Grenville, and soon the elections for the Convention Parliament showed the tide of monarchist feeling. More than a hundred Royalists got in, despite the Rump's attempt to disqualify them; no doubt others would have succeeded had not habitual caution led them to take the prohibition more seriously than it deserved. Where there were no Cavalier candidates Presbyterians were returned as the next best, and republicans of whatever shade were swamped in the torrent of feverish loyalism.[1]

On May 1 Grenville presented himself to the House of Commons

1. On the elections and the state of opinion between March and May 1660, see Davies, *Restoration*, chap. 16.

with the King's letters, and Morice's motion that the constitution resided in King, Lords, and Commons was passed without dissent. The tumultuous acclamations reached a new crescendo, receded only imperceptibly after the proclamation of the King in the following week, and returned in intoxicating fullness on the 25th when Charles disembarked from Mountagu's flagship at Dover. Four days later, his birthday, he entered London. The enthusiasm was enough to move even the normally temperate Evelyn to flights of joyous lyricism, although his conventional piety could not resist the addition of a characteristic but inapt biblical allusion. The King enjoyed his own again, and loyal hearts rejoiced. For the Royalist party, once again a party rather than a conspiracy, it was an exultant recompense for hateful memories of failure and frustration: for Marston Moor, Naseby, and Worcester; for Norfolk, South Molton, and Winnington Bridge.

Yet behind the bells and the bonfires and the fountains running with wine it is not being cynical to detect a certain sense of disillusion. As often happens in mass celebrations, those who shouted loudest had not necessarily done most for the cause "in the worst of times." Loyalty was now fashionable, Sir William Denny wryly admitted when he wrote to Hyde in April 1660, for the first time for several years. Denny was not the only one who discovered the use of his pen as the sun of monarchy began to climb the political sky. The extravagant outbursts of Royalist zeal that hectic spring were often symptoms of guilt, unhealthy and belated demonstrations of a fidelity which had previously, in too many cases, been only passive. Perhaps because the clergy had contributed less than their due share, some of the most hysterical declamations came from the pulpits, provoking the King to ask responsible men like Barwick and George Morley to use their influence for restraint. When Alderman Robinson warned Charles of the damage done by drunken rakes talking tipsily of revenge, the King advised him to put them in jail, where they would be better off than "governing in taverns." The more level-headed Royalists followed the King's instructions and issued public declarations stressing their moderation and disclaiming any desire for revenge.[2]

2. *CCISP, 4,* 636–37, 651, 680. *CISP, 3,* 715, 722. *Barwick,* pp. 517–20. Baker,

The story is well known of the King's shocked disgust when, amid the joyful enthusiasm of the Restoration, he was surrounded by crowds of clamoring place-seekers, demanding compensation for their loudly proclaimed sacrifices. "They were observed to be most importunate who had deserved least," Clarendon remarked drily. The degeneration of a conflict of principles and ideals into a sordid squabble for jobs and offices had not, of course, affected the Royalists alone. In December 1659 Brodrick noted the same unashamed predominance of personal over political motives in the Presbyterians. "Religion," he told Hyde, "though the sacred pretext to the earlier part of the War, they lay aside . . . treating of single interests. Can [the King] comply with each, whilst perhaps two (it may be three) aim at the same Office, Forest, Chase, etc?" Mordaunt also criticized this tendency in the Presbyterian lords, instancing Manchester's determination to secure the treasurership. "Dividing the skin before the beast be kild"—Mordaunt applied the common proverb.[3]

Mordaunt, however, was in no position to cast the first stone. Long before the Restoration, Royalists began to whet their knives for a share of the metaphorical skin. There had been a trickle of requests for future favors throughout the 1650's, but after the beginning of December 1659 the volume drastically increased. Mordaunt was not content with his viscountcy and angled for the post of Gentleman of the Bedchamber. Looking for something more lucrative, he, Peyton, and Sir Jeremiah Whichcott asked for a lease of the Newcastle coal-farm. Hartgil Baron wanted the place of Clerk Comptroller of the Household. Roger Whitley thought he deserved the lease of a hospital at Chester. John Heath and Robert Phelips' wife both demanded blank warrants for baronetcies, which they were sure they could sell; Heath also asked for a grant of part of a suicide's estate. The begging letters poured in: some reasonable, some pathetic, others merely funny. The King's irritation at the flood of petitions after he reached England was not, therefore,

---

pp. 722–23. White Kennet, *A Register and Chronicle Ecclesiastical and Civil* (London, 1728), pp. 120–21. See also Davies, *Restoration*, pp. 314–18.

3. *LBM*, p. 178. Clarendon, *Con.*, § 33. *ClSP, 3*, 629. See also Davies, *Restoration*, p. 352; Hardacre, *Royalists*, pp. 145–51.

altogether a sign of unprepared astonishment. After starving while their enemies enjoyed the fruits of office for twenty years, the Royalists were going to make up for lost time.[4]

The dilution of the old Cavalier ardency by selfish place-seeking did not, however, mean that by 1660 the Royalist party had entirely lost its soul. The tenacity of old loyalties in the face of persecution had on the contrary been impressive. One way of demonstrating this is by approaching the question from the other end and observing how few Royalists deserted their allegiance between 1649 and 1660. The great majority who fought for Charles I in the civil war lapsed into political inaction afterward; but nearly all remained loyal at heart, even if only passively so. The real deserters were those who would go to the lengths of giving active assistance to the other side, ranging from public statements of support to employment as spies against their former comrades. A brief summary of the known instances may help to illustrate the Royalists' general steadiness in the 1650's.

We can begin with the Royalists who openly deserted. Plenty of coats had been turned in both directions during the civil wars: Ashley Cooper, Broghil, and Monck are only a few of the most notable who began as Royalists and ended on the side of Parliament. After 1648 there was comparatively little movement across the political boundaries. There were many rumors, of course, sometimes spread by government agents to divide the opposition. The old canard about Hyde's pension from Cromwell often recurred. There was inevitably some social fraternizing between Royalists and their enemies, particularly in the heyday of the Protectorate: sometimes suspicions were aroused. Lady Dysart's relations with Cromwell were more than merely social, malicious gossip hinted, probably inaccurately.[5] The number of exemptions from the Decimation Tax indicates the existence of a fair proportion of Royalists willing to admit the error of their ways in return for special treatment, but the great majority resisted the tempta-

---

4. *LBM*, pp. 130–31, 168. *NP, 4,* 193. *CCISP, 4,* 571, 628, 685.
5. *Memoirs of Sir John Reresby,* ed. Andrew Browning (Glasgow, 1936), p. 121. Gilbert Burnet, *History of My Own Time,* ed. O. Airy (Oxford, 1897–1900), *1,* 438. See also Hardacre, *Royalists,* pp. 120–21.

tion. A few found it possible to accept offices bestowed by the rebel government: Fleetwood's kinsman Sir John Pettus, for instance, received the post of Deputy Governor of the Mines from Cromwell. In addition to the formal obligations involved in giving security, some Cavaliers made voluntary pledges of conformity, in return for the authorities' promise to refain from further molestation. The insulting epithet "Oliver's fiddler," which clung to Roger L'Estrange after an interview and an accidental musical evening with Cromwell in 1653, was the result of an agreement of this kind. Another who made his peace with Cromwell was the poet Abraham Cowley, until 1654 secretary to Jermyn in Paris. Cowley's indiscreet association with Thurloe's spy Bampfield brought him under suspicion of a more dangerous kind of disloyalty, but there is no evidence to convict him; Jermyn was equally careless. Cowley conformed peacefully enough, and justified himself in print, but went no further than a realistic, Hobbesian acceptance of the existing power.[6]

The open converts to conformity were only a small fraction of the Royalist party. Those who gave information were even fewer, but their importance was out of all proportion to their numbers. Few of the Royalists who betrayed their friends had motives as simple as those of the common spy who works merely for pay. Many, like the vast numbers of interrogated suspects, talked because they could not help it, but implicated their friends as little as possible. A handful gave general information about Royalist policies of which they disapproved: Sir Philip Monckton's criticisms of the assassination policy and the Spanish alliance spring readily to mind. The conduct of those who volunteered full confession in return for pardon was less excusable, for unless there were enough mental reservations to make it meaningless, such a promise inevitably led to the involvement of others. Thomas Coke's behavior in 1651 was the worst example of this, but there were other, less disastrous cases: Nicholas Bagenall in 1655, John Stapley three years later. The line between the suspect who gave only the information dic-

6. *NP*, 2, 219, 345. *TSP*, 4, 232. Rawl. MS A 16, p. 351. HMC, *Ormonde*, new ser. *1*, 316. Kitchin, pp. 37–41. For Pettus see *DNB*. Cowley's position is discussed by Nethercot, *Cowley*, pp. 142–63; and Firth, *EHR*, *52*, 636.

tated by circumstances and the one who supplied additional details in return for special treatment is not easy to draw. The instances named were the least reserved in their disclosures; they were hardly typical of the average Cavalier under examination.

Next in the scale of defection comes the considerable class of people who tried to secure themselves with Scot and Thurloe by promising information and then not giving it, or giving only trivial or misleading details. The plea that the alleged treason was merely a move in the popular game of trying to outwit the authorities was the stock defense of the uncovered spy: it was used after the Restoration by both Corker and Willys. In many of these oversubtle efforts by doubtful Royalists to safeguard themselves against the future it is quite impossible to penetrate to the real motive; often the individual may not have known himself. Some information would be offered as a means of standing well with the government, but as a precaution against discovery by other Royalists, and above all against the possibility of the King's restoration, it would not be enough to discredit the plea that the whole thing was a skillful deception. The most charitable defense of Robert Werden would be to put him into this category; according to Willys' own apologia he belongs there too, although both he and Werden went a good deal further than can be justified by this claim. Such men played a double or even a triple game, and only guesswork can suggest which side they were on; if indeed they were on any side at all.

The paid spies and trepanners are a simpler proposition. Most were poor men, servants like Pearce and Masten, obscure courtiers like Manning and Richard Palmer, obsessed with greed for Thurloe's gold. Some, like Bampfield and Sir John Marlay, harbored feelings of resentment against the Court for not satisfying their political ambitions, but even in these cases the pecuniary motive predominated. It is possible that the surviving records do not account for all the Royalist defaulters, that some managed to leave no trace of their activities. Yet it is unlikely that there were many. A remarkable feature of the defections, in view of the conventional tributes to Thurloe's ingenuity, is that almost all the traitors were suspected before the Restoration. Of the paid spies, only Priestman and John Walters were not unmasked. The argument from silence should not be pressed too far, but it seems likely that there were few deserters of consequence whose names have disappeared.

In 1660 Thurloe uttered a famous warning that if he was molested, he had "a black book which should hang half of them that went for Cavaliers." [7] The threat was effective, but with fuller knowledge than was available to the Council in 1660 we can be less impressed by the possible contents of the dreaded black book. Certainly Thurloe had been terrifyingly efficient, making good use of spies and "decoy ducks." He had achieved the ultimate triumph of infiltrating the Sealed Knot. But his control of the mails and skill in evaluating depositions of suspects and gossip picked up by agents around the town were at least as important as his employment of professional informers. The idea that a large proportion of the Royalist party had anything to fear from his disclosures is a baseless myth. Against the Corkers and the Willyses can be set the obstinate loyalty of men like Peyton, Rumbold, and a host of others who stoutly continued to conspire in spite of repeated imprisonment, poverty, and defeat. In the lists of suspected or convicted participants in the succession of Royalist designs, the same leaders recur with impressive frequency. Arundells, Grenvilles, and Wyndhams in the West; Littletons, Newports, and Vernons in the Midlands; Stanleys, Musgraves, and Darcies in the North—in such names are the histories of a dozen plots.

The Royalists' bitterest enemies paid tribute to their solidarity. There were exceptions, but the majority married within the party and largely confined their friendships to it. Sometimes there is a certain smugness in recollections of Royalist virtue written from the comfortable safety of the Restoration: "So steddy to their principles, so regular in their lives, and so exemplary to all, (tho' there were some drinking Hectors intermixt)" Sir Philip Warwick piously intones, "that they converted very many." [8] Yet how many did they actually convert? The whole history of the Restoration lies in the gradual shift of moderate opinion to the point where a King was the only practical alternative to anarchy. The Royalists, how-

7. HMC, *5th Report,* Appendix, pp. 184, 208. *Diary of Henry Townshend, I,* 41.

8. Warwick, p. 379. See also Hardacre, *Royalists,* pp. 81–82.

ever, did not take the converts to their bosoms. A few Presbyterians worked their passages during the 1650's and were virtually indistinguishable from the Old Cavaliers by the time of the Restoration: Massey, Willoughby, and John Booth are the best instances. But as late as 1659 most of the Presbyterian supporters of monarchy were outside the party in any strict sense, and even men like Waller and Major General Browne, who had tinkered with Royalist plotting for years, had not been assimilated. Memories of civil war and sequestration committees, the Presbyterians' reluctance to relinquish the limitations of the Treaty of Newport, the religious animosity—all perpetuated the old distinctions, however meaningless some had become. The small number of defections from the Royalist party is paralleled by the equally small number of new recruits. From 1649 to 1660 the Royalist party was strikingly homogeneous.

This isolated exclusiveness was at once its greatest strength and its greatest weakness. On the one hand, it stimulated a sense of comradeship between the small minority of regular conspirators, the greater number of occasional participants in local plots, and the large majority of the inactive. On the other hand, it made satisfactory cooperation with non-Royalist groups extremely difficult. In 1648 and again in 1651 many Royalists had held aloof out of disgust at the concessions to the Scots. For seven years after Worcester, although advances were made to prominent individuals like Fairfax, the Royalists attempted to pull down the republic alone. Repeated failures disillusioned some of the supporters of isolation and led to a greater interest in what the Presbyterians wanted: hence the discussions of 1658. It was not until Mordaunt's Great Trust supplanted the Sealed Knot, however, that the Presbyterian alliance was tentatively restored. Even in 1659 the old jealousies still smoldered, and there were many who shared the Knot's objection to Booth's rising as "totally Presbyterian." In spite of this, there is a noticeable difference between the level of cooperation in 1659 and the ineffective discussions of the previous year. Many Royalists, by their unwillingness even to talk about combined action, showed that nothing had been learned, nothing forgotten; but especially among the Trust's faction, the fog of suspicion was dispersing.

Next to the failure to maintain a working alliance with the

Presbyterians, the Royalists' most obvious weakness was their inability to mobilize their full strength in the various armed rebellions. The party was united on fundamentals, but when it came to action internal divisions neutralized its efforts. The repercussions of court politics contributed to this. There was a definite relation between the conflict of the Hyde-Ormond group with the Louvre and Swordsmen factions and the divisions in England. The more responsible and propertied Royalists, even the Duke of York admitted, supported Hyde's policies as far as they understood them; and James had no reason to magnify the Chancellor's popularity.[9] Hyde built up first the Sealed Knot, and when that failed, the Great Trust, in an attempt to control affairs in England. Although the Action parties, both before and after the March rising, were not unanimously hostile to Hyde, they contained men who were— agents like Davison, Pile, and Hopton were instructed to have no dealings with the Chancellor. Much of this antagonism was personal (Pile, for instance, looked to Nicholas, whose policy was identical with Hyde's), but through the years after 1651 one can detect rumblings of Louvre influence. The animosity of Gerard and the Swordsmen produced disruptive accidents like the plots of 1654 and kept up a continual whispering campaign against Hyde's ventures. The Herberts' pressure on Loughborough will be remembered.

The most flagrant example of internal division was, however, more than a matter of court politics. The Sealed Knot, until 1659 the King's only accredited council in England, was merely a pallid substitute for the ideal committee proposed by Sir Gilbert Talbot soon after Charles II's accession. Puritan East Anglia, an area of little promise for Royalists, was disproportionately overrepresented, and its members only rarely descended to the details of local planning. It is idle to point out that the Knot, in spite of the traitor in its midst, was usually right in its opposition to irresponsible violence. Some concessions were necessary to retain the confidence of the more militant Royalists, and once the Knot's excessive caution was recognized, as it was already in 1654, there was little hope

9. *Life of James II . . . Collected out of Memoirs Writ of His Own Hand,* ed. J. S. Clarke (London, 1816), *1, 273.*

of establishing it at head of a united party. Nevertheless, Hyde persisted with it until 1659. When he admitted its inadequacy, the Knot's lingering influence provoked first the damaging controversy over the August rising and then the dispute about Willys' treason. All political movements, whether peacefully or violently inclined, need both their hotheads and their "wary gentlemen": it was the Sealed Knot's tragedy that it never reconciled the two. The Trust was more successful, but by 1659 the damage was done.

The fissure between the activist and prudentialist wings of the Royalist party was more than a superficial difference over tactics. Behind it, and behind the division between those who conspired at all and those who conformed passively, can be seen the conflict of interest between the propertied and unpropertied. Like Defoe's Cavalier, the typical Royalist conspirator was a younger son. This was as true of the cautious members of the Knot as it was of the more flamboyant adventurers. Although Belasyse and Loughborough were both peers and men of substance, neither was the head of his family; the former's nephew Fauconberg married Cromwell's daughter, the latter's brother Huntingdon steered clear of political entanglements altogether. Although Northampton was drawn into the Trust for a time in 1659, it was the junior Compton who consistently ran the risks of conspiracy. Edward Villiers was a cadet of a Royalist family; Russell and Willys were younger brothers of moderate parliamentarians or neutrals. Many of the Action parties' supporters were of similar status: younger sons or brothers of men whose behavior was more politic than their own. Henry Norwood was a younger son. So too was Robert Phelips; his elder brother Edward flirted with conspiracy in 1651 and 1655, but kept out of real trouble.[10] Andrew Newport was more assiduous in conspiracy than his brother, the Lord of High Ercall. Mordaunt's brother, the Earl of Peterborough, followed a course of undramatic neutrality between 1649 and 1660. Such examples could be multiplied many times.

The high incidence of the younger son in the Royalist underground movement is only another expression of the fact that active

10. For Edward Phelips' contact with conspirators see Fea, *After Worcester Fight*, pp. 207–8; and *TSP, 3, 308, 428.*

conspirators were usually those who had little to lose if detected and most to gain by rewards from a grateful monarch. Conspiracies were repeatedly crippled by the abstention of their natural leaders among the aristocracy. Hertford and Southampton, the two most venerated Royalist peers, were loyal enough, but typical in that, as Clarendon tell us, they "industriously declined any conversation or commerce with any who were known to correspond with the king." [11] Hertford left it to his son, but Beauchamp died before his time. Through the defection of such men the Royalists lost the support of many who looked to the great lords for leadership and patronage, and also lost valuable financial resources which would have made both conspiracy and rebellion more effective. The most consistently energetic leaders were nearly all men of second rank. Sir Robert Shirley, with his generous share of the Devereux estates, is a conspicuous exception; Sir Richard Mauleverer, Sir Roger Cooper, and Sir Thomas Harris also had extensive properties. But on the other hand Mordaunt was still dependent on his mother when he first became involved in the resistance movement; and she allowed him only £500 a year. Lord Byron was worth only £1,200 when he succeeded to his title, and his predecessor had lost his lands in the first Act of Sale. Sir Humphrey Bennett and Sir Hugh Pollard were worth less than £3,000 each. Most of the lesser agents were too poor to have compounded at all.[12]

For a large part of the Royalist movement willingness to run risks varied inversely with economic security. One pressing argument for caution was the fact that many wealthy Royalists were subject to heavy security for good behavior, often for long periods of time: Sir Richard Fanshawe, for instance, regarded a bond of £4,000 as sufficient to justify his inactivity.[13] The prudentialist preference for passive resistance was strengthened by fears of the dangers to society that accompanied insurrections. Wavering Presbyterians like Popham and Manchester, it will be recalled, were worried about the consequences of disorderly tumults. In the anarchy of

11. *Con.*, § 22.

12. *CCC*, pp. 1287, 1308, 1324–25, 1944, 2027, 2030; Coate, *LBM*, intro., p. x; Firth and Rait, 2, 520. Cf. the estimates of E. Klotz and G. Davies, "The Wealth of Royalist Peers and Baronets," *EHR, 58* (1943), 217–19.

13. *Fanshawe Memoirs*, pp. 81–87.

December 1659, when Royalist zealots were encouraging the London apprentices to riot, John Ashburnham, a consistent advocate of caution, expressed scathing contempt for "the rabble of Apprentises and others in the Citty." He warned his son-in-law, Hugh Smyth: "Though we may continue still unfortunate, yet I hope it will (at length) be found, that our past miseryes will render us more prudent then to persue our utter ruine in such wayes as those." [14] The great majority of the Royalist gentry were prepared to emerge from political inactivity only when it was possible to do so with the least chance of detection, and if disorder could be reduced to a minimum. The lesser gentry, however, had "more honour than inheritance," (the words are Major General Berry's) and so were more willing to conspire. In 1656 the observed fact that the most desperate plotters were men of small estate was freely used as an argument for lowering the limit below which the Decimation Tax was not payable. One officer opposed reducing the exemption level, on the grounds that "the middling sort of men" were "almost all for the parliament, or neuters"; but although this was probably true, it does not disprove the proposition that most of the violent Royalists were also within this class. [15]

Another basic division within the Royalist resistance movement was between the older Royalists who had fought the civil war and the new recruits of the later 1650's. These included not only the Presbyterians but also the younger men, "new sprung up Cavaliers," like Mordaunt and Brodrick. They brought to the party the ardor and courage of youth but also a certain irresponsibility, a lack of discipline, and the debauchery which was their outlet for political frustration and a natural reaction to puritan repression. Mordaunt exhibits many of the unstable qualities of the new Cavalier, and although he did not share Brodrick's dissolute habits, it is not hard to see why so many regarded him as "a rash young man," an ill-mannered upstart. [16] The new Royalists sometimes tried to segregate themselves in factions outside the control of the author-

14. Ashburnham to Smyth, December 17, 1659: Long Ashton MSS (Bristol Archives), Box 3. I am indebted to my brother, P. T. Underdown, for this reference, and to the City Archivist for permission to photograph.

15. *TSP, 4,* 216, 225, 235, 257, 287, 308, 316, 333, 341.

16. Clarendon, *Con.,* §§ 30, 33.

ized leaders. Brodrick's circle in 1659 was such a one, and its existence added a further element of division. The creation of personal
cliques of this kind was no new thing, and it was not confined to the
new Cavaliers: John Denham tried to construct one which included older and more responsible men like the Ashburnhams.

All this would have made effective Royalist resistance to the
republic extremely difficult at the best of times; in addition, inseparably related to these other faults, was the party's chronic organizational weakness. The Knot's inability to make its leadership
effective, the ephemeral looseness of the two Action parties, and
the contest for authority when the Trust was established in 1659
were the worst symptoms. After the disorganization of 1649–53 and
the ill-prepared failure of 1655, there was a gradual realization that
hard work, discipline, and patience were essential. A few Royalists,
of whom Sir Robert Shirley was the most notable, had constructive
if impractical answers to the baffling questions of organization.
Shirley's proposal that the clergy should be the nucleus of the resistance movement was intelligible but omitted to take into account
the clergy's disinclination for such a dangerous role. The Anglicans
had not been a persecuted minority long enough to create the kind
of underground network that was for so long a part of the Roman
Catholics' normal existence. The bishops were old, feeble, and in
retirement; they were dying off so rapidly that there was grave
danger that the episcopal hierarchy would disappear without both-
ering to perpetuate itself. There was a militant minority, with men
like Hewett, Barwick, and Carleton setting examples of determined resistance. But most of the Royalist divines were content to
hold their services when they could, and spend the rest of their time
in study and the provision of spiritual refreshment to the families
of contemplative country gentlemen. Brian Duppa admitted it.
"But where ar we all this while," he asked Sir Justinian, "that we
have so much leasure to busy our selves in David's Psalmes? Parla-
ments and Armies, changes and revolutions fill the heads of other
men, and we like Archimedes are drawing lines, while Syracuse is
taking." [17]

17. *Duppa-Isham Corr.*, p. 179. On the bishops see Bosher, pp. 26–27, 89–
100.

Royalist conspiracy was thus left to the laity. There were frequent efforts to distribute commissions to local officers, but until January 1660 none of the central directorates ever tackled the problem thoroughly. Quarrels over precedence, uncertainties over disputed commands, and overlapping jurisdictions followed inevitably. In 1658 Roger Whitley suggested that the country should be divided into associations, each to provide regiments from the counties within it, the regiments in turn to be drawn from hundreds and parishes, with a recognized chain of command from top to bottom. This was relevant enough, but Whitley went on to outline in minute detail arrangements for enlisting and training men, which were comically unrelated to the conditions of conspiracy. "The Foote, & Horse of every Parish," he pompously recommended, "to meete, every Sunday & Holiday, neare ye Parish-Church, to be exercised, etc. All ye force of ye Hundred, to meete once a quarter at least. All ye force of ye County, once or twice in a yeare." Whitley omitted to supply a handbook of suggested answers to satisfy Protectorate officials who happened to observe the drilling. Absorbed in his subject, he went on to demand the selection of prisons for disciplinary offenders, and military hospitals for the wounded. Perhaps he was merely plagiarizing a manual of military discipline. That was the trouble: officers familiar with the simple tactical problems of the civil war were not always capable of adjusting to the more flexible needs of conspiracy.[18]

The Royalist leaders, in other words, did not make the best use of their material. Even if the full weight of the party had been mobilized in a series of perfectly organized conspiracies, it is hard to see how they could have reversed the verdict of the civil war alone. A few hundred regular conspirators, several times that number of occasional participants: at no time did more than a tenth of the total of known Royalists conspire, though the remainder may have prayed for their success. The disruption of the normal social patterns; the collapse of the aristocracy's traditional claim to lead-

18. Mainwaring MS (John Rylands Library), 24, pp. 81–83. This discussion of Royalist organization, under the heading "Native Force & Aydes," is in a MS volume marked "Bruges 1658." I am grateful to the Keeper of MSS at the John Rylands Library for permission to photograph. Whitley's paper is discussed by Jones, *John Rylands Library Bulletin, 39,* 417–26.

ership; the party's financial weakness: these were still inescapable facts, as inescapable as in 1646. The Cavaliers thus needed the support of substantial groups from other parties: the importance of the Presbyterians, neutrals, and moderates was vital. Hyde always argued that in the end victory for the Royalists was inevitable if only they kept their heads and waited for the madness of rebellion to spend itself. In practice he was not consistent, or he would not have encouraged the Action parties' preparations; but he did so because the alternative would undermine the loyalty of the enthusiasts. And the lesson of 1649–51 was clear: the Royalists must do the work alone. As the bankruptcy of successive republican experiments became plain, a Stuart monarchy on the lines of 1641 would become more and more attractive to moderate opinion. Furthermore, Hyde pointed out, through all its aberrations the nation was Royalist at heart: in the end a restoration would come by a "resurrection of the English loyalty and courage." [19]

This last claim has an important bearing on one of the fundamental questions underlying this study: why, in spite of the Royalists' weakness, did the country burst into the extravagant enthusiasm of 1660? Hyde was right to some extent: the majority of the politically articulate always had a vague emotional attachment to the old order. There were significant outbreaks of Royalist feeling even in the darkest days. Too much should not be made of the indiscretions of obscure citizens who so often betrayed themselves in convivial moments with toasts to the Scots King, and of confusion to the present power, yet in the context of other incidents they are not totally meaningless. When the Duke of Gloucester was dispatched from Cowes in 1653, some of the ships lying off shore were said to be "more free in their salutes than became them." [20] Supporters of the republic admitted that no jury, unless well packed beforehand and perhaps not even then, would convict Royalists for political offenses: hence the High Courts of Justice. Throughout the Interregnum Royalist agents moved in and out of the country, escaped from prison, and conducted complicated designs which must

19. Wormald, pp. 171–72, 186–98.

20. *CSPD, 1652–53,* pp. 162–63. Examples of seditious words in local court proceedings are legion. For some additional ones see *York Castle Depositions,* pp. 26, 39–40, 46–48, 50, 52–53, 55, 59, 70, 73–74, 80.

have come to the ears of many who were not Royalists, with curious impunity. Perhaps there was a sinister meaning in the obstinate persistence of a traditionalist country to observe the Popish festival of Christmas. An indignant member of Cromwell's Parliament observed on that day in 1656 how one could "pass from the Tower to Westminster and not a shop open, nor a creature stirring," and in the same debate Lambert was troubled by dark thoughts of Cavaliers "merry over their Christmas pies." Observers as remote from each other as the pro-Royalist Venetian ambassador Paulucci and the republican Harrington agreed that public opinion was overwhelmingly in favor of monarchy.[21]

There is, however, a vital difference between an historical sentiment and a political cause. The existence of vague conservatism and nostalgic preference for the established and traditional among the politically illiterate or unconcerned was only a negative factor in the Royalists' ultimate success. Strong political sympathies on either side were the property of a small and highly articulate minority, but this was the minority that counted. As long as the Protectorate succeeded in governing the country without too much disturbance, and without giving too much rope to puritan fanaticism, the apathetic mass might shed a secret tear for the King over the water, but otherwise let well alone. Other things being equal, even before Cromwell's death the moderates might have been ready to transfer their allegiance to a Stuart from a Cromwellian monarchy. But other things were not equal. The key to the situation was the Army, and the Army remained, as long as Cromwell lived, firmly under his control. The Army provided the massive guarantee of domestic tranquillity, and Cromwell did his best to cover it with a decent shield of constitutional respectability. In its later years the Protectorate did more than provide stability: it returned to Cromwell's earlier search for "settlement," although this time with a less conciliatory attitude to the Cavaliers. It followed that the natural response of the moderates was to support the Cromwellian regime, and it was for this reason that a striking number of the Presbyterian leaders of ten years before began to take their

21. *Burton, 1,* 229, 240. *Cal. State Papers, Venetian, 24,* 185. Davies, *Restoration,* p. 91.

places in the new Court party: Clotworthy, Glynne, and Jephson are typical examples.[22]

In the comparatively tranquil atmosphere of the Protectorate active conspirators were therefore regarded as wanton disturbers of the peace, moved only by a selfish desire to exploit the doling out of offices and perquisites that would follow the King's return. In 1657 the most acute Royalist observers were in mortal fear that Cromwell would accept the crown; if he did so the opportunist support that would accrue to him might banish the Stuarts forever. Cromwell did not take the fatal step, and the Presbyterians remained chronically divided: some, like Willoughby, Browne, and Waller, saw the best hope of stability in the return of Charles II; others, following Jephson and Glynne, continued to support the existing power; and the majority, like Fairfax and Manchester, tried to postpone the moment of commitment. Meanwhile, for all three groups, the Army supplied an effective deterrent to any attempt to change the status quo, and only when its discipline broke down in 1659 were the chances of civil peace greater under a Stuart monarchy. This overwhelming fact, entirely outside the Royalists' control, accounts for the futility of their conspiracies all through the 1650's; against the military Leviathan all resorts to violence were ludicrously ineffective.

The death of Cromwell, therefore, was the vital incident. But if victory was inevitable after September 1658, why were the Royalists so slow to achieve it? The answer is inherent in the political process itself. There is always a time lag separating historical effect from cause. The Protectorate managed to stagger on for a few months under the pathetic Richard. The breach between Rump and Army was delayed for another six months. The ferment of anarchy took time to overflow. Monck was slow in making up his mind. The internal weakness of the Royalist party was more disastrous than ever. For many neutrals and moderates the exhibitions of Royalist faction and bickering were unedifying enough to make them think twice about a premature transfer of their sympathies. Skillful trimmers like Popham, having shrouded their dealings with Royalist agents in an impenetrable web of evasion, resented

22. Hexter, *The Reign of King Pym*, pp. 169–73.

being endangered by loose talk of their having made nonexistent engagements. The decision to stake everything on armed rebellion in August 1659 also helped to delay the end. The breach between Army and Parliament might overwise have come a few weeks sooner, and the whole process have been accelerated. Without Oliver, however, the Army had nowhere to turn in any constructive sense: Lambert was not the only one to know what he was against, but not what he was for. As soon as the soldiers lost their taste for politics, lost confidence in their leaders, and were convinced that they would only be regularly paid by a free Parliament, the Restoration occurred. Yet, ironically, it was Monck and the only disciplined part of the Army that had the last word.

Are we then to conclude with Oldmixon and the Whigs that the Royalists, active or passive, were unimportant and played no part in the Restoration? On the contrary, the existence of an irreconcilable Royalist party was a fundamental cause of the impermanence of all republican regimes from 1649 to 1660. Triumphant Independents might repeat their incantations about the "Good Old Cause" of a free people and a free Parliament, but their actions belied them. As long as the Cavaliers remained unconverted, a freely elected Parliament was impossible unless the republicans were willing to sign their own death warrants. The alternative was military government, unpopular in itself and also as the origin of high taxation, puritan moralism, and petty local despotisms. For Cromwell's failure to achieve his goal of constitutional harmony, both wings of the Royalist party were partly responsible. The stubborn aloofness of the silent and static majority was important, but the conspiring minority cannot be dismissed entirely. Without them monarchist sentiment might have withered away, for every cause needs its martyrs and its zealots if it is to survive proscription. The conspirators, furthermore, directly provoked the most striking and most unpopular of all the constitutional experiments: the Major Generals. "It was nothing else, but the restless and invincible spirit of the Royal Party, that by keeping the Usurpers in a perpetual distraction, and Alarm, hinder'd them from proceeding to a final Establishment of their Power"—so Milton's nephew, Edward Phillips, concluded. There were other reasons for Cromwell's failure to reconcile his military past with his moderate present, but the existence of an implacable Royalist party was important. Thurloe advised Clarendon in 1660, not entirely out of flattery for the restored monarch, that fear of the Stuarts was the determining factor in Cromwell's foreign policy; the active survival of the Royalists was equally basic to the republic's domestic difficulties.[23]

The Royalist underground movement has a significance that goes beyond its contribution to the history of the Interregnum. Much of the political atmosphere and some of the factional conflicts of post-Restoration England have their origins in Royalist memories of the 1650's. The hysteria of the Popish Plot was an extravagant culmination of two decades of tension, in which fear of lurking conspiracy by republicans, by sectaries, by Papists, was part of the normal equipment of the politically conscious. The cloak-and-dagger atmosphere of the 1650's was by no means a new phenomenon, at a time when Fawkes and even the Catholic plots of Elizabeth's reign were still remembered; but the exaggerated fears of the years after 1660 were not completely unrelated to the Cavalier gentry's experience of conspiracy. The Royalists were used to plots. They had organized or sympathized with them themselves. Is it surprising that many regarded the use of spies and *agents provocateurs* as part of the standard procedure of government, and accepted their depositions at face value, or at least as convenient political ammunition?

A second important result of the years of conspiracy was the survival of Cavalier sentiment as a political force, and its subsequent incorporation into Toryism. It is impossible to disentangle this problem from the violent jealousies aroused by the King's treatment of his loyal followers after the Restoration; a brief digression into this familiar question is therefore unavoidable. The allocation of jobs and pensions, to say nothing of the vexatious land question, raised the matter of comparative services during the persecution. From an objective standpoint it can hardly be denied that the Royalists were as well rewarded as circumstances permitted. The distribution of court patronage was not based on loyalty and length

23. Baker, p. 670. "Concerning the Forraigne Affaires in the Protector's Time," *Somers Tracts*, 6, 329–31.

of service; nevertheless, many Royalists thought it ought to have been. It was impossible to satisfy everybody, but the chorus of protest at the favored treatment of Presbyterians who had come over only at the last minute while Old Cavaliers were left out in the cold is understandable. Even the formal recognition envisaged in the creation of a special order of chivalry, the "Knights of the Royal Oak," was quietly dropped as inexpedient.[24] The policy of conciliation was realistic; but it was pursued at the cost of much Cavalier bitterness. A few examples of the fortunes of some of the leading conspirators should help to illustrate the point.

The members of the Sealed Knot, naturally enough, did not go on to occupy the most elevated positions at Court. They had had Hyde's confidence and the chance, as the Chancellor hoped of Ned Villiers, "to rise in cloth of silver," and they had bungled it. Willys was mercifully ignored and allowed to disappear into lonely isolation.[25] The others were not disgraced, but neither were they promoted beyond their merits. Villiers became Governor of Tynemouth castle, and was granted the manor and royal house of Richmond; his niece Barbara used to stay there when the court got too hot for her. He was eventually knighted in 1680 and made Knight Marshal of the Household. Belasyse went furthest of all the members of the Knot—understandably, as he was a peer. He held some lofty offices in his county: Governor of Hull, Lord Lieutenant of the East Riding. He also became Governor of Tangier, but resigned on the passage of the Test Act. After imprisonment as one of the Catholic peers accused by Oates he was restored to favor under James and became a Privy Councillor and a Lord Commissioner of the Treasury. He died in 1689, the same year as Villiers. Compton and Loughborough both died within a few years of the Restoration: the former had time to be appointed Master of the Ordnance; the latter to be Lord Lieutenant of Leicestershire and to get a pension of £500 a year. Russell was the first colonel of the

24. See Thomas Wotton, *English Baronetage* (London, 1741), *4*, 363–80.
25. *CClSP, 3*, 36–37 (MS 50, fol. 51). William Winters, "John Foxe the Martyrologist and his Family," *TRHS*, 5 (1877), 79–81. It has been thought unnecessary to give full documentation for the biographical notes that follow, except where sources other than the standard reference works have been used.

King's Own Regiment of foot until 1681, but took no part in politics. Alan Brodrick remained in Hyde's service for a few years, sat
for Orford in both the Convention and Cavalier Parliaments, and
did well in Ireland, holding the office of Surveyor General, and
establishing the family fortunes on the sound basis of confiscated
land. Honywood was knighted and became Governor of Portsmouth. None except Willys sank into complete obscurity; none,
on the other hand, reached a position of great prominence.[26]

One member of the Trust, not surprisingly, did much better.
Grenville, who had handled the negotiations with Monck and carried the King's letters to Parliament at the end of April 1660, had
the greatest opportunities and the greatest rewards. Earl of Bath,
Steward of the Duchy of Cornwall, Lord Lieutenant of the county,
Lord Warden of the Stanneries, Groom of the Stole, Grenville be-
came one of the greatest men in the West and no mean figure at
Court. So complete was his grip on the Cornish pocket boroughs
that he became known as the "Prince Elector." He was one of the
two noblemen present when Charles II was received into the arms
of Rome on his deathbed. For Mordaunt, on the other hand, the
Restoration brought only frustration and disappointment. He and
Peyton got their lease of the Newcastle coal-farm. He wanted to be a
Commissioner of the Treasury but was ignored. Instead he became
Lord Lieutenant of Surrey, Constable of Windsor Park in reversion
after Secretary Nicholas, and in 1661 Governor of the castle. It was
hardly generous treatment and Mordaunt was correspondingly
bitter about it, the more so when in 1666 he was impeached for
misconduct in his management of Windsor. According to Clarendon, Mordaunt's comparative neglect was the result of his "unseasonable importunities" in demanding too much, and the vicious
jealousy of the other Royalists: "He was the butt, at which all their
arrows of envy, malice, and jealousy were aimed and shot; he was
the object and subject of all their scurrilous jests, and depraving
discourses and relations." Mordaunt's behavior before the Restoration was obviously not without future relevance.[27]

Of the other members of the Trust, Northampton's status was

26. *Pepys*, 7, 303. Lister, *3*, 202, 209 n.
27. Coate, *LBM*, intro., pp. xx–xxi. Clarendon, *Con.*, § 35.

already established by his earldom. The Lord Lieutenancy of Warwickshire, and various colonelcies and commissions led the way to
membership of the Privy Council in 1672 and appointments as
Constable of the Tower in 1675 and a Lord of Trade two years
later. Willoughby returned to his colonial ventures; he was
drowned in 1666 in an expedition to recover St. Kitts from the
French. Charlton was Speaker of the House of Commons for a short
time in 1673, and became a judge in 1680. William Legge, with a
much longer record of Royalist conspiracy, going back to the Army
plot of 1641, was reappointed Groom of the Bedchamber and got
the posts of Lieutenant and Treasurer of the Ordnance under
Compton. Peyton added to his share of the coal-farm a stipend from
the office of the Treasurer's Remembrancer of the Exchequer. He
was also a deputy lieutenant of his county and colonel of a local
regiment. It was not much, but it probably satisfied Peyton, who
could find more contentment among his books than some of the
others.[28] Andrew Newport's only appointments were the posts of
Esquire of the Body, Commissioner of Customs in 1662, and the
captaincy of a foot company at Portsmouth. His brother, Lord
Newport, who had been much less active as a conspirator, was more
successful: Lord Lieutenant of Shropshire, Comptroller and later
Treasurer of the Household, member of the Privy Council, and in
1694 Earl of Bradford. It was more important to be a peer than to
have been a conspirator.

Apart from the fortunate Grenville, the members of the Trust
did little better in the scramble for offices and honors than the
Sealed Knot. Some of the other activist leaders were recognized for
their services. Sir George Booth and Townshend got peerages at
Charles II's coronation, Richard Arundell soon afterward. The
men of 1654–55 for the most part received their deserts, but no
more. Sir Thomas Armstrong was reappointed Ormond's Quartermaster General of horse and got a monopoly to make Irish far-
things; he died in 1662 before he had time to make anything of a
career. Sir Hugh Pollard was made Governor of Guernsey and,
more significantly, Comptroller of the Household, thanks no doubt
to his ties with Grenville and Monck. Sir Richard Mauleverer was

28. Coates, *Journal of Sir Simonds D'Ewes*, intro., pp. xxxviii–xxxix.

appointed a Gentleman of the Privy Chamber and held some minor commissionerships. Sir Philip Musgrave was given back his command at Carlisle, and granted the farm of tolls in Cumberland and Westmorland. These were the typical records of the average country gentlemen in the later seventeenth century, owing little to their activities between 1649 and 1660.

Many Royalists complained vociferously of the inadequacy of their rewards. The most striking case is that of Sir Philip Monckton. In 1661 he managed to secure the post of Comptroller of the Customs at Dunkirk; it was not very lucrative, and became even less so a year later when the port was sold back to France. Monckton, like so many others, blamed Clarendon for his misfortunes, and retaliated by accusing him of favoring the King's enemies. Clarendon, not unjustly, dismissed Monckton as "mad and not fitt for any imployment." After Clarendon's downfall Monckton turned his attention to Belasyse, one of the reigning powers in Yorkshire, and threatened to accuse him of betraying Royalists to Cromwell. In spite of, or because of, his outspokenness, Monckton managed to enter Parliament for Scarborough in 1670, obtained a grant of the profits of the seignory of Howdenshire three years later, and in 1675 the less attractive honor of Sheriff of Yorkshire. His protests grew louder every year, and in 1676 he was sent to the Tower for defaming the King's ministers. Monckton, of course, suffered from a persecution complex; but there were others who felt almost as badly treated.[29]

Established country gentlemen of this kind might splutter indignantly while the Presbyterians waxed fat, but they were not entirely dependent on court patronage. The lesser men, the professional agents of the 1650's, were much more in need of help. Sometimes they got it, sometimes not. The faithful Rumbold returned to the Great Wardrobe and was deservedly appointed Comptroller; in 1663 he became Surveyor General of the Customs. A list of the household officers in 1663 includes many other familiar names: Robert Phelips as a Groom of the Bedchamber, John Scott and Edward Grey among the Gentlemen of the Privy Chamber, Thomas Ross as Keeper of the Library, James Halsall and Charles

29. *Monckton Papers,* pp. 76–81, 85–87, 100–2.

Littleton as Cupbearers in Ordinary, John Cooper as a Carver, Henry Norwood an Esquire of the Body, Dick Pile as a Serjeant Chirurgeon. A fair number of these appointments, it might be added, were made before the Restoration. Mordaunt's admirer Hartgil Baron was appropriately put in charge of the garden on the south side of Windsor castle. In 1661 he was given an annuity of £200 for thirty-one years.[30]

Two groups of conspirators had less reason than any to feel neglected after the Restoration: those who had aided the King's escape after Worcester, and the clergy. To the first Charles owed a personal debt of gratitude, which he showed occasional anxiety to repay; for the second, the road to preferment was much smoother because of the Church's greater resources, especially after the ejections of 1662. But orthodoxy counted for more than sacrifices during the years of persecution. Had it been otherwise Corker would hardly have gone back to Bradford. The pensions, gifts, and honors lavished on those who had saved the Worcester fugitive look impressive on paper. They were not always regularly paid, but then, nothing was, in Restoration England, and there was little logic in it. The Royalists who had helped the King had performed an important service, but the circumstances were such that they could hardly refuse. Many had been connected with the Western Association, and a few were involved in conspiracies later in the decade: Phelips, Wyndham, Mansel, and Gunter were the most active. But the assistants in the "miraculous preservation" were not the real mainstays of the resistance movement. They were rewarded because they had the King's ear, and once again it was influence rather than merit that counted.[31]

The controversy over rewards and offices was determined by the nature of the Restoration itself. Charles could not use conspiratorial rectitude as the only yardstick, because the essence of the settlement was to let bygones be bygones. If this appeared to give oblivion to the King's friends and indemnity to his enemies, the

30. *BIHR, 19,* 15–21. Egerton MSS 2542, fols. 255, 289, 343; 2551, fols. 13–17. *LBM,* p. 168 n.

31. For convenient summaries of the rewards given to the King's helpers after Worcester see Fea, *Flight of the King,* appendix; and *After Worcester Fight,* intro., pp. xxvi–xxxix, 151.

price had to be paid. The resulting bitterness was to color a good deal of the politics of the Cavalier Parliament. "The brand of the émigré is stamped on the generation after 1660," the modern historian of the Tories observes: the brand of the disappointed conspirator, one might add. The narrowly defeated pressure for a white terror, the frenzied Anglican intolerance, the fierce glee at the downfall of Clarendon the scapegoat for every Royalist frustration, the survival of a recognizable Cavalier group in Parliament into the 1670's and thus into Danby's Tory party—all owed much to collective memories of resistance before the Restoration.[32]

The Royalists' frustrations after 1660 suggest one more reflection about the significance of conspiracy. If Charles II had been restored by violence, the resulting constitutional settlement would have been unrecognizably different from the one that launched England on the road to 1688 and parliamentary sovereignty. Even Hyde, with his predilection for the mixed monarchy of 1641, might have been unable to resist the pressure toward absolutism, especially if a successful Royalist rebellion had been seconded by a Spanish army. The bitterness of post-Restoration recrimination should not obscure the fact that the prudentialists within the party had not been completely submerged by the activists, that the Gerards and even the Mordaunts had failed to carry more than a minority of Royalists with them in their desperate courses. Thus in 1660 the Cavalier leaders could support Charles II's relative moderation. Many of the penurious rank and file did not like it, but the exiles and the peers had never quite lost their grip on the party. Had the activists been in control in 1660, the white terror would not have been avoided, the land settlement would have plundered the former parliamentarians as mercilessly as they had once plundered the Royalists, and the moderates would not have been asssimilated by the judicious dispensing of offices and perquisites. The maintenance of the traditional distribution of power within the Royalist party, together with the fact that the Restoration was a negotiated settlement rather than a military coup d'état, combined to confirm Hyde's preference for conservative constitutionalism.

But we must return to our earlier conclusion, that although the

32. Feiling, pp. 78, 136, 143–45.

conspirators did not make the Restoration, without them it would
have been inconceivable. There is a certain monotony in the dis-
tressing sequence of failures in the plots of the 1650's. Yet however
ineffective, the very continuity of conspiracy helped to keep loyalty
alive, by dramatizing the fact that people existed who were willing
to risk their lives and fortunes. Political outlawry and religious
persecution, if neither as consistent nor as oppressive as indignant
Cavalier gentlemen liked to recall, nevertheless maintained the
self-conscious, segregated unity of the party. Only a minority actively conspired, but that minority provided an inspiring example
to the rest. Looking back on it after the disillusioning experiences
which culminated in dismissal and banishment, Clarendon could
not help seeing the consequences of the Royalists' exclusion from
responsibility, whether in England or in exile, as generally de-
moralizing and promoting cynicism and frivolity. Yet even in this
he conceded the importance of the Royalist experience, and its
impact on those "born and bred in those corrupt times, 'when there
was no king in Israel.' " [33]

33. *Con.*, § 37.

Appendix: Royalist Ciphers

CORRESPONDENCE BETWEEN ROYALIST conspirators was, of course, usually conducted wholly or partly in cipher. Most of the letters and documents used in this study had already been deciphered. Those in the Clarendon, Nicholas, and other Royalist collections were often deciphered by the recipients; and the officers of Scot and Thurloe broke through the ciphers of many that were intercepted. Modern editors have solved some of the remaining ones, often by constructing their own keys from deciphered letters. A large number of undeciphered letters can be found, however, on which the historical detective may exercise his ingenuity. Many of them are probably of little significance, but there are some not previously deciphered, dealing with the preparations for the 1655 rising, which provide new information about Royalist activities in that crucial period and which have been used extensively in the text. It is the aim of this Appendix to present the evidence for my deciphering of these and a few other letters. Let it be said at once that I claim no special skill in the art of cryptography: in most cases I was lucky to find the key.

Numerical ciphers used in the seventeenth century were of a simple and primitive kind: they presented few problems to the Parliament's cipher expert, John Wallis, and even fewer to the modern cryptographer. Little remains to be done in this direction, and to elucidate the text only three letters in numerical cipher need to be explained: the relevant passages are printed below in

A and B. In some ways even more elementary than the numerical ciphers, and yet impossible to decipher with certainty without a key, are the ciphers composed of pseudonyms and cant phrases, which Royalist agents used equally frequently. Internal evidence can often provide clues to the meaning, but it is impossible to be absolutely certain without the key. Macray, the editor of Volumes 2 and 3 of the *Calendar of Clarendon State Papers*, did his best to clarify many of the letters listed below, and Sir Charles Firth, in his articles on the 1655 rising, advanced other likely identifications. Both, however, made many errors, as will be seen when the selections from the cipher keys printed in C–G below are compared with their suggestions. Except in one instance, it has not been thought necessary to print the keys in full: only those pseudonyms and cant phrases found in surviving correspondence have been given. In each case a list of letters written in the cipher is appended.

A. CIPHER WITH "MR. SYMSON"

Two letters from the King and Hyde to the agent "Symson" in May 1654 contain passages in numerical cipher.

1. Hyde to "Symson," May 12/22, 1654: Cl. MS 48, fol. 217 (*CClSP*, 2, 357): ". . . Mr. Atkinson [obviously the King] is resolved to have
n o – g e n e r a l l   s e l e   l t g
47. 5. 43. 21. 12. 22. 1. 26. 11. 23. 51. but him 53. 20. 51. 1. nor 23. 8. 43. but Mr. Brooke" [the Duke of York]. Cf. fol. 215.

2. The King to "Symson," May 1654: Cl. MS 48, fol. 245 (*CClSP*, 2, 363): ". . . I must requyre you to communicate freely, as well the businesse
o f –?   a l l o t h e r s t o
5. 16. 17. Emstede [Ely?: cf. fol. 215] as 2. 23. 51. 9. 8. 29. 1. 3. 27. 44. 31.
         t h e
Mr. Drayton [Charles Davison?: cf. fol. 215] or to some one of 44. 29. 20.
– k n o t   N – A r m o r e r
43. 18. 47. 31. 44. and I would have 22. 43. 32. 3. 30. 31. 26. 1. 3. do the like, by himselfe or through you."

The solution was obtained by a comparison of the two letters with similar passages in the draft instructions to the Sealed Knot: Cl. MS 48, fol. 215. The principle on which the cipher is constructed is not obvious, but the numbers used give the following key:

1:E	2:A	3:R	5:O	8:T	9:O
11:A	12:E	16:F	17:Blank?	18:K	20:E
21:G	22:N	23:L	26:R	27:S	29:H
30:M	31:O	32:A	43:Blank	44:T	47:N
51:L	53:S				

B. CIPHER WITH JOHN WESTON

John Weston's letter to the King of August 30 [1657] contains several passages in numerical cipher: Cl. MS 52, fol. 222 (*CClSP*, 3, 169). The three printed below are referred to in the text. For the identification of the author as Weston, see above, p. 202, n. 2.

1. ". . . Mr. 10. 43. 25. 35. 44. 50. *[Hopton]* hath a freind whose name I know not but if it be 11. 27. 49. 35. 55. 49. 21. 36. 44. 71. *[Huntington]* perhapse I have beene too inquisitive after his character."

2. ". . . I was sent to by one Major 7. 5. 93. 36. 11. *[Smith]* of 6. 27. 87. 88. *[Suss]* 65. 31. *[ex]* a very honest man, who saies Coll. 6. 35. 9. 26. 97. 48. 14. *[Stapely]* of the same country, desiers an assurance of your pardon."

3. ". . . My freinds of the next county are all bespoken by Mr. 5. 57. *[Mo]* 60. 74. 66. 71. 36. *[rdent]*" [John Mordaunt].

Here again the principle is not obvious, but the following incomplete key seems to serve:

5:M	6:S	7:S	9:A	10:H	11:H	14:Y
21:G	25:P	26:P	27:U/V	31:X	34:T	35:T
36:T	43:O	44:O	48:L	49:N	50:N	55:I
57:O	60:R	65:E	66:E	71:N	74:D	87:S
88:S	93:I	97:E				

C. CIPHER WITH NICHOLAS ARMORER

The complete key is in Egerton MS 2550, fol. 14, endorsed "Cypher with Mr. Alton dd. Oct. 8th 1653."

Alton, Mr:	Nicholas Armorer	Baker, Mr:	D. of Buckingham
Archer, Mr:	Army	Browne, Mr:	Lord Belasyse

346

Appendix

Potts, Mr:		Trade:	Affairs
Purchases apace:	Grow very strong	Trulow, Mr:	Lord Wilmot
Radfield, Mr:	Ld. Loughborough	Utrecht:	Paris
Ramsey, Mr:	Ld. Newburgh	Wares:	Affairs
Row, Mr. Tho:	Thomas Ross	Westbury, Mr:	Edward Villiers
Salvage, Mr:	Highlanders	Wheatley, Mr:	Lt. G. Monck
Skinner, Mr:	Sir E. Hyde	Widow:	Government
Slow, Mr:	Ld. Cottington*	Williams, Phil:	Sir E. Nicholas
[S]pice:	Ammunition	Wilson, Peter:	Lord Belasyse
[S]tinton, Mr:	Sir J. Grenville	Woman, Old:	Lady
[T]obacco:	Money	Wool:	Money
[T]obacco, lb. of:	Hundred pounds	Worth:	Compton
[?]ken:	Letter		

Letters in this cipher:

1. [Villiers?] to "Mr. Desmond" [Hyde], [May 23, 1653]: *TSP*, 306–7. There is a glorious confusion here over dating. The MS (a ... by Thurloe's clerk) has "23 May 1623," but is endorsed ... May 1653," which is obviously correct. For some unknown ... son Birch assigned it to 1657. No conclusions about authorship ... be drawn from the hand, but the style is similar to Villiers', ... the repetition of his pseudonym "Westbury" is suggestive. ... know that he was in correspondence with Hyde at this time. ... The King to (a) [Belasyse], (b) [Willys], (c) [Russell], all ... ember 27/December 7, 1653: Cl. MS 47, fol. 120 (*CClSP*, ... 2).

[Villiers] to "M. Barsiere" [Hyde], January 12 [1654]: *TSP* ... Original in Villiers' hand.

...e starred persons were evidently replaced in the cipher before it ca... ...eral use. Hopton died in October 1652 (G.E.C., *Peerage*) and was repla... ...ipher by Sir Richard Willys (Cl. MS 47, fol. 120). Sir Thomas Gardi... ...d in October 1652 (*DNB*). The identity of his successor as "Clerkson... ...n, but it may have been Charles Davison: cf. *TSP*, 2, 144, 162; *ClSP*... ...; and Cl. MS 48, fols. 119–20, 155–60. Lord Cottington died in June ... *Peerage*) and was replaced in the cipher by John Russell (Cl. MS 47... ...r. Jeffreys" only occurs in correspondence using this cipher in a co... ...olles would be an impossible solution: *TSP*, 2, 162 (Holles was in E... ...e). Perhaps an error for "Ld. M." to whom Charles wrote an uncip... ...der this name: Cl. MS 47, fol. 120.

Chesne, M. du:	Lord Chandos	Lymington, Mr:	Sir M. Langdale
Commodity:	Commission	Mole, Mr:	Sir P. Musgrave
Florence:	France	Mosely, Mr:	Albert Moreton
Ghent:	Gloucester	Nanton, Mr:	Henry Norwood
Gloves:	Money	Needes, Mr:	Andrew Newport
Grapley, Mr:	Edward Grey	Normandy:	North
Greece:	Germany	Purton, Mr:	Parliament
Haverfordwest:	Hull	Sheep:	Foot
Kerby, Mr:	King of England	Stockings:	Money
Kinaston, Mr:	King	Swanley:	Shrewsbury
Kirkham, Mr:	King of England	Tisbury:	Tynemouth
Knight, Mr:	King	Upham, Mr:	Edward Villiers
Knockfergus:	Kent	Wade, Mr:	Ld. Willoughby
Knox, Mr:	King of England	Wilton:	Worcester
Liggens, Mr:	Ld. Loughborough	Youghal:	York
Lyme:	Ludlow		

Letters in this cipher:

1. [Nicholas] to "Mr. Grapley" [Grey], April 21/May 1, 1654: *TSP*, 2, 244. The writer is not identified, but Nicholas' notebook records a letter to Grey on this date: Egerton MS 2556, fol. 17.

2. The King to (a) [Moreton], (b) [Loughborough], (c) [Newport], (d) [Stephens], all September 12/22, 1654: Cl. MS 49, fols. 32–35 (*CClSP*, 2, 392–93).

3. The King to "Mr. William Worth" [Sir W. Compton], September 12/22, 1654: Cl. MS 49, fol. 36 (*CClSP*, 2, 393). There are drafts of two letters on fol. 36, to "Mr. Phillips" and to "Mr. William Worth," endorsed "The K. to Sr. W. Co. & Mr. War." Macray concluded that the first letter was therefore to Compton, but it is obvious from the contents that the endorsement has reversed the order. Compton's pseudonym in the Knot's cipher (below) is "Worth." "Phillips" may be Philip Warwick.

4. The King to [Sir Philip Monckton] and to [Sir Philip Musgrave], both September 26/October 6, [1654]: Cl. MS 49 fols. 64–65 (*CClSP*, 2, 399–400). These two letters are endorsed "The K. to Sr. P. M. & Sr. P. M." The second is to "Mr. Mole" (Musgrave), and Monckton is the only possible identification for the other: cf. ibid., fol. 49; 48, fol. 305.

5. [Henry Norwood] to [Hyde?], December 23 [49, fol. 258 (*CClSP*, 3, 2). Signed "H. Nutt," in N cf. ibid., 51, fols. 251, 309; and Rawl. MS A 43, begins "D. Ch." [ancellor?].

6. [Edward Grey] to Armorer, December 29, 1 fol. 275 (*CClSP*, 3, 5). "Mr. Grapley" is Gre Begins "Dear Nic," and endorsed as to Armorer

D. CIPHER WITH THE SEAL

Most of the key is in Egerton MS 2550, fol. tions in Cl. MS 94, fol. 28. The cipher is obvio the foundation of the Knot (three of the me the end of 1652), but it was used in letters t of the Knot with sufficient frequency to just although others also used it. This may have key Hyde was requesting early in 1653, to Villiers: Cl. MS 45, fols. 11, 32, 94, 102, 1

Appleby, Mr:	Lord Hopton*	Green, M
Ashwell, Mr:	Sir J. Grenville	Head, M
Beaujeu, M. de:	Sir E. Nicholas	Hill, To
Book-keeper:	Councillor	Hollanc
Bridges:	London	Hutchi
Calloway, Mr:	Col. E. Grey	Isaac,
Clerkson, Mr:	Sir T. Gardiner*	Jeffre
Complice:	Councillor	Kers
Crosby, Mr:	Cromwell	Lan
Cross, Mr:	King of England	Lip
Dale, Mr:	Col. E. Wyndham	Lor
Doleston, Mr:	Cromwell	M
Dovey, Mr:	Sir E. Nicholas	
Essex, Mr:	Lord Maynard	M
Factor:	Ambassador	M
Father:	The English	N
Flanders:	England	
Fond, M. du:	King of England	
Fry, Tom:	Sir C. Lewkenor	
Good, Mr:	Princess of Orange	

1:E	2:A	3:R	5:O	8:T	9:O
11:A	12:E	16:F	17:Blank?	18:K	20:E
21:G	22:N	23:L	26:R	27:S	29:H
30:M	31:O	32:A	43:Blank	44:T	47:N
51:L	53:S				

B. CIPHER WITH JOHN WESTON

John Weston's letter to the King of August 30 [1657] contains several passages in numerical cipher: Cl. MS 52, fol. 222 (*CClSP*, *3*, 169). The three printed below are referred to in the text. For the identification of the author as Weston, see above, p. 202, n. 2.

                H   o   p   t   o   n
1. ". . . Mr. 10. 43. 25. 35. 44. 50. hath a freind whose name I know
                H   u   n   t   i   g   t   o   n
not but if it be 11. 27. 49. 35. 55. 49. 21. 36. 44. 71. perhapse I have beene too inquisitive after his character."

                            S   m   i   t   h   S   u   s   s
2. ". . . I was sent to by one Major 7. 5. 93. 36. 11. of 6. 27. 87. 88.
e   x   S   t   a   p   e   l   y
65. 31. a very honest man, who saies Coll. 6. 35. 9. 26. 97. 48. 14. of the same country, desiers an assurance of your pardon."

                                        M   o
3. ". . . My freinds of the next county are all bespoken by Mr. 5. 57.
r   d   e   n   t
60. 74. 66. 71. 36." [John Mordaunt].

Here again the principle is not obvious, but the following incomplete key seems to serve:

5:M	6:S	7:S	9:A	10:H	11:H	14:Y
21:G	25:P	26:P	27:U/V	31:X	34:T	35:T
36:T	43:O	44:O	48:L	49:N	50:N	55:I
57:O	60:R	65:E	66:E	71:N	74:D	87:S
88:S	93:I	97:E				

C. CIPHER WITH NICHOLAS ARMORER

The complete key is in Egerton MS 2550, fol. 14, endorsed "Cypher with Mr. Alton dd. Oct. 8th 1653."

Alton, Mr:	Nicholas Armorer	Baker, Mr:	D. of Buckingham
Archer, Mr:	Army	Browne, Mr:	Lord Belasyse

Chesne, M. du:	Lord Chandos	Lymington, Mr:	Sir M. Langdale
Commodity:	Commission	Mole, Mr:	Sir P. Musgrave
Florence:	France	Mosely, Mr:	Albert Moreton
Ghent:	Gloucester	Nanton, Mr:	Henry Norwood
Gloves:	Money	Needes, Mr:	Andrew Newport
Grapley, Mr:	Edward Grey	Normandy:	North
Greece:	Germany	Purton, Mr:	Parliament
Haverfordwest:	Hull	Sheep:	Foot
Kerby, Mr:	King of England	Stockings:	Money
Kinaston, Mr:	King	Swanley:	Shrewsbury
Kirkham, Mr:	King of England	Tisbury:	Tynemouth
Knight, Mr:	King	Upham, Mr:	Edward Villiers
Knockfergus:	Kent	Wade, Mr:	Ld. Willoughby
Knox, Mr:	King of England	Wilton:	Worcester
Liggens, Mr:	Ld. Loughborough	Youghal:	York
Lyme:	Ludlow		

Letters in this cipher:

1. [Nicholas] to "Mr. Grapley" [Grey], April 21/May 1, 1654: *TSP*, *2*, 244. The writer is not identified, but Nicholas' notebook records a letter to Grey on this date: Egerton MS 2556, fol. 17.

2. The King to (a) [Moreton], (b) [Loughborough], (c) [Newport], (d) [Stephens], all September 12/22, 1654: Cl. MS 49, fols. 32–35 (*CClSP*, *2*, 392–93).

3. The King to "Mr. William Worth" [Sir W. Compton], September 12/22, 1654: Cl. MS 49, fol. 36 (*CClSP*, *2*, 393). There are drafts of two letters on fol. 36, to "Mr. Phillips" and to "Mr. William Worth," endorsed "The K. to Sr. W. Co. & Mr. War." Macray concluded that the first letter was therefore to Compton, but it is obvious from the contents that the endorsement has reversed the order. Compton's pseudonym in the Knot's cipher (below) is "Worth." "Phillips" may be Philip Warwick.

4. The King to [Sir Philip Monckton] and to [Sir Philip Musgrave], both September 26/October 6, [1654]: Cl. MS 49, fols. 64–65 (*CClSP*, *2*, 399–400). These two letters are endorsed "The K. to Sr. P. M. & Sr. P. M." The second is to "Mr. Mole" (Musgrave), and Monckton is the only possible identification for the other: cf. ibid., fol. 49; 48, fol. 305.

5. [Henry Norwood] to [Hyde?], December 23 [1654]: Cl. MS 49, fol. 258 (*CClSP, 3,* 2). Signed "H. Nutt," in Norwood's hand: cf. ibid., 51, fols. 251, 309; and Rawl. MS A 43, pp. 521–22. It begins "D. Ch." [ancellor?].

6. [Edward Grey] to Armorer, December 29, 1654: Cl. MS 49, fol. 275 (*CClSP, 3,* 5). "Mr. Grapley" is Grey in the cipher. Begins "Dear Nic," and endorsed as to Armorer.

D. CIPHER WITH THE SEALED KNOT

Most of the key is in Egerton MS 2550, fol. 32, with some additions in Cl. MS 94, fol. 28. The cipher is obviously of a date before the foundation of the Knot (three of the men listed died before the end of 1652), but it was used in letters to and from members of the Knot with sufficient frequency to justify giving it this title, although others also used it. This may have been the cipher whose key Hyde was requesting early in 1653, to decipher letters from Villiers: Cl. MS 45, fols. 11, 32, 94, 102, 136:

Appleby, Mr:	Lord Hopton*	Green, Mr:	Whitelock
Ashwell, Mr:	Sir J. Grenville	Head, Mr:	Prince Rupert
Beaujeu, M. de:	Sir E. Nicholas	Hill, Tom:	Lt. G. Middleton
Book-keeper:	Councillor	Holland:	France
Bridges:	London	Hutchins:	Seymour
Calloway, Mr:	Col. E. Grey	Isaac, Mr:	Presbyter
Clerkson, Mr:	Sir T. Gardiner*	Jeffreys, Mr:	Col. G. Holles*
Complice:	Councillor	Kersey:	Horse
Crosby, Mr:	Cromwell	Langston, Mr:	Sir E. Herbert
Cross, Mr:	King of England	Lipe, Mr:	Richard Pile
Dale, Mr:	Col. E. Wyndham	Lorne, Heer Van:	King of England
Doleston, Mr:	Cromwell	Manley, Mr:	Ormond
Dovey, Mr:	Sir E. Nicholas	Marriage:	Treaty
Essex, Mr:	Lord Maynard	Merchandise:	Letter
Factor:	Ambassador	Mother:	The Dutch
Father:	The English	North, Mr:	Duke of York
Flanders:	England	Ostend:	Newcastle
Fond, M. du:	King of England	Painter:	Papist
Fry, Tom:	Sir C. Lewkenor	Pieces of eight:	Horse
Good, Mr:	Princess of Orange	Poole:	Carlisle

Potts, Mr:	E. of Pembroke	Trade:	Affairs
Purchases apace:	Grow very strong	Trulow, Mr:	Lord Wilmot
Radfield, Mr:	Ld. Loughborough	Utrecht:	Paris
Ramsey, Mr:	Ld. Newburgh	Wares:	Affairs
Row, Mr. Tho:	Thomas Ross	Westbury, Mr:	Edward Villiers
Salvage, Mr:	Highlanders	Wheatley, Mr:	Lt. G. Monck
Skinner, Mr:	Sir E. Hyde	Widow:	Government
Slow, Mr:	Ld. Cottington*	Williams, Phil:	Sir E. Nicholas
Spice:	Ammunition	Wilson, Peter:	Lord Belasyse
Stinton, Mr:	Sir J. Grenville	Woman, Old:	Lady
Tobacco:	Money	Wool:	Money
Tobacco, lb. of:	Hundred pounds	Worth:	Compton
Token:	Letter		

Letters in this cipher:

1. [Villiers?] to "Mr. Desmond" [Hyde], [May 23, 1653]: *TSP*, 6, 306–7. There is a glorious confusion here over dating. The MS (a copy by Thurloe's clerk) has "23 May 1623," but is endorsed "23 May 1653," which is obviously correct. For some unknown reason Birch assigned it to 1657. No conclusions about authorship can be drawn from the hand, but the style is similar to Villiers', and the repetition of his pseudonym "Westbury" is suggestive. We know that he was in correspondence with Hyde at this time.

2. The King to (a) [Belasyse], (b) [Willys], (c) [Russell], all November 27/December 7, 1653: Cl. MS 47, fol. 120 (*CClSP*, 2, 282).

3. [Villiers] to "M. Barsiere" [Hyde], January 12 [1654]: *TSP*, 2, 19. Original in Villiers' hand.

---

* The starred persons were evidently replaced in the cipher before it came into general use. Hopton died in October 1652 (G.E.C., *Peerage*) and was replaced in the cipher by Sir Richard Willys (Cl. MS 47, fol. 120). Sir Thomas Gardiner also died in October 1652 (*DNB*). The identity of his successor as "Clerkson" is uncertain, but it may have been Charles Davison: cf. *TSP*, 2, 144, 162; *ClSP*, 3, 235, 238; and Cl. MS 48, fols. 119–20, 155–60. Lord Cottington died in June 1652 (G.E.C., *Peerage*) and was replaced in the cipher by John Russell (Cl. MS 47, fol. 120). "Mr. Jeffreys" only occurs in correspondence using this cipher in a context where Holles would be an impossible solution: *TSP*, 2, 162 (Holles was in Europe at the time). Perhaps an error for "Ld. M." to whom Charles wrote an unciphered letter under this name: Cl. MS 47, fol. 120.

4. The King to [Villiers], January 24/February 3 [1654]: Cl. MS 47, fol. 330 (*CClSP*, 2, 307–8).

5. [Villiers] to [Hyde], February 2 1653[-54]: *TSP*, 2, 64. Signed "Westbury."

6. [Villiers] to [Hyde], February 6, 1653[-54]: *TSP*, 2, 70–71. "Richard Eggleston" to "M. Barsiere."

7. The King to Loughborough, February 11/21, [1654]: Cl. MS 47, fol. 387 (*CClSP*, 2, 315).

8. [Villiers] to [Hyde], March 6, 1653[-54]: *TSP*, 2, 143–44. The MS is a copy, but the authorship is obvious.

9. [Villiers] to [Hyde], March 13 [1654]: *TSP*, 2, 162. In Villiers' hand.

10. The King to (a) the Sealed Knot and (b) [Belasyse], both [April 1654]: Cl. MS 48, fols. 157, 159 (*CClSP*, 2, 344–45).

11. The King to (a) the Sealed Knot, (b) [Sir W. Compton], and (c) [Belasyse], all May 1654: Cl. MS 48, fols. 244–45 (*CClSP*, 2, 363).

12. The King to [Villiers], July 6/16, 1654: Cl. MS 48, fol. 328 (*CClSP*, 2, 384).

13. [Stephens] to [Ormond], August 11, 1654: Carte MS 131, fol. 173 (*CClSP*, 3, 411).

14. The King to [Lord Maynard], October 13/23, 1654: Cl. MS 49, fol. 80 (*CClSP*, 2, 404). "Mr. Essex" is Maynard in the cipher.

15. [Nicholas] to [Sir John Grenville], October 24/November 3, 1654: *TSP*, 2, 691. "E. de Beaujeu" to "Stinton," Nicholas and Grenville respectively in the cipher.

E. CIPHER WITH WILLIAM RUMBOLD

The following cipher is printed in full (with the exception of a covering address for correspondence) because of its importance in establishing the membership of the Sealed Knot. The original is in Carte MS 194, fol. 43, endorsed "Cipher with Mr. Rumb."

The King — Westrope
The Lord Lieutenant
Sr. Edward Hyde

Lord Bellasis	Burton	
Lord Loughborow	Henry Lockington	
Sr. William Compton	William Cordwell	
Mr. John Russell	John Randall	—All by Mr. Roles
Mr. Edward Villiers	Edward Upton	
Sr. Richard Willis	Richard Watkins	
William Rumbold	William Robinsons.	

Letters in this cipher:

1. The King to the Sealed Knot, October 24/November 3 [1654]: Cl. MS 49, fol. 115 (*CClSP*, *2*, 413).

2. The King to [Rumbold], November 11/21, 1654: Cl. MS 49, fol. 160 (*CClSP*, *2*, 427).

3. The King to [the Sealed Knot], December 25, 1654/January 4, 1655: *TSP*, *3*, 76. Copy dated a day later: Cl. MS 49, fol. 265 (*CClSP*, *3*, 3–4).

4. [Hyde] to [Rumbold], December 26 [1654]/January 5 [1655]: Rawl. MS A 21, pp. 466–69.

5. Memorandum from [the Sealed Knot], [December 1654—January 1655?]: Cl. MS 49, fol. 267 (*CClSP*, *3*, 4).

6. [Villiers] to [the King], [January 1655]: Cl. MS 49, fol. 315 (*CClSP*, *3*, 11). In Villiers' hand.

7. The King to [the Sealed Knot], February 8/18 [1655]: Cl. MS 49, fol. 340 (*CClSP*, *3*, 16).

8. [Rumbold] to the King, February 8, 1655: Cl. MS 49, fol. 342 (*CClSP*, *3*, 16).

F. CIPHER WITH JOHN COOPER

The original is in Cl. MS 94, fol. 13, endorsed "Cipher wth Mr. C o o p e r 9. 39. 40. 44. 14. 49." The key is incomplete, but the letters in the Clarendon MSS can generally be deciphered with it. The letters in *TSP* for which this cipher appears to have been used are almost unintelligible, although a few names can be recognized.

Allen, Mr:		Conyers, Mr:	The King
Ascue, Mr:	E. of Rochester	Cloth (linen):	Foreign forces
Binns, Mr:	Lord Savile	Dixon, Mr:	Sir E. Hyde
	N. Armorer		

Ellis, Mr:	M. of Ormond	Redshaw, Mr:	John Cooper
Leake, Mr:	Sir H. Slingsby	Roberts, Mr:	Thomas Paulden
Martin, Mr:	Col. A. Gilby	Smyth, Mr:	Charles Burwell
Osborne, Mr:	Cromwell	Thompson, Mr:	James [John?]
Parsons, Mr:	Duke of York		Walters

Letters in this cipher:

1. [Cooper] to [Armorer], April 21 [1656]: Cl. MS 51, fol. 211 (*CCISP*, *3*, 119). For the identification of the writer as Cooper, see above, p. 207, n. 10.

2. [Cooper] to [Armorer], April 27 [1656]: Cl. MS 51, fol. 248 (*CCISP*, *3*, 124–25).

3. [Cooper] to [Armorer], May 1 [1656]: Cl. MS 51, fol. 277 (*CCISP*, *3*, 129).

4. Armorer to Ormond, May 9/19 [1656]: Cl. MS 51, fols. 298–300 (*CCISP*, *3*, 132).

5. Also possibly the letters from "Tho. Rawson," "Martin Lister," "Wilson," "Wm. Rawson," etc.: *TSP*, *5*, 310–11, 366, 414, 469; *6*, 89.

G. CIPHER WITH JOHN SKELTON

The original is in Cl. MS 94, fols. 14–15, endorsed "Cipher with Capt. Shelton."

Bennett, Mr:	Col. R. Arundell	Ponnstock:	Liskeard
Bridgeman, Mr:	The King	Rowe, Mr:	Sir H. Pollard
Buckhorn:	Horse	Sharpe, Mr:	Cromwell
Carter, Mr:	Lord Mohun	Shaw, George:	Sir E. Hyde
Hollocom:	Exeter	Tempest, Mr:	Sir C. Trevanion
Kerseys:	Ammunition	Tin:	Arms
Morestow:	Pendennis	Upton, Mr:	Sir J. Grenville
Poor John:	Foot		

Letter in this cipher:

[Skelton] to [Hyde], November 4 and 30, 1656: Cl. MS 53, fols. 27, 91 (*CCISP*, *3*, 199, 210).

Bibliographical Essay

ORIGINAL SOURCES

1. Official Records

The records of the Council of State cover the entire period of this study, in variable detail. For the most part the *Calendar of State Papers, Domestic Series, 1649–1660,* ed. Mary A. E. Green (London, 1875–86) can be relied on, but occasional use has to be made of the originals, State Papers Domestic, Interregnum, in the Public Record Office. There are also three volumes of Council proceedings for 1659 in Rawlinson MSS (Bodleian) A 134, A 259, and C 179, and a volume of warrants for 1654 in Rawl. MS A 328. For 1655–56 the records of the London Major Generals' Office, Add. MSS (British Museum) 19,516, 34,011–17, are valuable; some are printed by A. R. Bax, "Suspected Persons in Surrey during the Commonwealth," *Surrey Archaeological Collections, 14* (1899), 164–89.

Papers of individual public officials are even more important in tracing the history of Royalist plotting. Although Cromwell attained supreme power only in 1653, he was concerned in the problems of internal security from the beginning. His papers are collected and edited with distinction by Wilbur C. Abbott, *The Writings and Speeches of Oliver Cromwell* (Cambridge, Mass., 1937–47), which has a superb accompanying *Bibliography,* Cambridge, Mass., 1929. The person most immediately responsible for guarding the Commonwealth against conspiracy, both before 1653 and in 1659–60, was Thomas Scot. After the Restoration he wrote a useful guide to his intelligence system—"Thomas Scot's Account of His Actions as Intelligencer during the Commonwealth," ed. C. H. Firth, *EHR, 12* (1897), 116–26—but his papers have not been collected. However, for 1649–51 there is much information about conspiracy dispersed in *Original Letters and Papers of State Addressed to Oliver Cromwell . . . Found among the Political Collections of . . . John Milton,* ed. John Nickolls (London, 1743), and in the papers from Nalson's collection printed in Zachary Grey, *An Impartial Examination of the Fourth Volume of Mr. Daniel Neal's History of the Puritans* (London, 1739), and Historical Manuscripts Commission, *Portland MSS, 1* (1891). For the Protectorate we are more fortunate. Thurloe's papers in Rawlinson MSS A 2–67 are incomparably the most prolific source of information on the government side, including intercepted letters, reports of spies and intelligencers, and depositions of suspects under examination. Most are printed in *A Collection of the State Papers of John Thurloe Esq.,* ed. Thomas Birch (London, 1742), but frequent recourse has to be made to the originals and the unprinted papers. There are some supplementary papers in Add. MSS (BM) 4156–59. Two later accounts by men employed by Thurloe throw useful light on his methods: John Wildman, "A Brief Discourse Concerning the Businesse of Intelligence and How It May Be Managed to the Best Advantage," ed. C. H. Firth, *EHR, 13* (1898), 527–33, and Samuel Morland's paper in Historical Manuscripts Commission, *Buccleuch and Queensberry (Montagu House) MSS, 2,* Pt. I (1903), 49–51.

Less immediately concerned with conspiracy, but still indispensable, are *Journals of the House of Commons 1547–1714* (1803–), *6, 7; Acts and Ordinances of the Interregnum,* ed. C. H. Firth and R. S. Rait, London, 1911; and *A Bibliography of Royal Proclamations of the Tudor and Stuart Sovereigns,* Vol. *1: England and Wales,* ed. Robert R. Steele, Bibliotheca Lindesiana, *5,* Oxford, 1910. *Calendar of the Proceedings of the Committee for Compounding,* ed. M. A. E. Green (London, 1889–92), for all its editorial inadequacies, is a mine of information about the Royalists' financial affairs, and contains as well some details about Booth's rising not to be found elsewhere. *A Complete Collection of State*

Trials, ed. T. B. and T. J. Howell (London, 1816–28), *5,* contains the trials of some of the more notable conspirators.

2. Royalist Correspondence

The papers of the exiles attempting to direct conspiracy from beyond the seas are naturally the most complete. Hyde, who exercised general supervision after 1652, has left every historian in his debt for his careful stewardship of his papers as well as for his later writings. The Clarendon MSS (Bodleian) are the Royalist equivalents of Thurloe's papers. The *Calendar of the Clarendon State Papers,* ed. O. Ogle, W. H. Bliss, W. D. Macray, and F. J. Routledge (Oxford, 1869–1932) is usually reliable, but in the earlier volumes it is often necessary to go to the originals to clear up ambiguities and obscurities. The most thorough selection is *State Papers Collected by Edward, Earl of Clarendon,* ed. R. Scrope and T. Monkhouse (Oxford, 1767–86), and there is another useful one in T. H. Lister, *Life and Administration of Edward, first Earl of Clarendon* (London, 1837–38), *3.*

Next to Hyde, Nicholas was the exile most regularly involved in correspondence with the party in England. The section of his papers in the British Museum—Add. MSS 4180, 15,856, 41,202 A, and Egerton MSS 2534–56—is highly informative, and the selection in *The Nicholas Papers: Correspondence of Sir Edward Nicholas, Secretary of State,* ed. G. F. Warner, Camden Society (London, 1886–1920) is excellent. Some additional letters to and from Nicholas are printed in *Diary of John Evelyn,* ed. H. B. Wheatley (London, 1879), *4.*

Ormond was the third of the directing triumvirate, but although no account can ignore them his papers deal heavily with Irish affairs, and with conspiracy in England only occasionally. *A Collection of Original Letters and Papers, Concerning The Affairs of England, 1641–1660, Found among the Duke of Ormonde's Papers,* ed. Thomas Carte (London, 1739) prints most of the important documents, and there are many unpublished ones, including some cipher keys, among the Carte MSS (Bodleian). Ormond papers from Kilkenny castle are printed in Historical Manuscripts Commission, *Ormonde MSS, 1* (1893), and new series *1* (1902).

The most useful of the lesser collections of the exiles' correspondence is that of Sir Marmaduke Langdale, Historical Manuscripts Commission, *Various Collections, 2* (1903), Harford MSS. Others of occasional value are those of Lord Hatton, Add. MS (BM) 29,550, some printed in *Correspondence of the Family of Hatton,* ed. E. M. Thompson, Camden Society, London, 1878; Gervase Holles, Historical Manuscripts Commission, *Bath MSS, 2* (1907), and *Buccleuch MSS, 1* (1899); and Robert Long, Add. MS (BM) 37,047, and the calendar of his captured papers in Historical Manuscripts Commission, *Pepys MSS* (1911), pp. 294–307. *Memorials of the Civil War,* ed. Robert Bell (London, 1849), has some of the correspondence of Sir Richard Browne, ambassador in Paris. *Letters and Papers Illustrating the Relations between Charles the Second and Scotland in 1650,* ed. Samuel R. Gardiner, Scottish Historical Society, *17* (Edinburgh, 1894), prints some papers relating to conspiracy in England from the Clarendon MSS and the State Papers. *Memorials of the Great Civil War,* ed. Henry Cary (London, 1842), has miscellaneous correspondence of 1649–51 from the Tanner MSS (Bodleian).

Royalists in England, for obvious reasons, usually disposed of incriminating documents before they could fall into the hands of Thurloe's officers. The results of repeated inquiries to likely owners were therefore discouragingly fruitless. The most important exceptions to the general rule of immediate destruction are the papers of Barwick, Brodrick, and Mordaunt. Barwick's are printed in Peter Barwick, *The Life of the Reverend Dr. John Barwick . . . with . . . an Appendix of Letters,* trans. H. Bedford, London, 1724. Brodrick's, in Vol. *1* of the MSS of the Earl of Midleton, have not been published, apart from a few which appear, together with the much larger number of Brodrick's letters to Hyde from the Clarendon MSS, in *Clarendon State Papers, 3.* Mordaunt's can be found in Historical Manuscripts Commission, *10th Report,* Appendix 6 (1887), Braye MSS; and the admirably annotated *The Letter-Book of John Viscount Mordaunt 1658–1660,* ed. Mary Coate, Camden Society, London, 1945. Of less value are the correspondence of Andrew Newport and his family circle in Historical Manuscripts Commission, *5th Report,* Appendix (1876), Sutherland MSS; and the papers of the Seymour family in Historical Manuscripts Commission, *12th Report,* Appendix 9 (1891), Beaufort MSS. Sir Thomas Peyton's extensive correspondence in Add. MSS (BM) 28,003, 44,846–48 is tantalizingly devoid of references to his conspiratorial activities. However, both it and *The Oxinden Letters 1607–1642* and *The Oxinden and Peyton Letters 1642–1670,* ed. Dorothy Gardiner (London, 1933 and 1937) usefully illuminate his private affairs and his spells of imprisonment. Among several collections giving insight into the attitudes and behavior of the more passive Royalists, perhaps the best is *The Correspondence of Bishop Brian Duppa and Sir Justinian Isham 1650–1660,* ed. Sir Gyles Isham, Bart., Northamptonshire Record Society, *17,* Lamport, 1951.

3. Diaries, Memoirs, etc.

It is hardly necessary to discuss in detail the outstanding work by a participant. Clarendon so dominates the period that the most self-consciously critical reader can hardly escape being overwhelmed by his majestic synthesis. *The History of the Rebellion and Civil Wars in England,* ed. W. D. Macray (Oxford, 1888), and *The Life of Edward Earl of Clarendon . . . in which is included a Continuation of his History of the Grand Rebellion* (Oxford, 1857), in spite of their prejudices and lapses of memory still provide the essential starting point for any study of the Royalists. Most of the other well-known memoirs of the period are by or about Royalists who for one reason or another were outside the conspiring wing of the party. Newcastle (*Life of William Cavendish, Duke of Newcastle . . . by Margaret, Duchess of Newcastle,* ed. C. H. Firth, London, 1907) was abroad. Fanshawe (*The Memoirs of Ann Lady Fanshawe,* ed. H. C. Fanshawe, London, 1907) and Warwick (*Memoires of the Reigne of King Charles I with a Continuation to the Happy Restauration of King Charles II,* London, 1701) were in England, but inactive through most of the period, though the latter negotiated busily in 1659–60. Evelyn (*The Diary of John Evelyn,* ed. E. S. de Beer, Oxford, 1955) as usual cautiously avoided danger to life and limb, but his day-to-day comments on his experiences are sometimes valuable, and the magnificent editorial apparatus of this latest edition of his Diary must be gratefully acknowledged by any student of the period. Anthony Wood (*The Life and Times of Anthony Wood*, ed. Andrew Clark, Oxford Historical Society, Oxford, 1891–1900) preferred academic gossip to politics. The two chronicles—Sir Richard Baker, *A Chronicle of the Kings of England . . . Whereunto Is Added the Reign of King Charles the First, and the First Thirteen Years of his Sacred Majesty King Charles the Second* (London, 1674), and James Heath, *A Brief Chronicle of the Late Intestine Warr in the Three Kingdoms of England, Scotland and Ireland* (London, 1663)—provide occasional information of value, the former especially for the Restoration in the Continuation by Edward Phillips.

The most illuminating memoir by a conspirator is that of the embittered Sir Philip Monckton, *The Monckton Papers*, ed. Edward Peacock, Philobiblon Society (London, 1884), which is interesting for Yorkshire in spite of the author's persecution complex. *The Diary of Sir Henry Slingsby*, ed. Daniel Parsons (London, 1836) stops at 1649. Joshua Moore, "A Briefe Relation of the Life and Memoires of John Lord Belasyse," Historical Manuscripts Commission, *Ormonde MSS*, new series 2, 376–99, has little about Belasyse's role in the Sealed Knot, but is not entirely worthless. None of the other members of the Knot left memoirs, though Willys' defense is printed by J. G. Muddiman, *Notes and Queries*, 12th series *10* (1922), 123–24. A similar piece of self-justification by Francis Corker is printed in *The Retrospective Review*, 2d series *1* (1827), 292–95. The Presbyterian Royalists are best represented by Sir William Waller, *Recollections*, printed as appendix to *The Poetry of Anna Matilda*, London, 1788; see also *Vindication of the Character and Conduct of Sir William Waller* (London, 1793), which, however, deals mainly with the events of 1647. Two Presbyterian ministers left memoirs with important sidelights on Booth's rising: *The Life of Adam Martindale*, and *The Autobiography of Henry Newcome*, ed. R. Parkinson, Chetham Society, Manchester, 1845, 1852.

Works of this kind from the parliamentarian side are naturally less immediately relevant, but a few yield information or comment of significance. *Diary of Thomas Burton Esq. Member in the Parliaments of Oliver and Richard Cromwell,* ed. J. T. Rutt (London, 1828) has the debates of 1656–58 and 1659, in which government policy toward the Royalists was often discussed. *The Memoirs of Edmund Ludlow,* ed. C. H. Firth (Oxford, 1894) provides the impressions of a republican critic, as biased against Cromwell as any Royalist could possibly be. Bulstrode Whitelock, *Memorials of the English Affairs from the Beginning of the Reign of Charles the First to the happy Restoration of King Charles the Second* (Oxford, 1853) is mere chronicle, mostly repeating information available in the newspapers, but with a few additional items. Lucy Hutchinson, *Memoirs of the Life of Colonel John Hutchinson,* ed. C. H. Firth (Oxford, 1906) is not an important source for the Royalists but throws some light on events near Nottingham in 1659.

4. Newspapers, Newsletters, Tracts, etc.

The peerless Thomason Collection in the British Museum was carefully combed for information about the arrest and release of conspirators in the years 1651–58. For 1649–51 and 1658–59, absence from England compelled me to rely on the files of individual newspapers in American libraries. The following in the Sterling Memorial Library of Yale University were used systematically: *A Perfect Diurnall of Some Passages in Parliament,* Nos. 288–321 (1649); *A Perfect Diurnall of Some Passages and Proceedings of, and in Relation to the Armies,* Nos. 1–81 (1649–51); and *Mercurius Politicus,* Nos. 433–599 (1658–59). There are selections from the newspapers bearing on Cromwell's career, often with news of plots, in *Cromwelliana: A Chronological Detail of Events in Which Oliver Cromwell Was Engaged,* ed. M. Stace, Westminster, 1810. The most convenient collection of newsletters is in *The Clarke Papers. Selections from the Papers of William Clarke,* ed. C. H. Firth, Camden Society (London, 1891–1901), which also prints some scattered papers of the period of Booth's rising from Tanner MS 51 (Bodleian).

Information from newspapers, then as now, was not always reliable but is useful for corroborative purposes. The same is true of contemporary accounts in tracts often written for propaganda purposes. Besides many individual tracts consulted in the Thomason Collection, three volumes containing materials from Charles II's escape after Worcester deserve mention. Allan Fea, *The Flight of the King*, Pt. II, and *After Worcester Fight* (London, 1897, 1904); and *The Royal Miracle. A Collection of Rare Tracts, Broadsides, Letters, Prints and Ballads Concerning the Wanderings of Charles II after the Battle of Worcester*, ed. A. M. Broadley (London, 1912) all print contemporary narratives, but the editorial contributions are of little value except to the antiquarian. There are some essential materials for Booth's rising in *Tracts Relating to the Civil War in Cheshire*, ed. J. A. Atkinson, Chetham Society, Manchester, 1909.

SECONDARY AUTHORITIES

The great series begun by S. R. Gardiner, *History of the Commonwealth and Protectorate* (2d ed. London, 1903) still provides the most thorough and comprehensive account of the political history of these years. Carried on by C. H. Firth, *The Last Years of the Protectorate* (London, 1909), and Godfrey Davies, *The Restoration of Charles II 1658–1660* (San Marino, Cal., 1955), it puts this study in the necessary perspective. Gardiner, Firth, and Davies tend to ignore the continuity of Royalist conspiracy, and there are some minor errors of detail in all three, but their works contain the essential core of the period.

Of books dealing specifically with the Royalists, the most important is Paul H. Hardacre, *The Royalists during the Puritan Revolution* (The Hague, 1956), a suggestive introduction to the subject concentrating on social and economic history. The same author's "The Royalists in Exile During the Puritan Revolution, 1642–1660," *HLQ, 16* (1952–53), 353–70, indicates some further lines of study which might be pursued with profit. C. H. Firth, "The Royalists under the Protectorate," *EHR, 52* (1937), 634–48, is also valuable but covers a restricted period. Royalist myth and ideology are brilliantly treated by Keith Feiling, *A History of the Tory Party 1640–1714*, Oxford, 1924. Hyde's philosophy and policies are judiciously analyzed by B. H. G. Wormald, *Clarendon: Politics, History and Religion 1640–1660*, Cambridge, 1951. Robert S. Bosher, *The Making of the Restoration Settlement* (London, 1951) has some interesting chapters on the Church in the 1650's but exaggerates the effectiveness of the clergy as conspirators. Among older books are two by Eva Scott, *The King in Exile*, and *The Travels of the King* (London, 1905, 1907). In spite of a disconnected scissors-and-paste method, an absence of historical perspective, and many factual errors, these still provide the most detailed narrative account of politics among the exiles, and are not entirely worthless for the conspiracies in England.

Government policy toward the Royalists in 1655–56 is discussed by David W. Rannie, "Cromwell's Major-Generals," *EHR, 10* (1895), 471–506. There is no general study of the Secretary's office under Thurloe, though parts of Florence M. G. Evans, *The Principal Secretary of State* (Manchester, 1923) provide a useful introduction. Two articles studying Thurloe's intelligence system at close range, and in particular his employment of Sir Richard Willys, are Marjory Hollings, "Thomas Barret: A Study in the Secret History of the Interregnum," *EHR, 43* (1928), 33–65, and D. E. Underdown, "Sir Richard Willys and Secretary Thurloe," *EHR, 69* (1954), 373–87.

Articles describing specific conspiracies in isolation include many essays in local history, but few of real value. The best are W. W. Ravenhill, "Records of the Rising in the West," *Wiltshire Arch. and Nat. Hist. Magazine, 13* (1872), 119–88, 252–73; *14* (1874), 38–67; *15* (1875), 1–41, and J. E. Auden, "Shropshire and the Royalist Conspiracies between the End of the First Civil War and the Restoration, 1648–1660," *Shropshire Arch. Soc. Transactions*, 3d series *10* (1910), 87–168. A good general account of the plots of 1649–51, but concentrating on the Presbyterians, is Leland H. Carlson, "A History of the Presbyterian Party from Pride's Purge to the Dissolution of the Long Parliament," *Church History, 11* (1942), 83–122. The conspiracy of 1654–55 is treated in greatest detail by C. H. Firth, "Cromwell and the Insurrection of 1655," *EHR, 3*

(1888), 323–50; *4* (1889), 313–38, 525–35. A good but much briefer modern account is A. H. Woolrych, *Penruddock's Rising 1655*, Historical Association Publications, general series, G. 29, London, 1955. The only recent study of the rising of 1659, J. R. Jones, "Booth's Rising of 1659," *Bulletin of the John Rylands Library, 39* (1956–57), 416–43, is equally sound but lacking in detail.

Local histories such as the Victoria County Histories provide much biographical information but disappointingly little else. Easily the best of the local histories of the civil war, with excellent chapters on the 1650's are Mary Coate, *Cornwall in the Great Civil War and Interregnum*, Oxford, 1933; and A. C. Wood, *Nottinghamshire in the Civil War*, Oxford, 1937. Of the countless older books, John Latimer, *The Annals of Bristol in the Seventeenth Century* (Bristol, 1900) is mere chronology and suffers from a complete absence of documentation, but can be used with caution.

The standard biographical collections are sufficiently familiar to require no description. Three recent works are particularly valuable for the less prominent figures: C. H. Firth and G. Davies, *The Regimental History of Cromwell's Army*, Oxford, 1940; Mary F. Keeler, *The Long Parliament 1640–1641: A Biographical Study of its Members*, American Philosophical Society Memoirs, 36, Philadelphia, 1954; and A. G. Matthews, *Walker Revised. Being a Revision of John Walker's Sufferings of the Clergy during the Grand Rebellion*, Oxford, 1948. Matthews, *Calamy Revised. Being a Revision of Edmund Calamy's Account of the Ministers and Others Ejected and Silenced, 1660–62* (Oxford, 1934) is a similar mine of information on the Presbyterian clergy. Seventeenth-century collections written for polemical purposes, such as Walker's, and David Lloyd's *Memoires of the Lives . . . of those Noble Reverend and Excellent Personages That Suffered . . . from 1637 to 1660* (London, 1668), contributed to the growth of Royalist mythology but have little other value for the modern historian. Family histories, often written with much piety but little scholarship, are far too numerous to list exhaustively; the most helpful to this study are Roger Granville, *The History of the Granville Family* (Exeter, 1895), which has information about Sir John Grenville's movements not readily available elsewhere; E. P. Shirley, *Stemmata*

Shirleiana; or the Annals of the Shirley Family (London, 1873) for Sir Robert Shirley; and F. P. and M. M. Verney, *Memoirs of the Verney Family . . . from the Letters . . . at Claydon House* (London, 1892–99), describing the life of a circle of less active Royalists.

Biographies of individuals are also too numerous for more than a brief selection to be mentioned. It is striking that there is no single biography that provides an adequate insight into the career of a prominent conspirator. Maurice Ashley, *John Wildman: Plotter and Postmaster* (London, 1947) does so for the Leveller leader, but there is no Royalist counterpart. The early chapters of George Kitchin, *Sir Roger L'Estrange* (London, 1913) are useful for one who was at this period an inactive Royalist. Thomas Carte, *The Life of James, Duke of Ormond* (Oxford, 1851) is of great value for Ormond's mission to England in 1658. C. R. Markham, *A Life of the Great Lord Fairfax* (London, 1870) is disappointing for the General's years of retirement, and later lives add nothing to the *DNB* account. One of the few biographies of a second-rank conspirator is Sir Frederick Maurice, *The Adventures of Edward Wogan*, London, 1945.

Index

Major references of place-names are indexed by county; incidental references are not indexed.